MARK AS RECOVERY STORY

✠ MARK ✠
as
RECOVERY STORY

ALCOHOLISM AND THE RHETORIC OF GOSPEL MYSTERY

John C. Mellon

UNIVERSITY OF ILLINOIS PRESS
Urbana and Chicago

© 1995 by the Board of Trustees of the University of Illinois
Manufactured in the United States of America
C 5 4 3 2 1

This book is printed on acid-free paper.

Scripture quotations unless otherwise noted are from the Revised Standard Version of the Bible, copyright 1946, 1952, and 1971 by the Division of Christian Education of the National Council of Churches of Christ in the U.S.A., and are used by permission. Material from the book *Alcoholics Anonymous* is quoted with the permission of Alcoholics Anonymous World Services, Inc. Permission to reprint this material does not mean that Alcoholics Anonymous has reviewed or approved the contents of this book, or that Alcoholics Anonymous agrees with the views expressed herein.

Library of Congress Cataloging-in-Publication Data

Mellon, John C.
    Mark as recovery story : alcoholism and the rhetoric of Gospel mystery / John C. Mellon
        p.   cm.
    Includes bibliographical references and indexes.
    ISBN 0-252-02165-7 (alk. paper)
    1. Bible. N.T. Mark—Criticism, interpretation, etc. 2. Jesus Christ. 3. Twelve-step programs—Religious aspects—Christianity. 4. Drinking in the Bible. I. Title.
BS2585.2.M433   1995
226.3'08362292—dc20   94-24082
                                                           CIP

To
all who have sought Jesus
neither from above nor from below
but at the bottom,
in the etymologically primal cry,
"God, help!"

CONTENTS

PREFACE

This book proposes a radical recontextualization of the Gospel of Mark, an excursion beyond the horizon of current Markan studies into an unexplored realm of New Testament meaning. Specifically, it interprets the gospel according to typologies of alcoholism and recovery peculiar to today's Twelve-Step programs. These typologies, products of the twentieth century and familiar to large numbers of people, are essentially spiritual and hence potentially germane to the understanding of religious texts, but they have yet to be employed in research on the Bible. My reading has convinced me that looking at Mark from the viewpoint of addiction and recovery can prove surprisingly fruitful, both for comprehending the work as a whole and for responding to the particular questions that continue to puzzle Markan scholars.

But why apply to Mark's gospel a conceptual schema seemingly out of place in its time and alien to its content? I would have been as perplexed as anyone by such a proposal when, many years ago, I first looked into Mark in search of the pre-Christian Jesus. But the more I reflected on the gospel through my understanding of the alcoholic illness, the more questions like the following grew in significance:

- Might the enthusiast behaviors that nineteenth-century liberal biographers observed in the Galilean phase of Jesus' career reflect the same grandiose messianism often seen in newly sober alcoholics?
- Could the judgmentalness and righteous anger that Mark's Jesus exhibits in Jerusalem indicate what today's alcoholics label "mental drunkenness" and "playing God," attempts to change others rather than oneself?

- Do not Jesus' Passover utterances concerning wine and blood and drinking no more, together with his prayer in Gethsemane, bear uncanny resemblances to the words of an alcoholic "hitting bottom" and surrendering to a power greater than the self?
- Might the secrecy emblems in Mark, such as the cup of water, the water carrier, the donkey, the Elijah references, the Twelve, the desolating sacrilege, and so on, finally yield their meanings under analysis from a perspective of alcoholism?

At first I assumed that an interpretation of Mark prompted by such questions could be only personal, nothing more than a further demonstration of the gospel's ability to address the needs and experiences of successive generations of individual readers. But then I began to wonder whether a stronger hypothesis might be arguable, namely, that Mark's gospel may have originated within a community whose members' experience with drink had been one of addiction followed by release. Against all odds I asked the question: could Mark actually be the product of an unremembered fellowship of former drunkards?

Aware that such a position is unprecedented in academic literature and will evoke profound skepticism, I have tried to develop as precisely as possible the evidence necessary to evaluate this hypothesis from a scholarly point of view. My approach is mainly that of text-grammar. Given Mark's linguistic virtuosity, his knowledge of languages, dialects, puns, and ambiguities, I have examined the Greek text of the gospel in search of dual readings lost in translation and unrecorded in the annals of Markan interpretation, whose discovery would point to the writer's involvement with a primary audience separate from the Christ cult that finally adopted his work. I have also discussed certain historical data and a number of Hebrew and Christian writings intertextually related to Mark.

Anticipating a charge of anachronism, I begin the book by arguing that chronic drunkenness ("alcoholism," in the modern lexicon) existed among ancient wine and beer drinkers and that the idea of a sobriety fellowship in one corner or another of the Roman world, while historically undocumented, is not at all anachronistic. I then lay out seven kinds of evidence, most of it new and surprising:

1. unrecognized ambiguities in key passages of the Greek text of Mark, mainly of grammar, lexis, theme, speech act, and reference, whose content consistently corresponds to the transhistorical spirituality of today's Twelve-Step movement;
2. interpretations of Mark's notorious secrecy emblems, some of them enumerated in the preceding list, pointing to alcoholism as the book's camouflaged *Sitz im Leben;*

3. identification of the developmental progression of Jesus' persona—from euphoric to bellicose to pacific—as a characteristic pattern of recovery from active alcoholism;
4. genre features identifying Mark as a third-person narrative displacement of the age-old former drunkard's recovery story, including three-partness, the stage-one/stage-two motif, "bottoming out" and spiritual exaltation, and "turning-point" apocalyptic;
5. contrastive interpretive possibilities within the Passion narrative reflecting the spirituality of recovery, for example, paschal abstinence rather than ritual drinking, *psuchē* death rather than bodily death, Barnasha rather than Barabbas, Gethsemane rather than Golgotha, powerless servants rather than powerful hierarchs, and spiritual rather than corporeal resurrection;
6. interpretations of phenomena external to Mark that support the alcoholism reading, for example, the evangelist's cryptic nicknames, Jesus' Q community reputation as a drunkard, the apostles' Pentecost drunkenness, wine-free communions, the water of Cana, and donkey-headed graffiti;
7. relevant intertextual material from Isaiah's Zion poem and Servant figure, Luke's Pentecost story in Acts, the Yahwist's account of Noah's connection with wine, Psalms 16 and 116, Joel, Daniel, the primitive core of John, and Revelation.

Taken together, this evidence composes the problematic features of Mark and gives rise to an intellectually coherent and historically plausible interpretation of the gospel as a whole. It yields a fresh image of Jesus as a humbled and ultimately anonymous recovering person, an image that I think many readers will find more congenial than conventional religious views. And it provides grounds for a reconstruction of Christian origins significantly different from prevailing models.

Of myself as writer I should state that, in addition to being a longstanding student of Mark and Markan scholarship, I am a recovering alcoholic sober for many years. Regularly involved with other ex-addicts, I am versed in the spirituality and lore of Twelve-Step recovery. Although such a disclosure ordinarily would be out of place in a scholarly book, its relevance in the present case should be obvious.

This book is intended primarily for New Testament scholars specializing in the Gospel of Mark, the historical Jesus, and the sociology of first-century Palestine and for persons in the field of English involved in the critical study of religious literature. It should also find readers among religionists interested in the spirituality of the Twelve Steps and among religion teachers, ministers and rabbis, pastoral counselors, and other professionals alert for new ways of amplifying traditional images of Jesus. And I believe it will appeal to a broad spectrum of men and women in Alcoholics Anonymous and other Twelve-Step fellowships who are interested in reconciling received understandings about Jesus with the spirituality of recovery.

This book does not court sensationalism or seek to undermine religious belief. It does not involve personal testimony or esoteric symbolism. It is not anti-alcohol. Its analyses are principally literary, not historical. The picture of Jesus it develops neither impugns his character nor challenges Christian doctrines about his sinlessness and dual nature, nor is it in any other way irreverent. Nonetheless, despite my hope that all readers will find the book enlightening, I expect that many will at first experience the opposite. Misinformation and revulsion concerning alcoholism will sidetrack some, and rigid interpretive paradigms others. I offer three suggestions to facilitate reading:

- After reading chapter 1, stop and consider how the typologies of addiction and recovery discussed therein might shape the interpretive perspective of readers inclined to think in those terms.
- Read the three Mark chapters (2, 4, and 6) in whatever order is most comfortable. If chapter 2 seems too focused and technical at the outset, detour to chapter 4 and its broader and more conventionally academic beginning. Or turn to chapter 6, which starts with the commencement of Mark's narrative.
- If the alcoholism hypothesis becomes a stumbling block, set it aside for the duration and focus instead on the surprising translational possibilities the book brings to light, which are linguistically independent of the alcoholism hermeneutics.

Overall, the purposes of this book are to enlarge our thinking about the origins of a religion that ultimately defined an era and to look for common ground between the Markan fellowship of old and today's Twelve-Step movement, deemed by many the most important spiritual development of the present century.

Lastly, I am pleased to acknowledge a debt of gratitude to those who have helped me write this book, some unknowingly, some alcoholics and some not: To my family, especially Mary Gael and Christina, whose support of me and of the project that claimed so much of me never flagged. To Ed, whose story brought me into recovery and ultimately provided the hermeneutical key to Jesus' eucharistic words. To Leo, prince of twelfth-steppers, whose death taught me to seek the

Messiah not in a person but in the Program. To Joe at the Mustard Seed, who shared his skills of Bible translation and the work of his scholarly hero, the late Mitchell Dahood. To Bill, writing teacher and fellow sojourner in recovery, who cared enough about this book to point out the rhetorical shortcomings of early versions. To another Bill, who pastored me gently during the often unbearable enthusiast phase of this work. To the scholars and editors who kept me rewriting by ignoring my submissions, and to Bill, Carolyn, Charles, David, Thomas, and Richard, who took the time to respond to the work of a newcomer to Scripture studies. To Donald, who more than any other has given me the professional counsel and encouragement without which this book would not have appeared. To Don, my sponsor, who admonishes me, book or no book, to continue each day to make sobriety the most important thing in my life.

My thanks also go to the ancient people who began it all: the Yahwist; Elijah the water drinker; the anonymous prophet called Deutero-Isaiah; Jesus the founder and way-shower; the women who followed him; John nicknamed Mark, who first handed on his story; and the elder seer of Revelation. And to the persons of our own era who enfleshed the Program in the fullness of time—to Carl, who told it to Rowland, who passed it on to Ebby, who carried it to Bill in the kitchen of a Brooklyn apartment in the autumn of 1934, and to Bill and Dr. Bob and the one hundred men and women who named it and shaped it and gave it to the world in the book *Alcoholics Anonymous*. And finally to alcoholics around the tables of countless meetings, fellow sufferers whose words have so richly banqueted me with the multiplied bread and the new wine of recovery.

MARK AS RECOVERY STORY

✥ 1 ✥

INTERPRETIVE PERSPECTIVE

While men drink they remain drunk; when they abjure
their wine, their thinking is changed.
—Jesus, Gospel of Thomas 28

Despite an immense amount of scholarly attention in modern times, the Gospel of Mark remains an enigma whose provenance, genre, primary audience, and clandestine symbolism continue to escape detection. Recent studies have interpreted the gospel in contexts of the sociology of first-century Palestine, Hebrew Scripture, and research on the historical Jesus. For example, Howard Clark Kee has studied Mark's community from the perspective of Jewish sectarian apocalypticism of the two preceding centuries.[1] Vernon Robbins, seeing Mark's Jesus as a teacherly figure, examines the gospel within a context of ancient rhetoric and pedagogy.[2] Burton Mack characterizes Mark as a mythmaker who shaped memories of a Galilean Cynic sage into an origin myth incorporating motifs of the royal figure, rejection, and vicarious martyrdom intended for such diverse Jesus groups as the Q prophets, the Twelve in Jerusalem, the family of Jesus, the congregation of Israel, and the many Christ cults.[3] Mary Ann Tolbert interprets the gospel according to the conventions of popular literature of the Greco-Roman world, specifically the Hellenistic erotic novel.[4]

Other studies view Mark as a midrash on Hebrew Scripture. John Bowman, for example, considers Mark's master paradigm to be the Passover Haggadah;[5] Duncan Derrett sees the gospel's type in the Moses and Joshua story,[6] and Wolfgang Roth finds it in the Elijah and Elisha narrative.[7] Historical work by Dominic Crossan,[8] John Meier,[9] and Ron Cameron[10] has added knowledge about Mark's sources crucial to all future studies of Markan intention. Despite such scrutiny, however, the secret of Mark's gospel has survived intact. Its symbols remain undeciphered, its genre features obscure, its covert audience unidentified, its rhetorical exigence imprecisely defined, and its spirituality unrecognized.

Like archaeologists puzzled by an uninterpretable artifact, Markan researchers need to change tack, to stop asking what the social milieu of first-century Palestine can tell us about Mark and begin to ask what Mark, viewed anew, can add to our knowledge of the first-century social scene. This will mean departing from familiar interpretive frameworks and embracing alternative, paradigm-breaking hermeneutics not ordinarily associated with antiquity yet compatible with its cultures and its texts. It will mean turning from extracting textual meanings to generating them, from what scripturalists call exegesis to prudent uses of what is so often pejoratively labeled eisegesis, meaning here the creative and appropriate reading in of meanings. As a project in this sort of textual archaeology, the present book proposes an unprecedented theory of the Markan audience: its identity, its symbolism and spirituality, the genre features it discerned in the Markan text, the image of Jesus it memorialized, and the social conditions motivating its concern for anonymity and secrecy.

What are the unanswered questions about Mark that this or any theory of Markan audience must ultimately address? The following list enumerates the gospel's more obvious enigmas:

a. What is the purport of the evangelist's nicknames "Marcus" (Greco-Roman form of "Mark") and "stump-fingered"? Scholarship has provided no answers, whereas Mark's primary audience would have known their significance.

b. Why the idiosyncratic form of apocalyptic found in Mark 13, and what is the "desolating sacrilege" (13.14)? The guesses of scholars trivialize the meaning of this important image, whereas Mark's audience would have known its referent and assigned it apocalyptic centrality in the organization of the entire gospel.

c. What sort of lived experience backgrounds Jesus' baptism (1.9–11)? The question is typically dismissed for lack of evidence, but Mark's "insider" audience (4.11) must have known what lay behind this cryptic origin story.

d. What do the culturally anomalous words "This is my blood" mean in the Last Supper narrative (14.24)? Why is the order of events in Mark's account of the service of the paschal cup and the speaking of the wine words (14.23–24) different from the witnesses of Matthew and Paul-Luke? Mark's audience would have understood this uniquely Markan intentionality.

e. Is the surrender depicted in Gethsemane (14.32–39) self-immolating or self-assertive? It is often intuited as the former, but it is invariably interpreted as the latter, even in so-called literal translations of the original Greek. Mark's audience would have known its true character.

f. What is the referent of the mysterious "Twelve" (passim, especially 3.14–15 and 4.10)? Nonscholars presume that the term refers to twelve disciples, whereas scholars have recognized its referential obscurity but have failed to offer convincing explanations. Mark's audience could have explained the term.

g. What are the meanings of clandestine symbols such as the cup of water (9.41), the unridden donkey (11.2–7), the man carrying a jar of water (14.13–15), and the young man in a white garment (14.51–52 and 16.5–7), as well as of the many enigmatic events throughout the narrative, ranging from the wilderness temptation (1.12–13) and the attempt by Jesus' family to take charge of him (3.21) to the Elijah reference, the wordless cry from the cross (15.36–37), and the tearing of the Temple veil (15.38)? Mark's audience would have interpreted these puzzling symbols and events within a single coherent rubric as other than midrash.

h. Who was Barabbas (15.7–15)? Why the historically unattested Passover privilege (15.6)? Why a tomb of solid rock (15.46)? Why the empty tomb but no resurrection appearance (16.5–7)? Who are the female servant figures (14.3–9, 15.40–41, and 16.1–8)? Why are they afraid (16.8)? Mark's audience would have known the answers.

i. Why are Jesus' disciples, prefigures of emergent Christian clergy in Mark's own day, portrayed so harshly, failing to understand about the multiplication of bread (8.14–21), the Messiah (8.27–33), and service rather than authority (10.35–45), and shown forsaking Jesus and fleeing (14.50)? Why the anticlerical bias of the allegories late in the gospel?

j. Assuming John Mark of Acts to be the evangelist in his youth, why did he break with Paul (Acts 13.13 and 15.37–39)? Did Paul's developing Christ mysticism lead to the rupture, and how did it influence the christological content in Mark's book? Mark's audience would have known the story behind this conflict.

k. As genre features of the gospel, what is the purport of the stage-one/stage-two theme, of sequences of threes, of the exorcisms, and of Jesus' progression from euphoria to belligerency and then to peacefulness? Mark's audience would have recognized the interconnectedness of these features in constructing the gospel's meaning.

1. Why all the secrecy in the first place? Why did Mark camouflage his primary audience such that its identity would remain hidden (as it does even now) and a Christ cult intended only as a secondary or ostensible readership group, while aware of and perplexed by the gospel's enigmas, would from the outset regard itself as the sole intended audience?

Some of the foregoing questions are considered uninteresting relics of earlier periods of Jesus research, whereas others are dismissed as unanswerable, consequences of what Frank Kermode has called the "tacit understandings that existed between this dead writer and his dead audience."[11] This is not to suggest that the questions lack significance but only that researchers have failed to identify interpretive perspectives from which to address them productively. Obviously, bolder and more innovative solutions to the Markan enigmas must be explored.

Audience Hypothesis

Accordingly, this book will examine a hypothesis depicting Mark's secret audience as a heretofore unrecognized Jewish sobriety fellowship, a nonmessianic Jesus group consisting of former drunkards turned water drinkers who believed themselves to have been freed from their wine demons by the power of God. Members of this egalitarian community, both peasant and middle class, would have met regularly to celebrate their sobriety and spiritual awakenings and to carry a message of changed thinking to newcomers. Few outsiders would have known these Jesus people as nondrinkers, and those who did, apart from family members, would have thought them abstinent ascetics. Group members would have memorialized Jesus as a fellow sufferer and founder of their movement around 30 C.E. Overall, despite a separation of nearly two thousand years, these groups would have been comparable in experience, outlook, and spiritual praxis to the modern recovery fellowship known as Alcoholics Anonymous. Obviously, any interpretive framework arising from this hypothesis will involve a hermeneutics unprecedented in NT studies and foreign to nonaddicts, both scholar and layperson. Its topics will be drinking and not drinking, powerlessness and empowerment, textual hiddenness and ambiguity, apocalypse and *metanoia* (after-knowledge), anonymity, and egalitarian versus hierarchical polities.

Of the many skeptical responses to this audience hypothesis, probably the first to surface will be charges of anachronism and lack of evidence. It will be argued that since alcoholism and recovery seem absent from ancient thinking, their imputation to a first-century culture is therefore anachronistic. It will also be claimed that since these topics have never been discerned in the Markan text, the hypothesis lacks evidence.[12] This situation evokes the analogy of archaeologists pondering an "unreadable" artifact. The fact that they do not know *how* to interpret the artifact means that they cannot assert, in advance of examining a certain interpretive paradigm, what it does or does not refer to, what counts as evidence and what does not. Moreover, they expect each new "reading" of the artifact to be arresting and to evoke resistance. It is part of the experience of paradigm re-formation. Because a description of any new paradigm is necessary prior to its application, this chapter will outline the response typologies of the alcoholic reader as background that nonalcoholic readers will need in order to evaluate the proposed hypothesis.

Alcohol Addiction among the Ancients

First, however, the question of anachronism must be addressed. Here the archaeologist's criterion is "could not have been" rather than "not yet observed." For example, although groups of model-ship builders similar to today's hobbyist associations have never been observed in ancient Rome, the idea of such groups on the Roman scene would not be anachronistic, whereas the idea of model-airplane builders would. In the case of alcoholic beverages, although references to habitual drunkenness and voluntary abstinence from drink are plentiful in the ancient world, there seems to be no evidence of anything resembling the modern sobriety fellowship. Nonetheless, the hypothesis of a localized, perhaps short-lived, and previously undiscovered first-century recovery movement, probably situated in a region of heavy wine production, is both plausible and nonanachronistic. Its possible historicity depends solely on the acceptability of two propositions:

a. Alcohol addiction, whether or not much remarked by writers of the time, existed among beer and wine drinkers in the first century just as in all succeeding centuries, both before and after the advent of distilled spirits.
b. The grass-roots spirituality of recovery characteristic of Alcoholics Anonymous, which arose from popular genius in the 1930s C.E. and interpreted alcohol addiction as an illness responsive

to spiritual treatment, could just as readily have arisen in the 30s
C.E.

On the latter point, it is important to understand that nothing in
the concept of recovery is inherently modern. As used here, the term
recovery refers to the spiritual realm and not to the genetic and neu-
robiological subject matter of contemporary addiction science or to
the medical and psychological procedures used in the professional
treatment of addicts. Just as there was alcohol addiction in the ancient world, so too there could have been spiritual sobriety groups
whose members, like their modern counterparts, believed themselves
freed from their drink obsession by the grace of God. As it happens,
the founders of Alcoholics Anonymous borrowed heavily from the
practices of the Oxford Groups, a popular Christian movement of the
1930s whose express purpose was to rediscover the elementary and
untheologized spirituality of first-century Christianity.[13]
On the former point, no one doubts that chronic inebriety over-
arches the boundaries of time and culture. Ancient writers recognized
the addictive quality of wine while praising its medicinal value and
its contribution to union with the gods, as in Dionysiac circles.[14] Discussing the ancient practice of mixing wine with water, the historian
R. J. Forbes confirms the presence of alcoholics in antiquity by bluntly
reiterating the observation of numerous classical authors, "Only
'boozers' drank pure wine."[15] The Hebrew Bible speaks repeatedly
about habitual intoxication (see the discussion of Dt 21.18–21 later
in this chapter). Furthermore, the NT contains several words connoting more than ordinary drinking: *methusoi,* "drunkards" (1 Cor 6.10);
oinophlugia, "gross excess of wine" (1 Pt 4.3); *oinopotēs,* "winebibber,
excessive drinker" (Mt 11.19; Lk 7.34); *paroinos,* "habituated to wine"
(1 Tm 3.3; Ti 1.7); and *prosechō,* "to give oneself to or to be addicted
to," said of wine (1 Tm 3.8). The early rabbis report accounts of
drunkenness and hangovers in their injunctions connected with Passover drinking, leaving no doubt about the alcoholic content and effect of the wine drunk.[16] Early synagogue homilies dealt with the
problem of inebriety.[17] Tacitus writes that Caligula and Claudius were
forced to extend the feast of the Saturnalia to three and seven days,
respectively, and to provide wine at public expense, so great was the
thirst of the Roman mob.[18] Little more than a decade after Mark's
time, Domitian launched an attack against excessive drinking that
forbade the planting of further vines in Italy and ordered the acre-
age in the provinces reduced by at least half.[19] E. R. Goodenough has
catalogued widespread Jewish use of wine symbols between the time

of the Maccabees and the fall of Jerusalem in 70 C.E. and concludes that "the drinking of wine and the symbolism of the vine were everywhere an important part of Jewish observance and thinking."[20] Although the ordinary Palestinian, Jew or Gentile, would have thought the idea of a sobriety fellowship preposterous, there would have been no shortage of wine addicts as potential members.

From the third century B.C.E. on, techniques of viticulture had improved to the point where wine was available in grape-growing areas in quantities sufficient to make it cheap enough for all but the lowest classes of people. Palestine had been an agriculture center at least from the time of its hellenization, and wine was an important product. Seán Freyne describes the successful efforts of the Ptolemaic governor Appollonius to improve the regional vines, together with his agent Glaukias's report of a commercial Palestinian estate with 80,000 vines.[21] Ruth Amiran's catalogue of Palestinian pottery from the later Iron Age depicts a wide variety of wine vessels: storage jars, jugs, decanters, and amphoriskoi.[22] The historian Emil Schürer interprets the archaeological remains of Greek jars as evidence of the Palestinian vintners' practice of importing wine containers for use in their export trade.[23] Freyne writes, "What is really taking place is the transformation of Palestinian agriculture into agrobusiness, controlled and monopolized by outside agencies."[24] The geographer Harm Jan de Blij confirms that by Roman times wine had become a part of the daily diet, among common people as well as the upper classes, both in Rome and in provincial Roman cities where grapes were plentiful. Opportunity for addiction was therefore widespread. De Blij sees the Romans as responsible for industrializing viticulture: "Eventually a process all too familiar to small farmers began: the Roman capitalists bought out the grape farmers by the hundreds, consolidated their lands, and created huge wineries that drove remaining private growers out of business."[25] One effect of this development would have been to curtail the local peasantry's supply of a drink to which they were habituated or addicted, always a cause of alcoholic anger and civil unrest.

Firmly subjugated to Roman rule by the turn of the era, Galilee was a wine-producing region that experienced the development just described. Speaking indirectly of Galilean viticulture, Josephus describes the district thus: "Not only has the country this surprising merit of producing such diverse fruits, but it preserves them: for ten months without intermission it supplies those kings of fruits, the grape and the fig."[26] During the turbulent decades following Pompey's conquest of Palestine in 63 B.C.E., Roman capitalists must

have devoured the regional vineyards for their export trade, leaving
native Galileans both thirsty and disgruntled, a condition likely to
have contributed to the banditry and warfare that characterized first-
century Palestine.[27] The preallegorical version of the parable of the
wicked husbandmen (Mk 12.1–9; see chap. 6 herein) in the Gospel
of Thomas 65 clearly reflects absentee ownership of agricultural estates employing Galilean peasants as tenant workers. C. H. Dodd has
written: "The parable, in fact, so far from being an artificially constructed allegory, may be taken as evidence of the kind of thing that
went on in Galilee during the half century preceding the general
revolt of A.D. 66."[28] Significantly, the parable is not about grain or
olives but about wine. First-century Galilee was neither the first nor
the last instance when a frustrated thirst for alcohol sparked rebellion. To exdrunkards the region's double renown, wine and militancy, readily suggests the disease of alcoholism. Later in this book (chap.
6) Mark's story of the Gerasene demoniac possessed by a legion of
demons and at war within himself (Mk 5.1–20) is interpreted as a
displaced allegory about an alcoholic populace whose response to
latent addiction and social oppression is internecine fighting.

Given a climate of widespread alcohol addiction and religious fanaticism, first-century Galilee would have been a likely place for the
emergence of a recovery program based on the individual drinker's
admission of defeat and cessation of fighting. Inasmuch as such an
admission would have contravened the dominant Mediterranean
values of honor and shame, recently discussed by Dominic Crossan,
any such sobriety fellowship would have remained semi-underground
and anonymous, more or less like today's Twelve-Step programs.[29]
Similarly, the sense of liberation widely acknowledged to follow from
an admission of powerlessness would have confirmed and reinforced
the peasant egalitarianism certain to have been a salient feature of
any ancient Palestinian sobriety fellowship, just as it is of Alcoholics
Anonymous today. James Scott (quoted by Crossan) considers such
peasant movements to be transhistorical and transcultural, characterizing each as "a society of brotherhood in which there will be no rich
and poor, in which no distinctions of rank and status (save those
between believers and nonbelievers) will exist."[30] Also, the concept
of "healed healers," which Crossan applies to the Galilean Jesus
groups, applies equally well to today's recovering alcoholics, who
reinforce their own sobriety by carrying the message of wellness to
those who still suffer.[31]

Sepphoris, a Romanized city near the village of Nazareth, could
well have been home to exactly the kind of sobriety fellowship hypoth-

esized here. In noting the occasional association of particular emblems with synagogues, Emil Schürer mentions the curious fact that "in Sepphoris there was a 'synagogue of the vine.'"[32] A more appropriate emblem for the meeting place of an alcoholism group is difficult to imagine. Stranger still is the report by Josephus that Sepphoris, a center of rebellion after the death of Herod the Great in 4 B.C.E., by the time of the Roman-Jewish War in 67 C.E. numbered "the only people of that province [Galilee] who displayed pacific sentiments."[33] Although there are political explanations for this progression from bellicosity to peaceableness, it is not too much to think that a movement of sober alcoholics may have contributed to the nonmilitance that saved the city from destruction by Vespasian's legions. In any case, there is ample reason to conclude that alcohol addiction existed at all levels of society by Roman times. Moreover, conditions in first-century Palestine, particularly Galilee, suggest that the illness may have been epidemic in that region.

As for terminology, *alcoholism,* a word used throughout this book, is a modern term designating a spiritual malady of which unremitting drinking is the chief symptom. Naturally, the word will seem out of place when employed even hypothetically in reference to the first century, yet the argument advanced in this book is that Mark's secret community possessed the equivalent of the modern concept of alcoholism as a spiritual illness. What they seem to have lacked, or what may have been lost, is a name for their concept. Mark's community apparently referred to the illness by the notion of demon possession (though it may simply be Markan camouflage; see chap. 6). In any case, using the modern word to fill this apparent lacuna in the first-century lexicon presents a way around this linguistic impasse, given the unsuitability of available alternatives. Terms like *chronic drunkenness* or *inebriety,* while they sound less anachronistic than *alcoholism* when applied to ancient history, simply do not mean what the latter term means.

Finally, just as knowledgeable persons today distinguish sober alcoholics from self-willed abstainers, so it is important that the reader not confuse the first-century recovery groups hypothesized here with fanatical religious sects of the time, such as the Rechabites and Nazirites, or with professional ascetics like the Therapeutae and Essenes, whose practice of abstinence apart from addiction was, then as now, the antithesis of sobriety following active alcoholism. The conflation of these two kinds of groups would be understandable. Indeed, it provides a basis for reinterpreting certain well-known information about communities of early Christians who drank water instead of wine in their eucharistic rituals. Reasoning from second-century evidence, scholars have always identified these communities as ascetics, whereas the earliest of them, particularly those predating the Roman-Jewish War, could have been the alcoholism groups hypothesized here (see chap. 4 for discussion and references).

Generally speaking, biblical historians and sociologists doubtful about the present hypothesis should remember that they are no different from other readers in "seeing" what they are conceptually predisposed to look for and ignoring what they are not. They will have failed to see recovery from addiction as a possible cause of nondrinking among the ancients because, unless they happen to have a connection with recovery in their own lives, they simply do not think in those terms. A case in point is Bruce Malina's anthropological study of the nonconsumption of food and drink in the NT world.[34] Malina lists three forms of nonconsumption: abstinence (dieting, asceticism, and encratism), fasting, and socially commanded avoidance. But nowhere does he demonstrate any awareness of a fourth form, the kind practiced by ex-addicts freed from compulsive drinking. If the shoe were on the other foot and the former drunkard were the scholar, this form of nonconsumption would head the list. In any event, members of the hypothesized Markan sobriety fellowship would have been not teetotalers or ascetics but individuals who had drunk deeply of undiluted wine, known its addictive grip, come to a crisis and surrendered, and experienced healing empowerment and spiritual awakening.

Overview

Although the question of anachronism can be readily dispatched, the task of marshaling evidence for the historical actuality of a Markan sobriety fellowship is the work of this entire volume. It will have succeeded if readers who begin with the understandably skeptical question, How is it possible to see alcoholism in Mark? conclude by asking, How was it possible *not* to? As to method, the book employs what might be called the "metanoetics of recovery" as a hermeneutics for interpreting Mark's gospel and speculating about its audience, genre, origin, and message. The interpretation itself occurs primarily in three chapters:

- Chapter 2 discloses the alcoholism themes in the Markan Passion narrative, for example, the drinking ritual and disavowal of drink at the Last Supper, the figure of the cup and admission of powerlessness in Gethsemane, *psuchē* death as antitype to bodily death, the refusals of wine from the cross, Elijah as a clandestine figure of sober abstinence, and "Son of Man" as an anonymity appellative.

- Chapter 4 surveys scholarship on nonmessianic Jesus groups in Palestine before the Roman War and outlines a theory of provenance based on the identity of the Markan communities as a fellowship of water drinkers historically unrecognized among these Jesus people. It points to genre features identifying Mark as an encoding of the former drunkard's recovery story within a work intended for a Judean Messiah cult. Finally, it reconstructs the particular story on which the gospel is based, Jesus' first-person account of his career from its Jordan beginnings to his Jerusalem drunkenness and finally his definitive Gethsemane surrender.
- Chapter 6 decodes the alcoholism and sobriety emblems in Mark 1–13, ranging from demon possession to the "desolating sacrilege," and interprets the many allegories in Mark 14–16 as warnings about the corrupting influence of clerical structure in the Markan groups as well as in the Christ cult.

Taken together, these readings demonstrate the coherence of an interpretation of Mark in terms of recovery from alcoholism and lay groundwork for rehistoricizing the entire gospel.

The remainder of this book pursues the intertextuality of Markan thinking elsewhere in Scripture. The following are studied: Jesus' Q community reputation as an inebriate reported in Mt 11.19/Lk 7.34 read as a quotation of Dt 21.20 bluntly translated; the biblical etiology of addiction represented in the Yahwist's stories of the Fall and Noah's discovery of wine; the Deutero-Isaian Suffering Servant identified as derelict drunkard and addiction bearer for the many; Luke's story in Acts of Peter's Pentecost sermon on Joel and Psalm 16, together with the memory of the apostles as drunkards; material in the Gospel of John reflecting a protocommunity of water drinkers who understood the Cana sign not as a changing of water to wine but as the replacement of wine by water; and the wine bowl imagery and the references to Daniel 12 in the Book of Revelation as adumbrations of a bimillennial age of religious alcoholism destined to culminate in apocalypse and a subsequent age of sobriety.

Obviously, the idea of Jesus as an alcoholic, albeit recovering, carries with it a high potential for rejection prior to investigation. The puzzling Markan saying at the conclusion of Jesus' discourse on ego-death (see chap. 6), wherein Jesus acknowledges not just his message but also his person as possible objects of shame, speaks directly to this point: "For whoever is ashamed of *me* [italics added] or of my words" (Mk 8.38). Persons who accept the established medical view of addiction as illness will recognize that the imputation of alcoholism to Jesus neither defames his person nor calls into question the authenticity of his proclamation of the rule of God. Allowing Jesus to be alcoholic ratifies the fullness of his humanity without violating traditional Christian doctrines about his sinlessness and two natures. It points up the docetism of popular images of Jesus as an exemplar of moral rectitude who could not possibly be subject to an ugly human malady such as alcoholism. And it challenges each person to think of addiction as an affliction paradoxically ordained by God, for which everyone possessed of a human nature is eligible, rather than as a moral failure or a character flaw. Open-minded readers willing to see this book through to the end, though they may disagree with its conclusions and even its outlook, will recognize that the Jesus it presents, although he shares a dark past of alcohol addiction, emerges as no less founder and savior (Acts 5.31, *archēgon kai sōtēra*), and perhaps as a more accessible model of God-reliant spirituality, than the perfectionist and auto-empowered Jesus of more familiar religious conceptions.

Critical Method

The new possibilities of meaning that this book assigns to Mark's gospel are instantiated primarily through the identification of lexical, grammatical, and referential ambiguity, through retranslation of the original Greek, and as a consequence of indexing given readings to the emergent *Weltanschauung* of recovery. Biblical passages are approached from a reader-response stance, at times in contexts of form-critical analyses, and then explicated by means of text-grammar, typology, translational linguistics, and, in the case of the anticlerical materials in Mk 14–16, allegory. Finally, they are interpreted through the conceptuality of addiction and recovery. Occasionally these alcoholism interpretations are contrasted with traditional understandings, but no attempt is made to present the overall interpretive histories of the texts.

The critical stance adopted here is well known to literary critics. Scholars such as Louise Rosenblatt, Steven Mailloux, Susan Suleiman, and Jane Tompkins contend that meaning is generated in the reading experience rather than extracted from the text.[35] Edgar V. McKnight has argued the validity of reader-response approaches in postmodern biblical criticism.[36] Although biblical exegetes have conventionally thought of their work as drawing meanings "from" texts, the religionist Schuyler Brown, commenting on the applicability of a reader-based stance to the Bible, suggests that more and more scholars are finding such a stance to precipitate "a Copernican revolution in [their] interpretive theory" and no longer reject as mistaken the eisegetical reading of "subjective" meanings "into" texts.[37] Indeed, the literary critic Stanley Fish has argued that texts are actually "written" only when read, through acts of interpretation performed by readers. Whatever consistency and credibility attach to response-oriented readings result from the sharing of "interpretive strategies . . . for writing texts, for constituting their properties and assigning their intentions," by persons making up what Fish calls "interpretive communities."[38] The twin interpretive communities posited in this book consist of individuals whose hermeneutical perspective is defined by the shared experience of alcoholism and recovery. These communities and their response typologies are described in detail in the following section.

Two criticisms are often lodged against the reader-response approach: that it removes intention from the author's control and places it wholly in the hands of the reader and that it is valid only when undertaken as a form of divination wherein the reader serves merely as a conduit for whatever understandings spontaneously arise in consciousness. On the first point, the position here acknowledges that no reading of texts as pointedly structured as the Christian gospels can attain credibility if it assumes that their authors lacked intentions they could have stated, at least generally. Moreover, these intentions ought to be comprehensible historically. What reader-response criticism argues is that such intentions may turn out to be quite different from those canonized in the history of the texts' interpretations. This will be particularly true of works shrouded by secrecy, as is Mark, or much redacted, as is the primitive core of the Gospel of John.

On the second point, it is a critical commonplace that no reader ever engages a text empty-headed. Literary interpretation is like any other cognitive activity in that, for understanding to occur, perceptions must at some point interact with the reader's prior knowledge. What the reader-response approach subverts is the tyranny of the *pre*constructed interpretation. Every reading act, however, even those involving the supposedly free play of the mind, finally takes place within some conceptually representable perspective. Works are never decontextualized but repeatedly recontextualized. The multiple indexicality of texts, their ability to mean different things in different contexts, makes possible their many interpretations. Nor are reader-based responses and free play of the mind limited to deconstructing meaning; they also serve as heuristics for hypothesizing about previously undiscerned aspects of the intentionality of texts. Largely ignoring the role of reader perspective, Frank Kermode ends his essay on Mark by pronouncing its narrative unfollowable and its secrecy forever concealed behind "a door of disappointment."[39] Yet despite its storylike qualities, Mark's gospel is clearly intended as history, not fiction. Hence it must be possible to locate a perspective that renders its narrative followable and its secrecy transparent. The perspective studied here involves a recontextualization of Mark featuring as its covert audience an association of former wine addicts who remembered Jesus as the founder of their movement and a fellow sufferer.

Typologies of Addiction and Recovery

To follow the argument of this book, nonaddict readers should acquaint themselves with the response typologies characteristic of recovering alcoholics. A term used with increasing frequency over the past fifty years as a result of Alcoholics Anonymous and the Twelve-Step movement it spawned, "recovering alcoholic" designates a new type of human being present in contemporary society. Stereotypes of skid row derelict and town drunkard no longer characterize the alcoholic. Recovering alcoholics are just as likely to be career people who never lost their jobs or families, college students barely out of their teens, or homemakers who sipped their wine in secret. Diverse in age, ethnicity, education, vocation, social situation, and religion, former alcohol addicts following A.A.'s twelve-step program exhibit a remarkable uniformity in their understanding of recovery. They consider alcoholism to be a spiritual malady that cannot be remedied by willpower alone and attribute their sobriety to an admission of powerlessness and reliance on a power greater than self. Most call this higher power God. Recovery from alcoholism typically leads to an awakening of spiritual consciousness and profoundly changed thinking. Religious in character but not a religion, recovery affords a new and potentially illuminating perspective from which to interpret traditional religious writings.

Definition of Alcoholism

Since the meaning of the term *alcoholism* is a question hotly disputed within psychology, medicine, and sociology, it is important to dissociate this book from all such controversy. As used here, the word refers neither to a medical disorder nor to a psychopathic condition (although many drinkers do experience physical and psychological problems along with their alcoholism) but to a spiritual illness. Its symptoms are a chemical dependence on alcohol coupled with fear, anger, delusion, defiance, and dishonesty. Its pathology is self-will operating under a persistent illusion of auto-empowerment. At its core lies the radically individuated and narcissistic self, which in its efforts to achieve autonomy becomes its own deity and suffers in return the curative wrath of God. Addiction to substances is a result of this wrath. Active alcoholism is by no means limited to obvious inebriates but can afflict seemingly normal drinkers whose bondage is only vaguely sensed or, as is so often the case, obscured by denial.

Thus alcoholism is not subject to objective diagnosis but only to self-appraisal. There is no minimum drinking requirement, nor is the illness definable by physical or genetic criteria. It is not important to know whether a particular addiction is physiological or psychological, only that every addiction is mystical. Persons are alcoholic when they say they are, and not otherwise, despite appearances and professional diagnostic opinions to the contrary. Not all drunkards are alcoholics, and not all alcoholics are drunkards. Today thousands whom doctors and therapists would not have labeled alcoholic are finding new lives in Twelve-Step recovery. Countless others die each day from failure of self-diagnosis. The remedy for alcoholism is neither medical nor psychological but spiritual. It requires the surrender of self, the admission that the individual is not God, and the ultimate recognition that one's drug of preference, whether alcohol or another substance, only symbolized and catalyzed the deeper existential problem. Quitting drinking, although a prerequisite for sobriety, does not cure or even arrest alcoholism; it only enables the sufferer to commence the spiritual program necessary for recovery.

Response Typologies

Even though its underlying spiritual principles are timeless, the specific conceptuality of recovery common to Alcoholics Anonymous and other Twelve-Step programs is little more than a half-century old. Although studied by observers both inside and outside these fellowships, recovery continues to elude systematic description.[40] Its manifestations, however, are apparent. It can be read in A.A. literature such as the book *Alcoholics Anonymous*[41] and in programmatic statements known as the Twelve Steps, the Twelve Traditions, the Promises, and the Absolutes. It can be experienced in realities such as following a daily program, going to meetings, working the Steps, talking the talk, speaking, twelfth-stepping, sponsoring, inventorying and admitting, praying and meditating, maintaining A.A. contact, and service. And it can be heard in the body of living lore and tradition— some of it written, but most oral (stories, sayings, clichés, lingo, outlook, and ways of thinking)—that alcoholics invoke in their meetings, mutual communication, and daily living. Nonalcoholics have little idea of the richness of this tradition or the extent to which it is being shared on a daily basis by persons of every walk of life. The program of Alcoholics Anonymous is not cabalistic and contains no secret rites of any kind, yet it remains a mystery even to old-timers, just as all spiritual new-mindedness remains mysterious. Ultimately, it is a mystery living in each sober alcoholic.

Here now are the main response typologies that an interpretive community of recovering alcoholics unconstrained by conventional meanings would employ in reading the Gospel of Mark. Readers of Mark will recognize at once that all the textual features mentioned in these typologies are present in the gospel.

Intoxication Alcoholics distinguish two kinds of drunkenness, physical and mental. Although the term *mental drunkenness* is metaphorical, the condition it names is quite real.

    a. Physical drunkenness: textual features assigned salience will be references to drinking and not drinking, to water as opposed to wine, connections between wine and suffering, and drunken rage imaged in demonic terms.

    b. Mental drunkenness: salient features are rampant self-will, obsessive anger and judgmentalness, attempts to dominate and change others, contentiousness and fighting, self-pity, and grandiosity. Persons can experience mental drunkenness in the absence of physical intoxication. Textual features will be gurulike pronouncements and instances of "playing God" and judging others instead of one's self, together with anger images and "cup of wrath" metaphors.

Turning Point The turning point is the moment of grace in the depths of pain, suffering, and chaos when the drinker is offered the gift of recovery. Turning points are experienced and recalled in differing ways, but they are regarded by all as definitive life crises.

    a. Insight: moments of crisis, recognition, revelation, or apocalypse regarding alcohol. Material reported varies from seeing alcohol as enemy, to knowing one's self as alcoholic, to sensing the desire to stop dinking, or to experiencing the conviction of powerlessness over alcohol. Textual indications will be epiphanal statements reflecting new awareness relative to drink.

b. Admission of powerlessness: the moment of surrender, of admitting defeat in one's previously unrecognized contest with God on the issue of empowerment. Textual features will be baptisms, self-immolating prayers, or repudiations of will and willpower.

c. Asking for help: the moment of encounter with "Jesus" experienced anonymously in the realized etymology of his name (Jesus, *Yēšûa'*, consists of Hebrew roots meaning "God, help!"), worded in various ways but always an unconditional call for help to an other.

d. Quitting drinking: statements about not drinking, drinking no more, or drinking water rather than wine will be salient.

e. Changed mind: an awakening of spiritual consciousness and changed thinking, featured as a metanoetic awareness and a sense of life lived on a new basis. Textual references to *metanoia* will be significant.

God as Higher Power   Alcoholics need and ultimately find a power by which they can live, which must be a power greater than alcohol and hence greater than the self. Awareness of this power can range from a strong sense of spiritual visitation to the "still, small voice" experience, or it can be a retrospective recognition often said to be educational in nature. This power is the felt source of all guidance, love, and spiritual uplift. It is not defined theologically or professed creedally but known through personal awareness and spoken of communally using the phrase "God as we understand him." Textual references to power, requests for empowerment, and "power" *(dunamis)* used as a name for God will be significant.

Recovery   Alcoholics define recovery as surrender, asking for help, not drinking, attending meetings, turning their will and their lives over to the care of God, stopping fighting, inventorying and letting go of resentments and judgmentalness—in short, changing their thinking completely. Significant textual features will be calls for radical action, a changing of mind, joining in a following, leaving the multitude for meetings with other recovering people, the cessation of bellicosity, and similitudes stressing the overarching importance of recovery.

a. Two-stageness: recovery typically occurs in two stages, powerlessness over alcohol followed by powerlessness over self. All two-stage imagery will be significant.

b. Honeymoon: the joyful period immediately after release from alcohol but before the recognition of one's mental drunkenness. Premature and grandiose attempts to carry the recovery message to others often bring about an end to the honeymoon euphoria.

c. "The Program": a shorthand name for the spiritual content and dynamic of recovery. Designations like "the Way" and "the rule of God" will be understood as similar shorthands.

d. Twelve Steps: twelve specific precepts of recovery setting forth the attitudes and actions that lead to spiritual awakening and serenity. Any mention of "Twelve" as a possible set of formulations or precepts will assume significance.

e. Meetings: assemblies where recovering people hear one another's stories and discuss the Twelve Steps. Meetings are where persons hear the words that make them well. They may be open to everyone or closed to all except those having a desire to stop drinking. References to drawing apart from the crowds, gatherings with the Twelve, and hearing the Word will be meaningful.

f. Sobriety jargon: meetings as commensal table fellowship; the words of recovery as spiritual food embodied by persons who share their stories and then multiplied by others who offer follow-up comments. Parables about serenity, feeding, multiplication of bread, the priority of recovery, radical action, and embracing the program partially versus wholly will be significant.

g. Spiritual awakening: spiritual resurrection following the spiritual death of active alcoholism. References to being lifted up and empowered and to bearing witness for the benefit of others will be salient.

Recovery Story   The recovery story is the narrative all alcoholics tell of their defeat, surrender, conversion, and recovery, which is known to trigger the surrendered admission of powerlessness in hearers. It is a three-part story of suffering, turning, and sobriety. This tripartite structure is a significant feature of the recovery-story genre.

a. Part 1, the drunkalogue: the first part of an alcoholic's story consisting of chained anecdotes illustrating what the person was like before quitting drinking.

b. Part 2, the turning point: an account of the apocalyptic moment when the person "hit bottom," only to experience the grace of God expressed in the desire to stop drinking, followed by surrender, admission of powerlessness, and prayer for help.

c. Part 3, the gratitude song: this element tells what the person is like now, in sobriety, progressing spiritually and trying to carry the message to others and practice the principles of recovery in all their affairs.

d. Two story types: type-one stories depict a smooth progression from stage one to stage two of recovery via the six middle steps of the program. Type-two stories tell of a protracted descent into mental drunkenness following the honeymoon period, much additional suffering, and often a return to drink before the person hits bottom a second time and then surrenders not just his or her alcohol addiction but the entire self to God, takes the six middle steps, and finally attains stage two. Type-two stories are characterized by continually worsening mental drunkenness and self-willed action.

Recovery versus Religion   Even though alcoholics remain open to the good that religious people can offer, they take care not to mix religion with their recovery programs. Although both religions (here referring to Western religions, in particular the principal denominations of Christianity and Judaism) and recovery are spiritual in nature, religions feature drinking rituals and often seem to promote strife, empowerment by self-will, and submission to clerical authority, whereas recovery stresses stopping drinking, surrender, reliance on a higher power, and egalitarian freedom from hierachical governance. Textual features will be interpreted differently depending on whether they are viewed from the perspective of religion or recovery.

a. Service: basic service in recovery consists in carrying the message to those who have experienced apocalypse and the desire to quit drinking. Basic service in religion consists in ministering the wine cup to the many who are still drinking and awaiting revelation.
b. Membership: recovery attracts members by offering life in the eternal now, whereas religions solicit membership based on the hope of avoiding annihilation in a postmortem future. Religions may require the confession of a belief system as a condition of membership, whereas the only requirement for entrance into recovery is a desire to stop drinking.
c. Rank: religions generally contain two ranks of members, lay people and ordained clergy; recovery contains one rank, ordinary alcoholics.
d. Polity: recovery is thoroughly egalitarian, a benign anarchy wherein God rules directly and immediately within each person and in the collective conscience of the group. Religions are often hierarchies wherein overlords mediate the rule of God by means of authority and law.
e. Anonymity: recovery considers anonymity its spiritual founda-

tion, always reminding its members to place principles before personalities. Religions often exalt the personages and offices of their hierarchs.

f. Founders: founders of religions are often divinized and worshipped as messiahs. Thus far, founders of Twelve-Step programs are remembered only as their originating members.

g. Outside issues: religions engage in controversy and endorse and oppose causes, whereas recovery fellowships hold no opinions on outside issues.

In each of the foregoing categories, textual features indicating religion will be understood, perhaps allegorically, as pointers to the essential alcoholism of the religious perspective.

In addition to those listed above, other response typologies also figure in this book and are explained at the point where they govern the interpretation of the text in question.

Interpretive Communities

This book posits twin interpretive communities for Mark's gospel, one contemporary and known to be actual and the other ancient and hypothetical, with the typologies just listed governing the thought of both groups. The former community is the modern fellowship of recovering alcoholics, exdrinkers heretofore blinded by aporia to the alcoholism intentionality of Mark's gospel. The latter group is the first-century sobriety movement here hypothesized as having produced the Gospel of Mark. In their understanding of the Markan genre, the ancient and the modern communities share a common horizon of expectation. Both construe addiction and recovery as spiritual phenomena. Both embrace an image of God as an unnamed higher power manifest in the collective conscience of their egalitarian fellowship, open to individual understanding and encounter but not reducible to conceptual definition and seemingly indifferent to cultic sacrifice and other forms of religious mediation.

The minds of both communities comprise a distinctive argot, spirituality, metanoetics, and apocalyptic. Members begin their journeys to recovery in identical ways, by "hitting bottom" and recognizing alcohol as the cause of their troubles and then by uttering the cry for help etymologically concealed in the name *Jesus*. Both groups follow this soterial Jesus (implicitly in the case of the modern community) in turning from addictive drinking to imbibing the oxymoronic "new wine" of the rule of God. Both groups practice an open commensality whose "bread" is the healing word of recovery distributed communally by the meeting leader and multiplied in the comments of all present. Members progress from illness to wellness by following spiritual precepts known to the ancients as the Twelve (see chap. 6) and to modern alcoholics as the Twelve Steps. Finally, as witnesses to empowerment by God, the members serve as anonymous messengers of recovery to other sufferers.

Secondary Hypotheses

Although argued mainly in literary terms, the theory of audience advanced herein gives rise to a number of secondary hypotheses about Mark's gospel whose implications are historical and theological. The following thumbnail descriptions indicate how these secondary hypotheses will be developed throughout this book:

Exigence   Mark is hypothesized to have written his gospel in Judea during the crisis of the first Roman-Jewish War, in which he foresaw not only the disruption of regional Judaism but also the probable dissolution of the Markan movement itself. So viewed, his book represents an effort to preserve, albeit covertly, the story of his semi-underground sobriety fellowship and its distinctive memory of Jesus.

Ostensible Audience   In addition to writing for a primary if clandestine audience of former drinkers, Mark also targeted a Judean Messiah cult as his apparent or ostensible audience. The hypothesis here is that this cult was preparing, as a postwar survival strategy, to ordain a governing clergy in imitation of the gentile Christian churches to the north. Apparently Mark knew of the cultists' intention to downplay their Jewish identities and present themselves to the Romans as a reformed agency of theocratic governance prepared to maintain social order in a postwar Judea in which they expected Judaism to be outlawed. Hence Mark decided that a book of Scripture adopted by this newly legitimated Messiah cult would be a safe and practical place in which to encode, and thus preserve, the Markans' secret story of Jesus and his original following.

Genre   As to literary form, Mark's book is viewed as a third-person displacement of the recovering alcoholic's sobriety story, the account of worsening illness, turning point, and spiritual awakening told by former drinkers from time immemorial. These stories are particularly associated today with members of Alcoholics Anonymous. To its ostensible audience the gospel would present a perplexing collage of diverse genre features—precisely those that have confounded modern interpreters—which its secret audience would recognize as camouflaging yet at the same time confirming its identity as a recovery story.

Secret Symbols The notorious secret symbols in Mark's gospel, beginning with the writer's own surname, are explainable as Mark's "wink" to his alcoholic readers, coterie reminders of his real but veiled subject, which was unintelligible to outsiders yet readily interpretable in the light of recovery. The explanations given here are unprecedented in the history of Markan exegesis.

Portrait of Jesus Consistent with the trajectory of his career as depicted in the gospel's narrative, the Markan Jesus is limned herein as a wine addict who, like many who enter recovery today, undergoes a surrender experience, stops drinking, and enjoys an initial period of euphoric sobriety during which he prematurely attempts to carry the message of recovery to others, only to succumb to "mental drunkenness" followed by a return to actual drinking and an episode of violence when his grandiose messianism fails to convert others to his way of thinking. At the hour of his definitive turning point, Jesus dies to self and arises spiritually, surrendering not only his drink problem but his will and his life to a God he understands as Father and higher power, thereby attaining what the Markans, like recovering addicts today, understood as "stage two" of sobriety. Jesus' subsequent recovery story thus provided Mark the narrative outline for his gospel.

Psuchē Death Credited to the Markan fellowship is a spirituality identifying Gethsemane rather than Golgotha as locus of the atoning *psuchē* death required of all who seek release from the universal Edenic malady whose extreme is alcohol addiction. This spirituality runs counter to Paul's theology of physical death, resurrection, and substitutionary atonement and suggests that the Markans may have understood the facts of the Jerusalem crucifixion of 30 C.E. to have differed dramatically from those of the surface narrative in Mark 15.

Provenance In the scenario presented here (see chap. 4) Mark's writing is presumed to have been occasioned by the crisis of survival visited on Jewish society in Palestine, and hence on area Jesus groups, by Vespasian's initial military campaign of 67–68 C.E., which terrorized Jewish populations from south Syria to Judea and endangered the whole of regional Jewry. Prior to the Roman-Jewish War, during the period between 30 and 67 C.E., despite the banditry, messianic fervor, and insurrection abroad in the land, Mark's fellowship would have preserved its original Galilean character as a quietistic movement aloof from all political and religious controversy. The few outsiders who knew anything would have known only that the Markan groups consisted of individuals who had renounced wine for water, who met without fanfare in synagogues and homes, and who symbolized their gatherings by fish, bread, and vine.

By contrast, the Judean Messiah community originally based in Jerusalem, a brotherhood that traced its origin to the leader figures Peter, James, and John and to the other disciples who more enthusiastically than soberly followed Jesus from Galilee to Judea, would have repressed all memory of its founder's inebriety, denied its own alcoholic origins, and revised its history. By the time of Vespasian's campaign and Mark's writing, it was in process of becoming a hierarchical cult that was positioning itself to assume theocratic responsibility, under Roman oversight, for governing whatever might remain of regional Judaism, including the Jesus groups (loosely speaking, Jewish Christianity in Judea), in a postwar era sure to feature far stricter Roman demands for order within Jewish territories involved in the rebellion. Members of this increasingly public religion, on whose approval the acceptance of Mark's book depended, would have been the ostensible audience of his text, whereas the partially underground remnants of the anonymous sobriety groups descended from Jesus' original Galilean movement, shaken by Vespasian's brutality in northern Palestine, would have been Mark's secret audience. The hierarchical cult would have read Mark's book as the narrative of a heroic and authoritarian messiah, whereas the former drunkards would have interpreted it as a narratologically transformed and otherwise camouflaged version of the story of a fellow alcoholic and the messianic obsession he experienced on the way to recovery.

In short, Mark's gospel would have grown out of the writer's plan to preserve for his confreres the story of their founder's illness and recovery, along with word of their imperiled sobriety fellowship, by encoding them within a book apparently intended for followers of Jesus Messiah, members of an emergent religion about to be severed from Judaism by the sword of war, whose eucharistic liturgy, like that of the gentile Christians to the north, was a drinking ritual. Deprived of their niche in Judaism on account of its postwar suppression, the Markan groups in Judea probably died out by the end of the century. Apparently some were smothered in the 60s and 70s C.E. by an influx of penitent ascetics who mistook their surrendered abstinence for encratism, whereas others, harassed by increasingly dominical Christian clergies, simply disappeared underground. Although speculative, this scenario is no more conjectural than theories of Markan provenance that assume the gospel's "insider" audience to have been a Messiah cult. Chapter 4 develops this theory of provenance within relevant scholarly contexts.

Liturgical Wine Drinking Hypothesized as the core message of Mark's gospel is a theology of recovery based on the wine ritual that Jesus, recognizing sobriety as the eschatology of paschal drinking, enacts at the Jerusalem supper. It is a theology implicit in the Haggadah, present but veiled in the Christian Eucharist, and still unrecognized by Jew and Christian alike. Whole libraries of books have been written on the significance of Jesus' words and actions over the paschal bread and wine. The mainstream view among Christian theologians is that Jesus intended his followers to drink wine until the Parousia, the "second coming" of the Messiah. As a result, ritual drinking has been practiced over the centuries by nearly all the Christian churches.

Reasoning from the idiosyncratic features of Mark's Last Supper narrative, together with the Markan Jesus' paschal disavowal of drink, his admission of powerlessness and prayer for removal of the cup in Gethsemane, and his refusals of wine from the cross (all examined in chap. 2), the present book identifies Mark's audience as former drinkers who had stopped drinking, ritually and otherwise, in consequence of similar admissions of powerlessness and who had experienced in their own lives the parousia (*para*, "with"; *ousia*, "being"), or felt presence, of God. For the Markans, the end and aim of all drinking is that moment of surrender when one stops. Quitting drinking at the crisis point, the Markans had learned, leads to new-mindedness *(metanoia)*, a truth to which Jesus adverts in the Gospel of Thomas, logion 28, quoted in this chapter's epigraph: "While men drink they remain drunk; when they abjure their wine, their thinking is changed." Like recovering alcoholics today, Jesus and the Markans would not have despised drink or argued against its use; rather, they would have looked on it as the agent of the suffering necessary for one to know the joy of sobriety within the rule of God. Exactly this point is implied in the sapiential observation of alcoholics today, "If I hadn't started to drink, I never would have gotten sober."

Extrapolating from this view of the ironically salvific agency of wine, this book hypothesizes that Jesus (and Mark) regarded his recovery program as extending beyond obvious inebriates to implicate the crypto-alcoholism of humanity at large. To exploit this characteristic illness for the purpose of human redemption, Jesus at the Last Supper, at the apocalyptic hour of his surrender and influenced by Deutero-Isaiah's Zion Poem and Suffering Servant figure (see chap. 3), reinterprets the paschal wine duty as a drinking rite intended to addict many, whose salvific telos is each drinker's admission of powerlessness over alcohol, the first step toward spiritual awakening within the rule of God. Obviously, this theory of the Christian Eucharist differs radically from existing theologies of the Jerusalem supper and of the communal meal memorializing it in the churches. It motivates a new conception of the soteriological purpose of liturgical drinking, not only in Christian ritual, but in Jewish ceremony as well.

All the foregoing implications of the theory of Markan audience are developed and discussed in the remainder of this book. There are many new ideas to consider. The final section of this chapter turns to exegetical and interpretive work.

Preliminary Reinscriptions

Stanley Fish's idea of reading as writing corresponds to Jacques Derrida's term *reinscription*. The Bible scholar Dan Via has characterized Derridean reinscription as a reversal that "subordinates what was prominent and vice versa" and "leads to an irruptive new concept which could never have been included or understood in the previous regime."[42] To illustrate the process and at the same time begin reinscribing Mark from the perspective of addiction and recovery, this chapter now examines three items of biblical subject matter important to an understanding of Mark in the terms proposed: first, the evangelist's cryptic nicknames, "Mark" and "stump-fingered;" second, the block of Q material in which Jesus refers to the Son of Man's reputation as "a glutton and a drunkard" (Mt 11.18–19 and Lk 7.33–35); and third, the Yahwist's narratives of the Fall of Man (Gn 2.25–3.24) and Noah's drunkenness (Gn 9.20–27).

Markan Nicknames

It is generally agreed that the gospel's signatory title, "Mark," is actually a surname or nickname of the evangelist, who many believe was the John Mark of the Book of Acts (see chap. 4). In discussing the anthropology of the Mediterranean area, David Gilmore cites a number of studies on the dynamics of nicknaming.[43] Frequently arising from motives of deprecation or hostility and based on perceptions of deviance or weakness, nicknames, which are sometimes ironic or cryptic, are often perpetuated as much by the parties named as by the namers. Although "Mark" was one of the most common given names in the Roman world, the suggestion here is that its use as a surname/nickname in a Palestinian context could have denoted recovery from alcohol addiction. As Jews in Mark's fellowship would have recognized, "Marcus," the Greco-Roman form of "Mark," when heard in a Hebrew/Aramaic setting, sounds like a transliteration of the Hebrew *mar kôs*, "lord or master" *(mar)* of the "cup or chalice" *(kôs)*.[44] Now "cupmaster" is in several ways ambiguous. Ordinarily it has the transparent and in the first instance deprecatory meanings of tippler and ritual minister of the wine cup. To alcoholics, however, it will also have the esoteric meaning of one who has survived the ravages of drink and gained mastery over alcohol. Hence the surname "Marcus" could function in a Hebrew/Aramaic milieu, in the wordplay of exdrunkards who would contextualize it within their experience of addiction and recovery, as a coterie designation exactly equivalent to the modern term "recovering alcoholic." Indeed, "Marcus/Markôs" may have been a nickname for any member of the Markan fellowship. Just as today one hears "so and so is an A.A.," first-century Palestinians aware of the movement may have said "so and so is a Markôs." In sum, "cupmaster" would have been a deliciously ambiguous self-designation appropriated by members of the ancient sobriety groups hypothesized here.

Equally interesting, an even more cryptic nickname of the first evangelist motivates a similar alcoholism interpretation. The so-called Anti-Marcionite Prologue of the late second century speaks of "[Mark] who is called 'stump-fingered' [*colobodactylus*] because he had rather small fingers in comparison with the rest of his body."[45] Owing to its oddity, the name "stump-fingered" is generally assumed to be authentic rather than invented. But what does it signify? Surely the explanation given in the Anti-Marcionite Prologue is so obvious as to be suspect, but the perspective of recovery suggests an answer: the name "stump-fingered" could have referred to one who cannot grasp a drinking vessel, who cannot take up the wine cup. In other words, it would have served as a figurative designation for a person who cannot drink normally and so no longer drinks at all. Such an interpretation comports well with the understanding of "Markôs" just discussed. Those outside the Markan fellowship would have considered "stump-fingered" a deprecatory term connoting the shame of addiction, whereas insiders would have embraced it as an emblem of their wellness. Just as former drinkers in today's recovery meetings often say, "I am a recovering alcoholic, sober by the grace of God," members of the Markan groups may have said, "I am a Markôs, stump-fingered by the grace of God."

Alone, either of these nickname interpretations could be dismissed as a coincidence unrelated to any particular theory of Markan audience. The two names together, however, subsumed within a single interpretive rubric, constitute credible witnesses to the historicity of Mark's fellowship as a community of former wine addicts. Moreover, to read "Marcus" as *markôs* is to identify the image of the cup, arguably the central image of the entire gospel (Mk 9.41, 10.38–39, 14.23–25, and 14.36), as a key term in the book's very title. In short, to the insider audience of knowing Greek/Aramaic bilinguals who constituted its primary readership, the first gospel proclaimed "the good message of Jesus Messiah" (Mk 1.1) under the entitling signature, "according to the Cupmaster."

"Behold, a Glutton and a Drunkard!"

From an alcoholism perspective, a highly significant yet generally underinterpreted gospel text is the passage from the Sayings Gospel Q (Mt 11.18–19; Lk 7.33–35) wherein Jesus, in explaining the short parable of the children in the marketplace (Mt 11.16–17; Lk 7.31–32), overtly acknowledges his reputation as a drunkard:

> (Mt 11.18) For John came neither eating nor drinking, and they say, "He has a demon"; (19) the Son of Man came eating and drinking, and they say, "Behold, a glutton and a drunkard, a friend of tax collectors and sinners!" Yet wisdom is justified by her deeds.

Religious readers regularly ignore this surprising revelation, whereas alcoholics will consider the disclosure of Jesus' rumored identity as a drunkard the salient feature of the entire passage. Scholarly readers ordinarily bypass this disclosure as well, concentrating instead on other questions that the passage raises, such as the age of the parable compared to that of the explanation, the meaning of "Son of Man," the interpretation of the wisdom saying, whether Jesus fasted and how observant he was, and so on. Where present, discussions of the epithet "glutton and drunkard" generally euphemize its content. Olaf Linton, for example, has said that it indicates only that Jesus "took part in social joy" and was criticized for being "too devoted to food and drink."[46] Dominic Crossan asserts that the epithet taints Jesus solely by virtue of his commensality with undesirables, not because he was remembered as an actual drunkard.[47] Yet this is exactly the memory to which the saying on its face refers. In short, no one has really inquired into Jesus' self-admitted reputation as an inebriate.

Form and source criticism of the passage has already established the epithet's original independence from the "eating and drinking" context. Rudolf Bultmann reckons the explanation of the parable of the children (11.18–19) to have stemmed from an older source and to have been attached to the parable (11.16–17) only later in the tradition.[48] Norman Perrin contends that "glutton and drunkard," obviously the key phrase in any alcoholism reading, "belongs to the polemics of the controversy surrounding Jesus' earthly ministry during his lifetime, rather than to the circumstances of the controversies between the early Church and Judaism."[49] Accepting these form-critical conclusions serves to separate the epithet "glutton and drunkard" from the overall framework about "eating and drinking" into which it was introduced and also from the saying about "tax collectors and sinners" with which it was later conjoined in Q. Simply put, "glutton and drunkard" reflects a memory of Jesus older than and originally independent of its context and purpose in the Q material as finally developed.

As regards source criticism, Joachim Jeremias, echoing tradition, says that the phrase "glutton and drunkard" derives from Dt 21.20 and, as applied to Jesus, "stigmatizes him on the strength of this connection as 'a refractory and rebellious son' who deserved to be stoned."[50] Joseph Fitzmyer disputes Jeremias's claim on the grounds that Matthew's Q phrase, *phagos kai oinopotēs* ("glutton and drunkard"), "scarcely reflects" the Septuagint's *symbolokopōn oinophlygei* ("given-to-feasting drunkard").[51] Fitzmyer is referring to the grammatical differences between the two phrases and to the fact that *symbolokopōn* is a different word from *phagos*. Deuteronomy 21.20 is part of a longer passage (Dt 21.18–21) prescribing stoning as punishment for a son whose parents bring him before the elders and accuse him thus: "This our son is stubborn and rebellious, he will not obey our voice; he is one [here the Hebrew roots translate literally] squandering and drinking" (Dt 21.20). The question is, exactly what is being alleged by the original Hebrew? Widely translated in traditional versions as "glutton and drunkard," the Hebrew roots for "squander" and "drink" may be interpreted simply as naming attributes of a self-indulgent individual who insists on partying all the time instead of behaving responsibly. Some recent versions (e.g., the Jerusalem Bible and New American Bible), seeking greater fidelity to the original Hebrew, translate the roots as "wastrel and drunkard." Although this newer phrase distances itself from the inoffensive "eating and drinking" idiom, it retains the grammatical coordination of the older reading.

As to grammatical form, the writers of the Septuagint rendered the two Hebrew roots not as coordinate nominals (two names, an X and a Y) but rather as a single nominal following an intensifying modifier (an X-erous Y). Construing "squander" as a modifier of "drunkard" yields the phrase "squanderous drunkard," whose purport is quite different from versions in which the roots are rendered as conjoined nominals. Here the grammatical head of the phrase, and therefore its sole semantic base, is the nominal "drunkard" alone. "Squanderous drunkard" does not name someone a squanderer and a drinker; rather, it denotes a drinker whose drinking is squanderous, whose imbibing is extravagant or dissolute. In short, it names an out-of-control inebriate. It would be difficult to euphemize such a phrase, to hold that it designates only an innocent bon vivant. Translations in the idiom of modern alcoholism parlance would be "unbridled drunk" or "full-blown alcoholic." On this reading, Dt 21.18–21 prescribes stoning not for excessive banqueting but rather for incorrigible alcoholism, actually the likelier case, and surely the interpretation to which former wine addicts in the first century would have been drawn, including Jesus' confreres in Galilee.[52]

Here then are grounds for two conclusions: (a) the Q epithet in its original form, ascribed to Jesus in his own day, at the outset of what Edward Schillebeeckx calls the "primary Aramaic phase" of Q,[53] was indeed based on Dt 21.20, and (b) Galileans here identified in theory as former addicts in Jesus' recovery fellowship would have understood the original epithet to indicate that Jesus had once been, in fact as well as reputation, an out-of-control drunkard. In other words, they would have rejected the euphemistic reading of the Deuteronomic phrase "glutton and drunkard" in favor of the blunt alcoholism version, "unbridled drunk." The "glutton" part of the saying handed on by Matthew and Luke a half-century later would have been reintroduced in a subsequent phase of Q, partly to make the epithet conform to the less scandalous understanding of Dt 21.20 and partly to achieve semantic parallelism with the two-part expression "eating and drinking" in the John/Jesus framework into which the epithet was ultimately inserted.[54]

Reconstructing an original designation of Jesus as a "full-blown alcoholic" in this way brings to light a primal scene formerly lost to Christian memory, a scene presumably repressed by the Jerusalem brotherhood soon after Jesus' disappearance, known but transmogrified in the evolution of the Q materials and completely unheard of in the Pauline churches and the Jerusalem missions.[55] Of the early communities, only the Galilean recovery movement, whose tradition

Mark preserves clandestinely, would have remembered the epithet in its original form, even as it would have remembered the actuality of Jesus' alcoholism. According to the present theory, Mark omitted the saying from his book not because, as is ordinarily said, it belongs to a tradition he did not know (Q) but rather because he believed its inclusion might disclose the very secret he wished to conceal: word of Jesus' alcoholic illness and of the origin of the rule of God as a sobriety fellowship.[56] Mark would have been astonished to learn that later gospel writers (Mt 11.19; Lk 7.34) could quote what he understood as Jesus' admission of addiction without completely alienating their audiences.

The Biblical Etiology of Addiction

Recovering addicts will recognize in the familiar Genesis allegories of the Fall of Man and Noah's drunkenness the etiology of humankind's alcoholism.[57] Key elements in the story of the Fall are the tree of knowledge, the serpent, and the curses God places on the serpent and the soil on account of humans' self-willed disobedience. The Noah story introduces drunkenness per se and points to the inherited nature of alcohol addiction and to the servant role assigned the addict. Ordinarily unassociated, the two stories are in fact linked by a textual trace at Gn 5.29, which connects God's curse on the soil (3.17–19) with Noah's discovery of fermentation (9.20).

In the Genesis account of the Edenic tree of knowledge, Yahweh commands as follows (Anchor Bible version, hereinafter AB):

> (Gn 2.16) You are free to eat of any tree of the garden, except only the tree of knowledge of good and bad, of which you are not to eat. For the moment you eat of it, you shall be doomed to death.

Just what is this "knowledge," the eating of which causes death? A close look at the original language can bring new meanings to light. E. A. Speiser glosses the Hebrew root underlying "knowledge," *yd'*, as signifying a dynamic process, "to experience, to come to know, in the broad sense," "to be in full possession of mental and physical powers." He links this root to motifs of sexual awareness, wisdom, and natural paradise.[58] Claus Westermann says that *yd'* refers to functional knowledge about living and can also be translated "succeed."[59] So in modern terms, "knowledge of good and bad" in Gn 2.16 is by no means limited to morality. Rather, it connotes such things as intuitive mastery; effective coping skills; guidance to the next right action; satisfactory interpersonal relations, including sex; and the ability to handle baffling situations—in sum, all the competencies of successful living that sober persons sought but failed to attain as addicts but are promised in recovery.

Then why the commandment not to eat such wonderful fruit? Precisely because, in the Genesis allegory, our eating of the fruit represents our efforts to master successful living by our own hand. This is what the alcoholic calls "playing God." We truly live when we maintain conscious contact with God in the eternal "now" of divine presence, whereas eating of the tree of knowledge represents humankind's attempt to "know" our knowledge apart from the now and thus to live by concepts that misrepresent reality and reduce God to a theological construct, a theism to be believed or disbelieved as one chooses. Ultimately, eating the fruit of the tree of knowledge symbolizes humans' rejection of the Living God in favor of a false god of our own making.[60]

The serpent, a figure of fertility and wisdom borrowed from a Canaanite snake cult and traditionally identified with Satan, symbolizes the narcissistic extension of the self and division of consciousness in humanity's quest for auto-empowerment, resulting from a confusion of the contingent freedom of creaturehood with the autonomy of deity and a view of the "self" as a wise and omnipotent other. In other words, the story dramatizes the psychodynamic of playing God. The serpent says:

> (Gn 3.5) The moment you eat of the tree of knowledge your eyes will be opened and you will be the same as God.

The serpent's utterance represents humans trying "to god" themselves, to convince themselves that they possess a power and a wisdom they lack, that reality is other than what it is. This "mental drunkenness," as recovering alcoholics call it, constitutes the underlying pathology of all addiction.

The curses and punishments God visits on humankind, ultimately curatives, are the Yahwist's mythological way of portraying the addictive spell that falls on persons when, asserting the regnancy of the self, they attempt to usurp godhood. First comes the curse on the serpent:

> (Gn 3.14) God Yahweh said to the serpent: "Because you did this, cursed shall you be. . . . (15) I will plant enmity between you and all humans, and between your offspring and theirs; they shall strike at your head, you at their heel."[61]

E. A. Speiser points out that the meaning of the Hebrew root *'rr*, translated "curse" or "ban," is "to restrain (by magic), bind (by a spell)."[62]

The concept amounts to a primitive understanding of the deadly grip of addiction. Enmity between the serpent and humanity represents the inner conflict endemic to all mental drunkenness and experienced by every generation. Yahweh's curse condemns humanity to the consequences of its divided consciousness, constant agitation and inner conflict. Actually, it is not a curse *on* the serpent so much as the curse *of* a serpent placed on humankind. The alcoholic's term for this condition is "the bondage of self," a modern idiom that nicely renders the Hebrew root *'rr.*

God continues to enumerate the punishments inflicted on humankind:

> (Gn 3.16)· I will greatly increase your pain and your desire. . . .[63] (17) Cursed be the soil on your account. In anguished toil shall you eat from it all the days of your life. (18) Thorns and thistles shall it bring forth for you. . . . (19) By the sweat of your face shall you earn your bread.

No alcoholic needs an explanation of the "pain/desire" linkage. It is the emotional hallmark of addiction. The curse on the soil symbolizes combative struggle against every element of one's external environment, a companion to the conflict within one's divided consciousness symbolized by the curse of the serpent. Altogether, these curses and punishments allegorically represent the result of humanity's hubristic tendency to play God: unending agonistic struggle, both mental and physical, accompanied by unremitting desire and suffering. In modern terms, the curses identify the story of the Fall as an account of the origin of addiction. When recovering alcoholics say they have "stopped fighting everything and everyone," or are "powerless over people, places, and things," they are attesting to their release not only from desire but also from the serpent curse (psychic turmoil) and the soil curse (outward physical conflict).

But what of alcohol per se? In Gn 9.20, at the beginning of the episode of Noah's drunkenness, ordinarily considered a theologically insignificant coda to the story of the Flood, the Yahwist says of Noah:

> (Gn 9.20) And Noah, a man of the soil, was the first to plant a vineyard.

Sooner or later, most recovering people recognize that their alcoholism predates their addiction to drink. "Pouring alcohol" on their mental drunkenness was only another futile attempt to achieve happiness through self-exertion. From the perspective of recovery, therefore, Noah's turn to viticulture mythologically portrays the beginning of humankind's reliance on alcohol and identifies Noah as archetypal addict. Its connection to the story of the Fall would be arbitrary were it not for the textual thread the Yahwist has woven into the Priestly genealogy of the antediluvian patriarchs (Gn 5.1–32):

> (Gn 5.29) He named him Noah, which means, one who will bring us relief . . . from the very soil that Yahweh has cursed.

Thus Gn 5.29 connects Noah's discovery of wine (Gn 9.20) with the Edenic soil curse (Gn 3.17–19) by introducing Noah as a hero who will overcome God's curse on the soil by fermenting and drinking its produce. How quintessentially alcoholic to think wine more powerful than God! Most ancients looked on fermentation as a miraculous gift of the gods. Not so the Yahwist, who considers wine to be something we humans invented for use in our rebellion against God, a magical potion we deludedly believe will confer serenity short of atonement. What is represented in this primal scene of humans' proclivity toward drink is far graver than the happy thought of "wine gladdening the heart of man" (Ps 104.15) or wine as a comforting narcotic for misery (Prv 31.6–7). The discovery of wine only seems to portend what Gerhard von Rad has called "an amelioration of the severe [soil] curse."[64]

As if to illustrate this point, the Yahwist next relates the shocking story of Noah's drunken and naked sleep:

> (Gn 9.21) Noah drank of the wine, became drunk, and lay uncovered inside his tent. (22) Canaan then beheld his father's nakedness. . . .[65] (24) Then Noah woke up from his wine and learned that his youngest son had seen his nakedness. (25) He said, "A curse on Canaan! A slave of slaves shall he be to his brothers!"

Traditional interpretation considers Canaan to be the villain of the piece, but it was not he who exposed his father's nakedness but the drunken parent himself.[66] No alcoholic would interpret the story as casting blame on Canaan. The encounter is obviously innocent, and the truth here is in any case far more horrible than mere disrespect of a parent. What is depicted is the moment the alcoholic illness passes from father to son. Such was the Yahwist's point in recounting the present story. Noah's degradation, coupled with his subsequent anger, engenders not only fear but paradoxically guilt in his son Canaan, and so the curse of alcohol addiction passes from one generation to the next. Chapter 3 discusses this curse as interpreted by Deutero-Isaiah (54.9–10), who seems to understand it as coming not from Noah but from God.

The endings of these Genesis stories also introduce themes related to recovery that play important roles later in Scripture. In the Garden of Eden story, Yahweh concludes by assuring humanity that his curses will remain

(Gn 3.19) until you return to the ground, for from it you were taken.

In Hebrew, "ground" or "earth" ('*ᵃdāmā*) is a play on the name "Adam" or "human" ('*ādām*). Hence, humans will remain under God's curse until they find their true humanity by renouncing arrogated deity. Genesis 3.19 is usually understood as referring to physical death, but alcoholics will see it as pointing to the spiritual surrender and humiliation required for recovery. Nearly a thousand years later, Mark's Jesus would further illuminate this pathway to wellness through his own surrender on the ground of another garden, Gethsemane (see chap. 2). So too, the curse of servitude Noah places on Canaan (Gn 9.25), who represents all descendants of Noah destined to become alcohol addicts, signifies more than enslavement to drink. At a deeper level it identifies the alcoholic as a suffering servant to his nonalcoholic brothers and sisters. This is a theme theologized by Deutero-Isaiah (see chap. 3), touched on by Joel (chap. 5), incorporated by Jesus as an important but veiled part of his message about wine at the Last Supper (chap. 2), and emplaced as the cornerstone of the Markan theology of recovery.

Overall, it is tempting to conclude that the Yahwist was familiar with the drinking game, and perhaps with primitive ideas about recovery. He may have learned of alcohol addiction from the same Canaanite culture that had introduced the nomadic Israelites to wine in the first place. Conforming to the sequence of recovery recognized today, Mark in his gospel chiasmatically reverses the etiological order presented in the Yahwist's stories of the Fall and of Noah's drunkenness (onset of mental drunkenness followed by addiction to drink) by depicting in Jesus' paschal acts the order of recovery: disavowal of drink (the Last Supper) followed by a humbled renunciation of self-will leading to atonement (Gethsemane).

Recovery Criticism

As the foregoing reinscriptions demonstrate, viewing Scripture from a perspective of addiction and recovery not only leads to a focus on textual features ignored in conventional readings, it also culminates in radically different interpretations of the texts themselves and of the history implied by the texts. In reading Mark's gospel as the product of an unremembered Palestinian sobriety fellowship, the present book may be viewed as a prolegomenon to a theology of recovery similar to liberation and feminist theologies in the way in which, as Elisabeth Schüssler Fiorenza says, they "challenge historical-literary biblical scholarship to abandon the posture of scientific facticity, value-neutrality, and antiquarian mentality and to recover historical consciousness as remembrance for the present and the future."[67] The approach of this theology can be called recovery criticism. In hypothesizing that Mark's gospel was only ostensibly intended for the Christian communities that adopted it, recovery criticism develops a hermeneutics of secrecy and textual ambiguity. In portraying Jesus as a recovering alcohol addict, recovery criticism advances a hermeneutics of personal apocalypse and powerlessness, radical humility, and spiritual awakening. And in extolling anonymity and the placing of principles above personalities, recovery criticism proposes a hermeneutics that devalues messiahship and clerical office as devices for ordering the rule of God. All these topics have relevance not only for a new-historicist reconstruction of the Markan community but also for spiritual praxis in the world of the new millennium.

✛ 2 ✛

THE MARKAN PASSION

The paschal bread given by Jesus is the message his speaking
embodies: "This [wine] is [the cause of] my blood[shed],
yet also covenant blood, which I pour out for
[the recovery of] many."
—Alcoholism reading of Mk 14.22 and 24

The chief source of evidence supporting the hypothesis of this book
is the text of Mark itself viewed from a perspective of addiction and
recovery. Much of that evidence takes the form of systematic yet generally unrecognized linguistic ambiguities apparently intended to be
understood in one way by Jewish Messiah cultists and in quite another
by members of the Markôs fellowship. This chapter examines the
ambiguities in the Markan Passion narrative (14.1–16.8) because it
is here, at the climax of the gospel, that the alcoholism theme on
which these ambiguities turn, obscure throughout the first thirteen
chapters of Mark, becomes overt and apparent to readers willing to
set aside received interpretations and view the text as former addicts
would, through typologies of alcoholic suffering and recovery.

The chapter focuses on the four main scenes in the Passion: the
Last Supper, Gethsemane, the Crucifixion, and the Empty Tomb. As
they are traditionally construed, their respective dramatic functions
are ritual antedonation, agonistic interlude, climax, and conclusion.
From the angle of recovery, however, they function as epiphanal turning point, sacrificial conclusion, anticlimax, and denouement. In
them, the Cupmaster introduces drinking and not drinking as critical topics, the figure of the cup as an emblem of alcohol addiction,
self-repudiation as the key to atonement, and empowerment by the
spiritual power that Mark's Jesus calls *dunamis*. To recovering addicts

these are highly significant typologies. Although studied from many points of view, Jesus' words over the wine at the Last Supper, and his emphatic disavowal of drink, have never been scrutinized from the perspective of the alcoholic. Yet who knows better than exdrinkers the essential meaning of those utterances, the recognition of alcohol as the cause of one's troubles ("this [wine] is my blood . . . ," Mk 14.24), followed by the decision to stop drinking ("I will drink no more of the fruit of the vine . . . ," Mk 14.25)?

In fact, former addicts will see in the Markan Passion an illustration of the salvific irony of alcoholism: humiliation by drink can lead to exaltation by God. Consumed inveterately, alcohol ultimately deflates the drinker's pride and ego and so prepares each person for spiritual awakening. Obscured by more shortsighted explanations of religious drinking, this paradoxical truth provides an eschatological rationale for the presence of alcohol in religious ritual. For in church or synagogue, just as in drawing room or barroom, recovery begins by the grace of God, when drinkers recognize alcohol as both source and symbol of their problems and quit drinking. Until then, one's duty is to drink religiously, in both sacred and profane settings, suffer the often dreadful consequences, and await the intervention of God. In the present view, this is how the Markan Jesus at the Last Supper interprets the Passover wine ritual. Recognizing wine as the cause of his impending bloodshed, yet sensing the imminence of recovery, Jesus speaks the mysterious words over the paschal cup, Mk 14.24 as glossed later in this chapter: "This [wine] is [the cause of] my blood[shed], yet also covenant blood, [the message of] which I pour out for [the recovery of] many." Once established as the center of Christian worship, liturgical wine drinking, unlike all other drinking occasions, would always be accompanied by these veiled but saving words.

The Jungian theologian David Miller, studying the theme of drunkenness in Christian thinking, comes close to the position outlined here when he sees the archetype of Jesus in Silenos, the drunken teacher of Dionysus, who counseled unbridled drinking and the soonest possible death, once born, of ego.[1] Miller says, "The [self-willed] teetotaler and the [drinking] alcoholic make the same mistake! They are both intemperately temperate in their literalism. Neither is drunk in Silenos' radical sense" (p. 137). Miller rightly equates alcoholism (he means active alcoholism) with abstinence (he means the self-empowered abstinence of teetotaler or temperance advocate) as "both the same disease . . . from the silenic perspective. They are *theological* ailments in which one suffers a literalism" (p. 139). Such persons, says Miller, grasp the urgency of time, but they view their problem as "a concern of will and reason, a matter of personal control" (p. 139). They attempt to live life successfully "by doing something (drinking) or by not doing (abstinence)" (p. 139). What Miller's otherwise perceptive discussion overlooks is the third perspective, which lies at the heart of the argument here, that of the former drinker sober by the grace of God. In short, Miller overlooks the perspective of the recovering alcoholic, for whom sobriety is indeed the radical drunkenness of Silenos.

In focusing on the four major scenes named above, this chapter ignores other elements of the Passion, such as the woman with the perfume jar (14.3–9), betrayal (14.17–20), the stricken shepherd (14.27–28), Peter's denial (14.66–72), and the young man in white (14.51–52 and 16.5–7). Chapter 6 interprets these elements as anticlerical allegories, figurative reminders to the Markôs people in Mark's own day of how the original Jerusalem brotherhood had betrayed the memory of their Galilean fellowship by denying their alcoholic backgrounds and abandoning the role of servant for that of hierarch.

The Last Supper (14.22–26)

Mark's Jesus on the evening of Passover is a man in crisis. He has come to Jerusalem as a provincial exorcist and wisdom teacher with a reputation for personalist interpretation of Jewish religious law. Obsessed by his mission, he has attacked the Jewish religious leaders, seeking to change their thinking through contentious rhetoric (Mk 11.27–12.44), bellicose allegory (Mk 12.1–10), and vituperation (Matthew 23, though not in Mark). He has assaulted the Temple physically (Mk 11.15–18) and predicted its destruction (Mk 13.2). Recovering alcoholics, all too familiar with the extremes of self-assertion characteristic of addictive behavior, will perceive Jesus' actions as those of a man "drunk" on self-will. The Jerusalem authorities have little choice but to act against him.

Yet Jesus has reached the turning point. He has "sobered up" from this mental drunkenness and in an apocalyptic "hangover revelation," as it were (Mark 13, discussed in chap. 6), has seen that the God of Passover acts at the hour of catastrophe to convict religious drinkers of their powerlessness over alcohol, the first step toward recovery. Jesus further recognizes that the sign of God's initiative at this critical hour is a transformation within each person, a replacement of the compulsion to drink, ritually or otherwise, by the desire to stop drinking and to consume instead the figurative "new wine" of the rule of God (Mk 14.25). Aware of this message taking shape within him, Jesus approaches the Passover seder, the meal Christians were to call the Last Supper.

The oldest written accounts of the Supper, which portray the institution of the Christian Eucharist, are those of Mark-Matthew and Paul-Luke. Mark's version begins with preamble-like material in 14.12–21 (discussed later in this chapter and in chap. 6), followed by the meal narrative in 14.22–26. The latter consists of four parts: the words and actions over the bread (14.22), the giving of the cup (14.23), the words about wine (14.24–25), and a report of the singing of the Hallel psalms (14.26). Other canonical accounts of the Last Supper include elements not found in Mark: Matthew adds "eat" to Mark's bread words (26.26), and "to the forgiveness of sins" to the wine words (26.27). Paul has "which is for you, do this in memory of me" in the bread words (1 Cor 11.24), and "after supper," "new covenant," and "in memory of me" in the wine words (1 Cor 11.25). Luke adds "given" to Paul's bread words (22.19). Nonetheless, because the Markan forms, although not as old as the Pauline, are the least influenced by early eucharistic formulas, many scholars consider Mark's account, taken as a whole, closest to the actual words of Jesus.

Important in any discussion of the Last Supper is the linguistic and form-critical background provided by the work of Joachim Jeremias.[2] Concerning the eucharistic words per se, Jeremias (p. 192) considers Mark's to be the oldest attainable form of the bread words (14.22). As for the wine words, Jeremias in one place (p. 192) argues that "after supper" in 1 Cor 11.25 identifies the Pauline form as oldest, but in another place (p. 170–71), quoting Gustaf Dalman's dictum that the more scandalous the reading the more likely it will be historical, he points out that the susceptibility of Mark's "this is my blood" to a Thyestian (blood-drinking) interpretation and the possibility that Paul's "this cup is the new covenant" represents an attempt to ward off such an inference together weigh in favor of Mark's form as the oldest. But all such questions remain open. Some scholars (e.g., Werner Kelber) believe that the entire narrative outline of the Passion originates with Mark.[3] Others (e.g., Dominic Crossan) believe that Mark worked from a written source describing these events.[4]

"A Jar of Water" (14.13–15)

The Supper immediately follows the enigmatic reference to a man carrying a jar of water in Jesus' instructions to the disciples concerning Passover preparations. Commentators have never agreed on the significance of this reference. The view here is that it served as a reminder to knowing insiders that the Supper had been a gathering of the water-drinking Markôs fellowship:

> (14.13) And he sent two of his disciples, and said to them, "Go into the city, and a man carrying a jar of water will meet you; follow him, (14) and wherever he enters, say to the householder, 'The Teacher says, Where is my guest room, where I am to eat the passover with my disciples?'"

Traditionally the passage has been thought to show Jesus' ability to see the future, whereas contemporary interpreters stress the clandestine nature of Jesus' words. Howard Clark Kee, for example, writes that "secret signs and arrangements" such as this "seem to be part of Mark's intention *to portray the followers of Jesus as an esoteric group* [Kee's emphasis] . . . a secret society."[5] Just so, but what makes the passage noteworthy, beyond the mysterious prearrangement, is the anomaly of what the man is carrying, a jar. Commentators (e.g., C. S. Mann)[6] point out that only women carried jars, whereas male porters carried waterskins. From the alcoholism perspective, however, the oddity is not the vessel but what it contained: not wine, the ritual drink of Passover, but water, one's drink after renouncing wine. In other words, we would expect a person involved in Passover preparations to have been carrying wine for the celebration rather than water. So interpreted, the anomalous jar of water would have functioned as an in-group pointer to the Markans' memory of the Jerusalem seder as a meeting of their sobriety fellowship. Later sections of this book further discuss water as a sobriety emblem in Mark in connection with baptism (1.9–10), the cup of water (9.41), and Elijah as water drinker (15.35–36).

Bread-as-Word Embodied (14.22)

The meal narrative begins at verse 22. The Revised Standard Version (RSV) reads Jesus' words over the bread as follows:

> (14.22) And as they were eating, he took bread, and blessed and broke it, and gave it to them, and said, "Take, this is my body."

By most accounts these words reflect the blessing of the bread preceding the main meal of the seder. The uniqueness of the event stems from Jesus' equation of bread and body. As much as these words have been studied in the Christian tradition, the first question of interpretation here has been generally ignored: what does "this" refer to in the clause "this is my body?" So much time has been devoted to discussing the meaning of "is" that almost no one has noticed the referential ambiguity of "this" *(toutō)*. Readers invariably assume that "this" can refer only to the morsels of bread Jesus has just distributed or to the bread together with the other actions mentioned in the verse, without recognizing that it can also refer to Jesus' next utterance, his words over the cup of wine. Text-grammatically, the question is whether "this" is deictic (a pointer to an object outside the text, in this case the bread morsels) or endophoric cataphora (a pointer looking ahead to an upcoming block of text, in this case Jesus' next words). Usually the context of a statement precludes such ambiguities from arising. For example, a theatergoer who tells an intruder "This is my seat" is quite clearly referring deictically to the piece of furniture on which the person is seated, whereas a woman who responds to a marriage proposal by saying "This is my answer" is just as obviously referring cataphorically to what she will say next.

But with Mk 14.22, the context itself is ambiguous. Its definition depends on how one understands the meanings of "bread" *(artos)* and "body" *(sōma)*. The position here is that bread in Mark, at the Last Supper and in the three bread stories (6.31–44, 8.1–9, and 14–21), always symbolizes the Word of God, the message of recovery. Bread as a symbol of Word, of Torah, would have been a familiar idea to first-century Jews.[7] During the Passover meal, as Jesus begins the customary meditation over the matzo, he suddenly realizes that in so speaking he embodies, or incarnates, the Word that the bread represents. It is this realization that he voices in verse 22. For readers of the Markan text, therefore, understanding "bread" as symbolizing Word and "body" as indicating the embodiment of that Word by the speaker creates a context wherein "this" functions not as a deictic pointer to the bread but as a cataphoric reference introducing Jesus' words over the wine, reported in verses 24–25. In this context, the imperative "take" (*labete,* a verb with multiple senses) would mean not "grasp this matzo" but "take heed, pay attention, listen." Hence the following glosses would attach to verse 22 as read by RSV:

> Take [that is, attend], this [what I am about to do and say, which the bread I have given you represents] is my body [that is, the message I embody].

So understood, the verse can be retranslated thus:

> (14.22) And as they were eating, he took bread, and blessed and broke it, and gave it to them, and said, "Pay attention, this is the message I embody."

The message itself, the giving of the cup and then the words about wine, blood, covenant, and drinking no more, comes next.

Notice that this retranslation is not an interpretation of Mark's Greek but a straightforward reading keyed by the ambiguous reference of "this," and every bit as literal as the traditional version. In other words, the referential ambiguity motivates two plain sense readings. Ecclesiastical translators, perhaps without even noticing the ambiguity, have always selected the reading reflecting Christian eucharistic theology, "this [bread morsel] is my body," whereas translators seeking to represent the text as understood by readers focused on Jesus' following words about wine—former addicts, for example—will select the other reading, "this [that I am about to say] is what I embody."

In semiotic terms, the bread Jesus distributes is a sign of what he is about to do and say and, in doing and saying, will embody. Despite centuries of theological study of these words, Christians have always confined themselves to the assumption that Jesus was talking about bread somehow becoming his body and have never recognized that these words can also mean that by virtue of his ensuing speech act, Jesus' body becomes bread metaphorically realized in the Word his body utters, that is, in the message about wine that his speaking incarnates. This view directs attention away from the bread as a mystical object and toward the semantic content of Jesus' subsequent discourse on wine. Here, what happens as a consequence of the speech act is not a transubstantiation of bread to body but a transformation of thinking as Jesus comes to understand himself as Word embodied.

So read, Mk 14.22 provides a basis for harmonizing Jesus' self-image in Mark with that in the fourth Gospel. John's portrait of Jesus presupposes his self-awareness all along as Word incarnate, whereas Mark's Jesus displays no such awareness until the Last Supper, when he first comprehends the message about wine that he is destined to carry to suffering humanity. In identifying the bread of Passover as a symbol of the Word he embodies, Mark's Jesus sounds very much like his Johannine counterpart, the Logos enfleshed, who characterizes himself as "bread of life" (Jn 6.35 and 48) and "living bread come down from heaven" (Jn 6.51 and 58). It is not that Jesus becomes bread-that-is-really-body but that bread-that-symbolizes-Word becomes Jesus. Simply put, bread-as-Word is what Jesus is, what he incarnates, what his speaking makes real and present.

The Markan Bread Stories

A parabolic interpretation of the three bread stories in Mark supports the idea that Jesus considered bread to be a symbol of the Word of God, spoken or preached. In the first two stories (6.31–44 and 8.1–

9) Jesus responds to the people's need for food by breaking and distributing "five loaves and two fish," thereby feeding "five thousand men," and then "seven loaves" and "a few small fish," thereby feeding "about four thousand people." Despite the allure of literalness, readers have long seen bread in these stories as a metaphor for Jesus' teaching and its multiplied residue as Christian doctrine: "twelve baskets full of broken pieces and of the fish" for Jewish readers, and "broken pieces left over, seven baskets full," for gentile. For recovering alcoholics in today's Twelve-Step groups, however, the significance of the superabundance of bread is not the deposit of church doctrine but the idea that at meetings, the words of recovery are not just those of the meeting leader but the leader's words multiplied in the remarks of everyone present. Twelve-Step practice reflects this understanding. At group meetings, the person chosen as speaker distributes the bread-as-Word to the assembled members, who then multiply this "bread" in their shared comments within smaller groups.[8] All leave the meeting having "eaten their fill" and conscious of a miraculous leftover. Often they speak of being "fed" in these meetings, of receiving "spiritual food." Mark's stories of the multiplication of the loaves convey just this sense of bread as Word of God spoken through people and thereby multiplied.

In the third bread story (8.14–21) Jesus' disciples, prefigures of the Christian clergy emerging in Mark's day, have only one loaf in their boat and do not see how it can be multiplied. In reply Jesus warns them to beware of "the leaven of the Pharisees and of Herod." Viewed as a recovery trope, the image of one unmultiplied loaf suggests that the disciples' proclamation is limited to one spiritual principle rather than a number of principles organized programmatically (see the discussion of the Twelve in chap. 6) and that the disciples intend to do all the preaching themselves rather than allow the Word to be multiplied through the speech of others. Avoiding the leaven of the Pharisees and of Herod would thus mean refraining from preaching that is Pharisaic and Herodian, that is, moralistic and political. But the disciples do not understand this symbolism. In response Jesus reminds them of the superabundant residues in the earlier feeding stories, but his admonitions fall on uncomprehending ears. The allegory represents as trenchant a criticism of clerical sermonizing and myopia as Mark dared voice. All this supports the idea that the significance of bread in the Markan Supper narrative is not literal but symbolic.

The Cup Given and Drunk (14.23)

Mark next reports that Jesus gives the cup to the disciples, who all drink from it:

(14.23) And he took a cup, and when he had given thanks he gave it to them, and they all drank of it.

In his theological dissertation on the Last Supper, Albert Schweitzer identified the skeptic Bruno Bauer as the first scholar to notice that Mark presents as narrative what others present as a command from Jesus.[9] The command in Paul is to repeat the rite: "Do this, as often as you drink it, in remembrance of me" (1 Cor 11.25). In Matthew it is to drink: "Drink of it, all of you" (26.27). But in Mark there is no command of any kind, only the giving of the cup. Moreover, Mark portrays the disciples' drinking as an action narratively completed *before* Jesus utters his interpretive words about wine. By contrast, Matthew's participial form makes the "saying" of the command to drink simultaneous with the giving of the cup, and his version mentions nothing about whether the disciples drank. Thus, Mark's account differs substantially from the narrative that Christians are accustomed to hearing in the various congregational reenactments of the Supper. Schweitzer said of the Markan account: "Either it is a matter of an absolutely incomprehensible portrayal, which as a curiosity we need to consider no further, because it has absolutely no relationship with the established state of affairs, or we have before us the authentic account [of the supper] with which the investigation must begin."[10] Schweitzer chose the latter and concluded that Jesus did not intend to institute a eucharistic ritual.

The assumption here is that Mk 14.23 accurately represents the Markans' memory of the Last Supper, which presumably reflects the historical event. Its author, assuming him to have been the youthful John Mark of Acts, may have been present at the celebration, a newcomer to Jesus' fellowship and an eyewitness (see the discussion of Mk 14.51–52 and the Secret Gospel of Mark in chap. 6). On the other hand, given the significance of his ensuing words (14.24–25) as an eschatological interpretation of liturgical drinking, the view here is that Jesus did intend to institute a communal rite adapted from Passover drinking, one whose elements, however, he arranged as shown in the Markan narrative rather than in the order ultimately incorporated into Christian ritual. In other words, the Markan Jesus intended that the giving of the cup, and each recipient's decision to drink or not to drink, should occur unaccompanied by a command of any kind and before the speaking of the words about wine recorded in verses 24 and 25.

Relevant here is Eusebius's quotation of Papias's early second-century report of a remark by John the Presbyter, perhaps from the 90s

C.E., concerning Mark's gospel: "Mark . . . wrote down, although not in order, all that he remembered of what was said or done by the Lord."[11] The Presbyter's "not in order" is ordinarily presumed to refer to the sequence of events in Mark's entire book, but it is possible that what John had in mind was the problem of the ordering of the eucharistic narrative, which to an end-of-century elder would have seemed a troubling discrepancy indeed, in the light of the other Last Supper accounts and the emerging liturgical practice of the churches. In any case, as former inebriates, Jesus and the Markans would have known that persons must drink before they can respond appropriately to a message about quitting drinking, a fact that nicely explains the event sequence in the Markan Supper narrative. This order of events is further discussed at the end of this section.

The Message about Wine (14.24)

Jesus' words over the wine, which follow his giving of the cup, make up two sentences constituting the verbal part of the message to which he refers in verse 22. The RSV reads the first of these sentences as follows:

> (14.24) And he said to them, "This is my blood of the covenant, which is poured out for many."

Unlike "this" in the bread words (14.22), "this" in verse 24 is an unambiguous deictic reference to the wine in the cup of verse 23. Grammatically it is a demonstrative placeholder for the understood noun, *wine*. This wine is designated "my blood of the covenant poured out for many," a phrase formed of three syntactically abstract predicates (deep-structure sentences), each a different trope for wine:

1. This wine is my blood.
2. This wine is covenant blood.
3. I pour out this wine for many.

The first of these predicates is open to differing interpretations depending on the hearer's presuppositions about its function as a speech act and its thematic structure. Traditionally, "this wine is my blood" is construed as a performative utterance. Without altering the wine's sensible properties, the words are understood to change the wine in the cup into blood from Jesus' veins, the blood he will shed in crucifixion, which is given to his disciples as a way of allowing them to share vicariously in his sacrificial death.

Alcoholics, however, will hear "this wine is my blood" as an epiphanal utterance. The words convey Jesus' recognition of wine as the proximate cause of his impending bloodshed. Wine is what has brought him to this hour of catastrophe. The statement does not change wine into blood; rather, it metaphorically equates the two in a causal relationship. Technically a metonymy, it signifies the carnage and bloodletting associated with addictive drinking, the bloodshot eyes, cuts and bruises, internal bleeding, broken bones, damaged organs, and bloody fighting caused by alcohol. Hearing "this is my blood," and recalling the time they too recognized drink as an adversary unmasked, recovering alcoholics will find themselves face to face with Jesus as fellow sufferer.

Here again, Mark exploits ambiguity, not of reference, as with the bread words, but of theme. Ambiguity was a property of language recognized by Greek intellectuals at least as early as the fifth century. Susan C. Jarratt points to the Sophists' love of antitheses, puns, and other forms of language play as evidence of their awareness of linguistic indeterminacy.[12] Perhaps the first to recognize ambiguity as such, the Sophist Antiphon is remembered as saying, "No single statement has a single meaning." Writing for dual audiences, Mark believed that what the Christ cultists would understand one way, the Markôs groups would interpret another. In addition to issues of ambiguity, text-grammatical considerations such as topic and theme are beginning to find their way into Scripture commentary (e.g., in the work of Joseph Grimes).[13]

Jesus' words in Mk 14.24, lacking a prior discourse context, are thematically ambiguous. In the terminology of text-grammar, the theme of an utterance is its ideational focus, often called its "psychological subject," whereas the statement it makes is called its rheme. Its topic, which may or may not coincide with its theme, is the grammatically given element with which it begins. The distinction between theme and topic is explored in the work of František Daneš.[14] Here, wine is the topic in both readings of verse 24, but their themes differ. As traditionally understood, the theme of Jesus' utterance is blood:

Theme: my blood (the sacrificed blood of Jesus)
Rheme: is shared (in an unbloody way) by drinking this wine
(ritually)

By contrast, the alcoholism interpretation treats wine as the theme:

Theme: this wine (all wine, ritual or otherwise)
Rheme: is my blood (a figure for real bloodshed, the physical and
mental havoc caused by drink)

As canonically interpreted, therefore, Jesus' statement constitutes a subornation to wine drinking, a seduction to wine that plays into humankind's age-old efforts to counterfeit the presence of a seemingly absent God through the use of alcohol. To recovering alcoholics, however, the saying conveys Jesus' recognition that wine is not just the physical cause of his troubles but also their psychic catalyst. For wine does not merely intoxicate drinkers; it also aggravates their mental drunkenness. That is, it triggers the combative self-will uniformly characteristic of alcoholism—in Jesus' case, the messianism, judgmentalness, so-called righteous anger, and zealotic violence in the Temple that led to his indictment on capital charges. Because of this lethal combination of alcohol and self, his blood may spill in forfeit to the reactive anger of his compatriots. In short, "this wine is my blood" captures Jesus' insight that the wrath endemic to unredeemed humanity, when catalyzed by wine, leads to bloody destruction.

As with the bread of verse 22, the change effected by Jesus' words over the wine is tropological, not actual. Discussing the point from a different angle, Jewish students of the gospels, reasoning from a cultural perspective, have always insisted that the Jews' strong taboo against drinking blood makes it impossible that Jesus could have intended, or the disciples have understood, a metamorphosis of wine into blood.[15] Apart from formulations of Christian theology, the difference between ritual wine and ritual bread is that bread (as well as being a foodstuff) is only a tangible symbol, whereas wine (as well as being a drink) is more than symbolic: it contains real alcohol, ultimately a lethal toxin.

The second element of verse 24 is the predicate "this wine is covenant blood." This and the predicate "this wine is my blood" underlie the grammatically compressed double genitive, *haima mou tēs diathēkēs*, ordinarily translated "my blood of the covenant." To the Jew the phrase "covenant blood" would have called to mind the blood of circumcision or of animal sacrifice. Indeed, Heb 9.20 links Jesus' phrase "blood of the covenant" to the same phrase in Ex 24.6–8, which refers to the blood of animal sacrifice and is taken by many as the definitive exegesis of "covenant" in Mk 14.24. The view here, however, is that blood figures in the verse strictly as a metonym connecting wine with the physical carnage it brings on alcoholic humanity. Apart from this figurative use, blood per se, whether of animal sacrifice or otherwise, is not referred to in 14.24. Just as "this [wine] is my blood" is an original insight with Jesus, without parallel in Hebrew Scripture, so is the meaning of "this [wine] is covenant blood" a new idea on Jesus' part.

This is not to say that "covenant blood" is not a biblicism. The position here is that Jesus is referring neither to the circumcision covenant, the Passover covenant, nor the Sinai covenant but to the covenant in Is 54.9–10, wherein God promises never again to inflict his wrath on those he has saved. In identifying wine—the same wine he has just connected with his bloodshed—as covenant blood, Jesus may be interpreting this Deutero-Isaian scripture as a recovery covenant. The Isaian passage recalls "the days of Noah" and the Flood covenant (Gn 9.8–17) and introduces Yahweh's promise to forswear his oath of anger. The theory here is that Jesus connected this oath with Noah's drunken and angry curse on Canaan (Gn 9.25), interpreted here as the curse of alcohol addiction. The latter is the culminating event in the account of Noah's drunkenness (Gn 9.20–27) appended to the Flood story. The argument for this theory appears in chapter 3 of this book, which studies Deutero-Isaiah's Zion poem and Suffering Servant figure (Is 51.1–54.17).

In the light of recovery, the truth of Jesus' saying in 14.24 lies in its paradoxical juxtaposition of opposites: destruction ("my blood") linked with salvation ("covenant blood"); humiliation linked with exaltation (see Lk 2.34, "the fall and rising of many"); defeat linked with victory; and in the parlance of alcoholism, "bottoming out" linked with recovery. In English, "yet also" expresses this conjunctive relationship. Echoes of "this wine is my blood yet also covenant blood" can be heard in the sentiments of recovering alcoholics today: "The hell I went through with booze was necessary for the heaven I've found in sobriety." "I know now that the alcohol I thought was killing me was actually leading me to a better life." "I had to drink every drink I drank in order to know the joy of recovery."

Notice Jesus' two actions before speaking the words over the wine: he gives the disciples the cup, while he himself refrains from drink. If the Last Supper had been an ordinary seder, Jesus would certainly have drunk along with the others present. But it was not an ordinary seder; it was the Passover at which ipsissimal man gained insight into the salvific paradox of both drinking and not drinking. Jesus saw for the first time the eschatology of the Passover wine duty. Realizing from his own mental drunkenness that humankind's ultimate bondage is never to the presenting symptom of his enslavement (in modern terms, chemical addictions, mental obsessions, psychic pathologies) but always and finally the bondage of self, Jesus suddenly recognized how God uses wine to rescue humanity from the illusion of an autonomous selfhood, to beat the individual down to the point where the self is reduced to nothing. So Jesus gave his disciples a drinking ritual involving a new conception of covenant that describes wine in a cryptic saying destined to be understood one way by religious drinkers and in quite another by persons in recovery.

The third predicate underlying 14.24 is "I pour out this wine for many," usually cast as a relative clause in passive voice, "which is poured out for many." Its meaning is polyvalent. Realistically, "poured out for many" depicts real wine poured into a cup for everyone willing to drink it and follow Jesus' path into addiction and out again, to sobriety. Soteriologically, wine is a trope for blood, ultimately a figure for the addict's untimely death, a death died so that alcoholics unaware might turn to recovery before dying such a death themselves. Semiotically, pouring is a metaphor for the speaking of the message, the Word of life. So viewed, the RSV reading of verse 24 may be glossed as follows:

> (14.24) Then he said to them, "This [wine] is [the cause of] my blood[shed], yet also covenant blood, [the message of] which I pour out for [the recovery of] many."

Key here is the word *many*, with which Jesus links his situation to that of the Deutero-Isaian Suffering Servant (52.13–53.12), whose story immediately precedes the Isaian covenant discussed previously. Chapter 3 interprets the servant as a figure of the derelict alcoholic who suffers as vicarious addiction bearer for so-called normal drinkers and then "gives himself as a guilt offering" (Is 53.10), thereby showing the multitudes the path to atonement short of the painful extremes he endured. The term "addiction bearer for the many," an important element in Mark's theology of recovery, is discussed at length in chapter 3.

"I Will Drink No More" (14.25)

Turn now to the second sentence of Jesus' message about wine:

> (14.25) Truly, I say to you, I shall not drink again of the fruit of the vine until that day when I drink it new in the kingdom of God.

The saying is remarkable for its barbarous grammar, a triple negative in Greek (hence the retranslation below, "I will drink no more, no never again, . . .") conveying the strongest kind of intention to refrain from drink. Traditionally it is understood to mean "I will drink no more after I drink this cup" and was thought to convey Jesus' awareness of the imminence of his death and consummation in God. Many modern scholars, however, believe that Jesus did not drink from the cup, although interpretations vary widely. Joachim Jeremias cites a body of "widely accepted" exegetical commentary, much of it based on the pointed instruction in Lk 22.17 ("take this and divide it among yourselves") indicating that Jesus did not share in the cup.[16] By contrast, Edward Schillebeeckx, while acknowledging that "will drink no more" is the historical kernel of the saying, refers to the cup as "the very last cup Jesus will share with his friends."[17] Also disputed is the question of whether "truly [Hebrew/Aramaic *amen*] I say to you" identifies the saying as a vow of abstinence.[18] In the final analysis, however others may interpret the saying, alcoholics will hear it as expressing the central truth of recovery: addicts may recognize alcohol as the cause of their troubles, but until they are willing to quit drinking, until they decide to quit, and until they actually stop, they remain dead men and women. In Mk 14.25 Jesus demonstrates this truth by firmly and straightforwardly announcing his decision to quit drinking.

"New Wine" (14.25)

Verse 25 also contains a highly significant grammatical ambiguity, *heōs . . . auto pinō kainon* (literally, "until . . . it I drink new"), one version of which conveys Jesus' intention to replace real wine with the metaphorical "new wine" of the rule of God. Confirming this ambiguity, Robert Bratcher and Eugene Nida identify the adjective *kainon* ("new") as either the neuter accusative used adverbially ("until . . . I drink it new") or the masculine accusative modifying *oinos* ("wine"), which must be supplied in place of the pronoun *auto* ("until . . . I drink new wine").[19] Vernacular translations generally follow the former version and treat "new" as either a complement or an adverbial, rendering the final clause "when I drink it new" or "drink it anew," both of which mean "until I drink the same wine again." Fundamental to the Markans' understanding of Jesus' meaning, however, is the recognition that "fruit of the vine" and "new wine" are not co-referential. That is, they refer not to a single wine named twice but to two different wines. Linguistically, although *kainon* is an adjective, a transliteration of the Greek wording, "until I drink new it," is impossible in English because English almost never permits adjectives to modify pronouns. This fact, coupled with Christian translators' preconceived understanding that Jesus was referring to the same wine twice (indeed, a wine he would soon drink again), led to the traditional reading, "drink it new/anew." Some recent versions choose the alternative reading, supplying "wine" in place of "it" and rendering the clause "until I drink the new wine of the Rule of God."[20]

Still, the choice of reading is left to the translator, depending on his or her understanding of Mark's intention. Not surprisingly, the Markans would have chosen the second version just mentioned, rendering the verse as follows:

> (14.25) Truly I say to you, I will drink no more, no never again, of the fruit of the vine, until I drink the new wine of the rule of God.

Once again, the point is that *wine* in "drink new wine," unlike *it* in "drink it new/anew," clearly refers to a wine different from that referred to by "fruit of the vine." This referential distinction is crucial, for "the new wine of the rule of God," like the "smooth wine," "choice wine," and "superabundant wine" mentioned elsewhere in Scripture, obviously does not refer to real drink of any kind, fermented or unfermented. Rather, it is a figure, a metaphor for salvation, specifically, an oxymoron describing sobriety in terms of its opposite, actual wine drinking. What better way to express the joy of sobriety than by means of an ironically bibulous metaphor, "drinking new wine"? Indeed, newcomers to the Markôs fellowship may have begun their journeys to sobriety by professing this important saying.

Notice also that Jesus' expression "fruit of the vine" is a Jewish formula phrase referring to wine drunk in a religious rite.[21] Mark 14.25 as translated here thus parallels Ps 16.4–5, as emended in light of recent linguistic discoveries, wherein a Canaanite convert to Yahwism renounces his pagan wine liturgy in order to imbibe the "smooth wine" of Yahweh.[22] Psalm 16, therefore, although never recognized as such, very well may be the OT source of Jesus' concluding statement at the Last Supper, his announcement of his decision to switch from real wine drunk in ritual to the "new wine" of sobriety. (Chap. 5 discusses Luke's confusion about "new wine" in Acts 2 and Peter's use of Psalm 16 in his Pentecost sermon.) In any case, it is difficult to imagine a more straightforward statement than Mk 14.25 of a drinker's decision to stop drinking and to turn instead to God as the source of life.

Taken together, the foregoing retranslations of the Markan Supper narrative read as follows:

> (14.22) And as they were eating, he took bread, and blessed and broke it, and gave it to them, and said, "Pay attention, this is the message I embody": (23) Then he took a cup, and when he had given thanks he gave it to them, and they all drank from it. (24) He said to them, "This wine is the cause of my bloodshed, yet also covenant blood, the message of which I pour out for the recovery of many. (25) Truly I say to you, I will drink no more, no never again, of the fruit of the vine, until I drink the new wine of the rule of God."

Further implications of Jesus' paschal wine message are discussed at the end of this section.

Psalm 116 (14.26)

The Last Supper seder ended with the singing of the Hallel, Psalms 115–18. Psalm 116 is of special interest here because of the steps to recovery it contains. The Psalms scholar Mitchell Dahood characterizes Psalm 116 as the thanksgiving hymn of an anonymous individual whom Yahweh has saved from impending death. The opening verses, according to Dahood, indicate that the psalmist's peril was an illness:[23]

> (Ps 116.1) Out of love for me Yahweh did hear
> my plea for his mercy;
> (2) Truly he inclined his ear to me
> even as I called.
> (3) The bands of death encompassed me,
> and emissaries of Sheol overtook me.
> By anguish and grief was I overtaken.
> (4) But I invoked the name of Yahweh:
> "I beg you, Yahweh, deliver my soul!"
> (5) Gracious is Yahweh and just,
> and our God is merciful.
> (6) Yahweh is the defender of the innocent;
> I was brought low but he saved me.
> (7) "Return, my soul, to your rest,
> for Yahweh has treated you kindly.
> (8) For you, my soul, have been rescued from death,
> you, mine eye, from tears,
> you, my foot, from banishment.
> (9) I shall walk before Yahweh
> in the Fields of Life."

The proposal here is that the illness was a spiritual sickness akin to alcoholism. Verse 8 describes the malady as mental ("tears"), physical in its consequences ("banishment"), and spiritual ("soul death"), the triune hallmark of alcoholism. Verse 2 depicts the eagerness to save with which God awaits the drinker's prayer for help. Verse 3 powerfully conveys the feeling of remorse and "walking death" well known to practicing alcoholics. Verse 6 contains an image of the humbling low point that addicts, in a parlance unchanged in three thousand years, call "hitting bottom."

More pointedly, verses 10, 11, and 13, as emended here, exactly correspond to the first three steps of today's twelve-step recovery program:

(Ps 116.10) In faith I acted, even though it was to admit
"I am powerless, beset by unmanageability."
[Step one: We admitted we were powerless over
alcohol, that our lives had become unmanageable.]

(11) In my alarm, I came to understand,
"Everything of man is unreliable."
[Step two: Came to believe that (only) a power greater
than ourselves could restore us to sanity.]

(12) How can I return to Yahweh
all his favors to me?

(13) I will take the cup of salvation day by day,
and call upon God as I understand him.
[Step three: Made a decision to turn our will and
our lives over to the care of God as we understood Him.]

Clearly the psalmist's recovery began with a leap-of-faith admission of powerlessness. Dahood renders verse 10 as "I remained faithful though I was pursued, though I was harried by calamity." The initial root, *'mn,* means "firm, constant, reliable." The verb itself, translated as "faith," suggests reliance on God in daily living less than it does searching for God in a crisis, belief expressed through other-trusting action.[24] To render the hiphil form of the verb, which heightens its meaning in some way, Dahood yokes "remain" with "faithful." The version here retains the root meaning of enacted faith, with the hiphil indicating that the action occurred as an admission. So the Hebrew of the first half of the verse, *he'ᵉmantî kî,* is read: "In faith I acted, even though it was to admit. . . ."

In the second half of verse 10 Dahood reads, "I was pursued, I was harried by calamity." It is his discovery of *'ᵃdubbār* as the verb underlying "pursued" that supports an alcoholism reading of the verse. Other instances of this verb cited by Dahood indicate that anyone of whom it was said was utterly subdued, defeated, and subject to derision. In short, *'ᵃdubbār* captures exactly the sense of addicts' lack of power: alcohol has conquered them, pursues them without mercy, and renders them the object of scorn. Dahood's coupling of "harried" and "calamity" indicates that the psalmist was beset on every hand, nothing was working right for him. In other words, his life had become unmanageable. So read, verse 10 exactly conforms to A.A.'s step one, save only the absence of overt mention of drink.

Verse 11 captures the gist of step two. As Dahood remarks, if everything of man is unreliable, then all the more reason to rely on God. In step two, an individual's awareness of his or her own limitation leads to a belief that God as a higher power can be, may be, and finally is reliable.

Verse 12 poses a question that invites the decision mentioned in step three. Verse 13 then introduces the figure of the cup of salvation. The Hebrew for "salvation" consists of two root words, "God" and "saves." Etymologically, then, "taking the cup of 'God saves'" says exactly what step three says when it speaks of "turning our will and our lives over to the care of God." Verse 13 ends with *šēm yhwh*, usually translated as "the name of Yahweh." Because it lacked a word for "meaning," ancient Hebrew used *šēm* ("name") to signify not just the name of something but whatever meaning that name evoked to the person using it. So *šēm yhwh* would have meant to the psalmist exactly what the phrase "God as we understood Him" means to alcoholics reading step three. Finally, "salvation" in verse 13 is plural in the Hebrew text, always a puzzle to scholars. Perhaps the psalmist used the plural to convey the idea that the cup of salvation must be drunk on a daily basis, that step three must be taken each day. Thus the reading, "day by day."

The psalm then concludes:

> (Ps 116.14) I will fulfill my vows to Yahweh
> in front of all his people.
> (15) For Yahweh considers precious in his eyes
> the willing self-abandonment of his devoted ones.
> (16) "O Yahweh, truly I am your servant;
> I am your servant, your faithful son;
> you have loosed my fetters!
> (17) To you will I offer
> the sacrifice of thanksgiving,
> and your name, Yahweh, invoke."
> (18) I will fulfill my vows to Yahweh
> in front of all his people,
> (19) In the courts of Yahweh's house,
> in the midst of Jerusalem. Praise Yah!

Verse 15 contains an unexplained form of the word for death found nowhere else in the Psalms. In the context "precious in the eyes of God," dying to self is presumed, hence this version, "willing self-abandonment," the same self-abandonment Jesus demonstrates in his Gethsemane surrender. Verses 14 and 18 speak of fulfilling vows to Yahweh. Recovering persons will recognize here the obligation to carry the message to other alcoholics as set forth in step twelve. Verse 16 mentions the loosed fetters of recovery and declares the psalmist to be Yahweh's servant and son. "Servant" connects with Isaiah's Suffering Servant (52.13–53.12), and the phrase "your faithful son" connects with verse 10, "in faith I acted, even though it was to admit . . . ," suggesting that an admission of powerlessness is the criterion of sonship. Verse 17 stresses gratitude to God, something no recovering alcoholic may ever forget.

Traditionally said to depict Israel's deliverance from Egypt, Psalm 116 has received scant attention in both Jewish and Christian commentaries, particularly compared with the lavish concern devoted to Psalm 118, the messianic victory hymn that concludes the Hallel. In the light of recovery, however, the key to life after spiritual death is the archetypal alcoholism program contained in Psalm 116. At the Last Supper Jesus may have sung the solo part of the psalm himself. The theory proposed here is that he discerned in this ancient Canaanite poem a blueprint for his own imminent surrender in Gethsemane. Certainly it is reasonable to imagine that the psalm was very much in Jesus' mind, not merely because it was sung in the Hallel, but because of the pathway to recovery it reveals.

Summary

The following statements, which are given in the Markan order, separated from their original tropes, augmented by a fuller elaboration of the Suffering Servant link, and couched in the parlance of sober alcoholics today, paraphrase Jesus' message at the paschal seder relative to bread, wine, new wine, and recovery (Mk 14.22–25):

> (a) Command to attend:
> "Pay attention, this that I am about to do and say, which the bread I have given you symbolizes, is the message I embody."

> (b) Unworded action:
> After giving thanks for the opportunity of choice, Jesus gives the cup to all followers to drink or not drink, as they choose.

> (c) Spoken message about wine:
> "This wine is the agent of my suffering and downfall but also of my new life in recovery. That is how God's promised salvation works. Wine is thus the drink I pour out for all who would follow me into that life. It will bring many people there short of the extreme anguish I and other addicted servants must suffer. As for me, I will drink wine no more, for I choose sobriety instead."

Despite the many tropological interpretations of Jesus' utterance featured in Christian pieties, the wisdom of recovery suggests quite simply that it is humankind's thirst for wine, our essential alcoholism apparent in our unrecognized paradoxical desire at once to drink and to quit drinking, that over the ages has drawn so many to the Christian altar. The unleavened bread eaten there is but a symbol of the Word of God, but the wine, although a figure for the blood of Jesus and of the covenant, is as addictive as wine drunk anywhere.

Why does the Markan scenario, however, unlike the other accounts of the Last Supper, portray the giving and drinking of the cup without any command to do so and before the utterance of the words of interpretation? This is the question Albert Schweitzer posed to the twentieth century, whose response has mainly been to ignore it. The perspective of alcoholism suggests an answer based on a new interpretation of Mk 13.14, the central cryptic image not only of the Markan apocalypse (Mark 13) but of Mark's entire book, discussed at length in chapter 6:

> (13.14) But when you see the desolating sacrilege set up where it ought not to be—Let the reader understand!—then let those who are in Judea flee to the mountains.

Briefly stated, Mark's Jesus has come to the Supper focused on the apocalyptic insight conveyed by this verse, which is that recovery begins with the recognition of the wine of religion as a "desolating sacrilege," followed by the decision to "flee" from the altar to the "mountains," that is, to stop drinking ritually and turn instead to the Markôs sobriety program. Until then, persons must drink every drink they are destined to drink while awaiting their turning points. Thus, they must always be free to drink or not to drink, as divinely guided: All other admonitions, whether to imbibe or to abstain, corrupt this relationship between God and humans, compromise the salvific agency of alcohol, and prolong humanity's collective illness. For the alcoholic, self-willed abstinence can yield almost as much pain as unbridled drinking. This would explain why Mark's Jesus wordlessly gives the Passover cup to disciples and only after their decisions to drink or not drink voices his message about wine.

By contrast, the familiar rubrics of the churches, composites of the Pauline and Matthean accounts of the Last Supper, have traditionally included an explicit command to drink and an order of events opposite to the Markan and omit the material in verse 25 entirely. As a result, the commands to partake and to repeat the rite prompt some worshipers to drink beyond their turning points, since they are unaware that quitting drinking is the eschatology of the ritual. Many others, fearful of its holiness or its addictive property, approach the wine in an attitude of frightened abstinence. Consequently, entire churches celebrate the rite infrequently, or deny themselves the cup, or use unfermented juices, or sip from tiny glasses or small spoons, or barely wet their lips instead of drinking in an ordinary manner. Clearly, such voluntary abstinence and near-abstinence deprive persons of the salvific mediation of wine discerned by Jesus.

Moreover, the omission of verse 25 from the congregational celebration, to say nothing of readers' failure to recognize the grammatical and referential implications prompting the translational variant studied here, serves to further obscure the alcoholism intentionality evident in Jesus' paschal message. Viewed from the angle of recovery, Jesus' eucharistic words suggest his awareness of a divine covenant to save humankind from self-destruction by means of a wine ritual intended to addict many, so that, at the turning point, God can convict religious drinkers of their powerlessness and call them out of bondage and into recovery. What Jesus demonstrates in verse 25 is an apocalyptic response to that conviction and call—the decision to quit drinking. But the verse has always been omitted from Christian liturgical formulas. By contrast, the stories of recovering alcoholics, which do not mention this Markan text at all, stress its apocalyptic theme: turning from drink to sobriety at the appointed hour is the key to new and better life.

Gethsemane (14.32–41)

In the light of recovery, Mark's Gethsemane story recounts the concluding act of Jesus' ministry, to which the Crucifixion, ordinarily considered its conclusion, is but an antitype. Mark portrays Jesus as experiencing bodily death at Golgotha, but in Gethsemane it is his *psuchē* that dies ("my self is sorrowful as it approaches death," 14.34). A term first-century readers would have understood as "soul" or "inner being," *psuchē* names what we moderns call the "self." In the pathology of addiction, it is the radically individuated self trapped in the delusion of auto-empowerment. From an alcoholism perspective, therefore, Jesus' soteriological purpose in Gethsemane is way-showing, to model atonement via the surrender and immolation of his hubristic self, so that others might see and do likewise. The unawake disciples, however, fail to comprehend the significance of Jesus' words and actions.

As a result, Christian readers have construed the events in Gethsemane quite differently, as the following synopsis of its traditional interpretation illustrates:

> In the garden awaiting arrest, a deeply human Jesus suffers a fit of anxiety at the prospect of impending death. His purpose wavers and

his will fails. He asks God to cancel his destined execution, referred to by the image of the cup. Resisting temptation at last, he regains his heroic resolve and submits to the Father's will. He chides the disciples for sleeping instead of looking out for his captors and warns them, rather oddly under the circumstances, to guard against temptations of the flesh.

Although many have sensed that Mark intends the story to portray the immolation of self, it is invariably interpreted in the foregoing way, as depicting the opposite, an outward submission achieved through inner self-assertion. Reexamining traditional readings, especially that of the verb *parerchomai* in verse 35, and interpreting "cup" in verse 36 as a metaphor for addiction will bring to light lexical and figural ambiguities explaining the disparity between the perceived Markan intention and the traditional interpretation.

Preparation Prayer (14.32–35)

The initial part of the story shows Jesus' preparation for his surrender. Important at the outset is an explanation of the radically different sense of verse 35 proposed here. In this view conventional vernacular translations of the verse obscure Mark's alcoholism intention and establish an antisobriety context for understanding verse 36, the crux of Gethsemane. The RSV renders verse 35 as follows:

> (14.35) And going a little farther, he fell on the ground and prayed that, if it were possible [*ei dunaton estin*], the hour might pass from him [*parelthe ap autou he hōra*].

Particular questions concern the reference of "hour" and the dual meanings of *dunaton (dunatos)* and *parelthe (parerchomai)*.

First of all, though ordinarily assumed to refer to the time of Jesus' upcoming trial and execution, "the hour" can just as readily refer to the time at hand, the present moment in Gethsemane. Readers have always concluded that because Jesus is emotionally distraught (14.33) and sorrowful at the approach of death (14.34), the death he has in mind must be his crucifixion. Not necessarily. It can also be the death of the self, the *psuchē. . . thanatou* to which verse 34 overtly refers, a death about to occur in Gethsemane even as he speaks.

Next, the phrases with *dunatos* and *parerchomai* contain unseen ambiguities permitting an alternative reading of verse 35. *Ei dunaton estin* is a present tense indicative of direct address understood as a prayer requesting a desired outcome, "if (*ei*) possible (*dunaton*) it is/ be (*estin*)." But translating the adjective *dunaton* as "possible" weakens the request for power so important to Jesus at this juncture. In his discussion of Mark's uses of *dunamai* and *thelō* in weakened senses as the auxiliaries "could" and "would," C. H. Turner points out that the translator must decide from context when these words carry their full lexical meanings and when they are weakened.[25] Now Mark uses *dunamai* twice as often, proportionately, as Matthew and Luke, because a central issue in his understanding of the gospel story is power and who has it, humans or God. The possibility that Jesus in verse 35 is acknowledging lack of power and asking for help is obscured when *dunaton* is weakened to "possible." The phrase can just as correctly be understood as Jesus' prayer to be empowered, to receive God's *dunamis.* Hence an alternate reading, with *ei* rendered "might," *dunaton* translated in a verbal sense, and the implied dative "to him" supplied, would be: "he prayed that it might be powerfulled [to him]." The awkward English can be smoothed by substituting the phrase "to be empowered" or its idiomatic equivalents, "for the strength" or "for help."

Finally, *parerchomai,* a difficult verb with many senses, has the meaning "to pass by in time" or "to elapse."[26] Hence, in addition to being susceptible to the familiar readings, "pass him by" (New American and Jerusalem Bibles) or "pass from him" (New International and RSV)—that is, not happen to him, or idiomatically, that he not have to go through it—the Greek *hina . . . parelthe ap autou he hōra* can also read, "that . . . the hour elapse from him." English idioms for this sense of *parerchomai* would be "to get through it," "to get it behind one," or "to get it over with." Combining these alternative understandings of *dunatos* and *parerchomai* produces the literal but decidedly un-English reading, "he prayed that it might be powerfulled [to him] [that] the hour elapse from him." Substituting the idioms, however, and bearing in mind that "hour" can refer to the present moment, yields the following version of Jesus' prayer:

> (14.35) And going forward a little, he fell on the ground and prayed for the strength to get through the moment at hand.

Instantly one sees that verse 35 as retranslated does *not* represent a request for a change of destiny. Jesus' purpose in Gethsemane is *not* wavering. He is *not* asking to be spared the ordeal of the ominous hour or of crucifixion; indeed, he is not thinking of crucifixion at all.[27] Rather, Jesus is asking God's help to make the surrender he will enact in verse 36. And verse 36, in turn, liberated from the context set by verse 35 as ordinarily translated, now reveals its identity precisely *as* a self-repudiating surrender. Quite obviously, these alternate readings of *dunaton* and *parerchomai* open the door to a new and profoundly different understanding of the events in Gethsemane. Their importance cannot be overstated.

What we have in *parerchomai* is an ambiguity not of grammar, reference, or theme but of lexical sense, two possibilities of literal meaning operative in the original Greek but lost in translation whenever the target language lacks a verb having the same multiple senses as *parerchomai*. English, for example, has no single verb conveying the two meanings "pass by or pass from" (idiomatically, to be spared having to go through something) and "elapse from" (idiomatically, to get through something or get something behind one or get something over with). Mark counted on his two Greek-speaking audiences, Christ cultists and Markôs people, to interpret the text according to their differing understandings of Jesus' identity, the former without even noticing the ambiguity. What he did not reckon on was the probable loss of the lexical ambiguity in *parerchomai* once his book was translated into other languages. Had the Markans controlled the translation process, verse 35 probably would have been handed on more or less as retranslated here.

Christians have always missed the ambiguity of Mk 14.35 and hence of Jesus' basic disposition in Gethsemane. Hebrews 5.7 is the earliest evidence of the traditional understanding of Jesus' state of mind:

> (Heb 5.7) In the days of his flesh, Jesus offered up prayers and supplications with loud cries and tears, to him who was able to save him from death, and he was heard for his godly fear.

So certain have readers been that verses 35 and 36 ("remove this cup from me") unambiguously convey Jesus' requests for deliverance from suffering that K. G. Kuhn was able to base his theory that Mark's Gethsemane pericope comes from two sources, "Mark A" and "Mark B," in large part on the assumption that verses 35 and 36 are saying the same thing and hence represent a reporting of the same prayer from separate sources.[28] Werner Kelber's remark on verses 35 and 36 is typical: "But the request for the passing of the hour and the removal of the cup has every indication of a desire to bypass the cross."[29] Against this view, the lexical ambiguity discussed here indicates that the two verses can be understood as differing in purport not only from each other but also from their traditional readings.

By way of corroborating *parerchomai* as glossed here, notice how an often-remarked difficulty in another use of that verb, in Mark 6.48, is overcome by translating it with the idiom "to get through an event," that is, to pass through it successfully, or get it over with or behind one. In Mk 6.48 the disciples are having a hard time rowing their boat against the wind. The RSV reads:

(6.48) And he saw that they were distressed in rowing, for the wind was against them. And about the fourth watch of the night he came to them, walking on the sea. And he meant [*ethelen*, literally "wished"] to pass them by [*parelthein autous*].

Commentators have always wondered why Jesus would have wished to pass them by. It sounds rather a false note. *Parelthein* is the aorist infinitive of *parerchomai*, whose object is the accusative *autous*. The proposed idiom, used transitively, would render the final clause "And he wanted to get them through it." In other words, he wanted to help them successfully weather the storm and the arduous rowing. Jesus was not intending to pass them by but to come to them and help them. This is shown by what happens next: the disciples cry out in surprise (6.49), he identifies himself and calms their fears (6.50), and then he gets into their boat and the wind ceases (6.51). "To get them through it" smoothes a passage where the traditional reading of *parerchomai* creates a disturbance in the text.

Against this background, verses 32–35 of the Gethsemane pericope may be retranslated as follows:

(14.32) And they went to a place called Gethsemane, and he said to his disciples, "Sit here, while I pray." (33) And he took with him Peter and James and John, and he began to be amazed [*ekthambeō*] and strangely awestruck [*adēmoneō*]. (34) And he said to them, "My self [*psuchē*] is sorrowful as it approaches death [*heos thanatou*]. Remain here and continue watching [me]." (35) And going forward a little, he fell on the ground and prayed for the strength to get through the moment at hand.

"Amazed" and "strangely awestruck" convey Mark's descriptions of the distressing and confusing emotions he believed Jesus would have experienced on the threshold of *psuchē* death, as he realized that his ultimate encounter with God was about to occur. Perhaps Mark had known a similar experience in his own recovery. The sorrow Jesus acknowledges is the sadness so many feel at the turning point, the dying of one's old self. A man in A.A. sometimes plays a tape recording he made of himself during a hangover, on the night he decided to seek help for his alcoholism, which turned out to be the night of his last drink. The deeply sorrowful pauses and the tone of voice as he ruminates on his plight and reflects on his decision to ask for help are unforgettable. It is the voice of Jesus in Gethsemane. "Watch" in verse 34 is traditionally interpreted "be on lookout for my captors," whereas alcoholics will recognize that Jesus means "watch me, the surrender I am enacting." The "ground" in verse 35 is the same ground from which humanity rose up in our Edenic rebellion and thus the place appointed for our ultimate oblation to God. There Jesus asks for help to make his surrender.

Prayer of Surrender (14.36).

Next, in a simple but momentous prayer of atonement, Jesus abandons himself to the God of his understanding:

> (14.36) Then he said, "Abba (Father). You have all power [*panta dunata soi*]. Remove this cup from me. But not what I will, but what you will."

The first of four elements in the prayer, the Aramaic *abba*, a youngster's familiar word for "father," poignantly conveys Jesus' awareness of his being not God but rather the child of God, whom he understands as loving parent.

Second, the statement "You have all power" (*panta dunata soi*, literally, "all powers to you") is the same as saying, "I am powerless." It represents Jesus' rejection of the pathogenic illusion of self-empowerment. As suggested above, from the alcoholism perspective *dunamis* is an absolutely key word in Mark's gospel. It refers to spiritual power emanating from God, without which we humans are forever hostage to our angst. *Dunamis* allays fear, quiets anger, heals illness, lifts obsessions, dispels addictions, and removes the compulsion to judge, fight, and control. It confers acceptance and a sense of well-being. In Mk 14.62 *tēs dunamis* as a proper noun becomes, in effect, a name for God. Writing of this power in our own time, recovering alcoholics emphasize that its source is never the self but always an other greater than the self: "Lack of power, that was our dilemma. We had to find a power by which we could live, and it had to be a Power greater than ourselves."[30] To persons on the threshold of surrender, these same alcoholics tell how they appropriated *dunamis* in their own recoveries: "But there is One who has all power—that One is God. May you find Him now. Half measures availed us nothing. We stood at the turning point. We asked His protection and care with complete abandon. Here are the steps we took, which are suggested as a program of recovery: We admitted we were powerless. . . ."[31] These words from the book *Alcoholics Anonymous* exactly describe Jesus' situation and prayer in Gethsemane. *Dunamis* flows from God when we admit that we lack it utterly. Until then, we refuse to acknowledge our powerlessness.

Notice that the traditional translation of *panta dunata soi*, "all things are possible to thee" (RSV), though quite correct grammatically, fails utterly to capture any sense of Jesus' words as a recognition of his own lack of power. Matthew and Luke retreat even further from the implication of the Markan original. Luke omits *dunamai* entirely (22.42–44). Matthew's version (26.39) conflates verses 35 and 36 of Mark, and the only form of *dunamis* he uses is that in *ei dunaton estin*, which he takes not from verse 36 but from verse 35 of Mark. One has to conclude that Matthew and Luke simply could not bring themselves to accept the obvious implication of the Markan Jesus' words: "If God has all power, then I have no power."

Theologically, *panta dunata soi* conveys Jesus' repudiation of all claims to auto-empowerment spoken as a precondition of atonement. To persons who exalt Jesus as an idealized figure on whom to project an unrecognized belief in their own self-empowerment, this interpretation will doubtless seem threatening, but to those who have known the conviction of powerlessness and have come to look on Jesus as the archetypal recovering person, the words represent salvation itself. To the spiritually awakened, *panta dunata soi* is the masterstroke of Jesus' entire career. It signifies the death of his autonomous selfhood and the end of his pathological individuation. It is "the stone the builders rejected" of Ps 118.22, the cornerstone of the great victory gates of God through which Jesus is ushered, an event prophetically depicted in Ps 118.19–20 of the Hallel.

The third element in the prayer is the petition "Remove this cup from me." Here Mark exploits an ambiguity not of lexical sense but of figure. Traditionally "cup" is interpreted as a fixed expression, a dead metaphor referring to one's lot or destiny, and "remove this cup from me" is considered to be a paraphrased repetition of verse 35, with both verses understood as Jesus' request for a change of destiny. To the recovering alcoholic, however, "cup" functions as an active and emotionally charged metaphor, specifically, a metonymy referring to alcoholism by means of an object closely associated with it, the wine cup. In other words, the cup symbolizes Jesus' alcoholic illness, all the pain, fighting, and delusion that have led him to this moment. It is the cup of his earlier question to the disciples (10.38), "Can you drink the cup I am drinking? Will you be baptized with the baptism [the suffering] with which I am to be baptized?" It is the cup that Jesus has just given the disciples to drink at the Last Supper (14.23). And it is the cup discerned by Deutero-Isaiah, "the cup of anger and the chalice of reeling" (Is 51.17–23, discussed in chap. 3), that is, the cup of physical and mental drunkenness, of wine and the insanity accompanying wine, that bludgeons humankind into the surrender required for recovery. Hence, paradoxically, it is also the "cup of salvation" mentioned in Ps 116.13. "Remove this cup from me" therefore means, "take away my cup addiction, release me from bondage to drink."

Two points are worth noting about the cup figure. First, C. E. B. Cranfield's summary of OT cup metaphors highlights the prophets' use of the cup image not as a figure for suffering and death but rather as a symbol of intoxication referred to as the cup of "staggering" or "reeling" and of the chief emotion triggered by drink, anger or wrath.[32] Although Cranfield is correct to equate these images to drunkenness, the view here is that the prophets do not intend wine as a metaphor for wrath but rather wrath—or more fully, the wrath of God—as the consequence of wine. Like all Christian commentators, Cranfield interprets the cup in verse 36 not as something Jesus actually wants removed but rather as something from which he temporarily shrinks, "the cup of God's wrath against sin." Cranfield then points out that this interpretation does not square with Mk 10.39, where the cup metaphor seems to refer only to martyrdom for the two disciples. The figurative interpretation presented here, "cup addiction," not only comports with the prophets' use of the figure, but it also reconciles the disparity between 14.36 and 10.39 that arises when the Gethsemane cup is understood as signifying a theological concept like that mentioned by Cranfield. The cup of alcoholism is shared by Jesus' disciples, who drink from it at the Last Supper (14.23) and are never more alcoholic than when they want to lord it over others (10.37). As for Jesus, it is a cup that he, like all surrendered persons, most earnestly wishes to have removed.

The second point concerns Matthew's double use of *parerchomai* with regard to the cup, which he interprets as an expression referring to the ordeal of crucifixion (26.39 and 42). Matthew's usage suggests that he understands the words to mean neither a wavering of purpose on Jesus' part nor an actual request to have the cup "removed," as in Mk 14.36 (*parapherō*, "to take away," also Lk 22.42); rather, it indicates Jesus' desire to get on with things, to get his fated mission over with. Thus, in the sense of *parerchomai* brought to light here, which would have been as familiar to Matthew as to Mark, Jesus' dual mentions of the cup in Matthew would read:

> (Mt 26.39) My Father, enable me to get this cup behind me.

> (Mt 26.42) My Father, if I can't get this [cup] behind me unless I drink it, let thy will be done.

These Matthean readings comport with the thinking of the redactor of the Fourth Gospel, who also understands the term *cup* as a fixed expression for one's fate (Jn 18.11) but who tries to correct the story of Jesus' wavering, which he presumably felt unworthy of the exalted Messiah he associated with the Johannine community, by inventing a scenario in which Jesus actually seems to repudiate the Markan story by saying:

> (Jn 12.27) Now is my soul troubled. And what should I say? "Father, save me from this hour"? No, for this purpose I have come to this hour.

All this is evidence of the early Christians' bewilderment by Mark's Gethsemane story and their willingness to reject both readings of the Markan pericope because of the scandalous images of Jesus they convey. In other words, the Matthean and Johannine communities rejected both the Jesus who shrinks from his fate and requests a change of destiny (traditional Mark) and the Jesus who prays for help in surrendering, admits powerlessness, and asks for removal of his cup addiction (sobriety Mark).

Jesus' fourth and final petition in verse 36 is "But not what I will but what you will." These words need not, as is ordinarily assumed, express a sense of desire ("what I wish or want"). Nor need they signify Jesus' resignation to an outcome or his recantation of the prayers in verses 35 and 36. They can just as readily express his renunciation of self-will as a power source. Like every surrendering alcoholic, Jesus is admitting defeat in his battle of wills with God, acknowledging that the cup of his alcoholism can be removed not by dint of willpower but only by an other. From the day of his spiritual experience at the Jordan River, to his decision at Caesarea Philippi to go to Jerusalem, to his drunken assault on the Jewish religionists and the Temple, Jesus has resorted to greater and greater extremes of self-will in attempting to realize his vision for the world, the rule of God. Now he has hit bottom, thrown to the same earth, symbolically, from which his mythic primal ancestors rose up in their prideful attempt to grasp autonomy.

From an alcoholism perspective, then, Jesus' three prayer petitions—admission of powerlessness, request for the removal of his cup addiction, and renunciation of self-will—signal the beginning of the end of humanity's primordial rebellion against God. Verse 36 shows Jesus doing exactly what today's alcoholics do in the first three steps of their recovery program: First, they admit their powerlessness before the One who has all power. Second, they enact their faith in this higher power by asking him to remove their addiction. Third, renouncing self-empowerment, they turn their will and their lives over to the care of God, asking only that their surrenders might bear witness to others of God's wisdom and strength. So construed, Jesus' prayer may be retranslated as follows:

(14.36) Abba, as you have all power, so I am powerless; take away my
cup addiction, not through my willpower, but by your willing it.

In spiritual terms Gethsemane is thus the real locus of the atonement
miracle Christians celebrate at Easter, for there God comes to Jesus in
the prison cell of addiction, strives with his jailer alcohol, defeats it, and
shows its power to be a lie. Resurrected from the living death of alcoholism, Jesus rises from the ground of the garden a humbled man, a
new Adam in a redeemed Eden, a person now wholly reliant on a higher power who has discovered the secret of truly human living, no longer
a fearful individual pretending godlike autonomy but a true child of
God and son of man. In short, Jesus' Gethsemane resurrection is a type
of the spiritual awakening experienced by every recovering addict who
follows the Twelve Steps to sobriety and atonement.

The Sleeping Disciples (14.37–40)

The disciples do not see Jesus' way-showing surrender, however, because they are asleep. As newly translated here, Mark's text reads as
follows:

(14.37) Next he came and found them sleeping. And he said to Peter,
"Simon, are you asleep? Could you not watch [me] one hour? (38)
Watch [my actions], and pray that you may be spared the ordeal [*peirasmon*] of a ready spirit [*pneuma prothumon*] but a body that remains
inert [*sarx asthenēs*]." (39) So again he went away and prayed, saying
the same words. (40) And again he came and found them sleeping,
for their eyes were burdened down [*katabarunomenoi*] and they did not
know how they should respond to his actions [*apokrithōsin*].

The disciples' sleep is both a symbol of their spiritually unawake condition and the real consequence of the Passover wine they have
drunk. Hoping nonetheless that their time of surrender might have
arrived, that they might take the action necessary to follow the way
he has shown, Jesus attempts to awaken the disciples, again admonishes them to watch his actions, and repeats his prayer for their benefit. But to no avail.

Verse 38 requires special attention. The RSV translates this verse
as follows:

(14.38) Watch and pray that you may not enter into temptation; the
spirit indeed is willing but the flesh is weak.

Many commentators consider the verse less the historical words of
Jesus and more the early Church's paraenetic advice to Christians to
hold fast under persecution. It is based on *peirasmos,* meaning "ordeal

by suffering," and is generally interpreted as a strangely misplaced warning to avoid temptations ranging from apostasy to appetites of the flesh. All such interpretations seem unsatisfactory in the context of Gethsemane. The viewpoint of recovery suggests a different approach entirely, reflected in the version given above. Idiomatically, the "ordeal of a ready spirit but a body that remains inert" can be rendered as "pray that you may be spared having to learn the hard way" *(peirasmos)* what happens when you have "a ready spirit but a body that won't act." Every alcoholic will instantly recognize that Jesus is referring to the pain of sufferers who appear willing but refuse to act, who say they want help but will not ask for it, will not take the action necessary to receive it. It is characteristic alcoholic behavior, observable in the disciples' asthenia.

Betrayal to the Unawakened (14.41)

A final startling revelation is the identity of Jesus' betrayers. Verse 41 as here translated reads:

> (14.41) And he came the third time, and said to them, "Are you still sleeping and avoiding action [*anapauesthe*]? By such has come to pass [*apechei erchomai he hōra*] the son of man's betrayal into the hands of those who err [*hamartōlōn*]."

"Avoiding action," ordinarily translated as "taking your rest," comes from *anapauō*, which means "inactivity" or "inaction." Jesus' remark is not about sleeping in a literal sense; instead, it is yet another reference to the disciples' failure to follow his lead. *Apechei erchomai he hōra* is usually rendered as "It is enough, the hour has come." The present reading interprets *apechei*, often considered untranslatable, as an anaphoric reference to the disciples' failure to respond: "By such [your failure to act] has come to pass. . . ." *Erchomai he hōra* means not "the time has arrived" but rather "something has now come to pass." The sense is highlighted by omitting *he hōra* from overt translation. *Hamartōlōn*, etymologically translated as "those who err," is invariably rendered as "sinners," but the root meaning serves better here. Who are the Son of Man's betrayers? Who are those who err? They are not the Jewish religious figures about to arrest him but rather the spiritually unawakened disciples. The erring disciples are the ones who have betrayed Jesus.

Summary

The whole of Mark's Gethsemane pericope as retranslated from the perspective of recovery reads as follows:

(14.32) And they went to a place called Gethsemane, and Jesus said to his disciples, "Sit here, while I pray." (33) And he took with him Peter and James and John, and he began to be amazed and strangely awestruck. (34) And he said to them, "My self is sorrowful as it approaches death. Remain here and continue watching me." (35) And going forward a little, he fell on the ground and prayed for the strength to get through the moment at hand. (36) And he said, "Abba, as you have all power so I am powerless; take away my cup addiction, not through my willpower but by your willing it." (37) Next he came and found them sleeping. And he said to Peter, "Simon, are you asleep? Could you not watch me one hour? (38) Watch, and pray that you may be spared having to learn the hard way what happens when you have a ready spirit but a body that does not act." (39) Then again he went away and prayed, saying the same words. (40) And again he came and found them sleeping, for their eyes were burdened down and they did not know how they should respond to his actions. (41) And he came the third time, and said to them, "Are you still sleeping and avoiding action? By such has come to pass the Son of Man's betrayal into the hands of those who err."

All things considered, the frequency and pointedness of the ambiguities in the text of the Gethsemane story argue their intentionality. They may be summarized as follows:

Verse 35:

a. referential ambiguity: *he hōra* ("the hour") as impending crucifixion or as the present moment

b. ambiguity of mood: *dunaton* as the auxiliary "possible" or as the main verb "empowered"

c. lexical ambiguity: *parerchomai* as "be spared a fate" or as "get through a difficult moment"

Verse 36:

a. semantic ambiguity: *panta dunata soi* as Jesus' testimonial to God's all-powerfulness or as his admission of his own powerlessness

b. figurative ambiguity: *pōterion* ("cup") as an image of fate or as a metaphor for alcohol addiction

c. semantic ambiguity: *ti egō thelō* ("what I will") as volition or as willpower

Verse 38:

semantic ambiguity: *elthēte eis peirasmon* as "enter into temptation" or as "learn the hard way"

Verses 34, 37, 38:

lexical ambiguity: *grēgoreō* as "watch for enemies" or as "watch me"

Verses 37, 40, 41:
symbolic ambiguity: *katheudō* as sleep and nothing more or as a symbol of a spiritually unawakened state

Verse 41:
referential ambiguity: "betrayed into the hands of those who err" as referring to the Jewish theocrats of 30 C.E. or to the emergent Christian hierarchs of 68 C.E., whom the Gethsemane disciples prefigure

Notice that the nontraditional member in each pair of readings reflects the perspective of recovery and is thus the version that will be selected by an alcoholic reader aware of the ambiguity and detached from the traditional version. This consistency can hardly be accidental and lends strong support to the hypothesis of Mark's secret community as a sobriety fellowship.

Mark surely knew what he was doing in shaping the Gethsemane material. He crafted his story such that nonalcoholic readers would discern therein a Jesus whose image harmonizes with that of the Christ cults. This portrait, the interpretation of Gethsemane ultimately enshrined in Christianity, depicts Jesus not as a humbled and truly human being who shows the way to personal atonement but as a godlike hero who, though he falters momentarily, willfully propels himself toward crucifixion in order to achieve a substitutionary atonement. Necessary to guarantee the acceptance of his book, this picture nonetheless constituted a betrayal of the surrendered Jesus whom Mark has subtly limned behind the surface portrait.

Highly significant as a grace note to this reading of the Gethsemane pericope is an etymology of the name *Gethsemane* itself. According to the famed Aramaic scholar Gustaf Dalman, *Gethsemane* consists of the Hebrew/Aramaic word for "press," *gat*, together with the Greek *sēmeion*, meaning "sign." Dalman believed that the press at this particular site could well have been a winepress.[33] If so, how significant that the nondrinking (*colobodactylus*, stump-fingered) cupmaster (*Markôs*) locates the victory of Help-Me-God (*Y'shua*, Jesus) over the death force emanating from the agonistic human self (*psuchē*) at a place identified as the Sign of the Winepress (*gat-sēmeion*).

As for the disciples, Mark obviously depicts them as prototypes of Christian religious leaders, the clerical authorities he sees emerging in the Judean Messiah cults of his own day. Like so much in his book, his portrayal of the disciples as spiritually unawakened hierarchs is conditioned by the Roman-Jewish War devastating Palestine even as he writes. The time is presumably late 68 to early 69 C.E., during the lull between the Romans' military campaign in northern Palestine and their siege of Jerusalem.[34] Mark apparently foresees that the only Jewish-Christian communities to be tolerated in Jewish territory under the postwar Roman rule will be those whose leaders exercise strong hierarchical control for the sake of order. In this, Mark sees the end of the benign anarchy that has characterized the Markôs movement, as he knows it, from its beginnings. For Mark as for recovering persons today, authoritarianism is a form of mental drunkenness completely inimical to spiritual living.

In this connection Mark was doubtless aware of the final lines of the Deutero-Isaian drunkenness oracle (51.17–23; see the discussion in chap. 3), wherein Yahweh removes the cup from the alcoholic petitioner, just as from Jesus in Gethsemane, but then goes on to say (AB version):

> (Is 51.23) And I will put it [the cup of Is 51.17, symbolizing both real and mental drunkenness] in the hands of those who vex you, who said to you, "Bow down, that we may walk over you"; and you flattened your back like the ground, like a street for them to walk on.

Mark may have understood this oracle as illustrating what happens when leaders of spiritual movements abandon the servant role and start trying to govern. Perhaps he saw this kind of alcoholic behavior already driving the spirit from the Christian cults of his day. He consequently portrayed the disciples not only as intoxicated followers of Jesus awaiting their recovery and spiritual awakening but also as prototypes of religious authorities who inflict their mental drunkenness on those they govern. Thus the end of the Gethsemane story allegorically represents Jesus' betrayal into the hands of religious hierarchs: not the Jews of 30 C.E. but the increasingly authoritarian Jewish-Christian elders forty years later at the time of Mark's writing.

Crucifixion (14.62, 15.6–39)

In the light of recovery the final scenes in the Markan Passion appear problematic. Jesus' trial and crucifixion figure as an anticlimax in the narrative, illustrating how unsurrendered humans bring death on themselves by playing God and fighting others in their attempts to impose their wills on those around them. Dying is of course the inevitable end of physical life, but the death that opens into eternal life is death of the hubristic self, the death that Jesus experiences in Gethsemane, whereas death from crucifixion, like death from any form of execution or any other kind of mortal conflict, is the tragic end of unrenounced militance and agonism. Hence the question must be asked: did the Markans believe that Jesus, no political messiah but a Galilean wine addict who had publicly acted out an alcoholic obsession prior to his ultimate recovery, was actually crucified?

The answer suggested in this book, explored below and in chapters 4 and 6, is that they did not. The theory here is that the Markôs groups understood Jesus of Galilee and the Jewish insurrectionist crucified during the Jerusalem Passover of 30 C.E. to have been different persons. In this account the Markans believed that Jesus' original followers in Jerusalem, scattered at the time of his arrest and never to see Jesus again, had repressed (they would have said "denied") all knowledge of his alcoholic background and linked what little they knew of his prepaschal career with the crucifixion story of the insurrectionist messiah figure, thus providing Paul and other Christian apostles a basis for the crucifixion-resurrection theology and the Christ mysticism they so successfully promulgated. As for Jesus, the Markans perhaps believed that his Jewish captors on that long-ago Passover, recognizing he was only a drunkard and not a messianic claimant, had released him without ado and sent him back to Galilee, where he lived out his life in anonymity, sharing his recovery story with others in the Markôs groups. Indeed, it was presumably from the Markans' memory of the story Jesus told that Mark drew the narrative outline of his gospel, together with his accounts of spiritual events that would otherwise have been known only to Jesus, such as the baptism, wilderness, transfiguration, and Gethsemane. Chapter 4 of this book gives a first-person reconstruction of Jesus' recovery story as he would have told it later in Galilee.

Of course, Mark knew perfectly well that his Christian contemporaries would never accept a book that questioned Jesus' death on a Roman cross. Certainly he was aware of popular traditions about the Crucifixion. Thus his compositional problem was how to reconcile the disparity between his community's memory and that of the Christians. Mark's solution was to shape the remainder of his narrative such that Christians would regard it as portraying actuality, and the Markans, as allegory. In other words, every event from Jesus' trial by the Jews to the conclusion of the gospel functions allegorically, including the stories of the Crucifixion and the empty tomb. The single exception, the one event the Markans presumably considered an actuality, is the messianic witness in 14.62, discussed in the next section. For content Mark used prophetic elements from the Hebrew Bible and traditional material from what Dominic Crossan calls the Cross Gospel, the hypothetical original form of the Gospel of Peter,

together with his own fictions.[35] Some of these allegories are explicated here; the remainder, in chapter 6.

Messianic Witness (14.62)

Spiritually resurrected and freed of his messianism and righteous
anger, Mark's Jesus undergoes his arrest and trial virtually without
utterance, except for his response to the high priest's question, "Are
you the Messiah?" Jesus' reply is ordinarily rendered:

> (14.62) I am, and you will see the Son of Man sitting at the right hand
> of Power, and coming with the clouds of heaven.

Here Jesus quotes from two scriptural sources ("sitting at the right
hand" from Ps 110.1 and "coming with clouds of heaven" from Dn
7.13) and uses "Power" *(tēs dunamis)* as a circumlocution for the name
of God. Israelite kings were considered to be enthroned in a chair
to the right of God, symbolizing the source of their empowerment.[36]
Daniel's phrase "clouds of heaven" is a traditional image for the presence of God; if imputed to a person it would suggest an aura rather
than actual clouds. Discussions of "coming" *(erchomai)* usually revolve
around whether it means an ascent or a descent. *Erchomai* is a verb
with many senses, however, one of which is "coming and going," that
is, "going about."

Traditionally, "Son of Man" *(ton huion tou anthrōpou)* is considered
to be a self-reference by Jesus, and the entire verse is taken as a prediction of his second coming as God's messianic viceroy. Such a reading, however, serves mainly to reposition Jesus in precisely the sort
of power hierarchy he has just renounced in Gethsemane. The version given here presents a humbler picture. In Jesus' spoken Aramaic, "son of man" could just as readily have functioned as a general
indefinite noun referring not to Jesus alone but also to all redeemed
and sober people, people with a higher power who have the aura of
sobriety about them. Geza Vermes has studied the senses this term
had in Aramaic. Among them is the generic "man" or "any man."[37]
In commenting on Vermes' work on "son of man," Matthew Black
says: "No term was more fitted both to conceal, yet at the same time
to reveal to those who had ears to hear, the Son of Man's real identity. . . . In Aramaic the saying is skilfully ambiguous."[38] Mark has cap-
italized on just this ambiguity to both conceal and reveal the
subject(s) of verse 62. Refining the understanding, P. Maurice Casey
explains that "son of man" could be used in a general sense to say
something about oneself and a group of associates.[39] This is exactly
the generalized use discerned in Mk 14.62.

All this provides a basis for the translation and gloss of Mk 14.62 proposed here:

> (14.62) And Jesus said, "I am, and you will see recovering people [that is, people in Jesus' spiritual fellowship] empowered by God and coming and going [that is, going about living their lives] with a heavenly aura."

Reading *ton huion tou anthrōpou* ("son of man") as "recovering people" suggests that Jesus is not so much describing himself as the Messiah as he is envisioning the many people in recovery who will be seen living sober lives as the result of his messianic witness at the Last Supper and in Gethsemane. As ordinarily translated, Mk 14.62 is often regarded as a statement put into the mouth of Jesus by the early Church. This is not necessarily true; only its interpretation is the Church's. The words are Jesus' words handed on by the Markans and open to both the traditional version and the alternative but no less literal reading just indicated.

The assumption here is that the high priests and scribes understood the statement more or less as explained above. They recognized that Jesus was speaking spiritually, not theocratically, that he was not a political messiah figure but in fact only a peasant drunkard and enthusiast. So they released him. Presumably they instructed him to return to Galilee before he got into more trouble—and presumably he did. After all, persons who have undergone a Gethsemane experience have stopped fighting anything or anyone. Certainly the post-Gethsemane Jesus is a completely pacific figure. In this view Mark's conclusion of the trial scene, his account of the priest's charge of blasphemy and the condemnation by the entire council (14.63–65), would be a fiction introduced to satisfy Christian expectations. Chapter 6 more fully discusses the Markan understanding of "messiah."

Barnasha and Barabbas (15.6–15)

The historical issue underlying Mark's crucifixion narrative is not whether an execution occurred during the Jerusalem Passover of 30 C.E. but who was executed. The proposal here is that Mark, thinking allegorically, is offering his readers the same choice of victim that his narrative shows Pilate offering the Jerusalem multitude, the choice between Barabbas and Barnasha (Jesus), that is, between a figure of self-willed militancy and another of humbled anonymity. Wholly fictional, Mark's allegory would have been inspired by what he believed was the Christians' confusion of Jesus and the crucified insurrectionist. In the story Pilate offers to free a Jewish prisoner in honor of Passover and gives the crowd its choice of which man to free, Barabbas or Barnasha. *Barabbas*, the Aramaic nickname of an otherwise unidentified person sentenced to death for insurrection and murder, was a designation meaning "son of God" in an essentially inflammatory and self-appointed sense. *Barnasha*, on the other hand, was the Aramaic designation Jesus used (just discussed in connection with 14.62), sometimes for himself and sometimes for people collectively, translated as *ton huion tou anthrōpou* in Greek and "son of man" in English. The figurative contrast of these nicknames reinforces the idea that Mark intends the story of Pilate's offer, undocumented outside the gospel and historically unlikely, not as actuality but as allegory.

Relevant here is a line of scholarship that accepts as authentic the reading in certain manuscripts of Mt 27.17, "Jesus who is called Barabbas."[40] Hence *Barabbas*, like *Barnasha*, may have been another of Jesus' nicknames. Joseph Fitzmyer has called this line of thinking "idle speculation,"[41] but nothing is known of any Barabbas apart from the Markan story, and Jesus' conduct in Jerusalem certainly would have justified the rebel nickname "Jesus Barabbas." Those who knew both names would have recognized that Pilate's offer of a choice was not meant to be taken literally, since he would have been asking, in effect, "Which Jesus shall I execute?" The question is meaningful allegorically, however, if one assumes that Mark has personified the types represented by the names *Barabbas* and *Barnasha*, having discerned in the two appellatives names for the individual before and after surrender. Spiritually awakened readers will see Barabbas as the drunken self-willed zealot who plays God and seeks atonement in violent physical death, whereas Barnasha is the anonymous sober one who has found atonement in dying to self. In the course of his career in Jerusalem, Jesus exemplifies both types, just as all people carry within them the personas of Barabbas and Barnasha. Thus Pilate's offer as portrayed by Mark, construed allegorically, by no means applies solely to the Jerusalemites of 30 C.E. Readers of the gospel in every age must decide which death they ultimately choose for themselves, physical death or *psuchē* death, and which of their personas to sacrifice, Barabbas or Barnasha, just as they must decide which death to ascribe to the person they assume Jesus to have been. So understood, the allegory represents the quintessential recovery parable.

The Cry from the Cross (15.36–38)

Dominic Crossan has described a process by which the familiar details of the Passion evolved from an initial stage of minimal historical knowledge, to a prophetic stage of "multiple and discrete biblical allusions," to a final narrative stage combining and transforming these allusions into "a single sequential story" "flowing from the Cross Gospel, now embedded within the Gospel of Peter, into Mark," and from there into the other canonical gospels.[42] Mark's crucifixion narrative (15.21–39) begins with a collage of such details: Simon the Cyrene, the place-name *Golgotha,* Jesus' refusal of the drugged wine, the division of his garment, the inscription "King of the Jews," the two bandits, mockery by passersby and the high priests and scribes, and the quotation of Ps 22.1, "My God, my God, why hast thou forsaken me?" These provide a background for the key elements in the Cupmaster's cross story: the second offer of wine coupled with the Elijah reference, Jesus' refusal via his cry from the cross, the tearing of the Temple veil, and the centurion's profession.

True to his Last Supper decision to "drink no more of the fruit of the vine" (14.25), Mark's Jesus twice refuses the offer of wine, first in verse 23 and then again in 36–37. In describing the first offer, Mark rejected the biblical reference he found in the Cross Gospel (ultimately Gos. Pet. 16), an allusion to Ps 69.21, "they gave him wine to drink, mingled with gall" (the form later employed in Matthew 27.34), in favor of his own version, "wine mingled with myrrh." This phrase denotes not a lethal potion, as gall would have been, but simply a very potent drink-and-drug combination. Rather obviously, Mark's version of the first offer, followed by Jesus' refusal, reflects his community's understanding of Jesus as an ex-addict who had renounced drinking and drugging for good.

Surprisingly, the second refusal, never recognized as such, is the "loud cry" *(phonēn megalēn)* Jesus utters with his dying breath. The text reads as follows:

> (15.36) And one ran and, filling a sponge full of vinegar [*oxos,* actually sour or dry wine, as opposed to *oinos,* sweet wine], put it on a reed and gave it to him to drink, saying, "Wait, let us see whether Elijah will come to take him down." (37) But Jesus uttered a loud cry, and breathed his last.

How can the cry from the cross be interpreted as a refusal of the wine offered in verse 36? Many readers understand "gave it to him to drink" *(epotizēn)* to mean that Jesus did drink the proffered wine,[43] and some consider it the fulfillment of 14.25. The Greek verb, however, is apparently as ambiguous as its English equivalent, "to give to drink." It can mean either an offer of drink and the drinking that follows or an offer alone, without regard to whether it is accepted.

Ignoring for now the Elijah reference, one might expect the ambiguity of "give to drink" to be resolved by Jesus' response in verse 37, identified as a "loud cry," yet the function of the cry as a speech act is itself ambiguous. Many readers understand it as a final scream of pain, despite the fact that crucifixion involved death by asphyxiation and probably did not culminate in loud cries. Modern Bibles (but not RSV) typically format the text so as to make verse 37 begin a new paragraph and thus seem noncontextual with the offer of wine in verse 36. Most ancient manuscripts are unparagraphed, however, and the conjunction beginning verse 37 is *de* ("but"), not *kai* ("and"). True, *de* is a weak adversative often translated "and" or "then" when the context warrants, but here the only context is that provided by the reader in the process of disambiguating verses 36 and 37. The present reading of *de* as "but" treats verse 37 as an adversative intra-discourse response to verse 36, which in turn makes sense only if "gave it to him to drink" is understood as an offer alone without regard to any response and if the semantic function of the "loud cry" is construed as a refusal prompted by this offer. Text-grammatically, therefore, there is every good reason for understanding Jesus' cry in verse 37 as an emphatic refusal of the wine proffered in verse 36.

What is strange is that the content of the cry is missing, almost as if it had been deleted from the text. And that is precisely the theory proposed here. It happens that the Gospel of Peter does not include a verbatim recitation of Ps 22.1, "My God, my God, why hast thou forsaken me?" Rather, it has Jesus addressing *dunamis: "he dunamis mou he dunamis kateleipsas me,"* literally, "My Power, O Power, you have entirely left me" (Gos. Pet. 19). Both instances of the term *power* are taken as circumlocutions for the name of God, expressed as dual vocatives, and the statement itself is construed as a rough paraphrase of Ps 22.1. As already mentioned, Dominic Crossan believes the Gospel of Peter to be an expansion of a hypothetical document he calls the Cross Gospel, which, if actual, predated the canonical gospels and provided Mark with his one written source for the Passion narrative. Now the suspiciously awkward first-person *mou* ("my") suggests that the cry in the Cross Gospel, changed in the Gospel of Peter to second person in conformity to Ps 22.1, originally read as a third-person utterance, *"he dunamis mou he dunamis katelipe me."* Here only the second "power" would be a vocative circumlocution for God, while the first *(he dunamis mou)* would be a nominative referring to the speaker's own power. Hence the cry would have read, "My power, O Power, has entirely left me." In other words, "O God, I am powerless."[44] This utterance would linguistically echo Jesus' use of *dunamis* in Gethsemane (14.36) and is precisely the response a recovering alcoholic would give to the offer of wine.

But was the hypothetical Cross Gospel the origin of the foregoing cry? Perhaps not. Crossan acknowledges that material in the Gospel of Peter comes from both the Cross Gospel and the canonical gospels. Therefore, when a particular item occurs in the Gospel of Peter and in a canonical gospel, it is impossible to tell whether it originated in Cross Gospel or the canonical document. The position here is that the reconstructed saying, "My power, O Power, has entirely left me" ("O God, I am powerless"), is a Markan invention, a play on the wording of Ps 22.1 originally included in the first version of Mark's book (Secret Mark, discussed in chap. 6) immediately after the clause referring to Jesus' cry responding to the offer of wine. In other words, verse 37 in Secret Mark would have read, "But Jesus answered with a loud cry, 'O God, I am powerless,' and breathed his last." Presumably Mark excised the saying from verse 37 in later copies of his book (although not in time to prevent its adoption into the Cross Gospel/ Gospel of Peter tradition) after discovering that his intended ambiguity had failed, that emergent Christian clergy were reading the line not as a paraphrased doublet of the earlier recitation of Ps 22.1 but as a testimony to a powerless messiah, an image they indignantly rejected.[45] Why did Mark invent the saying in the first place? Apparently he intended it as an assurance to the Markôs coterie that their founder, were he to have been crucified, would have rejected drink even with his last breath.

Elijah (15.35–36)

Turn now to the Elijah references. Prior to recounting the offer of wine in verse 36, Mark, ever alert for linguistic nuances, reports that certain bystanders misunderstood Jesus' *Eloi, Eloi* ("my God, my God," verse 34) as a call to Elijah:

> (15.35) And some of the bystanders hearing it [*Eloi*, transliterated Aramaic] said, "Behold, he is calling Elijah [*Elias* in Greek]."

In verse 36 one of these bystanders offers Jesus the sponge of wine and goes on to say:

> (15.36) . . . "Wait, let us see whether Elijah will come to take him down [*kathaireō*]."

On its face the episode appears contradictory: the offer of wine seems to be a kindness; the Elijah reference, mockery. Apparently the anecdote reflects clandestine Markan lore about Elijah. First of all, the

Markans almost certainly would have honored Elijah as a fellow water drinker. They knew that his story begins with God's promise that he will drink water (1 Kgs 17.4). On meeting the widow of Zarephath, the first thing that Elijah requests is water to drink (1 Kgs 17.10). In his contest with the prophets of Baal, Elijah consecrates his altar with twelve jars of water (1 Kgs 18.33–35). En route to his revelation on Mt. Horeb, he receives from the angel of God a cake and a jar of water, which sustain him for forty days (1 Kgs 19.5–8, a prefiguration of Mk 1.13). When Elijah's spirit passes to Elisha, the latter's first miracle is to make wholesome the water of Jericho (2 Kgs 2.21).

Now Elijah's return was expected as a sign of the Messiah (Mal 4.5–6), and Mark's Jesus announces at the Transfiguration that Elijah has indeed come (9.13). The Crucifixion occurs at Passover, and part of the Passover wine ritual was—and is—to set for Elijah a cup that remains undrunk.[46] The theory proposed here is that over the years Mark's alcoholics, focused on the eschatological significance of "drinking no more" (14.25) coupled with their image of Elijah as a water drinker, had perpetuated a coterie interpretation of the undrunk Elijah cup as a sign not that Elijah has yet to appear but rather that Elijah *has* come but drinks no wine. In other words, they understood the undrunk Passover cup as a veiled sign of the Age of Messiah, a sign whose recognition depends on a metanoetic reversal of conventional thinking regarding drink, namely, that the joy of wine stems not from consuming it but from deciding to leave it undrunk. The invocation of Elijah in connection with Jesus' refusal of wine from the cross, neither an obvious biblicism nor material from the Cross Gospel, would thus be a Markan fiction reflecting this coterie understanding of Elijah as a figure of sobriety. It would have functioned within the Markôs groups in at least three ways: as a *metanoia* parable underscoring the import of undrunk ritual wine, as a key to the interpretation of 15.37 given above, and as a reprise of Jesus' disavowal of drink at the Last Supper.

This understanding of undrunk wine may represent a Markan exegesis of Jeremiah's cryptic oracle of the wine jar (AB):

> (Jer 13.12) Now speak to them this word: Thus says the Lord, the God of Israel: Every wine jar is meant to be filled with wine. If they reply, "Do we not know that every wine jar is meant to be filled with wine?" (13) say to them: Thus says the Lord: Beware! I am filling with drunkenness all the inhabitants of this land . . . (14) I will dash them against each other, fathers and sons together, says the Lord. . . .

John Bright understands the people's response to mean that "they are the jugs, and they mean to be filled with wine."[47] Just so, and the larger meaning of the oracle is that persons arrogant enough to talk back to God suffer not only drunkenness but wrath in the form of the violence they visit on one another. The recovering alcoholic, however, need not read beyond the initial oracle, "every wine jar is meant to be filled with wine." Its import is clear, since wine vessels stay full only so long as their wine remains undrunk: renounce drink at the apocalyptic moment and surrender to the will of God. The Markans may have based their understanding of Elijah's undrunk Passover cup on some such interpretation of Jeremiah's ever-full wine jar.

But how did Mark expect nonalcoholics to interpret verses 35–37? It appears that Christian readers have never understood these verses as Mark intended them. The theory proposed here is that the final *auton* ("him") in verse 36 originally read *auto* ("it"), referring not to Jesus but to the sponge of wine. This would permit an interpretation of the perplexing reference to Elijah as a sarcastic taunt by a person in the crowd based on Jesus's reputed decision to abstain from wine (Mk 14.25) in emulation of Elijah. Thus the original form of these verses in Secret Mark would have been the following:

> (15.35) And some of the bystanders hearing it [*Eloi*] said, "Behold, he is calling Elijah." (36) And one ran and filling a sponge full of sour wine, [tauntingly] put it on a reed and gave it to him to drink, saying, "Wait, let us see whether Elijah [referring *not* to Elijah but to Jesus and his reputed Elijah-like abstinence] will turn and resist it [*kathaireō*, "put down" the temptation to drink the proffered wine]." (37) But Jesus answered with a loud cry, "O God, I am powerless," and breathed his last.

Idiomatically expressed, the import of this sarcastic taunt would be, "Okay, Mister Elijah, now that you're parched and dry and all but dead, let's see if you go on refusing drink." So read, verse 36 could well be the source of the slander Origen attributes to Celsus, who described Jesus at Golgotha as "rushing with his mouth open to drink" instead of "bearing his thirst like an ordinary man."[48] So viewed, Celsus's odd remark emerges as a significant extrabiblical confirmation of Jesus' reputation as an inebriate.

In any case, what actually happened to verse 36 in Christian understanding is reflected in Matthew's version of Mark's original. Matthew depicts one person kindly offering Jesus the wine, while others mockingly admonish the spectators to see whether Elijah "will come to save (*sōzō*) him" (Mt 27.49). Matthew's substitution of *sōzō* for the Markan *kathaireō* has caused subsequent translators to construe Mark's verb in its technical sense, to "take down" a body from a cross. By contrast, the view here is that Mark wanted Christian readers to see the offer of wine not as a kindness but as the beginning of a taunt whose perpetrator sarcastically goes on to address Jesus as Elijah (hence the performance of both actions by one person). Unaware of the lexical substitution Matthew would later make, Mark expected these readers to understand *kathaireō* in its psychological sense, to put down or conquer or resist a temptation. He knew that Christians remembered Jesus to have abstained from wine at the Jerusalem supper. Thus he considered this derisive offer of drink, followed by mock suspense as to whether Jesus would, like Elijah, resist it, as appropriate embellishments of what he knew to be a fictional crucifixion scene. All this is predicated on Mark's originally having written the pronoun *auto* ("it"), not *auton* ("him"), as the last word of verse 36. The subsequent change to *auton* would have been a redaction conforming the passage to the Christian understanding of the event ultimately represented in the Matthean version.

The Torn Temple Veil (15.38)

Understood as Jesus' final refusal of drink and profession of powerlessness, verse 37 gives new meaning to the notice about the tearing of the Temple veil that follows in verse 38:

(15.38) And the curtain of the Temple was torn in two, from top to bottom.

The veil was the curtain screening either the Holy Place or the Holy of Holies, the innermost places within the Temple. Scholars have debated Mark's purpose in placing this notice immediately after Jesus' death cry.[49] The view suggested here is that Mark is further highlighting the conjunction of not drinking and apocalypse: God's presence is opened to all who refuse drink unto death. To Mark's audience of spiritually awakened Jews, who knew Jesus as a fellow alcoholic, the reference to the tearing of the Temple veil would have had parousial significance.

The Centurion's Profession (15.39)

The scene at the cross concludes with the centurion's profession of Jesus as "Son of God," which is traditionally interpreted as a confirmation of Jesus' identity as the Messiah:

(15.39) And when the centurion, who stood facing him, saw that he thus breathed his last, he said, "Truly this man was a/the [both readings are correct] son of God."

Mark may have included this incident to distract unawakened readers from the preceding events. As ritual drinkers, Christian leaders would be scandalized by the idea of Jesus as a surrendered alcoholic whose last words were a refusal of drink. They would have been quite comfortable, however, with the image of Jesus as a godlike ruler superior to mortals, and the latter is precisely the meaning that the centurion, like any Roman familiar with this secular sense of the term, would have assigned to the title "Son of God." Mark evidently calculated, quite rightly as it turned out, that the Palestinian Christ cultists of his day would overlook the possibility that Jesus' final act was the refusal of wine in their haste to interpret the centurion's remark as indicating Roman approval of a new religion based on exactly the imperious image of Jesus they sought to foster. So he took the centurion he found as tomb guard in the Cross Gospel (Gos. Pet. 31 and 38), positioned him at the foot of the cross, and placed on his lips alone the "Son of God" profession that the Cross Gospel attributes to the soldiers' collective post-resurrection report to Pilate (Gos. Pet. 45).

Altogether, the details of Mark's crucifixion scene, culminating in the two offers of wine, the cry from the cross, the Elijah reference, the tearing of the Temple veil, and the centurion's profession, constitute a tapestry cunningly woven partly of traditional materials and partly of whole cloth, by means of which Mark satisfied the expectations of his Christian readers while simultaneously entertaining his insider audience with cryptic details embellishing a story they knew was fictional.

The Empty Tomb (15.40–16.8)

As symbols the women at the end of the Cupmaster's gospel—unlike the male disciples, who prefigure Christian clergy—represent surrendered and spiritually awakened persons of both genders, followers of Jesus in recovery. Peter proclaims Jesus to be the Messiah (8.29) but refuses to follow him through suffering and *psuchē* death. By contrast, the woman at Bethany anoints Jesus as Messiah by pouring her costly perfume over his head and breaking its expensive jar, actions symbolizing self-abandonment and commitment to another (14.3–9).[50] Later on, the men run away when Jesus is arrested (14.50), whereas the women stand by him at the cross, cosufferers in his Passion (15.40–41). Ultimately the women seek to enter Jesus' tomb (16.1–3), but the men avoid it completely.

Recovery criticism views Mark's account of the burial of Jesus as an allegory representing an effort by the Judean Christ cult to con-

ceal the alcoholic Jesus by encrypting him in a tomb hewn of rock
(petra). The tomb itself symbolizes the theocratic religion Mark saw
emerging in Jewish Palestine even as he wrote, as the Romans prepared to besiege Jerusalem and conclude their destruction of regional Judaism.[51] Elements of Palestinian Christianity, separate from the
gentile churches and until that time a largely unorganized movement
within Judaism, were seeking to transform themselves in the crisis of
war into a hierarchical institution acceptable to Rome as an agency
of societal order replacing synagogue and Temple. Membership in
this cult would have required profession of Jesus as a dominical
messiah and submission to authorities ruling in his name. Such a
religion will have no place for an anonymous messiah who had quit
drinking, admitted powerlessness, and given over his will to a higher power. In short, the memory of Jesus as a surrendered exdrunkard would have become anathema, to be encrypted and forgotten.

Hence the rock tomb can be interpreted as Mark's ironic and clandestine version of the *"petra*/Peter" pun traditionally ascribed to Jesus.
In the familiar version of the pun as later told by Matthew (16.18), Jesus
responds to Simon's profession of him as the Messiah by saying, "You
are rock, and on this rock I will build my church." By contrast, the
frankly sardonic version of this pun implied in the Markan text signifies the following: although *petra*/Peter, symbolizing profession of an
authoritative messiah, may be the foundational "rock" of the Christ
cult, it/he is also the rock tomb encrypting and concealing the memory of the powerless savior professed by recovering persons.

In the Markan scenario Jesus remains entombed until sunrise of
the third day (16.1–2), when it is revealed that he has risen and returned to Galilee (16.6–7). This two-day entombment apparently represents Mark's prophecy of a two-era or two-millennium period during which Jesus will be imprisoned within religion and represented
to its adherents through a preached image of messianic power and
perfection, the antitype of the alcoholic Jesus. The empty tomb and
return to Galilee would thus signify Jesus' ultimate escape from hierarchical religion and return to his egalitarian and benignly anarchical recovery program, at the dawn of the third millennium. Chapter 7 suggests that the advent of today's Twelve-Step movement sets
the stage for the fulfillment of this prophecy.

In the story the women want to anoint the body of Jesus inside the
tomb but are blocked by a huge stone covering its mouth. Allegorically, the scene further represents religion barring the way to the spiritual Jesus. Although "very large" *(megas sphodra)*, the stone is rolled back
by the women's prayer, "Who will roll away the stone for us from the

door of the tomb?" (16.3–4). Once inside they meet a man clothed in white (see chap. 6 for discussion of the man's identity) who tells them that Jesus "is risen and is not here." The women are to tell Peter and the disciples that Jesus has returned to Galilee, where they will see him just as he promised (16.6–7). In other words, the man is telling these women, these spiritually awakened persons, that they are in the wrong place after all. They should not shut themselves up in this Jerusalem tomb, this confining church; instead, they should seek the free air of Galilee, the symbol of their recovery program.

So the women leave the tomb, filled with trembling *(tromos)* and astonishment *(ekstasis)*, yet it is plain fear *(phobos)* that keeps them from saying anything to anyone (16.8). But who or what did they fear, and why? These are questions left hanging at the close of Mark's gospel.[52] The view of recovery criticism suggests that the women were afraid of the disciples themselves, afraid that the disciples had already become like the religious overlords in Jerusalem with whom Jesus had warred, afraid they would transform Jesus' simple Galilean program into a religion of authority and domination. Allegorically, the women at the tomb represent recovering persons in Mark's own day, the covert audience of his entire book, unsure and troubled as they see the image of Jesus as they have known him being replaced by a figure of hierarchical governance. In essence then, Mark's final allegory constitutes a warning to his confreres to keep silent about the uncrucified alcoholic Jesus at this dangerous time, the beginning of organized Christianity in postwar Palestine.

In a widely read book, Thomas Sheehan views the empty tomb as depicting "absolute absence," neither a resurrected body to compel belief in divinity nor a corpse to be iconized, only an invitation "to *surrender Jesus:* to leave him dead and to see that the meaning of Jesus is that Jesus himself no longer matters."[53] Sheehan's "absence" theory might seem to resemble the anonymity mystique so important in the spirituality of alcoholics. Sheehan, however, is deaf to Jesus' message about alcohol ("This [wine] is my blood of the covenant," Mk 14.24), just as he ignores Galilee as a postpaschal locus of recovery and symbolic antitopia to religious Jerusalem. It is in Galilee, after all, where Jesus promises to be present as a resurrected person (Mk 14.28), a promise recalled by the messenger in the tomb (Mk 16.7). All this marks Sheehan's view as quite different from that of recovery criticism, in which Jesus' risen witness and promised Galilean appearances matter a great deal. Indeed, chapter 4 of this book reconstructs the first-person sobriety story that Jesus would have told later on in Galilee, which provided Mark the narrative outline of his gospel.

Conclusion

This chapter has identified the alcoholism themes in Mark's Passion narrative, content that will be apparent to readers willing to detach themselves from ingrained translations and understandings and to examine the Markan text from the perspective of addiction and recovery. The textual ambiguities motivating the interpretations presented in this chapter are linguistically straightforward, varied in kind, and surprisingly numerous, as follows:

> reference: 14.22, 25, 35, 41, 62
> lexis: 14.34 (pars. 37, 38), 35, 62; 15.36
> theme: 14.24
> speech act: 14.22, 24; 15.37
> grammar: 14.25, 35
> semantics: 14.36, 38; 15.37
> figure: 14.22, 36, 37 (pars. 40, 41)
> allegorical signification:
> 14.13–15 (water carrier as gender anomaly or as sobriety image)
> 14.3–9, 15.40–41, and 16.1–8 (women as women or as Markôs people of both sexes)
> 15.6–15 (crucifixion victim as Barnasha or as Barabbas)
> 15.35–36 (Elijah as messiah herald or as sobriety exemplar)
> 15.46 (tomb as burial vault or as ecclesiastical crypt)
> 16.1–6 (empty tomb as resurrection or as liberation)

The consistent directionality, content, and narratological coherence of these ambiguities suggest a clandestine readership whose spiritual outlook resembled that of recovering alcoholics today. In other words, they support the hypothesis that Mark's secret audience was a community of former addicts who memorialized Jesus not only as fellow sufferer but also as architect of their movement's distinctive spirituality.

Apparent throughout the Passion narrative, Mark's compositional genius lies in his ability to write for this insider group while seeming to address a broad spectrum of Jewish and gentile Christ cultists who were in positions to make or break his book and who, he believed, would imagine themselves to be its sole audience. In so doing Mark exploits ambiguity and allegory to conceal the portrait of a powerless and surrendered Son of Man behind the lineament of a heroic and self-assertive Son of God. Mark intended these pictures of Jesus for his two audiences, spiritually awakened followers of the alcoholic Jesus and pious worshipers of the Jesus of theocracy. To former addicts the Last Supper and Gethsemane depict crucial way-showing events in recovery. The Last Supper portrays an archetypal A.A.-like meeting wherein Jesus, as the exemplar of alcoholic humanity, voices his recognition of wine as the cause of his troubles and then announces his intention to stop drinking. Psalm 116 of the Hallel adumbrates the first three steps of the recovery process, and the scene in Gethsemane shows Jesus taking those steps—admission of powerlessness, appeal to God as a saving higher power, and self-immolating oblation to that power. To religious readers, by contrast, these scenes display the institution of a cultic ritual set in the context of a fellowship meal and a poignant interlude of seemingly human weakness in the divine hero Jesus' progression toward his substitutionary death.

Conversely, followers of the alcoholic Jesus see little of spiritual significance in the events of the Passion to which Christian piety ascribes such importance: Jesus' crucifixion, burial, empty tomb, and presumed bodily resurrection. These scenes function primarily as allegorical pointers to the essential alcoholism of the religious perspective. The crucifixion story, based on the execution of a messianic insurrectionist in Jerusalem around 30 C.E., allegorically depicts the death religious individuals inflict on themselves as a consequence of their fanatical and sooner or later bellicose attempts to impose their wills on their fellows. The entombment symbolizes the concealment of the powerless Son of Man by religious leaders who preach a powerful Son of God to justify their assumption of clerical authority. The empty tomb signifies Jesus' emancipation from theocracy and entry into spiritual life, timeless and ultimately spaceless. But it does not indicate a bodily resurrection. Emblematic of alcoholic humanity's denial of the unavoidable reality of physical death, resurrection is the fiction by which religion teaches its adherents to live as they drink their way toward *metanoia* and eternal life in God. Despite the many appearance stories extant in the oral tradition, to say nothing of the expectations of his Christian audience, Mark staunchly refused to compromise the principles of his spiritual movement by depicting a bodily resurrected Jesus.[54]

Where Mark's two audiences would agree is on the importance of Jesus' words and actions over the wine at the Last Supper. Jesus' wordless giving of the cup to all disciples and his consequent utterance, "This is my blood of the covenant poured out for many," remain centrally important events in the Passion. In them Jesus raises to prominence the Deutero-Isaian covenant based on the salvific telos of wine and the spiritual recovery program to which its renunciation leads (see chap. 3). Why has the alcoholism meaning of Jesus' statement remained so long obscured? Possibly by some higher design. At the human level, at any rate, it is partly because of its stunning conciseness, its scandalous irony, and the denial it evokes in hearers unwilling to acknowledge their own latent alcoholism. Mainly, however, it is because the words could not, until now, have been interpreted from the perspective of recovery, for no such perspective existed. Only at the close of the second millennium has the necessary interpretive community appeared, the fellowship of recovering alcoholics whose experience of addiction and release uniquely qualifies them to discern the covert intentionality of Jesus' words. Religious drinkers hear these words and drink their communion wine for the same underlying reason that addicts drink, to satisfy an unconscious desire for apocalypse and parousia. Recovering alcoholics refrain from drink, grateful for the sense of experiencing both.

✤ 3 ✤

ISAIAH'S SERVANT DRUNKARD

In return for the affliction of his soul he shall drink [the
wine of sobriety], deeply, until sated.
—Isaiah 53.11

Interpreters of Mark's Last Supper narrative (14.22–26) and the earlier related discourse on the cup (10.35–45) have always recognized how pointedly in those scenes Jesus alludes to Isaiah's enigmatic poem of the Suffering Servant (Is 52.13–53.12). Jesus' description of the Son of Man's service, "to give his self as a ransom/guilt offering for many," is a verbatim quotation of the Hebrew text of Is 53.10.[1] Similarly, the "many" *(polus)* for whom Jesus at the supper "pours out" both wine and the message about wine links Jesus' eucharistic words with Isaiah 53, in whose Greek version *polus* occurs repeatedly. Important indeed is Isaiah's Suffering Servant, both conceptually and typologically, to the Markan Jesus' understanding of atonement.

Traditionally Christians have seen the servant's suffering as a prefigurement of Jesus' Passion. Modern readers, however, have recognized how poorly Isaiah 53 conforms to the details of Mark's crucifixion narrative, since the servant apparently does not die physically but submits to death of the self and lives to see his offspring (53.10–11).[2] The following questions are of special significance to Markan studies: Who is the Suffering Servant? What image of Jesus did Mark believe he prefigures? Did his story serve as the model for Jesus' atoning *psuchē* death in Gethsemane? What is his particular connection with the Markan form of the eucharistic narrative? This chapter examines these intertextual questions through the lens of recovery criticism.

Specifically, the chapter argues three propositions: First, Isaiah 53 is not a freestanding work but has as its interpretive context the Zion poem of Is 51.1–54.17, whose thematic center is the alcoholism ora-

cles of 51.17–23 and 52.3. Second, glossed and interpreted in the light
of these oracles, the servant poem reveals a persona recognizable as
that of the derelict alcoholic, the public drunkard. Third, the servant
as alcoholic plays multiple roles in the redemptive plan backgrounding the Markan Jesus' interpretation of the Passover wine ritual:

  a. As vicarious addiction bearer for the many, the servant experi-
     ences the suffering deserved by all drinkers, religious and oth-
     erwise, as unwitting rebels against God.
  b. As derelict street drunkard frightening to behold, the servant
     quickens in such drinkers the realization that only by the grace
     of God are they spared his extreme addiction.
  c. As recovering alcoholic, the servant models the surrender of self
     for the many to emulate, when and if they choose sobriety and
     atonement.
  d. As cupmaster in the ritual adapted by Jesus from the paschal
     wine duty, the servant ministers the wine cup to the many, there-
     by affording them an occasion for their own admissions of pow-
     erlessness over alcohol.

This chapter also addresses a biblical question that has always puzzled NT scholars: given the importance of the Suffering Servant to
Jesus, why did the early Church fail to employ the persona of the
servant in its canonical writings?[3] The answer proposed here is that
the awareness that the servant was tainted by addiction scandalized
the original Messiah cultists and prompted a conspiracy of silence.

Interpretive Context (Is 51.1–54.17)

Any commentary on Isaiah 53 must take a position on three disputed questions: Is the poem to be interpreted apart from or within the
longer Zion poem that forms its immediate context? Is it connected
to the three other so-called servant songs, or is it separate from those
passages? Is the servant a collective persona or an individual? In 1892
Bernhard Duhm advanced the theory of four servant songs separate
from their Isaian contexts, which paved the way for modern interpretations of the Suffering Servant as an individual historical figure.[4]
After a century of acceptance, Duhm's theory has fallen into disfa-
vor, and the servant is again looked on as the personification of Israel, either the historical nation or its future idealization.[5]

  The present reading therefore views Isaiah 53 as an integral con-
stituent of the Zion poem of 51.1–54.17. This poem recounts God's
offer of deliverance to a people whose real problem is not their po-

litical exile in Babylon but rather the plague of alcohol addiction visited on them in consequence of their rebellion against God, expressed in their pretended self-sufficiency. As interpreted here, the oracles at 51.17–23 and 52.3 unmistakably describe the Israelites' condition as alcoholism, a malady that comes from God, can be removed only by God, and presents itself in the dual symptoms of anger and inebriety. The perspective of recovery thus provides an interpretive framework through which Deutero-Isaiah's account of the Israelites' Babylonian captivity may be viewed in an entirely new light.

Address to Captive Israel (51.1–16)

The Zion poem begins with God's words to the members of the captive community reminding them that he is their source, that he can turn their wasteland into a new Eden (51.1–3) and provide judgment, deliverance, and everlasting salvation (51.4–6). The prophet then addresses the community and exhorts its members to awaken from their stupor, call on Yahweh as their higher power of old, and so find redemption and joy (51.9–11). God speaks again, assuring the Israelites that his is a power greater than the power of their oppressor (51.12–13) and promising to redeem them and give them bread, symbolic of his Word (51.14) placed in their mouths (51.16). Everything said in these verses applies equally well to prisoners of addiction in any age or culture.

Oracle of the Cup (51.17–23)

This oracle is of the greatest importance. It plainly identifies the alcoholic illness that afflicted sixth-century Jerusalem/Israel during its fifty-year Babylonian exile. It points to God as both source and cure of the malady and prompts an understanding of the entire Zion poem as a story of alcoholism. It provides the thematic ground against which the figure of the servant is displayed. And it is the text to which Mark's Jesus alludes in Gethsemane, as he asks God to remove his cup addiction. The oracle has three parts: (a) the cup as signifier of alcoholism (51.17–20); (b) removal of the cup from Israel (51.21–22); and (c) transfer of the cup to Babylon (51.23).

Verses 17–20 These four verses read as follows, in the translation of J. L. McKenzie (AB):[6]

(17) Awake, awake! Arise, Jerusalem! You who have drunk from Yahweh's hand the cup of his anger! The chalice of reeling [too] you have drunk, you have drained.

(18) There is no one to guide her of all the sons she has borne; there is no one to grasp her hand of all the sons she has reared.
(19) These two [foregoing] things have encountered you—who will condole with you? Violence, downfall, famine, and the sword [have ensued]—who will comfort you?
(20) Your sons swoon, they lie at the head of every street like an antelope in a net; they are stuffed with the anger of Yahweh, with the rage of your God.

The call to awake in verse 17 is obviously metaphorical. Sleep is a figure for the denial that stupefies the thinking of alcoholics, the same figure Mark uses to describe the disciples' condition in Gethsemane. Two Hebrew words for the wine cup appear, ḳôs and kubba<at, the latter a rare word usually translated as "chalice." Two cups are named in parallel stichs: "the cup of wrath" and "the chalice of reeling" (drunkenness). Both are identified as coming from God. Traditionally most readers have understood "reeling" as a metaphor for God's wrath visited on Israel as a punishment for its immorality. The few who have interpreted the alcohol imagery literally speak of wine only as a source of potential enjoyment that, if abused, brings down the wrath of God.

From the recovery angle, both views fall short. Alcoholics will see that the two cups are not synonymous; rather, they refer to the twin hallmarks of alcoholism: physical intoxication ("chalice of reeling") and mental drunkenness ("cup of wrath"), that is, obsessive anger, judgmentalism, attempts to dominate, fighting, and outright warfare. So viewed, these cups parallel the primeval curses in Genesis. The cup of wrath reflects the Edenic serpent and soil curses (Gn 3.14–15, 17–19; see chap. 1) symbolizing inner and outward agonism and the anger accompanying it. The chalice of reeling reflects the curse of servitude placed on Noah's son Ham/Canaan and his descendants (Gn 9.25), realized in addiction to alcohol. Moreover, addiction is not incurred as punishment for abusing drink but is ordained by God to further a redemptive purpose. God gives the chalice of reeling to those he chooses as vicarious addiction bearers for the many. Once again, to the alcoholic the cups of verse 17 are neither synonyms nor mere metaphors but a realistic description of the plague of alcoholism that apparently befell Jerusalem at the time of its Babylonian captivity. The historicity of such a plague is supported by Lam 4.21, which implies that the drunkenness it predicts for Edom has already fallen on the inhabitants of Jerusalem ("to you also [Edom in addition to Zion] the cup shall be passed").

Verse 17 is the interpretive crux of the oracle, and its importance cannot be overemphasized. Text-grammatically, the critical question is whether "chalice of reeling" is a metaphor renaming "cup of wrath" (the traditional reading) or refers to a different cup, that is, whether it depicts actual addictive drinking in addition to and distinct from obsessive wrath. In terms of Hebrew poetry, the traditional view construes the topic of verse 17 as wrath, the two cup images as an instance of synonymous parallelism, and the language of drunkenness in verses 18–22 as an extension of the "chalice of reeling" metaphor. The alcoholism view, on the other hand, sees the dual cup images as a case of synthetic, or constructive, parallelism signifying the essential elements of the alcoholic problem: drink accompanied by pathological anger.[7] Either alone is only what it is; the two together identify the illness that the modern world calls alcoholism. Given the limitations of ancient vocabulary, it is difficult to imagine how Isaiah could have found a language more straightforward than that of 51.17 to denote this timeless human malady.

Following verse 17, verses 18–20 show that the epidemic of addiction Isaiah describes is meant to be taken literally. The synonymous stichs of verse 18 indicate that the young, whose filial duty it was to guide their drunken parents home after bouts of drinking, cannot perform this duty precisely because they have become addicts themselves.[8] Their parent is Jerusalem, here personified as a woman, hence all the more helpless. Both parent and children are intoxicated, a condition all too familiar today.

The phrase "these two things" in verse 19 is ordinarily read as a cataphoric reference to the next four terms taken as two pairs of synonyms: "violence, downfall, famine, and the sword." Despite the semantic ingenuity of a great many commentators, however, it is difficult to see how these four words can be sensibly grouped to mean two things. In 40.2, in the prologue to his work, Deutero-Isaiah says that Jerusalem "has received from Yahweh's hand double for all her sins." But the referent of "double" has never been identified. The view here is that "double" in 40.2, the two cups in 51.17, and "these two things" in 51.19 all refer to the dual symptoms of alcoholism. So viewed, "these two things" in verse 18 would function not as cataphora but anaphora, a back reference to the twin cups drunk from God's hand in verse 17, one of drunkenness and one of wrath. With "these two things" serving to remention the two cups (thus the emendation "foregoing"), "violence, downfall, famine, and the sword" would name their four outcomes (thus the emendation "have ensued"). Hence the phrase "these two things" not only supports the idea that Isaiah was speaking of two cups rather than one, but it also neatly explains the prophet's cryptic reference to the "double suffering" sent by God (40.2).

Verse 20   The image of young Israelites "swooning in the streets" further reinforces the interpretation that Isaiah's "cup of reeling" refers to actual drunkenness. The swooning and raging anger signify intoxication accompanied by crippling mental drunkenness. As Isaiah saw it, Israel was suffering an epidemic of alcoholism afflicting young and old alike.

Verses 21–22   Next the oracle announces God's decision and promise to remove from Israel/Jerusalem the cup of its alcoholic illness:

> (21) So listen to this aflicted one—drunk but not with wine;
> (22) Thus says your Lord Yahweh, and your God who defends the cause of his people: "Look, I take from your hand the cup of reeling; the chalice of wrath you shall not have to drink again."

In "drunk but not with wine" (51.21), Deutero-Isaiah quotes Isaiah of Jerusalem (Is 29.9), who a century before identified chronic drinking as the consequence of an earlier Israelite rebellion against God.[9] About as obvious a reference to mental drunkenness as it is possible to imagine, the phrase "drunk but not with wine" reflects the insight that in any epidemic of addiction, the great majority of affected people do not suffer the extreme chemical dependency of the street derelict or round-the-clock maintenance drinker, but they do act out the many forms of anger and fighting that tear families and nations apart and plunge society into chaos. Such behavior was doubtless rampant among the captive Israelites in Babylon. Recovering persons from whom the "cup of reeling" has been removed often acknowledge their residual mental drunkenness by saying, "Today I don't have a drinking problem, I have a thinking problem," or, "My problem is no longer alcohol, my problem is me." Conversely, nonaddicts who are "drunk but not with wine" deny their alcoholism totally.

In verse 22, likened to an advocate "defending the cause of his people," God proclaims the end of Israel's alcoholism. The "cups" God has given the alcoholic nation he now takes from it. They were given in the order of wrath first and drunkenness second (51.17), reflecting the fact that addiction first manifests itself as an emotional pathology, fear enacted in anger. Now the cups are removed in reverse order, that of reeling followed by that of wrath. Commentators consider this chiasmus merely a rhetorical turn, but alcoholics will see it as more than mere rhetoric. Recovery must begin with the removal of one's chemical addiction before it can progress to the gradual loss of fear and anger, which is exactly the order in Isaiah's text. The verse announces first a divine action, "Look, I take from your hand the cup of reeling," and then God's promise that Israel will never again have to suffer addictive anger, "the chalice of wrath you shall not have to drink again."

As discussed in chapter 2, Jesus' prayer in Gethsemane, "take away my cup addiction" (Mk 14.36), is a direct reference to Is 51.22; in this prayer Jesus humbly asks God to grant the mercy promised in this Isaian oracle, removal of the cup of alcoholism. Notice that Mark portrays Jesus as praying the same prayer a second time (not three times, as is sometimes thought), "And again he went away and prayed, saying the same words" (Mk 14.39). Assuming that the Markans based their theology of recovery on Is 51.17–23, it is not too much to think that Jesus had Isaiah's two cups specifically in mind, that "cup" in his first prayer referred to the cup of reeling and in his second, to the cup of wrath. Recovering alcoholics following today's twelve-step program often report a similar two-stage experience. At first they understand steps one through three as pertaining solely to release from alcohol. Later, after undergoing the inventory process in steps four through seven, they speak of taking the first three steps a second time for release from mental drunkenness. They call the result "stage two" of recovery. So viewed, the removal of the two cups in the Isaian oracle, Jesus' two prayers in Gethsemane, and the two stages of recovery all exemplify the same spiritual process.

Verse 23 The oracle of the cup concludes with God's revelation of what he does with the cup once removed: he gives it to others caught up by fear, anger, and the urge to dominate:

> (23) And I will put it [the dual cup] in the hands of those who vex you, who said to you, "Bow down, that we may walk over you"; and you flattened your back like the ground, like a street for them to walk on.

Taken literally, verse 23 indicates that the plague of addiction will pass from the Israelites to the Babylonians, and this may actually have occurred in the years just preceding Babylon's fall to Cyrus (see the next section). But the meaning of the verse is more basic than this. It suggests that addictive anger is not confined to chronic drinkers, that it also emblemizes the latent alcoholism, or codependency, of the wider world. Isaiah's point is not that controllers and dictators suddenly become alcoholic but rather that the recovering person now recognizes that is what they have been all along. Active alcoholics seek to dominate the world because they feel threatened by domination. Freed of this compulsion, recovering alcoholics see that others are as ill as they were and recognize the need to detach from this pervasive mental drunkenness. Verse 23 thus prepares the groundwork for 52.11–12, which admonishes Israel to detach from alcoholic Babylon and live out its recovery in freedom.

Liberation Now! (52.1–2)

In the light of the oracle of the cup, Isaiah repeats the call to Jerusalem/Israel to awaken from its addiction and claim its promised liberation:

(1) Awake, awake! Put on your strength, Zion! Put on your robes of honor, Jerusalem, holy city! . . .
(2) Shake yourself free! Up from the dust, captive Jerusalem! Throw the yoke off your neck, captive daughter of Zion!

Oracle on Alcoholism (52.3–6).

Verse 3 depicts the mystery of addiction and release via an oracular riddle recapitulating the sense of 51.17–23:

(3) You were sold for nothing and it was not for money that you were redeemed.

Applied to alcoholism this riddle means that alcohol pays nothing to possess the addicted, and no money is paid it to release them. In other words, God is master of alcohol. He calls into addiction whom he wishes and frees whom he pleases. Active alcoholism comes from God as he pursues an obscure but salvific purpose, and it is removed by the gift of grace. Hence the question asked by modern research on addiction, "why do some drinkers become addicted while most do not?" is misguided. It ought to ask, "why does not everyone who drinks become addicted?" Theologically, although no one seems to have viewed the matter thus, addiction ought to be seen as the norm for all drinkers, not the pathology, and temperate or "normal" drinking ought to be seen as the result of a special grace. (Verses 4–6 are glosses on verse 3.)

Rhapsody of Peace (52.7–10)

These familiar verses proclaim the good news of recovery, peace, and happiness under the rule of a higher power:

(7) How beautiful upon the mountains are the feet of the messenger of good news. . . .

(10) Yahweh has bared his holy arm in the sight of all nations; all the ends of the earth shall see the saving deed of our God.

Detach! (52.11–12)

As discussed in connection with 51.23, recovering persons living in an alcoholic world risk falling prey to the same codependency that plagues nonalcoholic family members and associates of the practicing addict. One avoids this trap by detaching from contexts of active alcoholism, declaring one's independence from situations of anger, conflict, domination, and so on. Detachment is primarily a mental phenomenon. To happen at all it must happen in the mind, and it may or may not involve physically removing oneself from the actual situation. Historically, verses 11 and 12 refer to the Israelites' departure from Babylon, now drinking the cup of alcoholism, and their return to Palestine. In the psychology of recovery, however, these verses refer to detachment as a state of mind.

Isaiah's Zion poem thus foretells Israel's liberation from bondage, not so much its political captivity in Babylon, though that captivity and release were of course quite real, but more significantly its bondage to alcohol and self, from the devastating scourge of drunkenness precipitated by the willful anger the Israelites experienced, presumably as a result of their impotence in the face of Babylonian might. Addiction and wrath fell on the people of Judah as a consequence of their attempted self-reliance, their unwitting warfare against God. To save the Israelites from themselves, therefore, God sent a plague of alcoholism on them, to be removed when he saw that their minds had been changed, that suffering had readied them for redemption. So viewed, the entire history of the Babylonian captivity is a story of alcoholism and recovery. Apparently this is what attracted the Markan Jesus to the Zion poem.

Babylon's Alcoholism

In removing the cup from the Israelites, God promises to give it to their oppressors (Is 51.23), the Babylonian nation and its final king, Nabonidus. Could such an outcome actually have occurred? Surprisingly, certain evidence suggests that in the years immediately preceding its fall to Cyrus and the Persians in 539 B.C.E., Babylon may have experienced just such an epidemic of addiction. From its zenith of undisputed Middle Eastern power under Nebuchadnezzar, Babylon in only twenty years degenerated to a point where the city fell to Cyrus without a battle. Its immense wealth and luxury in the sixth century,

the anxieties accompanying its ill-gotten gains, and the absorption
of its citizenry in "more or less continuous" religious festivals[10] would
have prompted widespread drinking. Isaiah himself connects the Israelites' alcoholism with ritual drinking in Babylon: the Hebrew word
glossed as "chalice" in Is 51.17 and 23 is probably a translation of a
Babylonian term that, according to G. A. F. Knight, named "a large
bowl . . . used in the service of Marduk."[11] Craving a drink stronger
than their native barley beer, the Babylonians had begun importing
grape wine from Lebanon.[12] D. J. Wiseman tells of sites in Judah,
during Nebuchadnezzar's siege of Jerusalem, where "royal estates
were left to supply wine to Babylon as they had previously to the royal household in Jerusalem."[13] One of Cyrus's first acts on capturing
Babylon was to repair the dilapidation of the people's houses,[14] which
suggests that the city had suffered from a loss of self-respect and social order consistent with widespread inebriety. The Chronicles of
Market Prices unearthed in Babylon suggests an inflation rate of up
to 200 percent in the decades following Nebuchadnezzar's death,[15]
an indicator of economic chaos possibly stemming from epidemic
alcoholism. In describing the fall of the city, Herodotus and Xenophon attribute the bloodless victory of Cyrus in part to the drunkenness of the populace at festival time.[16] Daniel (5.1–4) refers to the
same story in his account of the drunken feasting of Belshazzar and
his thousand courtiers, who desecrated the holy vessels taken from
the Jerusalem temple decades earlier. Both stories point to a situation of alcoholic dissolution. All these bits of evidence indicate that
Babylon, in its last years, experienced internal decay plausibly attributable to wholesale alcohol addiction.

Still more surprising is the story of King Nabonidus, who spent ten
years near the end of his reign hundreds of miles from the city, in
the Arabian oasis of Teima, leaving his son Belshazzar in charge of
the capital. The following items of information portray Nabonidus
as the classic alcoholic: thrust on the throne in a palace revolt, he calls
himself a nobody lacking the requirements for kingship but then singlehandedly opposes the established Babylonian clergy by installing
an alien god hateful to the people and attempting to curtail festival
drinking.[17] Here is the alcoholic's lack of self-esteem, coupled with
grandiosity, self-will, and projection of his own problem onto others.
His opponents in the Marduk priesthood write that "a demon alters
him," that he "confounds the rites," speaks against "the divinely-or-
dained order," and is afflicted with "wrath."[18] These are evidence of
intoxication, possibly delirium, together with alcoholic anxiety and
anger. The frontispiece of Paul-Alain Beaulieu's study of Nabonidus

is a stela in the British Museum depicting the king raising a wine cup to his mouth under the aegis of the moon god Sin.[19] Finally, threatened by popular revolt, Nabonidus deserts his capital city for a protracted stay at Teima, deep in Arabia.[20] Subject of much speculation, his move could have been the "geographical cure" par excellence, recovery slang for the alcoholic belief that moving somewhere else will solve the problems caused by one's drinking.

The most mysterious part of Nabonidus's story, however, is what occurred at Teima, where, according to "Verse Account," he was provided with "rainwater to drink,"[21] another instance of water as a counterimage to wine. An Aramaian fragment from Qumran called "The Prayer of Nabonidus" tells of a seven-year illness during which the king was smitten by a "bad inflammation" sent by God and then restored to health through the ministrations of an exiled Jew who heard the king's confession of faults and brought him to Yahweh.[22] Paralleling this account is Daniel's story of the recovery of the insane king called "Nebuchadnezzar" (4.25–37), whom many scholars now believe was actually Nabonidus.[23] Behind these bits of information may lie the story of Nabonidus's recovery from alcoholism: his bad inflammation (cf. Is 5.11, "inflamed by wine") and insanity could refer to intoxication coupled with an acute physical reaction to alcohol. The Jew who cured Nabonidus could have been a member of Deutero-Isaiah's circle familiar with the knowledge about addiction and recovery that informs the oracle of the cup (51.17–23) and the Suffering Servant poem (52.13–53.12). The king's departure from the capital city may have been not a "geographical cure" after all but the result of his decision to detach from the pervasive drunkenness of Babylon. Such a theory is highly conjectural, but no more so than other proposals attempting to explain Nabonidus's strange behavior,[24] and it obviously comports with the idea of rampant alcohol addiction in Babylon.

Moreover, Nabonidus's admission of alcoholism and turn toward recovery, assuming these events actually occurred, may have been triggered by the sight of the servant himself. G. A. Larue describes the great Akitu, or New Year, festival in Babylon and names elements in Isaiah 40–55 that he believes identify that festival as the historical background to the Zion poem. One such element is the scapegoat theme. Larue writes: "During this period [of the Akitu festival] a human scapegoat, perhaps a condemned prisoner, was paraded through the streets as part of a communal purgation rite. The expulsion and destruction of the scapegoat cleansed the community of guilt and made it possible to begin the year free of taint."[25] The scape-

goat could just as well have been a derelict drunkard from among the
Israelite exiles. Such a choice would have been quite fitting, assuming the Babylonians to have been experiencing epidemic drunkenness. Touched by an unknown power as he beheld the scapegoat,
Nabonidus may have reached out for help and established contact
with members of Isaiah's circle, who may have advised him to forsake
Babylon for recovery in the Arabian oases.[26] In any case, his acceptance of Yahweh as an unnamed higher power and confession of
wrongs recorded in "The Prayer of Nabonidus" are definite hallmarks
of the timeless regimen of recovery.

Nabonidus, therefore, may be the king referred to in the prologue
of the servant poem (52.15), "kings stand speechless before him."
More important, the sight of a drunkard used as a public scapegoat
by a citizenry of unwitting alcoholics, interpreted in terms of Isaiah's
emergent understanding of addiction and recovery, may have been
what inspired the prophet to link the concept of the scapegoat's vicarious suffering with the idea of the recovering person's way-showing atonement and exaltation. Thus the drunkenness of Babylon and
the recovery of its king would have been the seedbed of Deutero-Isaiah's unprecedented theological insights into God's plan to redeem
rebellious people from their alcoholic illness. How that redemption
occurs is the subject of the servant poem itself.

The Servant Poem (Is 52.13–53.12)

Text

Here is the text of Isaiah's poem of the Suffering Servant on which
the identification of the servant as derelict alcoholic is based, together
with brief notes on the readings. Versions consulted are from RSV,
New American Bible (NAB), New English Bible (NEB), D. J. A. Clines,
M. Dahood, J. L. McKenzie (AB), and D. W. Thomas.[27]

(52.13) Behold, the Exalted and Sublime Higher Power will prosper
his servant!
(14) Just as many were appalled when they saw him, so disfigured he
looked, he seemed less than human,
(15) So now the crowds are astonished at him, and kings stand speechless before him. For they see what was never told them, and ponder
what was never before heard.
(53.1) Who would have believed what we have reported? Where else
has the power of God been so fully revealed?
(2) To us he seemed like a scrub growth, like a stunted root in parched
soil. He had no beauty or splendor to attract us, no grace to charm us.

(3) He was despised by men, humiliated by suffering and tormented by his illness, a man who hid his face from others. We considered him a despicable nothing.

(4) And yet it was our sufferings he bore, our pains he carried, while we had counted him merely as stricken, as one smitten by God with affliction.

(5) But it was our rebellions for which he was wounded, our wrongs for which he was crushed. The penalty we should have paid fell on him, and by his pain we were healed.

(6) For we had strayed like sheep, each of us living by self-direction, while God laid upon him the guilt of us all.

(7) He submitted to his addiction and said nothing. He was carried away [by his illness] like a sheep to the slaughter, like a ewe dumb to the shearers.

(8) Unrestrained and intemperate, he was utterly carried away [by his illness], and who gave his life a thought? He was cut off from the land of the living, stricken for the rebellion of his people.

(9) A grave was assigned him with the wicked [on account of his addiction], a tomb among [other] demoniacs, even though he had done no violence nor spoken any deceit.

(10) Surely it was God who decided to crush him with pain. And yet: If he surrenders his self as a guilt offering, he will see his offspring and lengthen his days, and the plan of God will succeed in his hand!

(11) In return for the affliction of his soul he shall drink [the wine of sobriety], deeply, until sated. His knowledge of submission will have vindicated him, and will free the multitudes from bondage.

(12) So I rank him among the great, deserving of empowerment, because he recognizes his rebellion and submits to death [of self], while all along suffering for the wrongdoing of many and making entreaty for all the rebellious.

Notes

52.13: the version here is from Dahood, who reads third person, not first, and sees as divine appellatives three roots ordinarily thought to describe the servant's prosperity. This shifts the thematic focus from the extreme exaltedness of the servant to an emphasis on God as agent of his salvation. "Higher Power" replaces Dahood's "Most Lofty."

52.14: "disfigured" comes from NEB, Clines, and McKenzie. Dahood's repointing (vocalizing the ancient consonantal text) to yield an agentive phrase, "disfigured by men," along with "marred" from RSV and NAB, may result from attempts to read the scourging of Jesus into the poem.

53.1: the Hebrew "Yahweh's arm" is a figure read as "the power of God" by NEB, Clines, and Thomas.

53.2: "scrub growth" and "stunted root" are vegetation figures for the servant's disfigured and unsightly appearance implying how he grew rather than how he appeared as a result of injury from others. Neutral words like "young plant" and "sapling," widely used, miss the point that the servant's disfigurement comes from a flaw in his nature or a divine curse (see Dahood's note on verse 2 and his footnote 5).

53.3: owing to a probable defect of spelling in the traditional text, versions differ as to whether the servant turned away from others (NEB, Clines, Dahood, Thomas) or the others averted their faces from him (RSV, NAB, McKenzie). The reading here is from Thomas, based on the St. Mark's Isaiah Scroll.

53.4: the order of events is reversed here. The second colon expresses "our" initial belief, which was limited to thinking the servant to be just another sinner punished by God. The recognition expressed in the first colon actually came later, in the insight of conversion.

53.5: the vocabulary of "scourging" (NEB), "bruises" (McKenzie) and "stripes" (RSV, NAB, and Dahood) reflects the traditional preconception that the servant's experience prefigures the chastisement of Jesus. Since the Hebrew term is singular, the version here follows Clines in reading "pain." Nor need one assume that the grammatical passives "wounded" and "crushed" necessarily have people as their implied agents. The actions named by these verbs can just as well have been caused by the servant's illness.

53.6: all versions employ the English idiom "to go one's own way." The idiom used here, "to live by self-direction," says essentially the same thing and is frequently used by recovering alcoholics as yet another way to describe how rebellious humans attempt to be their own God.

53.7: the NEB, NAB, Dahood, and Thomas read the active voice "submitted," together with a passive form read "oppressed," "afflicted," or "harshly treated." Despite the progress of science, what the modern world calls addictions remain mysterious conditions that oppress and afflict certain people and treat them harshly indeed, hence the present reading, "he submitted to his addiction."

53.7: "he was carried away" is the first of several agentless passives in verses 7, 8, and 9 traditionally assumed by Christian exegetes to have as their implied agents a judicial court of the kind that acted against Jesus centuries later. In the context of an illness/affliction/addiction affecting the servant, however, it would be reasonable to conclude that the poet is describing how completely this illness "has carried him away," hence the bracketed gloss, "by his illness."

53.8: "unrestrained and intemperate" comes from Dahood's "without restraint and without moderation," nuances Dahood sees in traditional readings presumably thought to foremirror the unjust arrest of Jesus ("arrested and sentenced" in Clines, "perverted judgment" in McKenzie, "from prison and lawcourt" in Thomas, and "without protection, without justice" in NEB). Dahood assumes that the lack of "restraint and moderation" is on the part of others, whereas the version here imputes this lack to the servant himself, in consequence of his ungovernable addiction.

53.8: "carried away," "cut off" and "stricken," like "carried away" in verse 7, are agentless passives interpreted as having the servant's illness as their implied agents.

53.8: "cut off from the land of the living/of life" is the universal reading here. While death is clearly denoted, it is a completely open question what *kind* of death the poet had in mind at this stage in the progression of the servant's illness, whether physical or spiritual, body death or soul death. Lacking a purely spiritual vocabulary, persons often use strong physical metaphors to describe spiritual conditions. For example, veteran recovering alcoholics describing the spiritual death they experienced in the last stages of their drinking often use hyperbolic physical terminology that newcomers think refers to corpse-and-coffin death. Since verses 10 and 11 of the poem make it apparent that the servant ultimately lives, Christian interpreters have traditionally understood the servant's death as adumbrating Jesus' crucifixion and the material in verses 10 and 11 as a prophecy of his resurrection. Nonetheless, readers can just as validly construe verse 8 as a reference to the spiritual death of addiction and verses 10 and 11 as a prophecy of recovery.

53.9: Dahood notes the difficulty of determining the meaning of <*āšîr* in this context. It ought to mean "rich man" (as Dahood and RSV have it), but it is traditionally emended so as to parallel *rᵉšā<îm*, "wicked" (thus "evildoers" in NAB and McKenzie, "refuse of mankind" in NEB, and "criminals" in Clines). A case might be made for the reading, "whether a wealthy man or wicked." This would comport with an interpretation of alcoholism, since the malady strikes both rich and poor, good and bad. The present version, "a tomb among [other] demoniacs," comes from Thomas's reading of *sᵉ<irim bamatho* from the St. Mark's Isaiah Scroll. The assumption here is that many whom the ancients called demoniacs were actually chronically delirious or brain-damaged wine addicts (see chap. 6).

53.10: "if he surrenders his self as a guilt offering" contains the Hebrew >*āšām*, which denotes, according to J. Jeremias, a substitutionary offering made to free someone or something held in bondage.[28] Since his inner being is obviously what the servant gives in sacrifice—in modern parlance, his "self"—the bondage to which the guilt offering pertains would therefore be the bondage of self, the illusion of the self as God, arguably the underlying pathology of all addiction.

53.10: "if," read by McKenzie and NEB, suggests that the surrender may or may not happen. Assuming that self-surrender = physical death = Jesus' crucifixion, Christian exegetes regard this surrender as a foregone conclusion. Thus NEB reads, "The Lord . . . healed him who had made himself a sacrifice for sin." Dahood seems to deny the servant volition by reading an agentless passive, "certainly was his life made a guilt offering." The RSV and Clines avoid the issue, reading "when he makes. . . ." Thomas's passive concessive implies a divine agent, "though his own life be made an offering for sin, he shall see offspring. . . ." In the reality of alcoholism, however, the spiritually dead addict may or may not "surrender his self" and live. The same would have been true of the servant, hence the "if" of the present version.

53.11: Dahood and G. R. Driver apparently codiscovered *yirweh*, "to drink to satiety," as the verb underlying *yir'eh*, ordinarily understood to mean "see light" (NEB, NAB, and McKenzie).[29] "Light" is absent from the Hebrew text but present in the Septuagint and the Isaiah scrolls, where Dahood considers it to be haplography. This discovery is absolutely crucial to a reading of the poem keyed by alcoholism. Thomas ("drink deep of his anguish") and Clines ("drink deep of affliction") also read "drink" and together with Dahood ("with the anguish of his soul he was sated") see "anguish/affliction" as its semantic object, that is, as naming what the servant "drinks deeply of," failing to recognize that by verse 11 the servant's drinking days are over, a result of his surrender in verse 10. The present version reads a resultative relationship between affliction and drinking, "in return for the affliction of his soul, he shall drink, deeply, until sated." The drink referred to is the oxymoronic "satiating drink," that is, neither real wine nor the wine of affliction but their opposite, the purely metaphorical liquor of recovery following release from addiction, hence the bracketed gloss, "the wine of sobriety."

53.11: Clines understands *da'tô* as derived from *yd< II* as meaning "to be submissive, humiliated"; hence "knowledge of submission" is the key to freedom from bondage to both alcohol and self. The sense of knowledge is discussed in the following section.

53.12: although the versions differ but little, the reading here is closest to that of Dahood. The bracketed gloss, "death of self," identifies the kind of dying the servant undergoes in recovering from his addiction.

Discussion (Is 52.13–53.12)

Compositionally, the poem fulfills the prophecy of exiled Israel's deliverance from alcoholism. The servant, looked at apart from pre-conceptions equating him to the Christian Jesus, is immediately recognizable as the representation of an unfortunate human type found in drinking cultures everywhere, the derelict street drunk. One has only to reread the poem in this light to see the striking correspondence between the figure of the servant and that of the derelict. Thematically, the poem constitutes a theological reflection on a paradox perhaps more surprising than the servant's identity: God's use of the drunkard to redeem humankind from the mental drunkenness that we are condemned to suffer en route to atonement. Prophetic, enigmatic, incomplete in certain ways, the Suffering Servant poem has long awaited interpretation in terms of alcoholism.

Prologue (52.13–53.1)   The first four verses of the poem function as a prologue. Verse 13 introduces the figure of the servant as one who will prosper spiritually under the care of God, whom he serves. Verses 14 and 15 establish that the servant's story has a before and after. It is a message that changes the minds of many, kings and multitudes. (Again, the king whom Isaiah had in mind was perhaps Nabonidus of Babylon, whom the prophet may have known as a recovering wine addict.) In other words, the "before and after" of the servant's story, from his former appalling disfiguration to his wondrous appearance now, parallels a before and after in the thinking of the many who behold him. The message they ponder, unprecedented and stunning, is nothing less than the revelation that God's plan for the salvation of humankind involves his giving to each person, then removing, the cup of addiction. Verse 1 points to the total incredulity that must greet such a message and to the power of God, "the arm of Yahweh," uniquely revealed in recovery. (Some translators move the final distich of verse 14 to a place between 53.2 and 3.[30] Doing so destroys the before-and-after balance between verses 14 and 15 and so contravenes the Isaian intention.)

Dramatis Personae   D. J. A. Clines, in his literary reading of the servant poem, notes the following cast of characters: "I" (the prophet narrator), "he" (the servant), "they" (the unknowing multitudes), "we," and God.[31] Clines is quite correct in saying that the key to entering the world of the poem lies not so much in identifying the servant as in figuring out who "we" refers to and how to join their ranks, how to experience the changing of mind betokening the conversion to which "we" give witness. It is precisely this before-and-after perspective, this sense of "after-knowledge," of knowing one's mind to have been changed, that the Markôs insiders would have associated with the Greek verb *metanoeō*, invariably although misleadingly translated as "repent," which Mark places on the lips of Jesus (1.15) as the clarion call to the rule of God.

"Our" View Before (53.2–3)   These verses describe the servant as "we" saw him before the gift of insight and as "they" see him still. "Scrub growth" and "stunted root" imply that "we" thought the servant's condition to result from a natural flaw, an inborn deficiency or weakness of character. Obviously the image of the servant as a "despicable nothing" exactly reflects the attitude of many nonalcoholics toward the street drunk today. The servant's torment and ugly physical appearance realistically mirror the derelict's description: brown-skinned and befouled, stubble-faced and drooling, gap-toothed and horribly unkempt, eyes hollow and dazed, perhaps jaundiced or lame, incoherent and unsteady, utterly broken and degraded by drink. He often hides his face in shame, knowing that the world considers him just as loathsome as he regards himself.

The textual question of whose eyes are averted, the onlookers' or the servant's, will have to await further scholarly insight (see the note on verse 3). Many derelicts hide their faces in shame; others have no shame left. Similarly, observers often turn away instinctively when confronted by street drunks, not because of their ugliness per se, but because persons cannot look on such a one without for at least an instant realizing what their common humanity means: His plight could be mine! This, it is suggested, is Isaiah's whole point and the reason for the reading of verse 3 chosen here. For the "we" of the poem, persons gifted with after-knowledge, are precisely those who did *not* avert their gaze, who looked on the servant in his degradation and saw themselves, and thus achieved the salvific insight reported in verses 4–6.

"Our" Knowledge Now (53.4–6)   The thought in these verses is expressed in completely self-evident terms. "We," admitted alcoholics recovering by the grace of God, most of us spared the extremes of suffering and addiction the street derelict endures, although we first considered him to be a person smitten for no apparent reason (53.4),

now realize that the pain he bears is suffering we deserve. Needing no gloss or paraphrase, the simple clarity of verse 5 echoes across the ages: it is our rebellions for which he is punished. Verse 6 identifies the nature of those rebellions, which began in Eden and continue in every generation. It is not so much that we humans transgress against morality as that we attempt to live by self-direction, self-engendered wisdom, hence to be God for ourselves, often with the best of motives, thinking our actions pleasing to God.

As for alcohol, we recognize as illusory whatever control we thought we had over drink. We now see alcohol as a power far greater than ours, its spell a product of the Ham/Canaan curse that had befallen us, to which we would immediately succumb should God once again hand us the cup and the desire to drink again overwhelm us. Despite the hubris of modern science in studying the mystery of addiction, we now recognize that how alcohol does or does not affect us, how much or little we drink, are matters ordained by God. Whatever our imagined character or willpower, whatever our genetic makeup or family background, all of us who have drunk believing that we could do so safely, that we could control alcohol, deserved to become a street drunk—and would have, but for the grace of God.

Active Addiction (53.7–9)   In verses 7 through 9 Isaiah describes the iron grip of addiction. Here, in the grim reality of advanced alcoholism, we see the "walking death" endured by the derelict, from which sufferers with less severe cases are spared. In emphasizing the servant's silence, verse 7 eloquently points up the difference between the drunkard still fighting the illness, or loudly denying it, and the derelicts who have quit fighting and denying, who accept their lot and dumbly give themselves to drink, "like a sheep to the slaughter, a ewe dumb to the shearers."

Christians generally interpret verses 7–9 as foreshadowing the sufferings of Jesus. Verse 8 is ordinarily read as referring to a corrupt legal proceeding of the kind to which the Jewish authorities are believed to have subjected Jesus and to an execution similar to Jesus' crucifixion. Jewish exegetes, on the other hand, understand the verse as referring to the unjust and murderous treatment of Jews in the Christian era. Isaiah's use of passive verbs without agents establishes an indefiniteness of agency that permits not only the Christian and Jewish interpretations just mentioned but the alcoholism reading as well. By whom or what was the servant "carried away" (53.7 and 8)? By whom or what was he "cut off" and "stricken" (53.8)? By whom or what was his burial place "assigned" (53.9)? The answer proposed here is, not by other persons but by his illness. His alcoholism is what has "carried him utterly away," "cut him off," and so on.

As explained in the preceding notes to the text, "cut off from the land of the living" (53.8) need not indicate physical death; it can just as readily denote the spiritual death of addiction. "Death" intended nonphysically would have been perfectly understandable to sixth-century Israelites. Thomas's reading, "a tomb among [other] demoniacs" (53.9), is particularly revealing in light of the alcoholism interpretation, in that the ancients would have attributed many of the symptomatic behaviors of acute alcoholism, including delirium and psychotic anxiety, to demon possession. The emendation "other" highlights the servant's identification with fellow drunkards-demoniacs. The benign passivity expressed in the final distich of verse 9 is similarly interesting, since for advanced derelicts, their days of "violence" and "deceit" are over: no more sob stories or con jobs directed at passersby, no more jackrolling newcomers to the streets. All they do is drink what they can get and await death. Altogether, verses 7–9 display keen insight into the condition of street drunks in the final stages of their illness.

Recovery (53.10–11)   Verses 10 and 11 depict the servant's restoration to life and present an implicit theology of recovery for the multitude as well as for the servant. These verses answer certain questions and leave others unanswered:

First, what is the source of the servant's addiction? Answer: "it was God who decided to crush him with pain." In Isaiah's view the crushing affliction that turns strong men into helpless derelicts comes not from bad genetics, poor character, or weak willpower but from God.

Second, does the servant recover? Answer: yes, when he "surrenders his self as a guilt offering," a substitutionary donation to free another held in bondage, further discussed later.

Third, what are the consequences of the servant's giving his self? Answer: "he will see his offspring and lengthen his days, and the plan of God will succeed in his hand." The servant is redeemed from the spiritual death of addiction and prospers in recovery by carrying the message to other alcoholics.

Fourth, to what does "the plan of God" refer? The answer lies in a comparison of verses 10 and 11. Clearly, "surrendering his self" in verse 10 and "his knowledge of submission" in verse 11 refer to the same thing. Here "knowledge" refers not to propositional or intellectual knowledge but to the spiritual awareness experienced in any self-repudiating faith action. As the result of such an action, verse 10 says, "the plan of God will succeed in his hand," whereas verse 11 says that the multitudes will be "freed from bondage." Thus the "plan of God" refers to the freeing of the multitudes from bondage, not solely the political bondage of the Israelites in Babylon, but bondage to the crypto-alcoholism that from time immemorial has locked humanity in its vinous grip.

By contrast, two important questions are left unanswered in the Isaian text. First, how does the servant "surrender his self" and "know submission?" Second, how does his surrender "free the multitudes from bondage?" Historically, it remained for Jesus, in the persona of the recovering alcoholic, to answer the first question in his words over the wine and his repudiation of drink at the Last Supper, followed by his prayer in Gethsemane, an answer destined to remain obscured down the centuries. As for freeing the multitudes, the servant's unrestrained drinking and public intoxication, a spectacle described earlier in the poem, serve to convince others (the multitudes of verse 11) of their unrecognized alcoholism. Later, in sobriety, the servant tells his recovery story to the assembled people, thereby creating a moment of crisis when hearers can experience a changing of mind and admit their illness (see chap. 4 for a reconstruction of Jesus' sobriety story). The servant also prefigures Jesus' paschal role as cup minister in the wine liturgy intended for those in the multitude who need to drink still more before "hitting bottom" and surrendering. By contrast, those who choose to stop drinking, who encounter the crisis moment just mentioned, join the "we" in recovery. These are the outcomes of the servant's surrender of self, and this is how he proactively frees the many from bondage.

"Satiating [Wine]" (53.11)   A final question remains: how will the servant celebrate the joy of recovery? "He shall drink [of sobriety], deeply, until sated." "Satiating [wine]" makes explicit the alcoholism theme implied in the servant's description and links the poem to the oracle of the cup (Is 51.17–23). This satiating drink is not actual wine but metaphorical, yet another way of ironically describing the heady euphoria of recovery in terms of its opposite, drunkenness—hence the emendation in verse 11, "of sobriety." As indicated in the notes, the verb "drink to satiety" comes from a modern repointing of the ancient text, a profoundly significant philological insight. "Satiating [wine]" is similar to the "smooth wine" of Ps 16.5, the "overflowing wine" of Ps 23.5, the "sweet wine" of Yahweh "drunk deeply" in Ps 34.9, Yahweh's "salvation drunk deeply" of Ps 91.16, and the "mountains dripping new wine" of Jl 4.18. It looks ahead to the "new wine"

of Mk 14.25 and Acts 2.13 and the "choice wine" of Jn 2.10. All these expressions are figures representing the ecstasy of recovery after release from addiction. Today's alcoholics employ a similar metaphor when they call sobriety "the ultimate high" or describe recovery as "a higher high than any we ever got from drinking."

Envoi (53.12)   Isaiah's final words, "so I rank him among the great, deserving of empowerment," recapitulate the degradation-to-exaltation theme announced in the prologue. The words say about the former wine addict essentially what Jesus says about the Son of Man in Mk 14.62, "empowered by God and going about with a heavenly aura." Isaiah concludes by pronouncing the greatness of the servant, who ultimately surrendered and "died to self." Before that, during the period of his active alcoholism, he suffered horribly "for the wrongdoing of many," says Isaiah. The street alcoholic is no greater a rebel, no more a prey to self or enslaved by fear and anger, than are other people who consider themselves nonalcoholic, who have the occasional drink or two or drink ritual wine on Sabbath or Sunday. All deserve the drunkard's affliction, yet it is only the servants whom God chooses in every age and culture to suffer the agony of full-blown addiction.

A Recovery Covenant (Is 54.1–17)

Following the servant poem, Is 54.1–17 presents various images of recovery that conclude the Zion poem. Verses 1–6 speak of the prosperity and absence of fear and shame to be experienced under the higher power, imaged in spousal terms. Verses 8–10 describe Israel's illness as a flood of wrath reminiscent of Noah's flood. Verses 11–14 compare sobriety to the idealized, bejeweled city of the eschatological vision. Verses 15–17 are probably redactions.

Of greatest interest are verses 9 and 10, in which God compares the situation at hand to the covenant made with Noah after the Flood:

(Is 54.9) "This is like the days of Noah for me: As I swore that the waters of Noah should never again pass over the earth, so now I swear to you never again to be angry with you or rebuke you. (10) For the mountains may move, and the hills may totter; but my love will not move from you, and my covenant of friendship will not totter," says Yahweh, who has compassion on you.

If, as argued here, the Zion poem chronicles recovery from alcoholism, then God's "angry rebuke" in a context of "the days of Noah" after the Flood would refer to the curse of addiction on Ham/Canaan and his descendants (Gn 9.25), a consequence of Noah's alcoholic attempt to defeat God's curse on the soil by means of wine (Gn 5.29 and 9.20). Isaiah thus appears to have interpreted the Genesis text as identifying God, not Noah, as the author of the curse on Canaan, a possible reading of the Yahwist's Hebrew. Isaiah saw the derelict drunkard as inheritor of the curse, a slave to drink and a suffering servant to others. Hence he must have viewed the servant's recovery, which he witnessed in Babylon, as evidence that God had countervailed his curse of alcohol addiction by a covenant of recovery. In short, Isaiah understood God's vow "never again to be angry with you or rebuke you" as a promise never again to inflict the wrath of active alcoholism on those from whom he has removed the cup, just as God earlier promised never again to send the waters of Noah over the earth.

The proposal here is that this Deutero-Isaian "covenant" (54.10) is the covenant to which Jesus refers in his message about wine at the Last Supper (Mk 14.24). Jesus apparently understood the term in just this sense, as a promise of recovery from addiction based on the salvific telos of wine and the spiritual life to which its renunciation leads. The theme of Jesus' paschal words, "This [wine] is [the cause of] my blood[shed], yet also covenant blood, which I pour out for [the recovery of] many," which clearly refer to the servant and are immediately followed by a disavowal of further drink (Mk 14.25), indicates that it was this Isaian alcoholism covenant, and not the other "covenants" traditionally associated with his eucharistic words, that Jesus had in mind on this important occasion.

The Scandal of Alcoholism

The arguments thus far advanced for the Suffering Servant as derelict alcoholic are the following: the clinical accuracy of Deutero-Isaiah's alcoholism imagery throughout the Zion poem and particularly in 51.17–23; the historical possibility, however speculative, that Babylon in fact experienced an epidemic of addiction in its waning years; Nabonidus's conjectured alcoholism and recovery; the strikingly literal resemblance of the servant's portrait in Isaiah 53 to the stereotype of the street drunk; and the resonance of the "satiating [wine]" of Is 53.11 with the "new wine" of Mk 14.25. This last point, seen in connection with Jesus' pivotal reference to Isaiah 53 in Mk 14.24, "poured out for many" *(ekchunnomenon huper pollōn)*, supports the idea that Jesus understood the paschal wine ritual as intended to prepare the multitudes for redemption from their latent alcoholism without their having to suffer the ravages of advanced addiction.

To these may be added a final argument pertaining to the often-remarked absence from the Christian Scriptures of any sustained discussion of Isaiah 53. If Jesus actually identified the wine addict as archetype of Deutero-Isaiah's Suffering Servant, the scandal of drunkenness that would have tainted the servant would have been completely unspeakable to everyone other than Jesus' original followers (Markôs people, the Galileans whom Mark refers to as "insiders" and "women"). Any such interpretation of the servant would have been so thoroughly suppressed by presumed nonalcoholics in the Jerusalem church during its earliest years (along with any word of Jesus' own alcoholism) that scholars in the modern era would conclude that the Hellenistic churches of the late first century actually invented the Jesus-servant identification.[32]

Discussing the Suffering Servant christological motif in early Jewish Christianity, R. N. Longenecker puts the question thus:

> Having said all this, we are confronted with the problem with which every interpreter has wrestled: Why are not the suffering servant theme and Isa. 53, the only clearly redemptive suffering servant passage in the Old Testament, employed more explicitly in the canonical Christian writings? If indeed such an understanding permeates the whole of the Gospels and the earlier New Testament materials, we would expect the concept, together with its main Old Testament prooftext, to come to explicit expression frequently in the Christian literature. Yet in only three passages, Luke 22.37; Acts 8.32f.; and I Peter 2.21–25, is this done directly. "Here," as C. F. D. Moule points out, "is a phenomenon that still awaits explanation."[33]

Nor is the neglect of the Suffering Servant limited to Christian Scriptures; it also characterizes pre-Christian Jewish writings. M. D. Hooker concludes that "there was no pre-Christian doctrine of a suffering Messiah based upon Deutero-Isaiah."[34] Not even in the three apocalyptic works written specifically against the background of the Babylonian exile, 1 Baruch, 2 Esdras, and 2 Baruch (the Syriac Apocalypse), does she find reference to the servant or to the concept of vicarious suffering leading to the redemption of many. Hooker therefore concludes that the figure of the Suffering Servant remained an enigma to the Jews and that the idea of vicarious suffering was largely ignored in Jewish thought by the time of Jesus.[35]

Biblical theologians have proposed various explanations for the failure of early Christian writers to interpret the Suffering Servant. C. F. D. Moule suggests that Christian apologists avoided the idea of a suffering-servant messiah because they knew ahead of time that their opponents would refute it in a certain way.[36] W. Zimmerli and J. Jeremias say, on one hand, that the infrequency of citations argues the familiarity of the concept among early Christians and, on the other, that Jesus allowed himself to be known as the servant only in his esoteric teaching and not in his public preaching.[37] Some form-critical scholarship has concluded that it was neither Jesus nor his Palestinian followers but the Hellenistic church that equated Jesus and the Suffering Servant.[38] Hooker herself argues that Jesus was not more fully identified with the servant figure because no such figure existed as an independent concept prior to the Hellenistic writings; instead, from Moses on, only particular persons filled this role, and they were known simply as "servants of God."[39] Longenecker thinks the omission to be more a matter of circumstance than of theology. He likens the situation to Paul's awareness that the proclamation of Christ crucified was "a scandal to the Jews and foolishness to the Gentiles" (1 Cor 1.23) and concludes that, fixed though the Suffering Servant concept was in the consciousness of early believers, it "had little to which it could appeal in contemporary religious thought, and much that stood against it."[40]

Obviously, the scandal arising from the servant's degrading illness, as here interpreted, would explain the lack of servant references in postexilic Jewish writings. Alcoholism would also account for the paucity of servant references in Christian Scripture. Furthermore, it is clear from the vantage point of recovery that the concept of the servant as alcoholic informed the Markan Jesus' understanding of this mysterious Isaian figure. As one might expect, the cup is a central trope in the Cupmaster's gospel: in Mk 10.38–39 Jesus acknowledges that he is drinking the cup himself (*ho egō pinō*, continuous tense translated by the English present progressive, "which I am drinking"). He informs the disciples that the way to the exaltation they seek is through the same cup and prophesies that they too shall drink the cup he is drinking. Jesus enacts this prophecy at the Last Supper, in Mk 14.23, when he gives the cup to the disciples and they all drink from it. In Mk 14.36, in Gethsemane, a surrendered Jesus prayerfully asks God twice to remove "this cup" (interpreted not as an expression for lot or destiny but as a metonym for alcohol addiction), a demonstration of atonement lost on his unready followers. In each case, the term *cup* to Jesus would have signified the dual cups of Is 51.17 and 22, the cups of drunkenness and wrath given and removed by God, hallmarks of the alcoholic illness reserved for all disciples.

Apparently Jesus interpreted Isaiah's cup oracle and servant poem prophetically, in the light of his own alcoholism, and concluded that the "plan of God" mentioned by Isaiah (53.10) was, at some future apocalyptic time, to use the phenomenon of addiction to save his rebellious children, all the nations of humanity, from self-slaughter in the strife and warfare that result from mental drunkenness expressed in epidemic fear and anger. Thus, Jesus transformed the Passover wine duty into a drinking rite that came to epitomize the Christian liturgy. Consumed religiously, that is, ritualistically and insistently, which is to say, addictively, alcohol ultimately brings drinkers to the point where their only remaining choices are surrender or death. Surrender is painful and messy, the ominous "baptism" Jesus mentions in Mk 10.38–39, but beyond it lie recovery, freedom from fear and fighting, spiritual awakening, and joy.

In quoting from the servant poem in Mk 10.45, "The Son of Man came not to be served but to serve, and to give his self as a ransom/guilt offering for many" (see chap. 6), Jesus imputes to the drunkard servant multiple roles: service as addiction bearer, recovery messenger, and sobriety exemplar for an alcoholic world. Jesus identifies the paschal wine not only as "my blood" but also as "covenant blood" (Mk 14.24), apparently a reference to the sobriety covenant of Is 54.9–10, in which God promises never again to be angry with recovering people, never again to give them the twin cups of wrath and addiction. The wine itself Jesus pours out "for the many" (Mk 14.24). "Many" is both a biblical reference to Israelite and Babylonian alcoholics five hundred years earlier, members of the Isaian multitudes delivered through the self-sacrifice of the servant, and a prophetic reference to the many religious drinkers "drunk but not with wine" to whom the meaning of Jesus' message would ultimately be revealed. In Gethsemane (Mk 14.32–42) Jesus gives his self in sacrificial submission to God, even as the servant gave his self as a guilt offering and so lived to see his offspring (Is 53.10) and to model surrender for the many (Is 53.11). Finally, in the essential recovery metaphor, Jesus drinks "new wine" in place of real wine (Mk 14.25), even as the servant drank "satiating wine" in lieu of actual wine (Is 53.11).

These references argue the centrality to Jesus' thought of Deutero-Isaiah's Zion poem and the concept of the Suffering Servant: the wine poured out for the many; the cup given, the cup drunk, the cup removed; the passing of the cup to those who practice domination; the recovery covenant; the surrender of the self leading to atonement and the ransom of many; and the exaltedness of sobriety. Yet not one of them is so interpreted in Christian Scripture or in the ensuing centuries of Christian thought. The Markan cups are seldom highlighted and are connected with the Isaian cups only in passing. Jesus' words "this is my blood" (Mk 14.24) are never taken as conveying his recognition of wine as the cause of his own troubles or of the servant's suffering. "Covenant" (Mk 14.24) is always understood as the Sinai covenant, the circumcision covenant, or Jeremiah's "new covenant" (Jer 31.31–34), but never as the covenant of Is 54.9–10 connected with Gn 9.25. The import of "new wine" and of the ambiguous semantic structure of Mark's Gethsemane pericope has been overlooked from the outset, so far as we know. And the servant poem itself is invariably construed merely as a foreshadow of Jesus's trial and crucifixion. Thus did the scandal of alcoholism deter the early Church, including Mark's ostensible audience of Judean Christ cultists, from using the Isaian cup, servant, and covenant as interpretive concepts. By contrast, Markôs insiders and "women" would have understood the significance of these images and wholeheartedly approved Mark's boldness in featuring them so prominently in his book.

The Servant as Cup Minister

Every major city has its skid row and its skid row churches, many with early morning services. One can visualize the scene in the predawn darkness: communicants sipping from the wine chalice even as the winos in the street drain their bottles of port and muscatel. This juxtaposition of wretched gutter drunkenness and pious religious drinking points up the role of the Suffering Servant in the drama of human redemption. It is a role enacted by Jesus at the Last Supper yet denied and concealed at the outset of Christian history, forgotten almost at once, and forever uncast in the ensuing centuries of liturgical practice.

Like Deutero-Isaiah, Jesus viewed humanity's characteristic problem as the chronic inebriety of a few ("cup of reeling") coupled with the mental drunkenness of the multitudes ("chalice of wrath"). Everywhere he looked, Jesus must have seen this alcoholism propelling humankind toward destruction: bloody feuds, assaults and banditry, litigiousness, ethnic strife, adversarial sects and politics, Jew fighting Jew on the issue of collaboration with Rome, defiant patriots ranged against angry Roman occupiers, and his own war against the Jewish religious leaders. In this milieu Jesus apparently recognized that the deeper purpose of the Passover wine duty was to addict the nonaddicted and thereby prepare them to admit their powerlessness over alcohol as a prerequisite to stopping fighting. In other words, ritual wine would make actual alcoholics of the mentally drunk to qualify them for a recovery program wherein God could free them from bondage to their agonistic and fear-driven selves short of the physical ravages of advanced addiction and so save humanity from itself. What then, finally, is the connection between ritual drinking and the Suffering Servant? Interpreting Isaiah's poem from the perspective of his own illness, Jesus appears to have concluded that the servant's sacerdotal role was to inspire an impulse to recovery in all religious drinkers, the multitudes of alcoholics unaware. He would have recognized that Isaiah depicts the servant first as a type of the public drunkard and then as a recovering person who has surrendered his self and replaced actual wine by the satiating wine of sobriety. Jesus presumably believed that the servant, in each of these personas, would promote recovery in others. Before his recovery, the spectacle of the helpless derelict drunk prepares nonaddicts to admit their latent alcoholism by prompting the realization that "there but for the grace of God go I." After victory over alcohol, the servant exemplifies the self-surrender and joyous living that today's alcoholics call "working the program."

As for liturgical drinking itself, Jesus' paschal actions as portrayed by Mark indicate that he discerned yet another persona for the servant, that of apocalyptic cup minister to the many. This is the role Jesus enacted at the Last Supper, giving the cup to disciples, inviting them to drink or not drink as they chose, and then metaphorically identifying wine as his blood and announcing his intention to turn from drink to "the new wine of the rule of God." These actions can trigger in beholders the recognition of ritual alcohol as "a desolating sacrilege set up where it ought not to be" (Mk 13.14a; see chap. 6), followed by the conviction of powerlessness, whereupon God can remove the cup (Is 51.22, par. Mk 14.36) and free these drinkers to detach from religious fanaticism and other forms of organized anger and domination and turn to recovery (Is 52.7–12 and "flee to the mountains" in Mk 13.14c).

Many kinds of experiences involving the servant figure can trigger apocalypse for religious drinkers. One would be to behold the street derelict face to face, to look with unaverted eyes at the skid row drunkard and ponder the fact that his fate might have been one's own. Another would be to discern that every alcoholic's recovery story is encapsulated in the eucharistic words characterizing ritual wine as "my blood of the covenant poured out for many" (Mk 14.24). Another would be to see persons living their recovery programs in sobriety. Still another would be to recognize in the Christian deacon, who ministers the cup without drinking from it himself, the persona of

Jesus as the servant drunkard who disavows further drink in favor of the satiating wine of sobriety. The ultimate apocalypse, anticipated in the giving of the wine cup (Mk 14.23), would be conviction by the desire to stop drinking at the moment of taking communion.

As it happened, all these avenues to revelation except the first have remained closed to disciples throughout the two millennia of Christian history. Although the Markôs program survived long enough in the first century to produce the Cupmaster's gospel, except for a brief moment in the original Jerusalem fellowship and perhaps a decade or two within the primitive Johannine community in Galilee (see chap. 7), no former addict from then until now would witness to recovery at a Christian Eucharist. The alcoholism intentionality of Jesus' message would remain veiled, his disavowal of wine (Mk 14.25) would be excluded from the liturgy, and the identity of the servant would go unrecognized. Nonetheless, it is possible that God's plan for human redemption is being fulfilled today, in a world increasingly riven by addiction and strife. Signs of this fulfillment may be seen at meetings wherein anonymous exdrinkers who have suffered far less than the derelict drunkard proclaim themselves alcoholic, where liturgical wine has been replaced by the "new wine" or "satiating [wine]" of sobriety, where the authority of the Twelve Apostles has given way to the spirituality of the Twelve Steps, where the clerical sermon has been supplanted by the stories of recovering alcoholics, and where the many, detached from an addicted and violent world, are finding serenity and joy.

✣ 4 ✣

THE PROVENANCE, GENRE, AND STORY OF MARK

> . . . a cup of water to drink that you might know the
> meaning of Messiah.
> —Markan entrance rite, Mk 9.41

In the light of the exegetical possibilities uncovered in Mark's Passion narrative and Deutero-Isaiah's Zion poem, this chapter begins by examining sociocultural research on first-century Palestine to assess the likelihood that the hypothesized Markan audience existed. It asks to what extent the metanoetic spirituality attributed to the Markôs groups harmonizes with the character of other group movements on the ancient cultural landscape. The chapter then presents a conjectured scenario of the provenance of Mark's gospel consistent with the ethological context depicted in the sociological research and with facts pertaining to the onset of the Roman War. It then lays out certain extra-Markan material interpretable as evidence that the primitive Jesus fellowship could have been, in fact, a sobriety movement. Next it looks at research on the genre of Mark and points to features of the Markan text whose recognition by an audience of recovering alcoholics, including members of the Markôs community, would prompt such readers to identify the gospel as a displacement of Jesus' own recovery story, a story similar in form to those of alcoholics today. Finally the chapter reconstructs Jesus' first-person story as memorialized by the Markans.

Ancient Self-Help Groups
Sociological Research

Despite extensive study, important questions about Mark's gospel remain unanswered. What community produced the gospel? What was the set of circumstances that prompted its writing? Who was its intended audience? Could that audience have been multiple? What is its literary genre? Whence came its narrative order? What is the purpose of its secrecy theme and the many clandestine symbols it contains? What is distinctive about its apocalyptic content? How much of the narrative is Markan composition and how much is traditional? Well aware of such questions, Howard Clark Kee began his landmark 1975 study of the sociocultural setting of Mark's gospel as follows: "'Ultimately a cloud remains over the question of Mark's aim. . . .' Those are the disheartening but apposite words pronounced by W. G. Kümmel towards the end of his comprehensive survey of the hypotheses adduced in the past three-quarters of a century concerning 'The Literary Character and Theological Aim of the Gospel of Mark.'"[1] Seán Kealy's exhaustive series of thumbnail sketches of Markan research prior to the 1970s confirms Kümmel's conclusion.[2] Kee further asserted that in Mark, "we are dealing with an anonymous work of unknown provenance," and labeled most conclusions about Markan aims and origins, whether ancient or modern, "guesses" and "conjectures."[3] Kee proposed a new approach: "The 'horizon' of Mark must be extended to include not only the literary and conceptual models with which biblical scholars have been accustomed to deal, but models from the realm of social history as well, if we are to determine Mark's actual 'intention.'"[4] For Kee and others this meant turning from the question of how the Church originated to research on the cultural setting and social dynamics that yielded the anonymous text called the Gospel of Mark.

Antecedent concerns about the social setting of early Christianity are reflected in studies by Gustaf Dalman,[5] Shailer Mathews,[6] and Shirley Jackson Case,[7] and more recently S. G. F. Brandon,[8] Joachim Jeremias,[9] and E. A. Judge.[10] In a seminal article L. E. Keck argued the value of an ethological approach to the study of Christian origins.[11] Twentieth-century archaeological and manuscript discoveries have added new knowledge about Palestinian Judaism, which now seems a more likely source of Mark than the gentile community traditionally posited in Rome. In addition to the work of Kee, sociocultural studies appeared by Eduard Lohse,[12] John Gager,[13] Abraham

Malherbe,[14] Gerd Theissen,[15] and Bruce Malina,[16] all of whom employ sociological and anthropological approaches. Important too is the work of Martin Hengel indicating that Palestinian Judaism was not insulated from Hellenistic culture, as formerly thought, but experienced the same societal trends observed in the eastern Mediterranean region generally.[17] One such trend, highly relevant here, was the rise of various kinds of groups or associations in the Greco-Roman world of the first century, many of which, like Alcoholics Anonymous today, included a component of conversion or spiritual awakening.

Conversion as Self-Help

In his classic study of conversion in antiquity, Arthur Darby Nock argued that, whereas conversion was otherwise quite specialized and rare, Christianity drew people into its ranks by uniting the sacramentalism and philosophy of the time, satisfying desires for escape from Rome, fate, and death and offering fulfillment of social needs and security against loneliness.[18] Although these groups were often spiritual, their impetus was not, strictly speaking, religious. According to Kee, "craftsmen and those attached to the cult of various divinities formed associations called *collegia* . . . to foster the common welfare of the group, or to honor a divine benefactor."[19] Referring to Nock's study, Kee writes: "Although the Roman establishment on the whole regarded these cultic movements with mingled disdain and hostility, there were various modes of propaganda that attracted numbers of people who felt themselves to be marginal, as Nock has pointed out. The cults grew through personal testimony of individuals who had experienced deliverance ('salvation') from sickness or fear or both. . . ."[20] Although aware of this broader phenomenon, Malherbe speaks only of the Pauline cults, and Lohse confines himself to seven distinctively Jewish groups—Sadducees, Pharisees, Zealots, Essenes, Qumran sectaries, Therapeutae, and Scribes.[21] As for the Christian groups, Gager points to their sense of community as contributing to group strength in troubled times: "From the very beginning, the one distinctive gift of Christianity was this sense of community. Whether one speaks of 'an age of anxiety' or 'the crisis of the towns,' Christian congregations provided a unique opportunity for masses of people to discover a sense of security and self-respect."[22] In modern terms, these *collegia* or associations seem to have ranged from trade unions and professional organizations at one extreme to religious cults and self-help groups at the other.

Studying the increased incidence of conversion in first-century Palestine, Alan Segal writes: "No matter how common or important was conversion within the general Jewish community, it was significantly more so to the emerging sects in Judaism, and spectacularly so to Christianity."[23] Segal argues that persons convert because they "feel deprived of something, either material or spiritual, that seems present in the lives of others" and then lists various threats that Christian converts sought to escape, such as millenarianism, antiwitchcraft cultism, status ambiguity, and the demonization of the public religions.[24] Segal also examines the phenomenon of commitment that often follows sudden spiritual change, writing that "the highest degree of commitment is apparent only when sudden conversions are followed by and supplemented with other members' thorough education to the values of the group."[25] Segal's findings on commitment are paralleled in modern sociological studies of Alcoholics Anonymous. For example: "Our description of the process of affiliation also illustrates that A.A. . . . actually achieves a radical change in the affiliates' world view and identity through their acceptance of the A.A. philosophy and through their total absorption in the A.A. community and way of life. . . . Such a radical reorganization of identity, meaning, and life . . . is profitably viewed as conversion."[26] The foregoing conclusion by David Rudy reflects phenomena identical to those Segal observed in first-century conversion groups.

In arguing that Mark is more indebted to nonmessianic Palestinian Jesus movements than to the Christ cults, Burton Mack attests to the variety of these popular groups formed around old traditions and new interests: "Mystery cults, clubs *(koinōniai,* or 'associations'; *collegia),* theosophical societies, communes, gnostic sects, and other forms of social concentrations clustered to fill the void left vacant when the gods departed from the temples. Palestine was not excluded from this form of questing. As the hated Roman presence was prolonged, a restlessness set the climate for smaller sects to form."[27] Mack identifies five kinds of groups, each with its own sense of purpose, that remembered Jesus as a teacher, sage, or charismatic reformer but not as Messiah or a dying and rising god. These were: (1) itinerant Cynic-like Galilean preachers; (2) the Jerusalem community Paul called "pillars;" (3) a Transjordan movement connected with James and the family of Jesus; (4) a northern Palestinian "Congregation of Israel" whose miracle stories were based on the Elisha-Elijah archetype; and (5) house-based Jesus people who considered themselves a reform movement within synagogue Judaism.[28] It is in this mélange of Jesus groups, to say nothing of other kinds of spiritual and religio-political sects and associations dotting the Palestinian landscape, that the Markôs groups theorized here would have existed. Their membership would have been the clandestine "insider" audience of Mark's book, until now invisible to history.

Richard Horsley discusses the conflicts and imminent societal break-down that began in Palestine with the local revolts following Herod's death in 4 B.C.E. and culminated in the 60s C.E. in the push toward rebellion provided by arrogant Roman governors and the greed of Jewish priestly families.[29] Horsley critiques Theissen's structural-functional explanation of how the Jesus movement contained aggression during this period and then shows how the Jesus groups answered the crises of rampant debt by teaching mutual forgiveness of debts, of familial disintegration by substituting egalitarian nonpatriarchal communities for families, and of despair by renewing individual and group spirits. About the psychic and spiritual domains, Horsley writes: "in response to illness, self-blame, and possession by alien spiritual forces, for example, the Jesus movement continued the healing, forgiveness of sin, and exorcism initiated by Jesus."[30] Notice that "illness, self-blame, and possession" all but define addiction. Pathological drinking was doubtless a widespread response to the anger and angst of the times, especially in wine-rich Galilee, and hence the symptom of many persons drawn to these Jesus groups in search of serenity. Given the behaviors resulting from the combination of drink with fear and anger, it is possible that referring to demon possession had become a vernacular way of speaking about chronic intoxication, later adopted by Mark as a code word for addiction.

Markôs Groups

Against such a background, it is reasonable to believe that the sobriety group was one of the types, perhaps even the original type, comprised by the Jesus movement from the outset. Partly underground and little known to outsiders, these groups would have expanded, by the Roman War, south into Samaria and Judea and north into the Transjordan and Syria. Of the membership of the Jesus groups in general, Mary Ann Tolbert says, "the emerging consensus on the social description of early Christian communities seems to view them as a cross section of Greco-Roman society with the very top level and very bottom level omitted."[31] Hengel echoes this position: "We may assume that those men who bore the new message from Jewish Palestine to Syria and Asia Minor and indeed to Rome came neither from the illiterate proletariat nor from the aristocracy but from the creative middle class, which nowadays is so readily dismissed as 'petty-bourgeois,' a social milieu from which Jesus and Paul probably came."[32] Although Galilee was an almost entirely rural area containing mostly small towns, with many peasants and few if any aristocrats, its middle classes would have included unhappy drunkards aplenty as potential group members, drawn from the ranks of artisans, merchants, landed farmers, boat-owning fishermen, tax collectors, agents, overseers, innkeepers, stewards, brigands, women of all walks of life, and even rabbinic disciples. The next section of this chapter describes how the Gospel of Mark could have arisen from peasant and middle-class Jesus groups devoted to sobriety after addiction.

Demise of the Movement

Given the plausibility of regional sobriety groups as one manifestation of the original Jesus movement, what would explain their historical invisibility and presumed disappearance? The answer suggested here involves asceticism and denial on the part of nonalcoholics of the times. Apparently the sobriety groups were overwhelmed during the 60s and 70s C.E., at least within Judea, by a tide of Jewish-Christian ascetics traumatized by fear and guilt stemming from the Roman War and the destruction of the Temple and attracted by the quiet spirituality of these Jesus people. If so, the surrendered disavowal of drink characteristic of former addicts would have been replaced within the groups by the self-willed abstinence of fanatical nondrinkers. No sooner would these nonalcoholics have put the stamp of asceticism on the Markan groups than they in turn would have been vilified as water-drinking "gnostics" and expelled from the end-of-century churches by "catholic" Christians striving for liturgical uniformity. History has always known of these Jewish and Jewish-Christian ascetics. Jacob Neusner, for example, mentions a Talmudic report "that when the Temple was destroyed, ascetics who would not eat flesh or drink wine multiplied in Israel."[33] Scholarship has never looked into the difference between surrendered and self-willed abstinence, however, or imagined Mark's secret audience as exdrunkards joined in recovery groups. Yet the Jesus who at the moment of *psuchē thanatos* prays "[As] you have all power [so am I powerless], remove my cup [addiction]" (Mk 14.36) and who in his refusal of drink from the cross may have said "My power, O Power, has entirely left me [O God, I am powerless]" (Gos. Pet. 19) sounds very much like a surrendering alcoholic and antitype of ascetic self-empowerment.

Then as now, the doctrine of powerlessness espoused by alcoholics would have been incomprehensible to ascetics and repugnant to the educated aristocrats, both Jewish and gentile, and others of the intelligentsia from whose ranks end-of-century Christian *episkopoi* presumably came. Pointing out that not only Christianity but also rabbinic Judaism drew on the Socratic humanitarian tradition, Martin Hengel mentions as desirable features "the command to love all men, the stress on study, an almost Cynic asceticism, and a striving for autarky."[34] Alcoholics would probably respond that "striving for autarky," the antithesis of the rule of God, was what got them drunk and kept them drinking. All things considered, it is impossible to overstress the denial that alcohol and alcoholism cause in the minds of humans. The same is true today. For example, notice the presumably unconscious omission of abstinence from drink in Vincent Wimbush's recent list of ascetic behaviors in the ancient world: "In varying degrees and in different times and contexts, vegetarianism, fasting, sexual continence, general dissipation of the body, political quietism, and even physical retreat from society and construction of an alternate social world characterized the ethic of these movements."[35] Almost certainly the Jewish ascetics of the 70s and 80s, and the increasingly theocratic Jewish-Christian clergy of that time, would have denied, repressed, and completely forgotten the identity of the prewar Markôs people as groups of exdrunkards, exactly as the gentile Christ cults had after dissociating themselves from those groups earlier in the century.

The Pharisees who attained spiritual ascendancy within Judaism following the Roman War, while not ascetics, would have been similarly repulsed by the former wine addicts. Those who honored Jesus would have been only too ready to quash any rumors that the Markan groups traced their origins to Jesus' ministry. Pharisees drank ritual wine out of religious duty but condemned intemperate drinking. In contrasting the Pharisees and the "untouchables," the *am haaretz*, or peasants, to whom Jesus went, Robin Scroggs could just as well have been contrasting Pharisees and recovering people.[36] Bruce Malina's discussion of clean and unclean as a purity concept used by the Pharisees for setting boundaries, while it does not mention drink beyond noting that the oozing of fermentation was considered unclean, leaves little doubt that the chronic drinker, whether drinking or sober, would have been outcast.[37] Mark's story of the Gerasene demoniac (5.1–20) symbolizes the legion of outcast drunkards within humankind. Jesus' casting these demons into the herd of pigs represents the removal of the stigma of uncleanness from addicts once they enter recovery (see chap. 6).

In any case, it is entirely understandable how a citizenry frightened by the social chaos of the 60s and 70s, motivated by an exaggerated sense of guilt, and desperately seeking penance and spiritual consolation could have mistaken the exdrunkards' abstinence for asceticism and joined their groups in large numbers. In discussing the composition of the Gospel of John, chapter 7 herein suggests what happened when a manual of Markan proto-Johannine recovery parables came under the control of these ascetics. Sober members remaining in the Markôs groups, whose alcoholic origins had been increasingly ignored by nonalcoholic Jesus people before the war, would have been so completely overshadowed by the postwar influx of ascetics as to be wholly unknown to the new Christian hierarchs, whether Jewish or gentile. These officials, oblivious to the meanings of the nicknames *Marcus* and *stump-fingered*, would have been quite incapable of acknowledging a memory connecting Jesus with a movement of provincial exdrunkards. By the turn of the century those sobriety groups that had gone underground to escape the ascetics would have died out for lack of newcomers. The only remaining Markôs people would have been isolated old-timers.

In summary, given the existence of self-help groups and associations in first-century Palestine, including nonmessianic Jesus groups, coupled with social conditions in Galilee ripe for an epidemic of alcohol addiction, it is perfectly reasonable to assume that one kind of group in the region of Galilee would have been associations of former wine addicts, individuals who, from the depths of despair, had called out the name of Jesus ("God, help!"), turned from wine to water, and experienced metanoetic spiritual awakening and a return to healthy and productive living.

Scenario of Provenance

Mark's gospel is widely held to be an original document based on recollections of Jesus' sayings and possibly texts of the parables and the Passion narrative.[38] Although it contains no clear information about audience or place of composition, readers generally agree that the gospel incorporates a special form of apocalyptic; that its tone is one of urgency and crisis; and that it embodies a secrecy theme and clandestine material, is Palestinian in focus while pretending not to be, and was occasioned by the first Roman-Jewish War. Within this context the following scenario aims to demonstrate that a conception of Mark's book as an alcoholism recovery story hidden within a religious tale is fully compatible with conventional ideas about its timing and purpose and its seeming identity as a Messiah narrative.

The Times

The social climate in the Jewish regions of Palestine in the 60s C.E. was a mixture of religious frenzy, civil unrest, economic dissolution, banditry, and apocalyptic foreboding. Comparing Palestinian and Hellenistic Christianity in the 60s, Gerd Theissen calls the former "a powder barrel within which the Mediterranean cities kept the tensions within bounds," in contrast to the latter, which remained "largely in accord with the political structures of its environment."[39] The anxiety and anger of the times would have been both cause and result of widespread alcoholic drinking. In its various manifestations, the legacy of Jesus the Nazarene was exhibiting impressive vitality. Jesus communities ranged from Christ cults involved in ritual drinking to sobriety fellowships helping former wine addicts remain abstinent. Sayings of Jesus were heard in the synagogues, itinerant Cynic preachers called people to conversion in his name, and hymns and tracts proclaimed him to be the Messiah. Always a source of dispute, Jesus' words at the Jerusalem Passover were memorialized in some quarters but banned in others, and communal meals of bread and wine (but probably not of fish and bread; see chap. 7) were eaten in his memory.[40]

As for the political sphere, war with the Romans seemed imminent. Richard Horsley attributes the outbreak of rebellion in 66 C.E. primarily to "the deteriorating economic conditions of the peasantry and the disintegrating social structure, at both the village and the society-wide levels."[41] Horsley also cites the influence of certain prophets and messiah figures, repressive measures by Roman forces and particularly by the governor Gessus Florius (64–66 C.E.), the terrorism of the intellectualist group known as Sicarii, and the predatory behavior of the high-priestly families and the Herodians. Judean revolutionaries, who were fast gaining an upper hand, doubtless claimed Jesus as a freedom fighter against Roman tyranny, while their opponents, collaborators who believed that war would mean genocide, presented Jesus as a pacifist. The sobriety groups would have remained aloof from all such controversy.

The Writer

In the present view, Mark was a native Judean who began writing his book sometime in 68 C.E., in the wake of Vespasian's conquest of northern Palestine, perhaps shortly after Nero's suicide in June of that year, during the hiatus in the fighting that resulted from the ensuing civil conflict in Rome. Mark believed that the Romans would emerge victorious and were prepared, as the ultimate postwar reprisal, to prohibit all public expressions of Judaism in the rebel cities. He wrote in response to this situation, which he saw as an imminent threat to the existence of his Galilee-born Judean sobriety program, which the Romans considered a Jewish sect and to which he had belonged since early adulthood. An anecdote in his book, the curious mention of the "young man who fled naked" after the arrest of Jesus (Mk 14.51), has been called "a bit of autobiography" composed by the evangelist.[42] The assumption here is that this young man is Mark himself. The same is presumed true of the "John Mark" of Acts (see chap. 6, discussion of Mk 14.51–52).

If Mark was around twenty years old in 30 C.E., he would have been in his late fifties in 68. His mother, Mary, was a Jerusalem householder (Acts 12.12). Mark 14.51 suggests that Mark was on the scene with Jesus during the Jerusalem ministry. He may even have been present at the Last Supper, which was perhaps the occasion of his entry into the sobriety fellowship. In the 40s Mark traveled on missionary journeys with Paul and Barnabas (Acts 12.25, 13.5 and 13, 15.36–41). He must have been familiar with the gentile churches and with the Jewish Christ cults and Jesus groups, many of which, until the Roman war, remained in the embrace of synagogue Judaism. In a well-known passage in Eusebius, Papias quotes John the Presbyter to the effect that Mark wrote as Peter's interpreter. Other testimony locates Mark's contact with Peter in Rome around the time of the latter's death in the 50s and identifies Mark as a missionary in Egypt until the early 60s. Mark could have traveled to Rome to interview Peter almost anytime in preparation for a future book, and Alexandria may have been the refuge he later chose in which to escape the war in Judea and write his gospel. Contrary to positions often taken, the fact that Mark differed with Peter on questions of hierarchy does not mean that he could not have obtained material from the apostle, nor does his going to Rome to do so mean that he must have written for a community in Rome.

Despite his presumed lack of higher education, Mark had ample literary ability to shape the Jesus materials in the ways that the goals of his writing required. An Aramaic speaker of considerable linguistic sophistication, he recognized northern and southern Aramaic dialect differences and knew Greek and Latin.[43] Often called an untutored writer, Mark in fact wrote grammatically accomplished Koine Greek in a plain style readable by middle-class Aramaic-Greek bilinguals. The inelegance of his prose also served to remind his insider audience that his book was a transformation of oral discourse, specifically, Jesus' own recovery story. Of the tricky question of writing for multiple audiences, Mark knew that ambiguity and allegory can be used as devices of literary concealment, that readers will read a text exactly as their preconceptions dictate, and that a trusted omniscient narrator can exercise a powerful yet unseen control over interpretation on the part of unknowing readers.

The Markôs Fellowship

As argued in chapter 1, the popular Roman name *Marcus* functioned in a Palestinian setting as a coterie nickname identifying John Mark as a former wine addict. His fellow alcoholics, seeing an opportunity for wordplay with the Hebrew/Aramaic *mar kôs*,[44] employed the name as a universal in-group locution used for mutual identification, much like *Jacques* with French revolutionaries or *comrade* among communists. Similarly, the curious nickname *stump-fingered* may have been another coterie appellative designating one who cannot take up the wine cup, that is, who no longer drinks.[45] Mark had recovered from his addiction during his young manhood in Jerusalem, in a fellowship of exdrunkards who referred to themselves as *Yĕhôḥānān Markôs*, "cupmaster by God's grace," just as modern alcoholics say of themselves, "sober by the grace of God." Anonymous and detached from all religious and political disputes, Mark's fellowship located its origin around 30 C.E. in Galilee, in the teaching of another former addict, Jesus, son of Mary, the same Jesus hailed in the Messiah cults. As time passed, these recovery groups had spread south to Samaria and Judea, and perhaps north as well. Romans and other cultural outsiders would have considered the Markan fellowship merely another Jesus group within regional Judaism.

Like other Jesus people, the Markans congregated in synagogues and homes. They may have followed meeting formats adapted from the Haburah, the Jews' traditional bread-and-wine fellowship and thanksgiving meal. Jewish religious groups would have known only that Markan people were former drinkers reputed to interpret Jesus' teachings oddly and to abstain from wine in their Haburahs. As is true today, many alcoholics, including Mark, would have met with Christian groups on occasion, but few of the nonalcoholic Christ cultists were acquainted with practices within the recovery groups. As time passed Mark would have observed the increasing disparity between the spiritual understanding of Jesus' story heard in his recovery meetings and its religious interpretation being shaped by the Christians.

Mark served early on as a Pauline missionary, and he may have continued his travels later in service to the sobriety groups. Presumably he had contact with all kinds of Jesus communities. Accomplished at secrecy, Mark may have represented his abstinence to nonalcoholic Jesus people as a form of asceticism. What makes John Mark such a shadowy figure in Acts is his dispute with Paul. Mark broke off a missionary journey for no known reason, leaving Paul and Barnabas at Perga and returning to Jerusalem (Acts 13.13). Afterward, according to Luke, Paul refused to allow Mark to accompany him on mission (Acts 15.36–41). Paul may have heard about the memory of Jesus cultivated within the sobriety groups and been appalled by it, or Mark may have chosen to dissociate himself from Paul's emergent Christ mysticism and crucifixion-resurrection teaching. Rumors of Jesus' inebriety and that of the original disciples may be the reason Paul avoided contact with the latter and disdained any knowledge of Jesus' prepaschal career.[46]

Members of Mark's fellowship spoke a coterie idiom perplexing to outsiders. The nicknames *Marcus* and *stump-fingered* were items in this in-group parlance. The Markans' rite of admission, obliquely referred to in Mk 9.41, ". . . a cup of water to drink that you might know the meaning of Messiah," was the giving of a drink of water signifying the end of wine drinking. Members followed certain principles of spiritual living called "the Twelve" (Mk 3.14, 4.10, and passim). They called their fellowship "the Way" and "the rule of God" (Mark, passim). They spoke of sobriety as "drinking new wine" and called the words of recovery "bread" and members "fish." In their meetings they recalled Jesus' recovery story, especially the crisis points at Passover and in Gethsemane, just as they told their own stories, thanked God for spiritual empowerment and exaltation (Mk 14.62), and carried the message of a conversion of mind (*metanoia*, Mk 1.15) to the newly sober. (Chap. 6 includes detailed discussions of the foregoing references.)

The Crisis of War

What prompted Mark to write his gospel? Historically, the war fever that had been rising for years finally erupted into conflagration. Societal unrest and anger had combined with Roman willfulness to bring holocaust on Jewish Palestine. In 67 C.E., in response to news of a successful rebellion in Jerusalem, an enraged Nero had ordered the recapture of that city and the destruction of the Temple. For this task he chose the premier general of the empire, Vespasian, who with his son Titus and lieutenant Trajan set out from Antioch with three legions of soldiers to crush the rebels once and for all. The fury of the Roman invasion was the worst the region had seen in the two centuries following the persecution of Antiochus IV Epiphanes. Josephus writes that Vespasian's campaign of 67–68 C.E. ravaged entire Jewish populations from south Syria to Judea, garrisoning conquered towns and doubtless destroying their synagogues.[47] Jewish lawlessness had kindled such a hatred of Judaism among the Romans that they clearly meant to stamp it out completely, in its homeland if not in the Diaspora. Geopolitically, Palestine had too great a strategic value for Rome to risk its loss to the waiting Parthians. Despite the pause in hostilities caused by Nero's death and the ensuing civil unrest in Rome, every Jew undistracted by fanaticism or denial knew, in the second half of 68 C.E., that the capture of Jerusalem and the destruction of the Temple were inevitable.

Aware of this crisis, Mark would have realized that the impending demise of regional Judaism threatened the existence of his alcoholism program. He may have heard what happened to northern groups unlucky enough to have been found out by Vespasian's men. Not only would the movement lose the cover afforded by the synagogues, but the postwar Romans would surely regard it as just another Jewish sect to be outlawed with the rest. Fearing the worst, Mark decided that the surest way to preserve for future hearing the story of the alcoholic Jesus and the origin of their recovery program was to write it in a book, quickly.

Plan

Books can be proscribed as well as sects, however, and Mark's would certainly encounter not one opponent but two, the Romans because of its Jewishness and the Christians because of the scandal it would cause by disclosing Jesus' alcoholic malady. So he cast about for a hiding place where the Jesus story as he knew it would be both protected and accessible in a postwar country likely to be policed by far stricter Roman occupiers and devoid of all public manifestations of Judaism. Pondering his dilemma at the outset of the eighteen-month hiatus (until early 70 C.E.) in the Roman-Jewish War, Mark surely recognized that Jewish Christian groups in Judea were also seeking ways to survive in the postwar period. Aware that the gentile "churches" to the north were tolerated by Rome because their clergies guaranteed the people's civil obedience, the Judean Christians still unscathed by war presumably began preparing to disavow Judaism publicly, ordain clergies like the Gentiles, and profess themselves lawabiding Christians wishing only to worship in peace.[48] Their leaders perhaps imagined themselves hierarchs in a new theocracy founded on the ruins of synagogue and Temple, a New Israel under the banner of Jesus Messiah.

Mark must have expected that these new churches would retain the book orientation of their Jewish heritage and would therefore require a work of Scripture recounting the story of Jesus. Such a book, acceptable to both Romans and Christians, might provide exactly the place of concealment he sought for the Jesus story as he knew it. So the course Mark decided on was to write a politically inoffensive religious narrative of a spiritual messiah intended for Jewish Christians but to conceal within it, for the benefit of both his recovery fellowship and readers in a future apocalyptic time, the secret story of the alcoholic Jesus. It was a bold plan of camouflage. If it succeeded, Mark's Christian friends would read in his book the narrative of a Cynic-like teacher revealed as the prophetic wonder-working Son of God, while his ex-addict cohort would discern the hidden recovery story of an anonymous alcoholic Son of Man.

Audiences

Mark's task would not have been easy. The success of his project hung on the question of audience. His book would have to satisfy the requirements of not two but at least four different readerships. To win Roman approval it would have to attack the Temple, distance itself from the Jerusalem establishment, and show what happens to a messiah figure unwise enough to engage in social protest. For the Jewish Christians it would have to valorize Jesus' Jewish origins and orientation yet also highlight their separation from Judaism by explaining Jewish customs and Aramaic vocabulary from the viewpoint of a seeming outsider, and to depict the Messiah finally as spiritual and not political. To satisfy the gentile Christians who Mark supposed would ultimately read it, it would have to comport with their Pauline eucharistic ritual and Christ mysticism and accurately present the teachings and parables of Jesus enshrined in oral tradition and various collections of sayings. Finally, to serve Mark's alcoholic confreres it would have to couch the story of Jesus' recovery and their clergy-free program in a framework of ambiguity and cryptic allegory uninterpretable by outsiders. In short, what Mark's text needed from the Romans was an imprimatur; from the Judean Christians, identification and use as a scripture verifying their separation from Judaism; from the gentile clergies, a judgment of christological authenticity; and from the alcoholics, recognition that its clandestine symbolism signified the presence of Jesus' sobriety story. It was a tall order, which Mark ultimately filled by producing history's most ingenious work of literary concealment.

Place

Where Mark wrote his book is immaterial. Indeed, he took pains not to disclose the location to avoid any impediments to the acceptance of his work that a local identification might create. Even his celebrated errors in reporting Galilean geography may have been deliberate.

Thus it is irrelevant whether he wrote in Rome, as traditionally held on account of his connection with Peter, or Antioch, rural south Syria, Jerusalem, or Alexandria.[49] Mark's sole aim was to complete his text, have it copied, and distribute scrolls or codices to as many of the still-intact Judean congregations as he could in whatever time remained before Titus, commanding in Vespasian's stead, finished the conquest of Judea and Jerusalem. The need for haste would account for the gospel's brevity and sense of urgency. Mark knew more Jesus sayings than he included in his manuscript. The fact that a copy of Mark soon came into Matthew's hands and another into Luke's, and that both writers incorporated major portions of the work into their own gospels, suggests that it was widely circulated and accepted. The so-called Secret Gospel of Mark was probably an early version of the manuscript later modified in response to complaints by Christian censors (see chap. 6).

Outcome

It will probably never be known how many congregations of traumatized Judean Christians succeeded in using Markan scrolls to convince Titus's and, later, Trajan's soldiers of their dissociation from Judaism, thereby saving themselves from Roman wrath and continuing to worship openly. As for the alcoholism groups, some disappeared, while others maintained their identity and, like the Christians, used Mark's book to ward off Roman persecution. As discussed above, many of these groups were soon overwhelmed by guilt-ridden Jewish Christians who recognized the alcoholism intentionality of Jesus' eucharistic words but had stopped drinking by willpower, before hitting bottom and admitting defeat. So burdened, the groups foundered in what has been called "the wave of ascetic enthusiasm which culminated in a whole group of similar movements classed by modern scholars as Encratite."[50] The sudden influx of ascetics may have taken Mark's alcoholics by surprise. Some probably went underground to escape these fanatical abstainers. There they may have developed the prophecy of a coming alcoholic church and its distant apocalyptic crisis, which later became the Book of Revelation (see chap. 7).

It is important to remember that although most of the foregoing scenario is not known fact but nescient conjecture positioned in the "gaps" of history, the same is true of *all* theories of Markan provenance. Although it goes beyond conventional thinking, the picture given here violates no historical data. In fact, despite its novelty, it achieves greater plausibility than many other theories of Markan origin, owing to its straightforward account of such traditionally problematic elements as the gospel's clandestine content, its allegorically consistent anticlericalism, the oddly conflicting titles it assigns Jesus, its peculiar conflation of genres, its anomalous apocalyptic content, and its idiosyncratic paschal narrative, to name but some.

Extra-Markan Evidence

Richard Horsley has observed that a large part of the problem of researching Christian origins prior to the Roman War is "the paucity of texts that would provide any direct evidence concerning the concrete social form of the Jesus movement in Palestine."[51] The position here is that the Gospel of Mark, read from an alcoholism perspective, may be construed as direct textual evidence that certain of the early Jesus groups were composed of former wine addicts. Yet Mark represents but one source of data. Following are eight kinds of extra-Markan material interpretable as historical evidence supporting the alcoholism hypothesis.

"Unbridled Drunkard"

A direct mention of Jesus' addiction occurs in the Q material recalling his reputation as an "unbridled drunkard" or "full-blown alcoholic," uneuphemized forms of the phrase in Mt 11.19/Lk 7.34 ordinarily translated "glutton and drunkard" (discussed in chap. 1). This memory is corroborated by his family's calling him "manic/not sober" (*exestē*) and the scribes' identifying him as "possessed," Markan code for chronically intoxicated (Mk 3.21–22; see chap. 6).

The Events at Pentecost

In his handling of the Pentecost story in Acts, presumably historical, Luke unintentionally confirms the apostles' reputations as Galilean drunkards. This and the alcoholism theme of Joel and Psalm 16, the texts employed by Peter in his Pentecost proclamation, are discussed in chapter 5, which reconstructs the historical core of the Pentecost event and Peter's speech.

The Rule of God

The phrase "rule of God," the name of Jesus' program, has no known source. Neither a Pauline invention nor a derivation from existing Jewish concepts, it is, according to Burton Mack, "most probably an early construction of some Jesus movement."[52] Mack mentions (p. 72) what he holds to be the only authentic rule-of-God sayings: Lk 11.20

and 17:20–21 and Mt 11.12. All three lend themselves to an alcohol interpretation: The first speaks of exorcisms without mentioning healings, which is original Markan code referring to alcoholism cures (see chap. 6). The second is the much-disputed text "the rule of God is in the midst of you/within you," which exactly reflects the dual locus today's alcoholics assign to what they call "the Program." The third is Matthew's strange statement that, from the days of John the Baptist, the rule of God (Matthew writes "Heaven") "has suffered violence, and men of violence take it by force [*biazetai kai biastai*]." *Biazō*, ordinarily rendered as "to suffer violence," actually names any strong, radical, dramatic, upsetting action. What Jesus originally said was, "The rule of God [the program] is gotten by taking action, and it is the active ones who seize onto it." This urgency is echoed in modern recovery parlance spoken to newcomers, "Take action! Do whatever is necessary to get this program! The only chance you have is to grab hold of this program!" *Biazō* also occurs in Lk 16.16, where it is translated as persons "forcing" or "pressing" or "entering violently" the rule of God. Its location immediately after the parable of the radical action of the unjust steward indicates that Jesus meant that those who get the rule of God are those who want it badly enough to take strong action. Generally speaking, given the crucial importance in today's sobriety program of turning one's life over to the care and direction of God, "rule of God" seems exactly the term one might expect as the self-designation of an ancient sobriety movement based on similar principles of spiritual living.

Wine-free Eucharists

Numerous Jesus communities existed whose members abstained from ritual wine or drank their Eucharist in water only, a practice both symbolic and concretely representational of recovery. Scholars ancient and modern routinely interpret this practice as evidence of gnostic asceticism, fanatical Encratite abstinence. Although teetotalers had always existed in the ancient world (e.g., Nazirites and Rechabites), the position here is that abstinence can also be viewed as evidence of sobriety groups living in the shadow of the Christ cults and other Jesus movements.

The Thomas Groups   The alter-Jesus Thomas ("twin") groups would have been one manifestation of the movement. Logion 28 of the Gospel of Thomas attributes to Jesus the following:

> I took my place in the midst of the world, and I appeared to them in the flesh. I found all of them drunk; I found none of them thirsty [for

the water of sobriety]. And my soul became afflicted for the sons of men. . . . So for the moment they are drunk. But when they abjure their wine, their minds will be changed.[53]

Abjuring wine and a changing of mind *(metanoia)* were central to the thinking of the Markan groups. Although most gnostic-ascetic writings are dated to the second century and later, Helmet Koester says that the Gospel of Thomas originated perhaps "as early as the second half of the first century."[54] In any event, this and certain other logia from Thomas smack more of recovery than of asceticism.

Heb 10.29   Edward J. Kilmartin discerns a first-century chalice dispute behind Heb 10.29, which promises severe punishment for the Christian who "deems unclean the blood of the covenant by which he was sanctified," that is, who refuses to drink the eucharistic wine.[55] Neither Pharisees nor ascetics regarded fully fermented wine as unclean, but exdrunkards might well have employed some version of that concept as an ironic coterie locution referring to ritual wine, which they surely avoided at all costs, along with wine on all other occasions. Dating from the mid-50s, Heb 10.29 could thus represent a Christian anathema directed at the abstinent sobriety groups before the ascetics took them over. A similar admonition to water drinkers may lie behind the core of 1 Tm 5.23, "drink no water but a little wine."

Spiritual Seders   Joachim Jeremias discusses a line of scholarship based on the Epistula Apostolorum (140–70 C.E.) to the effect that the earliest Palestinian Christians emulated Jesus' Last Supper abstinence and neither ate nor drank at their Passover seders.[56] If what was remembered was the double disavowal of bread and wine later recorded by Luke (22.16 and 18), the practice may have been that of ascetics. If it was the disavowal of wine alone (Mk 14.25), however, it could reflect groups of former wine addicts turned water drinkers for whom bread was a spiritual symbol of the word of their recovery program. Jeremias explains this abstinence as fasting motivated by expectation of the Parousia, an explanation based on religious fundamentalism, as is the statement in the Epistula that the fast was broken at dawn. Apart from explanations on grounds of religion, if one regards the Lukan double disavowal as an invention of ascetics later in the century, and the Markan single disavowal as authentic, then the fasting that Jeremias mentions could well have been the abstinence of sober alcoholics patterned on Jesus' disavowal at the Last Supper.

Acts of Thomas   In the pseudepigraphic Acts of Thomas, in the tenth
act titled "How Mygdonia Receives Baptism," the convert Mygdonia
rejects the offer of wine from her handmaiden, whereupon Thomas
anoints her in oil. The following rite ensues:

> Now there was a spring of water there, and going to it the apostle bap-
> tized Mygdonia in the name of the Father and the Son and the Holy
> Spirit. And when she was baptized and clothed, he broke bread and
> took a cup of water, and made her partaker in the body of Christ and
> the cup of the Son of God, and said, "Thou has received thy seal, and
> thy eternal life."[57]

Günther Bornkamm believes that this and other liturgical content in
the Acts of Thomas point to a gnostic sect: "The Eucharist which is
celebrated in the *ATh* is a communion in the bread alone (cc. 27, 29,
49f., 133), and the cup associated with it a cup of water (c. 120)."[58]
Issues of gnosticism aside, this cup can be seen as the same cup that
alcoholics would have recognized as the contextually obscured but
highly significant referent of the seemingly innocuous cup of water
mentioned in Mk 9.41, an element of the entrance rite practiced in
the Markan movement from the outset (see chap. 6).

Daily Baptists   Glenn Koch's study of the Panarion discusses Epiphanius's belief that the Eucharist was celebrated without wine not only
by Ebionite groups but also by sects mentioned by Marcion and Tatian
and by various Encratite groups. He has heard of an Ebionite sect he
calls "Daily Baptists." Epiphanius takes literally the idea that this
group performed a ritual bath each day and also says they "use water only" for that part of the eucharistic mystery opposite the bread.[59]
Three hundred years after the fact, Epiphanius assumed that the
Daily Baptists were ascetics. Chapter 6 discusses the notion of baptism as Markan camouflage signifying the addict's surrender experience. So the Daily Baptists could have been Markôs people who replaced wine by water "one day at a time," to use the modern idiom.
Further, the "man carrying a jar of water" on Passover eve (Mk 14.13,
discussed in chap. 2) certainly identifies the Markans as water drinkers, ritually as well as realistically.

Further Witnesses   In his study of non-Pauline eucharistic practice,
Hans Lietzmann cites references to the use of bread but no wine not
only in the Acts of Thomas but in the Clementine Homilies, Acts of
Peter, Acts of John, and an epistle of Cyprian, concluding: "From all
this we learn, with regard to the oldest stage of this type of eucha-

rist, that there existed a form of the rite which contained only the consecration of the bread, and knew nothing of the blessing of the wine."[60] Lietzmann goes on to suggest that Paul invented the wine ritual, a conclusion completely opposite to the present position, which attributes it to Jesus at the Last Supper.

Historians of the Christian liturgy were quick to refute Lietzmann. Gregory Dix, for example, claims that none of the witnesses to wine-free Eucharists date from earlier than 150 C.E. and then says, "all the apocryphal 'Acts' which furnish the evidence for these peculiar eucharists also teach the 'Encratite' view of sexual intercourse,"[61] thereby implying that such rites are the inventions of second-century gnostic ascetics. The fact that the surviving witnesses are late and clearly Encratite, however, does not mean that the practices they report did not originate in the first century before the entrance of ascetics into the Jesus groups. Indeed, it is unlikely that so many witnesses to wine-free Eucharists would have appeared if they were not somehow connected with actual practices antedating the Roman War. Dix seems to think that accepting Lietzmann's view means that one must abandon the Pauline and Markan accounts of the Last Supper, but that is not the case. The position here is that Jesus did institute a wine ritual intended for all disciples, but only until they experience the conviction of powerlessness over drink, from which point on their communions would be free of wine, as was Jesus' at the Last Supper. In short, one need not give up a traditional picture of the primitive Eucharist to believe that liturgies without wine occurred in the Markôs groups from the very beginning.

The Gospel of John

Chapter 7 argues that the earliest Johannine community knew the Cana story, minus the redacted participle "made wine" in Jn 2.9, as an account of the replacement of wine by water oxymoronically labeled "choice wine." So read, the story echoes Jesus' Last Supper replacement of real wine by "new wine" and supports the idea of Proto-John as a collection of recovery parables for the newly sober. Apparently the primitive form of John emerged within the Markôs fellowship soon after Jesus' disappearance. This community had no bread-and-wine Eucharist and imaged Jesus as the personification of divine wisdom that kept them sober, much as today's alcoholics might say that the words of the A.A. program represent the wisdom of sobriety. Later versions of the Johannine text leave sobriety issues behind, reflecting as they do a subsequent conflict with ascetics, a postwar dispute with non-Christian Jews, and a final catholic redaction (see chap. 7).

The Wine Bowls of Revelation

Chapter 7 also interprets the wine-bowl septet and the bowl angel's prophecy in the Book of Revelation as the work of a writer in touch with the Markôs movement in its final years. From the alcoholism angle, Revelation's wine-and-wrath imagery strongly implies a community familiar with the alcoholic illness. Overall, the Book of Revelation emerges as a prophecy of a bimillennial church age marked by drunkenness and violence and destined to culminate in crisis, apocalypse, and sobriety for the chosen—exactly the sort of view one would expect from an end-of-century Markan.

The Servant Figure

Given Jesus' allusions to the Isaian servant, interpreted in chapter 3 as a type of the derelict alcoholic and hence as addiction bearer for the many, the absence of a Jesus-servant linkage within the Jerusalem church is explainable by the theory that that community had denied and suppressed this very important connection, even as its members denied and suppressed every memory of Jesus' alcoholism and their own. How might this have happened among the Jerusalem brotherhood? As their Pentecost enthusiasm waned, some of the sober drunks saw the futility of playing street-corner evangelist and returned to the anonymity of their sobriety program, while others in their number, together with nonalcoholic converts eager to exalt the personage of Jesus, began transforming their community into a Christ cult wherein the topic of Jesus and the Suffering Servant as alcoholics became forbidden matter. The two factions would have separated and remained apart until the Roman War and the ascetics' takeover of the sobriety groups. In short, denial and forgetting would have had their way with truth in the Jerusalem church. Certainly the "pillars" with whom Paul conferred on his second visit to Jerusalem around 48 C.E. (see Galatians 2) gave no evidence of the concerns of recovery.

Miscellaneous Clues

Various other material also counts as evidence of Jesus' alcoholism and points to his primitive groups as a sobriety fellowship:

A *"Fertilizing Spring"* Josephus's strange reference to "Capharnaum," which Matthew calls Jesus' "own city" (9.1), not as a town at all but as a "highly fertilizing spring called by the inhabitants Capharnaum"[62] may, unknowingly to Josephus, reflect a local memory of that city as the birthplace of the Galilean sobriety movement founded by Jesus, of which the water image "fertilizing spring" would have been a coterie emblem.

Donkey-headed Graffiti   Certain rather peculiar second-century anti-Christian ass's head graffiti[63] may reflect an unrecognized drunkenness idiom referring to Christians as "donkey heads," a locution stemming from the north-Aramaic "donkey/wine" paronomasia which in turn underlies the secret donkey business in Mark's story of the Jerusalem entrance (Mk 11.1–7). The linkage to wine is reinforced by Justin's claim (*First Apology*, par. 32, 262) that the disciples found the ass tied to a vine (Gn 49.11). This "donkey/wine" pun and the possible drunkenness idiom are discussed at length in chapter 6.

Celsus   Origen quotes Celsus as describing Jesus at Golgotha as "rushing with his mouth open to drink" rather than "bearing his thirst as an ordinary man" (see chap. 2, note 48), a slander whose source could well have been Jesus' reputation as a drunkard.

Paul's Silence   Paul's remarkable and quite unexplained refusal to hand on any biographical information about Jesus, and his equally curious avoidance of contact with any apostles save Peter and James in his parley in Jerusalem around 35 C.E. (Gal 1.18–19), may stem from his knowledge that Jesus and the first disciples were tainted by alcohol addiction, hence somehow unclean or unworthy. In the Christ mysticism he infused into the gentile churches, Paul apparently substituted the cross of Barabbas for the inebriety of Barnasha as source of the "scandal and foolishness" of the Christ event.

Taken together, the foregoing material provides extra-Markan evidence supporting the principal hypothesis of this book: the Markôs groups constituted a sobriety fellowship that remembered Jesus as a former wine addict.

The Genre of Mark
Sui Generis

The issue of genre has concerned modern Mark scholars almost as much as matters of provenance have. Among the first applications of modern literary-critical theory to Mark were T. Boomershine's rhetorical study and Dan O. Via, Jr.'s, tragicomedic structuralist analysis.[64] Werner H. Kelber focused on literary aspects of the gospel in explaining Mark's choice of the story form to confer authority on a Jerusalem community Kelber believed had disappeared in the Roman-Jewish War.[65] Although he considers the Passion narrative to be an example of a fabula, Frank Kermode finds the startling intercalations and oppositions in Mark 1–13 unfollowable as narrative, the consequence of unrecoverable understandings between a long dead writer and audience.[66] David Rhoads and Donald Michie analyze the various literary components of Mark, particularly the narrator's role and characteristic patterns such as two-step progressions and items in series of three.[67] Jack Dean Kingsbury employs a literary analysis of the secrecy motif in Mark as a way of construing the christology of Mark.[68] Howard Clark Kee begins his sociocultural study by reviewing research on claims for the genres of aretalogy (deeds of a god), tragedy, origin myth, Hellenistic romance, comedy, martyrology, and chria (sayings of a sage) and ends by agreeing with Amos Wilder that Mark created a "wholly new" genre.[69]

Writing from a viewpoint of classical rhetoric, George A. Kennedy identifies a variety of Hellenistic rhetorical forms in his survey of New Testament Scriptures.[70] Also arguing from the perspective of ancient rhetoric, Vernon Robbins contends that the genre of Mark is that of the memorabilia of a sage *(apomnemoneumata)* and that the interchanges between Jesus and the disciples reflect the teaching process between a sage and his students involving Hellenistic pedagogical forms.[71] In a comprehensive analysis, Mary Ann Tolbert rejects the Jewish forms of apocalypse and midrash as too limited in their application to Mark. About the three genres she then discusses—aretalogy, biography, and memorabilia—she concludes that "each . . . by emphasizing so strongly one aspect of Mark's story, of necessity must omit or undervalue other parts of the story. In fact, if one could *combine* [her emphasis] an aretalogy's focus on miracle-working, a biography's focus on the character of Jesus, and a memorabilia's focus on the teaching cycle between Jesus and the disciples, one would have almost created an adequate generic formulation for the Gospel of Mark."[72] Tolbert goes on to argue her thesis that Mark is a work of ancient popular culture, a novel or romance similar in pattern and technology to extant works recounting the misadventures of young lovers at the hands of the god Eros. Of greatest relevance here, however, as indicated below, is Tolbert's suggestion that a combination of forms conceivably might compose the gospel's genre.

Conventional notions about genre undergo surprising revision in reader-response criticism. For example, the critic Adena Rosmarin writes that "genre is the most powerful explanatory tool available to the literary critic." For Rosmarin, genre should be defined pragmatically and rhetorically rather than naturally or representationally. Genre terms become topoi for literary interpretation. The operative issue is not avowed authorial intent but how well the chosen genre explains the work. The critic "manipulates his genre, deducing particulars from it until he thinks his readers will 'recognize' a particular text." Rosmarin quotes E. H. Gombrich's remark that the interpretive task consists not in finding accurate comparisons but in "inventing comparisons which work."[73] As discussed later, the genre to which Mark's gospel is compared herein is that of the recovering alcoholic's sobriety story. The particular story in question is Jesus' account of his own illness and recovery.

What makes the Markan genre puzzle so baffling is that Mark had to conceal Jesus' recovery story from nonalcoholic readers by making it appear to be other than what it was. How did he achieve the necessary camouflage? First of all, Mark transformed Jesus' first-person story as memorialized by the sobriety groups into a third-person narrative controlled by an omniscient and seemingly trustworthy narrator. Second, Mark knew his literary forms, and he knew how the nonalcoholic Jesus groups and the Christ cults, both gentile and Jewish, typologized their understandings of Jesus and therefore what genres they would select in recognizing the gospel's text and assessing its validity. Thus he resorted to exactly the combinatory strategy Tolbert alludes to, shaping his materials so that his diverse audiences would see just enough aretalogy, biography, and memorabilia, not to mention midrash and apocalyptic and Roman Son-of-God political vocabulary, to satisfy their expectations. Lastly, confident that his secret was safe, Mark included in the final episodes of his book certain allegories not in Jesus' original story, which his alcoholic readers would interpret as critical of the politically expedient religious hierarchicalism that sooner or later, Mark believed, would come to dominate the Jesus movement in postwar Palestine.[74] In short, Mark transformed and embedded Jesus' sobriety story within a carefully constructed collage of forms familiar to different groups of readers, whose complexity would endlessly intrigue text analysts, thus diverting them from the hidden recovery story.

Indirectly supporting the recovery-story theory is the fact that literary commentators frequently mention features of Mark's gospel pointing to its original identity as an oral story and to the atypicality of its narrative form. Kermode discusses its lack of coherent narrative form.[75] Rhoads and Michie point out that Mark is terse and quick-paced, marked by a "brevity of style and rapidity of motion [that] give the narrative a tone of urgency."[76] Martin Hengel labels Mark a "dramatic narrative" and speaks of the "apparent artlessness" of "individual pericopes strung together one after the other."[77] C. S. Mann cites a work by Franz Nierynck "calling attention to a phenomenon which appears characteristic of spoken style—that of making a broad statement in one sentence and then proceeding to refine it by words or phrases in succeeding sentences."[78] C. H. Turner noted the "autobiographical" flavor of Mark, how it seems to record "the experience of an eyewitness" wherein the many instances of the third-person "they" in the text have replaced the first-person "we" of the original account.[79] All this underscores the gospel's oral quality while reflecting the continuing search by readers for the gospel's genre. Turner and others, of course, think that the orality stems from Peter's eyewitness recollections. No one has seen that it could have come directly from Jesus, as a transformation of his story first told at the Last Supper and then postpaschally in Galilee and memorialized in the Markôs groups.

As for Mark's narrator, Rhoads and Michie characterize the effect of his omniscience as follows: "The unlimited knowledge of the omniscient narrator, unbound by time or space and able to know the minds of the characters, gives the narrator tremendous authority with the reader, who comes to trust the narrator as a reliable guide in the world of the story."[80] In Mark the narrator's main function is to confine nonalcoholic readers to the world of the religious gospel. A crucial example was observed in the Gethsemane pericope (Mk 14.35; see chap. 2). What it reports is not direct but indirect discourse, a device of Markan concealment wherein the narrator's linguistic ambiguities ensure that an unknowing audience will read the verse not as Jesus' request for help in making his surrender but as signifying a moment of wavering on Jesus' part wherein he shrinks from the violence he sees approaching and asks to be spared his destined crucifixion. Mark expected religious readers to trust the narrator completely, confident that his alcoholics would not be misled in the slightest.

In summary, the position argued here is that the textual surface of the Gospel of Mark displays no recognizable genre identity. In other words, its distinctive genre feature is that it is sui generis. From the perspective of recovery, Mark is a pastiche of elements of different genres camouflaging an underlying alcoholism story so as to conceal it from religious readers who, were they to have recognized its actual character, would have anathematized the book and thwarted Mark's very purpose in writing it.

Mark as Sobriety Story

The alcoholism story is basically a type of the fundamental biblical narrative: prisoners to the Edenic curses, humans attempt to live by self-empowerment, produce suffering and chaos, hit bottom and cry out, and are rescued by a nameless and invisible other they ultimately call "God." The story of the Israelites' Egyptian captivity and exodus follows this pattern, as do psalms such as 16 and 116. Elijah's encounter with God is a paradigm recovery story (1 Kgs 19.4–12): brought low and thinking of dying (hitting bottom), Elijah falls asleep (spiritual death), whereupon an angel (messenger of sobriety) invites him to eat bread (hear the word of recovery) and drink water (not wine), not once but twice (stage one, then stage two), journey forty days (the suffering in recovery), meet God on a mountain (sobriety), and know him via a still, small voice (inner awareness of the living God). Ancient or modern, recovery stories can change lives. By sharing their stories alcoholics progress in sobriety and carry a message of *metanoia* to those who still suffer.

A Rhetorical Genre To identify the recovery story concealed in Mark, nonalcoholic readers must become acquainted with the genre features of such stories. As oral discourse prompted by a particular social exigency, recovery stories are best studied from a perspective of rhetorical criticism. In a way that literary criticism does not, rhetorical criticism stresses the role of social situation in any definition of genre. For Karlyn Kohrs Campbell and Kathleen Hall Jamieson, "the rhetorical forms that establish genres are stylistic and substantive responses to perceived situational demands."[81] Carolyn R. Miller argues that "a rhetorically sound definition of genre must be centered not on the substance or the form of discourse but on the action it is used to accomplish."[82] Miller believes that classification of discourse should be based "upon recurrent situation or, more specifically, upon exigence understood as social motive."[83] Miller identifies three ways that a collection of discourses may fail to constitute a genre: "First, there may fail to be significant substantive or formal similarities at the lower levels of the hierarchy [of rules for symbolic interaction]. . . . Second, there may be inadequate consideration of all the elements in recurrent rhetorical situations. . . . The third way a genre may fail is if there is no pragmatic component, no way to understand the genre as a social action."[84] These criteria serve to highlight features of the recovery story as a rhetorical genre.

The alcoholic's story is a first-person monologue of three parts telling "what we were like, what happened, and what we are like now."[85] These three parts respectively depict a speaker's descent toward the "bottom" of his or her alcoholic illness, then the turning-point experience, and lastly a paean of gratitude celebrating sobriety. This tripartite structure is a highly stable feature of the recovery story. Part one of the story, generally its longest part, is often called the "drunkalogue." Drunkalogues recount the worsening of the speaker's condition through a chain of anecdotes illustrating the progressive nature of addiction. The phenomenon of chained anecdotes explains the defective narrative form frequently remarked in the textual surface of Mark. For readers employing the interpretive schema of worsening alcoholism, however, chapters 1 through 13 of Mark will appear as well-formed discourse.

Social Effect   The recurrent social situation in which the recovery story is told is meetings of former drinkers conducted for the purpose of hearing speakers tell their stories. Falling outside the three kinds of rhetoric named by Aristotle—deliberative, forensic, and epideictic—the recovery story constitutes a fourth kind, which may be termed metanoetic. The substance of metanoetic rhetoric consists of recollection as its element and crisis (radical decision) as its aim, while its form consists of identification. Two kinds of auditors are ordinarily present, sober alcoholics whose minds have been changed and others, both wet and dry as to drink, who are awaiting the changing of mind and sobriety. For sober auditors the story's social motive is its celebration of sobriety; for all others it is getting sober. The action the story accomplishes for sober persons is the active experience of gratitude; for others it is the receipt of new-mindedness *(metanoia)* relative to drinking.

Fully describing the situational element of the recovery story requires further attention to the two kinds of auditors, sober persons and those awaiting sobriety. Nonsober hearers identify the drunkalogue as a jeremiad narrating the woes they have known as a result of drink and unredeemed self. For most it is the first time they have heard such matters acknowledged openly. If their identification with the jeremiad is strong enough, the turning-point narrative triggers an epiphanal crisis opening the hearer's mind to spiritual intervention manifest in an awareness of other and a new freedom to act radically and differently, specifically, to stop drinking and start working a recovery program. The third part of the story, the gratitude song, if heard at all, serves mainly to evoke wonderment.

By contrast, sober auditors of the recovery story hear the drunka-logue as a jeremiad turned comedic by virtue of their having survived the woes of drink it portrays. This explains in part the laughter characteristic of A.A. meetings and the faintly derisive tone of the term *drunkalogue* itself. For sober hearers the turning-point narrative triggers memories of their own *metanoia* moments. These in turn quicken an awareness of gratitude that allows these hearers to rejoice along with the speaker in the third part of the story, the paean of gratitude, actually an epideictic celebration of recovery. So the overall social effect of the recovery story is that the nonsober get sober, while the sober are confirmed in sobriety and exercised in joy.

Beyond accomplishing these social actions, the sobriety story possesses certain additional genre features observable in the Markan text. Two formal features are tripartite structures at various levels and two-stage events. These point to the tripartite structure of the recovery story and the two-stageness of recovery as a spiritual process. A substantive feature is the apocalyptic content of the story, which corresponds to the apocalyptic material in Mark.

Three-partness As noted, a salient feature of the recovery story is its construction in three parts. "Three-partness" has been widely observed in Mark, for example, the three boat scenes, three bread stories, three Passion predictions, Jesus' three returns to the sleeping disciples in Gethsemane, the three hours mentioned in connection with the Crucifixion, Peter's three denials, and so on. Rhoads and Michie point out that the idea of progression is key to this genre feature: "a threefold series is no mere repetition of similar events, but involves a progressive development. . . . The reader is thereby prepared to view the three episodes of a series in relation to each other. That is, when the series unfolds, the reader then looks back from the perspective of the third scene and understands more clearly the issues involved in the first and second scenes."[86] These three-item series serve as Markan signposts reminding the knowing reader that three-partness is a heuristic feature of great importance both to their identification of the text as a recovery story and to their recognition of its parts.

The three parts of Mark's narrative, which is to say, of Jesus' recovery story, are as follows:

1. drunkalogue: chapters 1 through 13 (the last of which adumbrates Jesus' turning-point apocalypse);
2. turning point: the supper and garden pericopes, 14.22–26 and 32–42;

3. paean of gratitude: evidences of Jesus' sobriety and spiritual awakening following the garden pericope, in 14.43–16.8, passim.

Apparently the traditional characterization of Mark as a passion narrative with a lengthy introduction arose from a sense of the structural unity and preamble-like function of the part of Jesus' story identified here as the drunkalogue.

Stage 1/Stage 2   Another feature of the sobriety story is its two-stageness, which reflects the recovery process. Most alcoholics experience their recovery in two stages separated by a time interval. Stage one of getting sober involves relief from habitual intoxication, and stage two involves recovery from mental drunkenness as evidenced in catastrophic attempts to live by self-empowerment. The basic event sequence sees alcoholics hit bottom, ask for help, and enjoy an ecstatic "honeymoon" period free of drink, only to realize, as a result of working the six middle steps of the twelve-step recovery program, that they are victims of a more profound kind of bondage even than alcohol, bondage to self. Both Isaiahs spoke of the phenomenon of mental drunkenness apart from physical intoxication: "Be drunk, but not from wine; stagger, but not from strong drink" (29.9) and "Listen to this, afflicted one, drunk but not from wine" (51.22). Ultimately persons hit bottom a second time, humbly surrendering not just their alcohol problems but their wills and their lives to God. This is the ego-death involved in a person's definitive third step, the transition to stage two of sobriety. Afterward, persons progress to the final three steps of the program, which specify continuing inventory and prayer, spiritual awakening, principled living, and efforts to carry the message of recovery to others.

The passage to stage two of recovery can be relatively painless, or it can be just the opposite. Some people must suffer greatly from mental drunkenness before their spiritual awakenings. The differences are dramatic enough that it is possible to discern "type-one stories" and "type-two stories." The event sequence just given describes the type-one story. By contrast, the type-two event sequence sees persons conclude their sobriety honeymoon without completely giving themselves to the recovery program. Their mental drunkenness becomes pronounced, marked by paranoia and increasing self-will. Endeavoring to carry the message to others, they grow progressively angrier and more dictatorial when their efforts fail. Victims of a pitfall called "two stepping," these persons try to stay sober on steps one and twelve alone, not drinking but fanatically taking others' inventories instead of their own and attempting to give away what they do not have. Frequently they return to drink, with terrible consequences. After further suffering, they may finally hit bottom and acknowledge powerlessness over self as well as alcohol. Those who do will ultimately attain stage two of sobriety. Readers will have recognized that Jesus' story is of type two. That is, it exemplifies the second type of event sequence in the two-stage progression to recovery.

Commentators have always recognized that Mark relies on stage one/stage two as a structural motif, but they have never agreed as to its purpose. Examples are the movement from the Galilean to the Jerusalem ministry; the three two-stage parabolic stories just before the juncture between these ministries (the dual responses to the Syro-Phoenician woman in 7.24–30, the healing of a man's deafness and then his muteness in 7.31–37, and the cure of the blind man who first sees partially and then fully in 8.22–26); the second baptisms referred to in 10.38–39; the first and second prayers for removal of the cup in Gethsemane; and two-stage progressions in discourse elements such as statements, questions, imperatives, and descriptions.[87] The position here is that Mark was fully aware of stage one/stage two as a motif constitutive of the recovery-story genre.

Mark announces the stage-one/stage-two motif at the outset, in the prologue of his gospel, which speaks of Jesus Messiah, late Isaiah, the Babylonian captivity, *metanoia*, and baptism in the spirit (1.1–8):

> (1.1) The beginning of the Gospel of Jesus Christ, the Son of God. (2) As it is written in Isaiah the prophet, "Behold, I send my messenger before thy face, who shall prepare the way of the Lord. . . ." (4) John the baptizer appeared in the wilderness, preaching a baptism of repentance [*metanoia*, after-knowledge] for the forgiveness of sins. . . . (7) And he preached, saying, "After me comes he who is mightier than I. . . . (8) I have baptized you with water; but he will baptize you with the Holy Spirit."

The key to Mark's intention lies in seeing each of the elements of the prologue as the stage-two member of a stage-one/stage-two pair that becomes apparent when each element is expressed in terms of contrastive foci: not John the Baptist, who came first, but Jesus, who came second; not early Isaiah but late Isaiah; not the earlier Egyptian captivity but the more recent Babylonian; not first knowledge but after-knowledge; not water baptism, which initiates recovery, but spiritual baptism, which culminates it. In short, the multiple stage-two emblems at the beginning of the gospel serve to alert alcoholic readers that the gospel recounts the second stage of Jesus' sobriety story, not the first, which would have covered his prebaptism drunkenness.

Apocalyptic Yet another substantive genre feature of the recovery story important in Mark's gospel is its apocalyptic content. A key issue in Markan studies concerns the kind of apocalyptic the gospel contains. As is often pointed out (see chap. 5, note 16), the apocalyptic in Mark does not fit the traditional pattern depicting God as siding with a good Israel against its evil enemies, for the cataclysm Jesus seemingly predicts falls on Israel itself. Dan Via sees Mark as formally and thematically "quite atypical of apocalyptic." For Via, "Jesus' whole story is the paradigm which gives the clue to the content and quality of existence in history."[88] And the essence of Jesus' story, as seen from the perspective of alcoholism, is inner change. Via agrees, stating that Jesus at the outset of the narrative is not who he is at the end, but through a dying-rising process he becomes the saving Son of Man/Son of God prepared to carry the message of life to others ready to follow him and undergo the same death and resurrection in an ongoing temporal process.[89] Just as it is in Mark's gospel, apocalyptic understood as radically changed thinking *(metanoia)* is a theme in both the recovery process and the sobriety story.

Ancient apocalyptic consists of warnings about impending revelatory crises and the dire consequences of the critical choices involved, descriptions of the signs of these crises, and accounts of the crisis experiences, all represented in a veiled and symbolic manner. Recovery stories typically feature such important apocalyptic moments as the following: recognition of alcohol as adversary; conviction of powerlessness; decision to quit drinking and to ask for help; recognition of self as the ultimate enemy; and a final ironic understanding of alcohol as friend indeed, a goad to recovery. Also featured are insights such as the importance of keeping watch for the revelation and taking action when it comes, and of looking not to personages but to spiritual principles for help. These are precisely the insights and revelations the Markan Jesus communicates in his apocalyptic discourse (Mark 13) and in the Last Supper and Gethsemane pericopes viewed from the perspective of alcoholism. The downside of apocalyptic, of course, is that persons who refuse to watch and act often perish, both individually and as nations, which is what the cataclysm imagery of apocalyptic depicts.

Hence it should be clear why warnings, consequences, and signs of apocalypse are voiced throughout the alcoholic's drunkalogue. For example, speakers often say that continued drinking leads only to death or insanity, while sobriety requires a complete change of thinking. These warnings parallel the outer and inner cataclysms portrayed in biblical apocalyptic. Beyond the physical carnage caused by drunkenness, another sign of impending apocalypse is the recognition that alcohol is not working anymore, is not the effective nostrum it once was. This sign is found in the apocalypses of Joel (1.12; see chap. 5) and first Isaiah (24.7–11) and is the deeper meaning of the "failed wine" of Jn 2.2. A stage-two revelation is that fighting, pain, and suffering result from efforts to change and control other people. This is Jesus' referent in Mk 10.38–39 when he speaks about the second baptism awaiting all disciples who seek to lord it over others. Finally, all of Mark 13 is a collection of apocalyptic admonitions clustered around the image of the "desolating sacrilege" (13.14), whose implied recognition by Jesus provides the basis for everything he says and does at the Last Supper and in Gethsemane (see chap. 6 for an exegesis of Mark 13). Overall, the issue of apocalyptic, given short shrift in so many theories of Markan intention, represents yet another topic of correspondence between recovery conceptuality and Markan thinking manifested as a genre feature of Mark's book.

Jesus' Story Reconstructed

Jesus as Addict

Although images of Jesus have abounded in diversity from antiquity to the present, no one has noticed that Jesus' career bears the earmarks of alcoholic suffering and recovery. Among modern writers, for example, Jaroslav Pelikan has surveyed Jesus' place in the history of culture;[90] Hans Küng has catalogued the Christs of piety, of dogma, of the enthusiasts, and of literature;[91] Dennis Duling has studied christological conceptions of Jesus through history;[92] John Hayes presents a continuum of modern interpretations ranging from Son of Man to superstar;[93] Patrick Allitt has described pseudoscholarly American images of Jesus shaped by special interest groups such as urban reformers, socialists, capitalist boosters, secular humanists, promoters of racial pride, and temperance advocates;[94] and Anton Wessels describes perceptions of Jesus in Asia, India, and Africa and among Jews, Moslems, Hindus, and Taoists.[95] Scholars such as Günther Bornkamm, Michael Grant, Paula Fredriksen, Dominic Crossan, and Marcus Borg have studied Jesus from religiously neutral historical perspectives.[96] Contemporary christological conceptions of Jesus generated within the field of religious studies have viewed Jesus as a Galilean charismatic, rabbi, Pharisee, Essene, and end-time prophet.[97] Jesus has also been imaged from other diverse perspectives: psychology, ancient magic, Marxism, myth, sexuality, feminist biology, popular reification, and Mesopotamian drug culture.[98] Recent studies regard Jesus as rhetorician, Cynic sage, faith catalyst, hero of an ancient novel, married founder of a European bloodline, Qumran priest, Mediterranean peasant, preacher of Jewish restoration eschatology, and antinationalist Jew.[99] But no one has seen Jesus as an addict.

Traits of alcoholism have been observed in Jesus, however, although never named as such, since apart from chronic drinking, symptoms of the illness have only recently been identified. For example, famous nineteenth-century lives by Ernest Renan and David Friedrich Strauss represented Jesus pathologically, as a fanatic and a man obsessed.[100] H. J. Holtzmann noted a psychological movement from success to suffering to failure.[101] In his medical dissertation Albert Schweitzer refuted certain biblically naive psychiatric studies that had characterized Jesus in terms such as paranoia, delusion, and hallucination.[102] What alcoholics call "mental drunkenness" is exactly what was sensed in these liberal biographies and psychiatric studies. Warner Fite applied to Jesus an alcohol idiom supposedly first said of Spinoza, calling him "der Gottbetrunkene Mensch" ("the God-intoxicated man").[103] Schweitzer's famous image of Jesus crushed beneath the great wheel of human history onto which he has hurled himself is fraught with unrecognized alcoholic grandiosity.[104] Mid-twentieth-century Jewish scholarship viewed Jesus as a Zealot driven by the belief that, since God must rule and not the Romans, he must overthrow the Romans to allow God to rule.[105] Recovering alcoholics would regard such obsessive and violent behavior in a former drinker as evidence of untreated alcoholism. Although Adolf Holl finds Jesus at home in various kinds of "bad company,"[106] and Lee Snook uses the term "anonymous Christ" to emphasize the multiple dimensions of salvation operative in the postmodern age,[107] the image of Jesus as a member of an anonymous sobriety fellowship would probably be foreign to the thinking of both men. The Jungian Edward Edinger characterizes Christ in psycho-spiritual terms meaningful to alcoholics, but in examining the symbolism of the blood of Christ, he completely ignores the salience that recovering alcoholics would assign to blood as a symbol of the physical carnage connected with wine.[108] The view of the present book, of course, is that Jesus' story is the alcoholic's story par excellence.

"Writing" Jesus' Story

Recall the maxim of reader-response criticism that texts are "written" only when read. How then to write the text of Jesus' story? Accord-

ing to the critic Wolfgang Iser, text production in readers progress-
es from the arousal of expectations to retrospective modification of
authorial artistry in the text the reader realizes. Readers' expectations
comprise features constitutive of the functional categories called
genres.[109] To enter the textual world of Mark's hidden gospel, therefore, nonalcoholic readers must bypass the narrator's pronounce-
ments, query the alcoholic reader as to relevant features of the recovery-story genre, look beyond those parts of the narrative that are
Markan camouflage and allegory and then listen for the voice of Jesus
speaking in prosopopeia, and construct their realizations of Jesus'
story accordingly.

Although Jesus may have recounted his entire story numerous
times after his return to Galilee (Mk 14.28 and 16.7), the theory
advanced here is that he told its initial part, the drunkalogue, for the
first time at the Last Supper. It has been observed that a lacuna occurs in Mark's account of the paschal seder at the point in the text
between the words over the bread and those over the cup.[110] Mark's
alcoholics would have recognized that Jesus' drunkalogue belongs in
this lacuna as a preamble to the wine message. In other words, Jesus
at the historical supper, in a spoken meditation occurring after the
words about bread (later memorialized as Mk 14.22) and before the
giving of the cup (later Mk 14.23), told of his descent into worsening alcoholism, starting with his Jordan experience and culminating
with the events in Jerusalem that had brought him to the hour at
hand (Mark 1–13). The content of this meditation is what later became part one, the drunkalogue, of his full story. Jesus then proceeded to enact or experience what Mark's narrative recounts as the wine
message (14.24), disavowal of drink (14.25), Hallel singing (14.26),
and Gethsemane surrender and prayer (14.35–39). These events
provided the content of part two, the turning point, of Jesus' story,
whenever he told it later on. Taken together, Jesus' drunkalogue and
his words about wine symbolically represent the "main meal" of the
paschal seder.

Here then is a reconstruction of Jesus' sobriety story as he would
have told it afterward in Galilee. Its purpose is to enable readers of
the gospel, both alcoholic and nonalcoholic, to visualize Mark's narrative as a first-person account and to hear it prosopopeially, as if told
by Jesus himself, exactly as the Markôs groups memorialized it before
Mark's writing. It is not, however, meant as a representation of Jesus'
speaking style or *ipsissima vox*, nor is its vocabulary keyed to the ancient language(s) Jesus spoke, whether Aramaic, Hebrew, or Greek.
Scriptural references are mostly to Mark. Important exceptions are

"unbridled drunkard" from Q, the Lukan version of the rejection at Nazareth (placed in the Markan order), and the Matthean accounts of the sending out of the disciples and the cursing of the unbelieving towns—content omitted by Mark presumably because he considered it a tipoff to Jesus' alcoholism and likely to scandalize his religious readers. Chapter 6 discusses in detail the exegeses implied by this reconstruction.

Drunkalogue

At the Last Supper Jesus introduced his drunkalogue by saying, "Pay attention, this is the message I embody" (14.22). But later on in Galilee, as the Markan nicknames came into use (see chap. 1), Jesus may have begun like this:

> "My name is Jesus and I am a Markôs (cupmaster), stump-fingered (sober) today by the grace of God.
>
> "Of my drinking in Galilee there is little to tell. I was an unbridled drunkard (Mt 11.19/Lk 7.34). My family finally cast me out (Dt 21.18–21). My wanderings took me to the Jordan and the man known as John the Baptist (1.9). A lifelong nondrinker (Lk 1.15), John knew how to put drunkards in touch with the power from above.
>
> "John charged me to let my mind be changed (*metanoia*, 1.4). He told me to stop trying to master wine and to drink water instead (1.8). No sooner had I drunk the water John gave me than I felt changed (1.10–11). Today I believe it was the action of God acknowledging me as his son in virtue of my admission of powerlessness (Ps 116.10 and 16).
>
> "My withdrawal from wine was a forty-days-in-the-wilderness experience. I hallucinated wild animals. John's disciples repeated the message of powerlessness to me until my cravings subsided. They kept me from yielding to the temptation to return to willpower instead of relying on God to handle my drink addiction (1.12–13).
>
> "Soon I began to carry the message to others. I called it the good news of the rule of God. I cried out to addicts, 'The time is now! The rule of God is within your grasp! Change your minds and catch hold of this good message!' (1.14–15). Then I gave them a cup of water to drink that they might know the meaning of Messiah, the ineffable joy of recovery (9.41).
>
> "At once men and women began leaving their families and work for fellowship in our sobriety program (1.16–20). When I would bid a drinker to admit his powerlessness, his release from the drink obsession was often as violent as if a demon had come out of him (1.21–26). Later I told a riddle about the effect of drink on humanity at large. I likened it to an outcast man possessed by a legion of demons, so strong no one could subdue him and insanely bent on destroying himself, yet altogether pacific and charged with gratitude after he sobered up (5.1–20).

"On my first return to Nazareth, the townspeople heard about my arrival in the company of other reputed drunkards and made a commotion. My family got word of it and came to take charge of me as they had always done, thinking I was drunk again (3.20–21). Some officials from Jerusalem said that my success with drunks proved only that I was drunk myself, but I explained in riddles that a drunk drunk cannot possibly get another drunk drunk sober (3.22–27).

"Soon all kinds of sick and hurting people began coming to us. They got better because they were willing to admit they needed help. I would say, 'Your act of trust has made you well.' The crowds got so large that we had to draw apart by ourselves for our sobriety meetings. The officials began accusing us of violating the law (1–3, passim).

"Still, it was a joyful time, that first season in Galilee. I codified the principles of sobriety into twelve propositions that we followed ourselves and conveyed to newcomers for the cure of drunkenness. We called them 'the Twelve' (3.14–15). I composed parables about the importance of the rule of God that I thought might catch the interest of persons still awaiting the conviction of powerlessness (4.1–41). I made a riddle about our group meetings. It compared the word of recovery spoken by the meeting leader to bread distributed to the multitude and the responses of group members to the multiplication of that bread feeding the many (6.35–44 and 8.1–10).

"I had a wonderful sobriety honeymoon, but it was not to last. On another visit to Nazareth I experienced my first bout of mental drunkenness, which ultimately led me to drink again. It was in the synagogue on the Sabbath. They asked me to read the messiah prophecy from the Isaiah scroll. I do not know why I did what I did next. It must have been fear. I felt it was wrong but did it anyway. At the end of the reading, I proclaimed the fulfillment of that Scripture in the hearing of those present! An uproar broke out. Who did I think I was? They said I was drunk and should heal myself before trying to heal others. I accused them of failing to honor my prophecy just because I was a local man they knew from before. The people got angry, I became more fearful and agitated, and they threatened to throw me off the cliff! I left town shaken and ashamed (6.1–6; Lk 4.16–30).

"From then on, things steadily grew worse. Angry at my rejection, I sent out the disciples to proclaim the rule of God in the surrounding towns. But I was so blinded by resentment and hurt pride stemming from the Nazareth debacle that I predicted their persecution and rejection while assuring them that a messianic theophany would occur before they were finished. I was oblivious to the insanity of my actions (6.7–12; Mt 10.16–23). When the disciples returned with nothing to report, no persecutions, no theophany, no conversions (6.30), I became enraged and cursed the unbelieving towns (Mt 11.20–24).

"By now the ecstasy of my newfound sobriety had vanished. Mental drunkenness commenced to run wild. I forgot that our program requires individual conversion. I decided that the way to bring the people to the rule of God was to convert their religious overlords. So I began disputing with these men, arguing my own interpretations of the law (7.1–22). Even worse, I concluded that my disciples were incapable of understanding me, and so I rejected them (8.14–21). I then left Galilee for Caesarea Philippi (8.27).

"What happened there sealed my fate. I learned that my disciples, confused by my mental drunkenness, were prepared to proclaim me the Messiah! This triggered such an attack of addictive self-will that even now I shudder to recall it. I knew I was not the Messiah, yet I began acting messianically. I could not help myself. I concluded that my compatriots would grasp the rule of God only if I went to Jerusalem and singlehandedly forced it on their religious leaders. There I would demonstrate the death of self through an act of heroic self-will. The absurdity of this decision was apparent, yet I was incapable of governing my actions, so drunk was my thinking (8.27–38).

"Looking back, I see that I was following only two of our twelve sobriety principles, the first and the last, not drinking and trying to carry the message. But the remaining principles were missing from my program. While I talked a good game (9.14–10.52, passim), I had forgotten completely about surrendering to the higher power and judging myself, not others, about powerlessness over self, and about prayerful contact with God. I was as drunk dry as if I had returned to drinking.

"Nor was it long before that unhappy event came to pass. Somewhere en route to Jerusalem I started on the wine again. I was drinking as I lectured my followers about service (10.35–45) and as I played the messianic guru in various ways during our journey to the holy city (9.14–10.52, passim).

"I was wine drunk on entering Jerusalem, as you well know, although those outside our fellowship, unaware of the 'donkey/wine' pun in our local speech, say that I was riding a donkey (11.1–10). My drunken actions ranged from cursing a barren fig tree to an act of public violence, seizing worshipers' drinking vessels in the Temple (11.11–17). I assaulted the priests and scribes verbally, with my parable about the vineyard (12.1–12) and with rhetorical ploys aimed at persuading them to renounce their religious offices and accept the rule of God (11.27–33 and 12.14–44). But my efforts changed no minds and only strengthened the officials' resolve to do away with me (11.18 and 12.12–13).

"Through all this I suffered terribly, not just from my drinking and self-contempt, especially after tasting sobriety, but because I knew I was out of control and unable to help myself or to ask for help, and all the time afraid that a horrible end was coming soon. I felt that sense of impending doom present in our apocalyptic writings.

"But that was my last drunk. For the next day, hungover and remorseful, I experienced a revelation. I saw that my problem was not the religious authorities or my followers or the people or even wine itself; my problem was me. I had hit bottom at last."

Turning Point

His drunkalogue concluded, Jesus would have proceeded to tell the turning point of his story, events recorded in Mark's supper and garden pericopes (14.22–26 and 32–42):

> "What happened was that I arrived sober for our Passover seder (14.17). As I distributed the matzo, I realized that it symbolized the message of sobriety I would embody in telling the story of my drunken career from the Jordan to Jerusalem (14.22). At the end of my recitation, I gave thanks and passed around the wine cup. All my followers drank from it (14.23). As the cup went round, I remembered my hangover revelation: wine was the cause of my likely bloodshed, the source of my misfortunes, and the catalyst of my insanity.
>
> "Then Isaiah's Suffering Servant came to mind. Before he could know the 'satiating wine' of sobriety (Is 53.11), he had to drink the wine of drunkenness. What wine had done for the Servant it was now doing for me, humbling me that I might be exalted (Mt 23.12; Lk 14.11). The drink I had thought an enemy I now saw as the instrument of our promised salvation. The blood of the grape was both the cause of my bloodshed and the blood of the Isaian sobriety covenant (Is 54.9–10).
>
> "Next I remembered the prophecy about the 'many,' the multitudes who follow the Servant's example of submission and so escape bondage (Is 53.11). Somehow I connected this prophecy with the wine of religion. At once I understood the purpose of ritual drink. God intends it to bring the nonaddicted many to the same surrender point that we drunkards encounter. I saw the multitudes finding sobriety at the brink of self-destruction, as a result of drinking religious wine.
>
> "As I again held the cup, these thoughts bodied forth in the words about wine I spoke to the assembled company: 'This wine is my blood yet also covenant blood poured out for many' (14.24).
>
> "I knew I had taken my last drink. On no account would I again resort to the cup. I remembered Psalm 16 and the man who renounces ritual wine for the 'smooth wine' of Yahweh (Ps 16.4–5). So I quoted the words of that ancient brother: 'I tell you, I will drink no more of religious wine, no never again, until I drink the new wine of the rule of God' (14.25). Even as I spoke I saw the meaning of Elijah's undrunk cup at Passover: Elijah comes but drinks no wine! (15.36)
>
> "We ended our seder by singing the Hallel (14.26). Psalm 116 stood out, the story of another suffering brother, a beaten man who dies to self, surrenders to God, and admits his powerlessness. I saw that I must do likewise. So I took my disciples and went to pray at the place we call the Sign of the Winepress (Gethsemane) (14.32).
>
> "I felt great sorrow and distress at the dying of self (14.34). But I fell on the ground and asked God for the strength to get through that difficult moment (14.35). Then I prayed: 'Abba, as you have all pow-

er so I am powerless; remove my cup addiction, not through my will but yours' (14.36).

"I had asked Peter, James, and John to watch me pray (14.33), thinking they might follow my lead, yet I found them drunk and asleep (14.37). Again I prayed, this time for freedom from mental drunkenness: 'Abba, I am powerless, release me from the bondage of self, through your will not mine' (14.39). Still the disciples slept their drunken sleep, continuing their betrayal of the twelve sobriety propositions that guided my actions (14.40–42).

"As for me, I arose from the ground a free man. A peace came over me. My sanity had returned. I realized that my problems had been of my own making. I knew that I had ceased fighting everything and everyone, even drink. I prepared to leave Jerusalem and return to Galilee, a reborn child of God and a truly human being at last (14.28)."

Gratitude Song

Any reconstruction of the conclusion of Jesus' story will be entirely conjectural. The rest of Mark's narrative only hints at the serenity Jesus found in recovery: his surrendered silence during his trials (14.61 and 15.5) in contrast to his earlier bellicosity (chaps. 11 and 12), his testimony to empowerment and exaltedness (14.62), and his spiritual awakening and escape from religious bondage and strife signified by the allegory of the empty tomb (16.1–8).

The following version is based on the assumption that Jesus, risen from the ground of Gethsemane, returned to Galilee exactly as Mark says he would (14.28 and 16.7). There he would have pursued his program in anonymity, telling his story to whoever would listen. Surely Jesus noted the drunkenness, anger, and social dissolution reaching crisis proportions in the land. Thus it is reasonable to believe that he kept alive his revelation about ritual wine and the nonaddicted "many," ending his story with the apocalyptic exhortations that later became Mark 13:

"Today I am grateful to be free of the compulsion to drink or to play God and act out my mental drunkenness. I am thankful I can choose to live simply as a son of man.

"For me, Jerusalem is only a memory. Yes, they arrested me that Passover night, and the nonsober among my disciples forsook me and fled (14.43–50). When the high priest asked if I was the Messiah, I replied that 'Messiah' would be signified by numbers of anonymous recovering people empowered by God and coming and going exalted in sobriety (14.62). When they saw I was only a drunkard and not a messianic claimant, they let me go and I returned to Galilee.

"Our movement has produced widespread spiritual awakening. Many who know my name are not former drunkards. Some of our number, like Peter, James, and John, hold that I was crucified and miraculously resurrected. Mystics like Saul of Tarsus have proclaimed me Messiah. As for me, I'm grateful to be sober and anonymous.

"I end with a word to those awaiting their turning point: watch for the moment when you recognize the ritual wine cup as a desolating sacrilege (13.14a). That will be your signal to flee from religion to recovery to escape the wrath unleashed by clerical dominance and self-willed fanaticism (13.14b–19). No one but God knows when your revelation will come, so watch for it (13.32–36). God has shortened the days to your apocalypse, so that you will not perish before it arrives (13.20). Remember, the Messiah will not be a person but a spiritual program (13.21–23) borne by a host of sober messengers (13.26–27). So I say to all, watch for the moment! (13.37)."

In terms of the trajectory of his overall story, Jesus' relapse from sobriety honeymoon into mental drunkenness explains the distinction his nineteenth-century biographers observed between the sunshine of Galilee and the darkness of Jerusalem, for example, Ernest Renan's notion of idyll become obsession; David Friedrich Strauss's idea of a psychopathic progression; H. J. Holtzmann's picture of psychological development from successful real-world messiah to a suffering messiah who fails tragically; and Albert Schweitzer's theory of a messianic hero who abandons the idea of a secret kingdom in the natural order for an apocalyptic eschatological vision toward which he endeavors to bend history, which crushes him for his presumption.[111] Though discredited on account of their biblical naïveté, the early psychiatric studies of Jesus criticized by Schweitzer had a kernel of truth: Jesus' behavior in Jerusalem was not that of a well person.[112] More recently, certain Jewish scholarship has argued for Jesus' involvement in the Zealot movement.[113] Although Jesus did act the insurrectionist, he did so not against Roman rule but against the leaders of his religion and the idea of hierarchy within spiritual congregations.

In any case, the grandiosity, judgmentalness, righteous anger, and contentious efforts to change the thinking of others so apparent in the Jerusalem half of Jesus' story are hallmarks of mental drunkenness and the consequences of humans' attempts to play God. The end of this malady is either violent collective destruction or individual surrender and *metanoia*, alternatives fully in keeping with Markan apocalyptic. Comparing the revelational consciousness in Mark with that associated with recovery today, only the surface imagery differs. Understanding Jesus' story as depicting his stage-two recovery from alcoholism neither modernizes nor psychologizes that story and comports well with the apocalyptic character of the Markan text.

Conclusion

Reasoning from the alcoholism theme so evident in Mark's Passion narrative, this chapter has proposed a theory of Markan provenance and genre characterizing the gospel's secret audience as members of a nonmessianic Jesus movement, Jewish and Palestinian, devoted to sobriety after release from alcohol addiction. It has posited the occasion of Mark's writing as the predicted severing of Judaism and Palestinian Christianity in the aftermath of the Roman-Jewish War and the consequent loss by the sobriety movement of its haven within Judaism. Mark's intention was to preserve Jesus' recovery story as memorialized within the Markôs groups by concealing it in a religious narrative presenting Jesus variously as Messiah, wonderworker, hero, and sage. Mark knew that religious readers would see his gospel as a collage of genre features belonging to the several images of Jesus they perceived in the surface narrative. By contrast, alcoholic readers would identify the genre of the hidden or secret gospel as that of the alcoholism recovery story, a first-person testimony consisting of drunkalogue, turning point, and gratitude song.

To assist the modern nonalcoholic reader in penetrating the surface of the religious tale and hearing the voice of a former addict telling his story, this chapter has reconstructed Jesus' sobriety story, hypothetically, as preserved within the Markôs groups. The import is not just that Jesus lived the events reported by Mark's narrator but that he lived to tell about them in the evangelistic idiom of recovery and that memories of that telling survived within the Markan movement and provided Mark the outline of his narrative.

Discussed exegetically in chapter 6, this new view of the Jesus story can trigger surprising reversals of thought: What has previously seemed a serene Jordan baptism may now be seen as a painful admission of addiction. What has been considered the ministry of a divine messiah may be thought the expression of a man's messianic obsession. What seemed an effort to reform an authoritarian religion now looks like an absurd attempt to control controllers into relinquishing control. What has been considered an unbloody ritual sharing of a bloody self-sacrifice may have been an epiphanal recognition of alcohol as both emblem and cause of human bloodshed generally. Words that have been thought to change wine to blood may be the ghosts of the turning-point narrative of a former wine addict's sobriety story. What seemed a superhero's resolve in Gethsemane is revealed as a humbled man's repudiation of self-empowerment. Wine itself, a drink that seems first a friend and then an enemy, turns out to have been a friend all along, just as an illness that seems a curse is revealed as a blessing. Lastly, a gospel that readers have considered a genre muddle is seen as a well-formed, albeit camouflaged, sobriety story.

✣ 5 ✣

NEW WINE AT PENTECOST

> These men are *not* drunk as you suppose. For it is the
> third hour of the day spoken of by the prophet Joel!
> —Peter, Acts 2.15–16

Elements of the Pentecost story in Luke's Acts of the Apostles point
to the historicity of Jesus' Galilean movement as a sobriety fellowship.
The narrative moves from the story of tongues to the exchange between Peter and the multitude as to whether the apostles' ecstatic
speech signified their drunkenness (2.1–15a) and finally to Peter's
kerygmatic sermon based on the apocalypse of Joel and Psalm 16
(2.15b–36). This chapter studies these parts of the Pentecost narrative from the perspective of recovery criticism.

Scholars generally agree that the discourses in Acts are Lukan
compositions commingling historical recollections with material of
Luke's own invention, though which is which and the kinds of sources
available to Luke remain unsettled questions.[1] In examining the Pentecost narrative this chapter reinterprets the stories of tongues and
intoxication and deconstructs the understanding of Joel and Psalm
16 on which Luke based his composition of Peter's inaugural speech.
Two propositions are argued, consistent with the theory of Markan
audience advanced here. The first is that the accusation of drunkenness results neither from misapprehensions about the apostles' glossolalia nor from certain onlookers' mention of "new wine" but from
a prior awareness by the Jerusalem multitude that the Galileans speaking were notorious drunkards. The second is that Peter's sermon was
actually a proclamation of Jesus' sobriety program based on the apocalyptic "new wine/smooth wine" metaphors of Joel 4.18 and Ps 16.5
(Dahood's translation),[2] in emulation of Jesus' paschal reference to
"new wine" (Mk 14.25).

The Pentecost Event (Acts 2.1–15a)

Luke's account of the part of the Pentecost story preceding Peter's inaugural sermon is traditionally understood as follows:

> Gathered together in a house, the apostles receive a spiritual anointing manifest in tongues of fire and the miraculous ability to speak in foreign languages. Next the polyglot multitude outside hear the apostles telling of God's mighty works in their own languages. All are amazed and ask about the meaning of this event, while certain others mock the apostles and accuse them of being drunk from new wine. Peter then addresses the multitude and assures them that the apostles are not drunk, as the people suppose, for it is only the third hour of the day, 9:00 A.M.

The position here, consistent with widespread scholarly thinking,[3] is that Luke has seriously distorted the actual event by conflating two blocks of material, one historical reportage and the other a popular fiction. Specifically, Luke has inserted the story about the apostles' miraculous acquisition of foreign languages into an otherwise unified eyewitness report of the actual Pentecost happening. The story is almost certainly an invention of popular imagination, whereas the eyewitness material is oral history handed on to Luke. What this history recounts, as interpreted herein, is the apostles' ecstatic attempts to evangelize the Pentecost multitude in the Markôs sobriety idiom, a coterie parlance that the people found largely incomprehensible.

In contrast to the traditional understanding, the following items summarize Luke's eyewitness material, minus the folk story, glossed from the perspective of recovery:

a. Sober and meeting together in a home, the apostles awaken spiritually and begin to speak in a "different tongue" *(heteros glōssa)*, a phrase referring to the spiritual parlance of their recovery movement, an idiom unknown to outsiders (2.1–4).

b. Approached by the apostles, the perplexed crowd members wonder what they are talking about and accuse them of being drunk—an inference from verses 12 and 15a, but *not* from the reference to "new wine" in verse 13, as is ordinarily assumed.

c. Certain "others" *(heteroi)* in the crowd, sober Galileans in Jesus' movement who understand the strange idiom, attempt with good humor to explain the apostles' speech as a consequence of their being filled with "new wine," which is recovery talk for the ecstasy of sobriety following active alcoholism (2.13).

    d. Peter assures the onlookers that the apostles are *not* drunk, as
       the crowd members (excluding the knowledgeable "others"),
       aware of the apostles' reputations or appearance as drunkards,
       have concluded *(hupolambanō)* they are (2.14 and 15a).
    e. Peter then begins his sermon with the proclamation, "For it is
       the third hour of the day spoken of by the prophet Joel" (2.15b
       and 16).

What follows are detailed examinations of the verses on which the
foregoing summaries are based.

The Idiom of Sobriety (Acts 2.1–4)

Viewed in terms of recovery, the events beginning the Pentecost story depict the apostles' spiritual awakening and call to carry the message. Verses 1–4 occur inside a house where the apostles are meeting apart from the festival crowd:

> (2.1) When the day of Pentecost had come, they were all together in
> one place. (2) And suddenly a sound came from heaven like the rush
> of a mighty wind, and it filled all the house where they were sitting.
> (3) And there appeared to them tongues as of fire, distributed and
> resting on each one of them. (4) And they were all filled with the Holy
> Spirit and began to speak in other tongues [a different tongue], as the
> Spirit gave them utterance.

What an amazing scene! One will recall that the final appearance of
the twelve disciples in the Markan narrative is on the night of Passover, when drunk from the wine Jesus gave them and asleep through
his way-showing surrender, they forsake their master and flee from
Gethsemane at the hour of crisis. Yet here they all are a mere fifty
days later,[4] quite sober, as Peter will soon testify, meeting in what
modern alcoholics would call a "home group," possibly in the house
of Mary, the mother of Mark (see Acts 12.12). Even more surprising,
notwithstanding the distracting physicalization of spiritual phenomena characteristic of Luke (see Lk 3.22), what the text represents is
the apostles' spiritual awakening and call to carry the message to
other alcoholics. In short, Luke's eyewitness material recalls the
moment at which the apostles experienced the equivalent of step
twelve of today's recovery program.[5]
    Now what of the "other tongues" named in verse 4 *(heterais glōssais)*?
Luke has pluralized the phrase (also in verse 11) to make it comport
with the folktale of the apostles' acquisition of foreign languages, but
the original form would have been singular, "a different or other

tongue." Some modern scholars identify it as a kind of glossolalia, but the view here is that the original phrase, unknown to Luke as he pondered his source materials, referred to the coterie idiom spoken by members of Jesus' fellowship, a timeless parlance alcoholics learn in the course of overcoming their illness. Many find it mystifying at first, almost like a new language. Recovering people today speak of learning "to walk the walk and talk the talk." At meetings one hears the motto "sobriety spoken here." In short, the "different tongue" that rested on the spiritually awakened apostles represented the distinctive argot of sobriety, in whose terms they had commenced to proclaim the message of recovery to the many.

The Folktale (Acts 2.5–11)

At this point Luke shifts the setting outdoors to the gathered multitude of Pentecost pilgrims. According to the folktale, they have somehow heard the loud rush of spirit within the house and find themselves being preached at by the apostles "each in his own language" (*idia dialectō,* not the same term as *heterais glōssais* in verses 3 and 4). Whence the folktale? It would have originated early in the tradition, as the Jerusalem community replaced the scandalous memory of the apostles' alcoholism by a legend that converted their sobriety parlance into foreign languages supernaturally acquired and explained away their reputation as drunkards by passing it off as nothing more than a mildly humorous misperception on the part of the Pentecost multitude. Fifty years later Luke used the story to make a biblical connection, that "the Pentecostal Spirit overcomes the ancient division of men's tongues that began at Babel."[6]

The Actual Occurrence (Acts 2.12–15a)

To see what really happened when the apostles addressed the multitude, one must read Luke's account without the folktale (2.5–11), quoted here with verse 4 repeated for continuity:

(2.4) And [the apostles] were all filled with the Holy Spirit and began to speak in a different tongue, as the Spirit gave them utterance. ... (12) Now [the people in the multitude] were amazed and perplexed, saying to one another, "What does this mean?" (13) Then certain others present laughingly explained, "They are filled with new wine." (14) Then Peter, standing with the eleven, lifted up his voice and addressed them, "Men of Judea and all who dwell in Jerusalem, let this be known to you, and give ear to my words. (15a) For these men are *not* drunk, as you suppose [that is, as you have accused them of being]."

Instantly one sees that this version gives just the opposite of the impression given by the uncut Lukan version, namely, that the people did *not* understand the apostles. The crowd was confused not because it heard foreign languages, for the apostles were not speaking the languages of foreigners (*idia dialektō*, now deleted), but because the apostles spoke in "a different tongue," that is, in the coterie idiom of recovery that they had so recently acquired. In their eagerness to carry the message, the ecstatic apostles must have waded into the crowd of festive Pentecost pilgrims and zealously begun, as today's alcoholics would say, to twelfth-step whoever would listen. Naturally, their jargon only confuses the people, who ask, "What does this mean? What are they saying?"[7]

"Filled with New Wine" (Acts 2.13)

In response, certain unidentified "others" or "different ones" (*heteroi*) in the crowd laughingly attribute the apostles' incomprehensible speech to their being "filled with new wine." Bible commentators have often asked who these others were, without answer. The view here is that the others were sober alcoholics, in the Jerusalem crowd but not of it, just as the converted "we" in Isaiah's Suffering Servant poem were part of the Babylonian multitude yet radically different from it.[8] They belonged to "the company of a hundred and twenty persons" mentioned earlier (Acts 1.15), the recovering alcoholics in the original Jerusalem community, most having followed Jesus from Galilee, who are gratified to see that the apostles have finally gotten sober.

They do not "mock" the apostles, as *diachleuazō* is regularly translated; rather, they merely laugh good-naturedly at the confusion the apostles' sobriety idiom causes the people. Based on *chleuē*, "jest," *diachleuazō*, ordinarily translated "to mock," can indicate degrees of humor short of ridicule or derision. Barclay Newman and Eugene Nida discuss the difficulty of translating subtle shadings of meaning when derision is used as humor.[9] Here the others know that the crowd members do not understand "new wine" as they do. Their humor spoofs the pneumatic enthusiasm of the apostles, who do not recognize that their coterie idiom is incomprehensible to the multitude. These others are not mocking the apostles, however, or for that matter the crowd; they're merely enjoying a little humor at the expense of both.

It is absolutely crucial to recognize, therefore, that in saying the apostles are "filled with new wine," these others are *not suggesting drunkenness*. Everyone from Luke up until the present has understood the remark as a scornful accusation of intoxication, but it is not. For

as readers know by now, "new wine" is recovery parlance for the ecstasy of sobriety following active alcoholism. It signifies the complete
opposite of actual drunkenness. This point is important for two rea-
sons. First, it verifies that the disciples in the Jerusalem community
at Pentecost, including those Luke designates "apostles," shared with
Jesus an understanding of "new wine" as a coterie locution. In fact,
it serves as an illustration of the sobriety parlance, the different
tongue that so perplexed the crowd. Second, it provides historical
support for the theory that Jesus' original Galilean movement was in
fact a recovery program. For if "filled with new wine" is not an accusation of drunkenness, and if Peter would not have thought it such,
then Peter's statement to the multitude, "These men are not drunk
as you suppose," cannot have been prompted by the new wine remark. It must have been triggered by other comments from the crowd
on the subject of the apostles' putative inebriety, not alluded to in
the Lukan narrative, which can have stemmed only from the crowd's
prior knowledge of the apostles' reputations, and perhaps their appearance, as public drunkards.

Luke, however, knows nothing of the apostles as ex-inebriates and
is unaware of the metaphorical significance of the phrase "new wine."
The latter is shown in three ways. First, Lk 22.18 omits Jesus' mention of new wine from his disavowal of drink at the Last Supper, as
originally reported by Mark (14.25).[10] Second, only Luke attributes
to Jesus the odd saying at Lk 5.39, which derogates new wine: "And
no one after drinking old wine desires new, for he says, 'The old is
better.'"[11] Third, the word Luke uses for "new wine" in verse 13 is
gleukos, which signifies fermenting grape juice still essentially nonalcoholic and unlikely to cause intoxication. Not only is *gleukos* not the
proper term to convey the metaphorical sense of "new wine" intended by Mark, which would have been *oinos kainos,* but it is inappropri-
ately used even if intended only in its literal sense, since Pentecost
occurs well before the grape harvest in Palestine, and there would
have been no fermentation in process, hence no supply of *gleukos*
available for drinking.[12]

As a result of his ignorance, Luke interprets the reference to new
wine he found in his source materials as an accusation of festival
drunkenness leveled by persons who, the evangelist would have his
readers believe, cannot differentiate between foreign languages and
the slurred speech of drunkards. Overall, Luke's representation of
Pentecost fails in significant ways. Not only does he present the apostles as accused of being drunk on a substance he must have known
was nonintoxicating and would not have been available at Pentecost

in any case, but he also appeals to their supposed speech in foreign tongues as the basis for the accusation. To be sure, alcohol promotes incoherent speech, but certainly not the mastery of foreign languages. Apparently Luke felt compelled to include the embarrassing references to drunkenness because they continued to live in the oral tradition, so he organized them around the story about foreign languages, thereby producing the inconsistent, almost burlesque[13] account contained in Acts 2.

"These Men Are Not Drunk!" (Acts 2.15)

Nonetheless, Luke's ignorance is fortuitous, for it is only because of it that he preserves the most significant remark in the entire pericope, Peter's denial of the apostles' drunkenness in verse 15a, "These men are *not* drunk, as you suppose." As explained above, the crowd's supposition is wholly unrelated to the new wine reference in verse 13. Taken independently, then, Peter's remark prompts the conclusion that the crowd must have had *a completely separate reason* for believing that any unusual behavior by the apostles would betoken drunkenness. It would be one thing for Luke to hand on the harmless story that some foolish onlookers mistook the apostles' evangelical zeal and their receipt of foreign tongues for festival tipsiness, but quite another for him to preserve a remark testifying to the apostles' appearance or reputations as chronic inebriates. Peter's statement can be interpreted only in the latter sense, however, once one recognizes that the apostles' different tongues were not foreign languages but sobriety talk and that the mention of new wine was a reference not to intoxication but to the joy of recovery.

Hence Peter's remark must refer to murmurs from the crowd, implied in verse 12 (RSV's "amazed and perplexed," *existēmi* and *diaponeō*, could just as correctly be read as "beside themselves and deeply troubled"), concerning the apostles' unsavory reputations. This conclusion is borne out by the meaning of the verb in Peter's statement, "as you suppose." *Hupolambanō*, regularly translated "suppose," "think," or "imagine," ought to be rendered in its sense of "say," "answer," or "claim." After all, Peter was not a mind reader. He could not have known what the people supposed, only what he heard them say. And what they said (implicit in verse 12) was, in effect, "How dare these men talk to us in this strange, pneumatic way about God? They are public drunkards, and we accuse them of being intoxicated now!" And Peter answers, in effect, "No, these men are sober men now, enspirited men, no longer the drunkards they used to be." Everything considered, although Luke interpreted it quite differently, Peter's reference to the crowd's protestations (2.15a) strongly supports the historicity of the apostles' alcoholism.

The Day of the Lord (Acts 2.15b–16)

Finally, by way of explaining the apostles' sobriety as a prolegomenon to his great proclamation, Peter identifies this Pentecost day as the "Day of the Lord" prophesied by Joel. Luke, however, unconscious of his cover-up of the apostles' alcoholism, misreads his source and construes Peter's words quite differently. The RSV reads:

> (2.15) For these men are not drunk, as you suppose [have said they are], since [*gar*] it is only the third hour of the day; (16) but [*alla*] this is what was spoken by the prophet Joel.

By introducing the awkward conjunction "but" at the beginning of verse 16, Luke truncates the clause of reason introduced by "since" in verse 15 such that it seems to mean only that the early hour (9:00 A.M.) explains why the apostles are not drunk.

The suggestion here, by contrast, is that Luke's source materials actually said the following:

> (2.15a) For these men are not drunk, as you have said they are. (15b) For it is the third hour of the day (16) which was spoken of by the prophet Joel.

Here "but" has been omitted as a spurious Lukan addition, and verse 16 has been translated as a relative clause modifying "day," with the result that verses 15b and 16 together constitute a single independent clause explaining why the apostles are not drunk. In other words, Peter's reference to the "third hour of the day" is not intended to suggest that it is too early in the morning for drinkers to be drunk, even at a festival (as if that were true).[14] Rather, it indicates something far more momentous, namely, that it is now the third hour of the "Day of the Lord" prophesied by Joel, the apocalyptic day when, according to the alcoholism hermeneutics Peter will momentarily use in interpreting Joel, the first sober and spirit-anointed persons will proclaim a recovery program to suffering humanity based on the etymological meanings of *Joel* ("God is the highest power") and *Jesus* ("God, help!"). Hence Peter is saying that the sobriety of these known drunks and their commencing to carry the message of recovery to an alcoholic world constitute the beginning of the fulfillment of Joel's prophecy. All this indicates how much the actual Pentecost event differed from the version ordinarily inferred from Acts 2.1–15a.

Apocalyptic and Sobriety

Prior to reconstructing Peter's sermonic exegesis of the Book of Joel, it is important to point out the similarities between apocalyptic and the message of sobriety. The position here is that apocalyptic of the kind represented by Joel and Mark 13 and modern statements about alcoholism and recovery paint the same portrait of unsurrendered humankind, both the individual and the aggregate, as addict. Apocalyptic has been defined as a prophetic style "in which heavenly secrets about a cosmic struggle and eschatological victory are revealed in symbolic form and explained by angels to a seer who writes down his message under the pseudonym of an ancient personage."[15] This definition overlooks the fact that apocalyptic has a psychic "inside," a psychological dimension just as important as its physical "outside." The cosmic signs-in-the-sky symbolize mental upheavals every bit as real as physical ones. The following paragraphs compare apocalyptic and the message of recovery on the following points: the human dilemma to which they pertain, the ensuing struggle, the forces at odds, the climax, the victory, and the action of God at the turning point.

Dilemma

In their address to sufferers, apocalyptic prophecy and the message of recovery describe the human individual's dilemma in essentially identical terms: "You have a mortal illness, manifest in your rebellious attempts to be God for yourself. If you do not change your thinking, you will kill yourself and perhaps others as well. Either way, a cataclysm will certainly befall you: destruction of your outer world and physical self if you continue your defiance, or destruction of your inner thought-world if and when you surrender."

Struggle

The violent upheavals involved in apocalyptic and alcoholism are both physical and mental. Lacking the concepts of modern psychology, apocalyptic conveys both kinds of cataclysm, outer and inner, via a semiotic vocabulary of cosmic end-of-the-world symbols. The lingo of alcoholism portrays the psychic element more discursively, though no less apocalyptically. For example, ancient apocalypticists would have instantly comprehended the following remark, versions of which are spoken to bottomed-out drunks still unconvinced that they want to quit drinking: "You had better find a way to get either a new mind or a new body, because the way you are heading, one or the other is going to self-destruct, and soon!"

The physical violence that alcoholic humanity brings on itself has always been apparent. The devastation that periodically fell on Israel resulted from its rulers' insistence on playing God in the face of powers greater than theirs. Underlying Mark 13 is Jesus' awareness that his probable execution is a consequence of alcoholic wills in conflict: his messianism exacerbating the fears of the Jewish hierarchs, their arrogance exciting his obsessive anger. Forty years later Mark was appalled by the destruction of Jewish Palestine resulting from the clash between the fanaticism of the Jews and the anger of the Romans. The smoke from the fires of war must have obscured the sun and moon exactly as the prophets foresaw. Today we see nuclear armaments, overpopulation, religious and ethnic strife, terrorism, and epidemic addiction as harbingers of physical doom. Such violence is never redemptive, only horrifying and life-destroying.

Inner destruction, by contrast, is less well understood and if anything more frightening than outer destruction. The cataclysm within *is* redemptive, yet people who testify to ego deflation and spiritual surrender, who speak about being entirely new persons on the inside, about powerlessness and a higher power that has changed their way of thinking, are usually dismissed as religious eccentrics. One place to hear about inner change is the recovery stories of ex-addicts, whose conclusions tell what these persons are like now that their thinking has changed. Anyone who has experienced the passage from defiance to humility, however, can bear witness to inner apocalypse.

Forces

The opposing forces depicted in apocalyptic arise from conflicting dynamics. It is God's impulse, curative and liberating, that urges us toward surrender, while the addictive forces of the unredeemed self, a manifestation of the Edenic curses, are what prompt us to continue our denial and fighting and bring us ever closer to physical destruction. Western religious conceptuality projects the animus of the self onto external beings called Satan and demons, whereas modern science employs psychological terms such as *obsession* and illness metaphors such as addiction as ways of speaking about the death force unleashed whenever human beings succumb to the primordial urge to be their own god.

Climax

The climax of the struggle occurs when sufferers reach the turning point and confront their ultimate alternatives: either physical death in the holocaust of their outer world or surrender and acceptance of the equally painful cataclysm of their inner thought-worlds.

Victory

The eschatological victory occurs when persons stop fighting and admit powerlessness. This event culminates in the "after-knowledge" of *metanoia,* the term Mark uses to name the changing of mind preached by John the Baptist and Jesus (Mk 1.4 and 15). The essential baptismal experience, *metanoia* is the result of surrendering and asking for help at the climactic moment. Thus it betokens the final victory of God over self, in the eschaton of an individual's life and ultimately in the collective life of humankind.

God's Action

In recovery as in apocalyptic, God directly intervenes and offers the gift of surrender. This gift, the conviction of powerlessness and the willingness to ask for help, enables persons to change their thinking and put their lives on a different footing. Its acceptance results in the basic spiritual experience and constitutes the first step toward conscious contact with God. Only God knows the time appropriate for this intervention. Too soon and the gift will be rejected; too late and the person, or humanity at large, will already have perished. (Apocalyptic is further discussed in chaps. 6 and 7.)

Peter's Inaugural Sermon (Acts 2.15b–36)

Turn now to Peter's sermon. Much attention has been devoted to the composition of the speeches in Acts, attributed not only to Peter but also to Stephen, Philip, James, and Paul, but many questions remain unanswered. Did Luke base these speeches on a lost collection of missionary testimonies to Christ? If not, if they are compositions in the manner of Greek historiography, is their content wholly a Lukan invention or the transcription of living tradition in the communities known to Luke? Does Luke's use of the Septuagint in representing Old Testament texts effectively establish the sermons as Lukan inventions? (Peter as an Aramaic speaker probably would have quoted the Hebrew version.)

The position here is that Luke's identification of Peter's texts as Joel and Psalm 16 is historically accurate but that his representation of the content of the sermon differs significantly from the charismatic interpretation that Peter, as a recovering alcoholic endeavoring to twelfth-step the nations on the Day of the Lord, would have placed on these readings. As composed by Luke, Peter's sermon focuses on Jesus as the central persona of a new religion, on his resurrection from physical death and his exaltation as mediator of the Holy Spirit, Lord, and Christ. By contrast, Peter as a sober alcoholic would have focused not so much on the person of Jesus as on the principles embodied in Jesus' spiritual program. He would have underscored the mortal nature of the alcoholic malady and then proclaimed the good news that a recovery program was available.

Which Peter?

Any reconstruction of Peter's speech at Pentecost will depend on prior conclusions about his spiritual condition at this juncture. What is the character of the Peter who, Luke tells us, delivers the first Christian sermon?

The Peter of Religion Is the Peter at Pentecost the Peter of Mark's surface narrative, the faithful disciple who, although slow to understand (Mk 8.14–21), professes Jesus as Messiah (Mk 8.29) and repents of his momentary denial of the Lord (Mk 14.72)?

Peter as Active Alcoholic Is he the Peter whom Mark's fellow alcoholics would have recognized in the secret Markan narrative as an active addict, a disciple who, although strongly attracted to Jesus and Jesus' anonymous recovery program, proclaims Jesus to be a messianic hero (Mk 8.29), refuses to admit powerlessness (Mk 8.32–33), denies the etymological Jesus ("God, help"; Mk 14.66–72), drinks again (Mk 14.23), drunkenly sleeps through Jesus' Gethsemane surrender (Mk 14.37 and 40–41), and finally succumbs to fear and runs away (Mk 14.50)?

Peter as Allegorical Figure Is he Peter portrayed allegorically as a type of the clergy Mark sees emerging in the Christian communities of his day, hierarchs obsessed by ecclesiastical authority (Mk 10.35–37), given to moralistic and autocratic preaching (Mk 8.14–15), and addicted to liturgical alcohol (Mk 14.23–24), who have encrypted all memory of the alcoholic Jesus in a Petrine (rock, *petras*) tomb (Mk 15.46)?

Venerable Peter Finally, is he the Peter that the evangelist Mark would have encountered in Rome in the middle or late 50s C.E.,[16] an old man greatly venerated yet utterly carried away by the tide that in twenty-five years had transformed their recovery program into a religion, a person so saturated in the new idiom of "church" that he could barely recall Jesus' simple program or his own recovery in those long-ago days following their fateful Last Supper and who had resumed the practice of ritual drinking?

Sober Peter   The view here is that Peter at Pentecost differs from all the foregoing characterizations. For whatever he may have been or would become, the Peter depicted in Acts 2 is spiritually awakened and recovering. In the fifty days since Passover, he has become sober, begun to follow the Jesus program in a nurturing community of former drunkards, and on this Pentecost day is practicing its twelfth step. He understands Jesus not as Lord or Messiah but rather, as Luke quotes him later on (Acts 5.31), as *archēgon kai sōtera,* "founder" of their recovery program and thus their "savior." Emulating Jesus' disavowal of wine, Peter has stopped drinking. He understands the new wine mentioned by his fellow alcoholics in the crowd as a reference to Jesus' paschal saying (recounted later on in Mk 14.25). To the nations assembled for the feast of Pentecost, a traditional celebration of the covenant, Peter is about to proclaim Jesus' recovery program as the solution to the problem of humankind's existential alcoholism. It is Peter's finest hour.

Peter's Texts

As texts for his sermon Peter chooses Joel and Psalm 16. Why these selections? Looking beyond the excerpts in Acts to the works in their entirety, one immediately sees their relevance to alcoholism and recovery. Joel proclaims an answer to the problem of chronic inebriety (1.5) and speaks of "new wine" (*tirosh* in Hebrew), not in its *gleukos* sense, but in its *oinos kainos,* or recovery, sense (4.18). Psalm 16 depicts an ancient man's disavowal of liturgical drink in order to imbibe the "smooth wine" of Yahweh (16.4–5), a sobriety metaphor exactly equivalent to "new wine." As a consequence, the psalmist receives the gift of life without experiencing physical death. Moreover, Joel is an important biblical source of Jesus' apocalyptic sobriety prophecy (recorded later on as Mark 13, discussed below in chap. 6), and Psalm 16 is the model for Jesus' Last Supper renunciation of liturgical wine (later, Mk 14.25). These coincidences cannot be accidental. In his speech Peter would have elucidated these connections as he recounted Jesus' paschal message about drinking and not drinking.

The Apocalypse of Joel (Acts 2.15b–21)

The interpretive hypothesis here is that the unredacted core of the Book of Joel, less than half its content, consists of an apocalyptic oracle telling of Israel's alcoholic illness and its possible destruction in suicidal warfare and proclaiming recovery based on a surrendered call for help to the higher power implicit in the name Joel ("God is the most high"). Ostensibly, chapters 1 and 2 of Joel depict a locust plague visited on Israel, shown in chapter 1 via images of agricultural devastation and then reprised in chapter 2 via martial imagery identifying the locusts as the army of God. Chapter 3, the verses Luke attributes to Peter at Pentecost, presents God's promise of spiritual awakening on the Day of the Lord to all who call on his name. Chapter 4 tells of eschatological struggle and judgment and the beginning of a peaceful era under the rule of God.

Ancient religious redactors have added so much cultic material to the core prophecy in Joel that it is common to hear the writer described as a person intimately familiar with Temple worship, perhaps even a priest. These redactions include descriptions of Temple rituals, exhortations about fasting and offerings, and a conception of the Day of the Lord as destroying Israel's enemies and vindicating Israel without the cataclysmic change of thinking characteristic of *metanoia*. All these religious redactions are ignored in the following commentary.

Figuratively, the locust plague is the vehicle in a metaphor comparing the ravages of alcoholism to the swarms of locusts that periodically laid waste to Palestine—terrifying, unconquerable, devastating, maddening. Grown huge in imagination, the locusts represent in particular the horrors of alcoholic compulsion and delirium and, more generally, the depravity of humanity divorced from its creator. Suggestive of the fighting to which addiction leads, their transformation into invincible warriors signifies alcoholism's telos in unwinnable warfare, ultimately against God. Interpreted theologically, the locust plague represents the salvific wrath of a fatherlike God seeking to redeem ill and deluded children.

The overt alcohol images in Joel are the promise of an end to addictive drinking (1.5), the failure of alcohol to produce its vaunted joy (1.11–12), the "winepress of wickedness" as an emblem of alcoholic anger and destruction (4.13), and "new wine dripping from the mountains" as a vinous image used in a sobriety metaphor (4.18).

There Is a Solution! (Jl 1.5)

Although never translated or interpreted as such, Jl 1.5 actually conveys the proclamation awaited by all suffering alcoholics who want to stop drinking but cannot, the announcement of a solution to their alcoholic problem:

> (1.5) Awake, you weeping drunkards, you wailing drinkers of wine, because further wine will be withheld from your mouths.

In other words, you won't have to drink anymore! Help is coming! Needless to say, verse 5 is always read differently, as meaning that because the locusts have devoured the vines, there will be no new wine, *tirosh,* understood in the sense of the Greek *oinos neos.* Without altering the pointing of the Hebrew roots, however, the alcoholism translation indicates that the lament of the drunkards arises not from the lack of wine but from their painful inability to stop drinking. Thus the future passive verb "will be withheld," together with its subject "further wine," which comes from translating *tirosh* in its *oinos neos* sense, conveys the promise of recovery.

As typically read, Jl 1.5 is oddly derisive in tone and a seeming intrusion into the text. Proponents of the received meaning must explain why the prophet should inject a comic address to drunkards into a litany of ruin and pious talk of fasting, saying in effect, "Oh, by the way, all you drunks had better weep and wail, for there will be no wine produced this year." Why should the prophet sarcastically depict the prospect of unsatisfied craving on the part of Israel's alcoholics? Such derision seems totally out of keeping with the remainder of his book. From the alcoholism perspective, however, the verse emerges as the central proclamation of the entire Book of Joel: there is a solution to your problem! It may very well have been the quotation with which Peter began his actual speech to the Pentecost multitude.

Locusts (Jl 1.4, 6–7)

These verses metaphorically characterize Israel's illness in terms of a fearsome locust plague:

> (1.4) What the cutting locust left, the swarming locust has eaten. What the swarming locust left, the hopping locust has eaten, and what the hopping locust left, the destroying locust has eaten. . . . (6) For a nation has come up against my land, powerful and without number; its teeth are lions' teeth, and it has the fangs of a lioness. (7) It has laid waste my vines, and splintered my fig trees; it has stripped off their bark and thrown it down; their branches are made white.

Cutting, swarming, hopping, and *destroying* translate different Hebrew words for the four stages of the locust's life cycle and illustrate the precise lexical distinctions persons can make about phenomena eliciting morbid fascination. What was true of locust plagues is no less true of epidemics of addiction. The lion imagery testifies to the power the locusts held over the popular mind, hence to the power of the addictive plight the locusts represent. The "wasted vine" and "splintered fig tree," traditional symbols of God's people, signify the ruin brought about by widespread alcoholism.

When Wine Fails (*Jl 1.12*)

This verse conveys the emotional bleakness occurring in advanced alcoholism, when wine has ceased to be the palliative it once was:

> (1.12) The vine withers, the fig tree languishes, pomegranate, [date] palm, and apple, all the trees of the field are withered; and gladness fails from the sons of men.

Superficially the failure of gladness results from the locusts' destruction of the fruit trees mentioned. In viniculture, however, grapes, figs, pomegranates, dates and apples are all used to make wine, which produces gladness and joy. Hence it is the "gladness" of wine, not of the trees, whose loss is lamented. Advanced alcoholics have long since ceased to find joy in alcohol. Recovering persons describing the last stages of their drinking often say, "Alcohol wasn't working for me anymore, but I kept on drinking anyway." This is the deeper intention of verse 12. The prophet is saying what his compatriot alcoholics cannot admit: wine is no longer the source of happiness it once seemed. The verse recalls the apocalypse of Isaiah of Jerusalem, who in an earlier epidemic of addiction also linked the failure of wine with the demise of joy (Is 24.7–11).[17]

The Day of the Lord (*Jl 2.1*)

In chapter 2 of Joel the prophet introduces the imagery of warfare to describe the bellicose teleology of alcoholism:

> (2.1) Blow the trumpet in Zion; sound the alarm on my holy mountain! Let all the inhabitants of the land tremble, for the Day of the Lord is coming, it is near.

This is the danger alarm, the trumpet signaling an attack. The cause of the alarm is not an invading enemy, however, but the nearness of the great "Day of the Lord." Joel uses the prophetic concept of Judgment Day to voice the same apocalyptic warning spoken to many a drunk the first time they are twelfth-stepped: "Surrender or perish! If you don't stop fighting your drink urge, the day is fast coming when you will either go insane or die!"

Locusts as Warriors (*Jl* 2.2–9)

These verses reprise the locust plague, transforming the figure used from omnivorous insects to an army of invading incendiaries. The locusts become "war-horses" drawing "rumbling chariots . . . a powerful army drawn up for battle." They "charge like warriors . . . unswerving from their paths." They "burst through the weapons and are not halted. . . running upon the city walls" and "entering through the windows." In chapter 1 the locusts represented the psychic furies of alcoholism. Here the martial metaphor signifies that alcoholism is not just an individual malady typified by anger and fighting but a collective illness that leads whole societies into suicidal warfare.

Cataclysm (*Jl* 2.10)

The warfare imagery gives way to the first of Joel's three formulaic references to cosmic cataclysm:

> (2.10) The earth quakes before them, the heavens tremble. The sun and the moon are darkened, and the stars withdraw their shining.

Religious readers typically interpret this and similar verses as representing God's unilateral destruction of the cosmos, the so-called end of the world. The alcoholic will see the cataclysm as ambiguous, however, with both outer and inner events as its potential referents, and as resulting from humanity's actions as well as God's, either cooperative or rebellious. Outwardly the verse foretells the obscuring of heavenly bodies by clouds of pitch-blackened smoke from burning cities, an image of genocide chillingly familiar today, after a century of world wars, firebombings, oil-well fires, and potential nuclear winters. Inwardly the image represents the breakup of one's conceptual cosmogony, the cataclysm of one's alcoholic thought-world that occurs with surrender. Drunkards cannot recover without this inner change, nor can alcoholic societies whose members refuse to change escape outward destruction.

Curative Wrath (*Jl* 2.11)

This verse presents surprising information about the locust plague, alcoholism, and the wrath of God:

> (2.11) The Lord utters his voice before his army, for his host is exceeding great; he that executes his word is powerful. For the Day of the Lord is great and very terrible; who can endure it?

The locusts are revealed as God's army. Ironically, then, the devils of alcoholism and the hell of warfare are sent by God, not to kill, but to cure. It is therefore God's powerful wrath against which alcoholics fight, propelling themselves closer to the day of reckoning. Nor is God's wrath punishment; rather, it is the product of the immutable truth embodied in the First Commandment. Our self-empowered attempts to remove our fears and live in peace are forms of playing God, and our addictive nature condemns us to learn this lesson the hard way, through long suffering.

The remainder of chapter 2 (2.12–27) consists of a cultic redaction calling for national repentance. In response, God will defeat both the locusts and the northern invaders, restore the produce of the land, and declare Israel vindicated before its enemies. What is represented is the kind of "magic" salvation alcoholics pray for before surrender, wherein God "changes his mind," cancels his wrath, and deems people justified without any change on their parts. The idea that it is God and not humanity that needs to change, typical of a certain kind of religious thinking, is pure untreated alcoholism.

Spiritual Awakening (Jl 3.1)

Chapter 3 (2.28–32 in RSV) resumes the original sobriety oracle with material describing the spiritual awakening that awaits sufferers in recovery:

> (3.1) And it shall come to pass afterward, that I will pour out my spirit on all flesh; your sons and your daughters shall prophesy, your old men shall dream dreams, and your young men shall see visions.

Luke saw this verse as a prophecy of the giving of the Holy Spirit, which he believed the miracle of the tongues fulfilled at Pentecost. As an alcoholic Peter would have understood it as prophesying a spiritual recovery program culminating in a felt sense of conscious contact with God.

The Servant Theme (Jl 3.2)

This verse is ordinarily understood as extending the promise of the Holy Spirit to the serving classes, to demonstrate the universality of the gospel offer: "Even upon the menservants and maidservants in those days will I pour out my spirit." The view here is that the verse bespeaks a different intention and should be translated as follows:

> (3.2) Upon all who serve, men and women, will I pour out my spirit in those days.

So read, the line alludes to the servant theme found in Deutero-

Isaiah, which will become central to Markan recovery theology. Alcoholics serve by suffering full-blown addiction for others to see and then, in recovery, by carrying the message of sobriety to fellow sufferers. This reading brings to light yet another reference in Joel to alcoholism and recovery. More important, it links Joel with Deutero-Isaiah as texts contributing to Jesus' conclusions about the importance of service.

Cataclysm Assured (Jl 3.3–4)

These verses again present the cataclysmic imagery first seen in 2.10:

> (3.3) And I will give portents in the heavens and on the earth, blood and fire and columns of smoke. (4) The sun shall be turned to darkness, and the moon to blood, before the great and terrible Day of the Lord comes.

Joel apparently knew that his alcoholic listeners would try to imagine a way to receive the Spirit short of dying to self, so he again points out that cataclysm is inevitable. Alcoholic humanity must die to receive the gifts of recovery and spirit. There is no easier, softer way. Either we continue fighting on the outside until we destroy ourselves physically, or we capitulate and submit to the destruction of our old ways of thinking.

The Name of the Lord (Jl 3.5a)

The first half of Jl 3.5 contains the chief directive of recovery, the invitation to supplication concealed within the divine name:

> (3.5a) And it shall come to pass that all who call upon the name of the Lord shall be delivered.

Over and over in the stories of recovering alcoholics one hears the turning point when sufferers, all their human resources exhausted, cry out in abject surrender: "Help me, God!" "Jesus!" "Help!" "Anyone out there, help me!" "If there is a God, will he help?" This is the apocalyptic moment when one discovers the meaning that the name obscures. Here *Joel* is erased as name and replaced by the insight concealed in its Hebrew etymology, "God is the most high," the available higher power, the source of all help. Similarly, the erasure of *Jesus* as a religious name leads to an encounter with the Hebrew roots underlying the name, which mean "God, help!" As a speech act, this cry is not a pious profession of Jesus as Lord but a call to a nameless other. It is surrender through agnosis, supplication to a nameless reality apprehended only as "not I," "Yahweh," the Anonymous

Present One who empowers in crises. For "the name of the Lord" finally means that God has no name by which he can be known and conjured, that he is rather a presence and a power responsive only to unconditioned appeal.

War (*Jl 4.9–12*)

Following additional redactions (4.1–8), Joel's oracle predicts warfare as humankind's illness runs its course: "Prepare war. . . . Let all the men of war draw near." Alcoholics fight to the bitter end in the vain hope of proving that they can learn to drink like other people, or quit drinking, by willpower. Only later do they see that their struggle was actually warfare with God. It is this fighting that Joel's verses depict. The warlike saying, "Beat your plowshares into swords, and your pruning hooks into spears," is just the reverse of the pacific saying in Is 2.4 and Mic 4.3. The ironic protestation of the weak, "I am a warrior," points up the alcoholic's deludedness, for alcohol is a power far greater than even the strongest human will. Finally, "The nations . . . come up to the valley of Jehoshaphat," a name that means "God judges." All persons and all warring nations ultimately come to their day of reckoning, the crisis point at which their fighting ends, whether in holocaust or surrender. And strange to say, when such conflict involves the spiritual realm, it is the unwon war, defeat not victory, that triggers the self-immolating surrender that makes true supplication to the Anonymous One possible.

Vinous Anger (*Jl 4.13*)

This verse presents the third overt alcohol image in Joel:

> (4.13) Put in the sickle, for the harvest is ripe. Go in, tread, for the wine press is full. The vats overflow, for their wickedness is great.

The image associates the anger and wrong enacted by alcoholic and warlike humanity with the crushing of grapes at harvest time. It is difficult to imagine a more pointed connection between wine and bellicosity. Much later it will become the "grapes of wrath" image in the Book of Revelation (14.15–20). Superficially the passage says that even as there comes the time to make wine, so too there comes the time to judge the alcoholic illness stemming from wine. Because wine catalyzes the illness, however, and brings drinkers to a saving crisis they might not otherwise know, the deeper ironic meaning points to the salvific purpose of alcohol. Exactly this idea illuminated Jesus' thinking as he reinterpreted the paschal wine duty at the Last Supper.

Decision Time (Jl 4.14–15)

The oracle again speaks of the valley of Jehoshaphat, here translated "valley of decision," the moment of crisis experienced by every recovering alcoholic:

> (4.14) Multitudes, multitudes in the valley of decision! For the Day of the Lord is near in the valley of decision. (15) The sun and the moon are darkened, and the stars withdraw their shining.

The decision is the same for every addicted person, surrender or physical death. The Day of the Lord as the day of personal decision is a theme Peter would have stressed in his appeal to the Pentecost multitude, even as Joel speaks here of "multitudes, multitudes." The term further links Joel's prophecy with Isaiah's Suffering Servant poem. Both describe a recovery program sent by God, available to each person in the multitude. In hindsight, then, the thought in verse 14 is not ominous but a prophecy of the universal offer of sobriety. Again, the cataclysm imagery (4.15) adumbrates the choices entailed in one's decision: mortal physical destruction if one continues fighting, salvific psychic destruction when one surrenders.

"New Wine" (Jl 4.18)

Because verses 16–17 and 19–21 are probable redactions, Joel's original oracle effectively ends with verse 18, which contains his fourth and final alcohol image:

> (4.18) And in that day the mountains shall drip new wine, and the hills shall flow with milk, and all the stream beds of Judah shall flow with water.

This is "new wine" in its *oinos kainos* sense. The metaphor scarcely needs further comment. Its pairing with "mountain" heightens its salvific overtones. The "mountains dripping new wine," clearly a metaphor of recovery, are the same mountains to which Jesus in Mk 13.14 admonishes persons to flee once they have recognized the identity of "the desolating sacrilege" (see chap. 6). "The hills flowing with milk" is redactional; "stream beds flowing with water" is the proper parallel to the "mountains dripping new wine" stich. Like new wine, water is a sobriety image. Just as new wine is a figurative opposite to real wine, so is water its realistic counterpart, one's drink after renouncing alcohol.

Verse 18 goes on to predict the appearance of a fountain issuing from the Temple:

(4.18) And a fountain of water shall come forth from the house of the Lord, and water the valley of Shittim.

The fountain prophecy also occurs in Ez 47.1–12 and Zec 14.8 and is recapitulated in Rv 22.1–5. An elaboration of the water symbol, the fountain prophecy is an allegory of the ultimate transformation of religion ("house of the Lord") into a sobriety program ("fountain of water") at some indefinite future time following a period of religious alcoholism. "Shittim" in verse 18 means "acacia trees," whose wood was used to make the Temple furniture. Thus "and water the valley of Shittim" looks like a cultic redaction aimed at neutralizing the fountain allegory by making it seem to support the priestly establishment. Over half the verses in Joel are redactions of this kind. Clearly, the priestly conservators of the Hebrew Scriptures went to great lengths to domesticate Joel's radical alcoholism oracle.

Psalm 16 (Acts 2.22–36)

Conflicting Exegeses

In Acts 2.22 Peter's sermon shifts from explaining the gift of spirit just received by the apostles to the topic Luke assumes Peter must have developed next, the proclamation of Jesus' crucifixion and resurrection. Luke finds these events foreshadowed in Psalm 16, the other scriptural text he believed played a part in Peter's sermon. Ignoring the reference to liturgical drinking at the beginning of this psalm, Luke focuses on verses 8–11. His argument runs as follows: since David, the presumed psalmist, died and was buried, then verse 10, which speaks of the writer's assumption to God without prior death, must be a prophecy of Christ's resurrection. But this ignores the fact that the Jesus of Christian belief *did* die a painful death and was buried, whereas verse 10, according to Mitchell Dahood, is quite explicit in its waiver of the death experience: "The psalmist firmly believes that he will be granted the same privilege accorded Enoch and Elijah; he is convinced that God will assume him to himself, without suffering the pains of death."[18] Clearly, Luke's exegesis of Psalm 16 leaves much to be desired.

Luke's version aside, how would Peter as a newly sober alcoholic have interpreted Psalm 16? The assumption here is that Peter applied to this psalm the theory of sobriety advanced by Jesus in his paschal message about wine: drinking rituals prepare alcoholic humanity for the Day of the Lord, when the gift of powerlessness is offered and persons renounce drink in favor of the "new wine/smooth wine" of sobriety. This explains why Jesus offered the disciples wine to drink before he announced his own disavowal of further drinking. Peter may have heard Jesus identify the language of his disavowal (later recorded as Mk 14.25) as a quotation of Ps 16.4–5. Believing that the Day of the Lord had arrived on Pentecost, Peter would have proclaimed not Jesus' crucifixion but rather his recovery and recovery program. Recounting Jesus' paschal message about wine, Peter would have cited Psalm 16 as the source of Jesus' disavowal saying. In addition, he may have pointed to the resultative relationship between hitting bottom and drinking "smooth wine" implied in verse 5 of the psalm and to the idea in verses 10–11 that recovery is the beginning of eternal life.

The Psalm

Psalm 16 was composed not by David but by an anonymous convert to Yahwism well before David's time. The psalmist's conversion occurs with his repudiation of the liturgical wine drinking he formerly practiced in the service of false gods. Dahood's path-breaking translation of verses 1–5, quite different from traditional versions, is as follows:

> (Ps 16.1) Preserve me, O El,
>   for I have sought refuge in you.
> (2)   I said, "O Yahweh, you are my Lord, my Good,
>   there is none above you."
> (3)   As for the holy ones who were in the land,
>   and the mighty ones in whom was all my delight:
> (4a)   May their travail-pains be multiplied,
>   prolong their lust.
> (4b)   I surely will not [anymore] pour libations to them from my
>   hands,
>   nor will I [again] raise their names to my lips.
> (5)   O Yahweh, you have portioned out my cup of smooth wine,
>   you yourself have [made falling low] my lot.

Verses 1 and 2 contain the psalmist's profession of Yahweh as El, the higher power. Verses 3 and 4 refer to the Canaanite and Phoenician gods the psalmist has renounced. Verse 5 introduces smooth wine as a metaphor of sobriety, a consequence of his "falling low," that is, of hitting bottom, as it were, in his ritual drinking.

Dahood identifies the travail-pains and lust of verse 4 as follows: "This curse harks back to Gen iii 16 and employs essentially the same terms: *harbāh 'arbeh 'iṣṣ ᵉbōnēk wᵉhērōnēk*, 'I will greatly increase your travail-pains and your lust.'" Traditional readings of Gn 3.16 (see chap. 1, note 63) construe the curse as connected to childbirth and sexual desire, but those do not appear to be the meanings the psalmist has in mind. The psalm is essentially about freedom from bondage to the gods of addiction. "Delight" in verse 3 refers to the joys experienced early in one's drinking career, while "pain and lust" in verse 4a refers to the excruciating craving addicts experience later on. The psalmist declares his freedom by directing the curse of addiction back onto the gods whence it came.

Stopping Drinking

In verse 4b the psalmist renounces further liturgical drinking, abjuring the wrathful wine drunk to the false gods. Of "raise their names" Dahood says, "This is the metaphor of drinking a chalice." The hypothesis here, never advanced before, is that the Markan Jesus bases his disavowal of drink on just this verse of Scripture: "Truly I say to you, I will drink no more, no never again, of the fruit of the vine, until I drink the new wine of the rule of God" (Mk 14.25). As discussed in chapter 2, Jesus' fruit of the vine reference points to wine drunk in religious ritual, as does "raise their names"—the names of false alcohol gods—in Ps 16.4b. Moreover, Jesus' "new wine" exactly parallels "smooth wine" in Ps 16.5. After giving the linguistic basis of his translation, Dahood says, "The smooth wine symbolizes a tranquil and happy existence as opposed to the cup of fury that Jerusalem received from the hand of Yahweh (Isa li 17). . . ." Exactly so. Dahood mentions an ancient Canaanite goblet recently unearthed at Ras Shamra depicting the god El giving his children wine to drink and saying, "Eat, o gods, and drink, drink still more!"[19] How close Dahood comes, and how close Psalm 16 comes, to seeing what Isaiah and Jesus saw: that the god of wine is in the end not the false god the psalmist and others have thought him but El the Banquet Giver, the higher power who offers his sons and daughters wine to drink to prepare us for the eschaton, when, after much drinking and suffering, we come to the turning point readied to renounce wine in favor of eternal life in sobriety.

Hitting Bottom

Dahood translates verse 5b as "you yourself have cast my lot." He goes on to say that the root underlying "cast" is "*ymk*, a by-form of *mkk*, 'to sink, fall.'" Dahood has chosen "cast" in view of "lot," to render the familiar idiom of casting lots. From the alcoholism perspective, however, "falling low" would render the familiar alcohol idiom "hitting bottom." It seems perfectly possible linguistically, and it makes far better semantic sense in terms of the thematic content of the psalm, hence the emendation given above, "you yourself have made falling low my lot." It is this falling low that triggers the conviction of powerlessness and defeatedness discussed above in chapter 2 in connection with Ps 116.10, the Hallel psalm Jesus presumably interpreted in terms of recovery as a result of just this link with Psalm 16. In any case, the significance of the parallel between Mk 14.25 and Ps 16.4b–5 cannot be overemphasized. It offers compelling support for the alcoholism intentionality of Mark's narrative.

Recovery

The remainder of Psalm 16 reads as follows:

> (Ps 16.6) The lines have fallen for me in pleasant places,
>   and the Most High has traced out my property.
> (7)   I will praise Yahweh who counsels me,
>   and whose heart instructs me
>   during the watches of the night.
> (8)   I keep Yahweh continually before me,
>   indeed, from his right hand I will never swerve.
> (9)   And so my heart rejoices,
>   my liver leaps with joy,
>   and my body dwells at ease,
> (10)   Since you will not put me in Sheol,
>   nor allow your devoted one to see the pit.
> (11)   You will make me know the path of life eternal,
>   filling me with happiness before you,
>   with pleasures at your right hand forever.

The dominant theme here is the joy of sobriety under the rule of a higher power kept in contact through prayer and meditation. Dahood's understanding of verse 10 as referring to assumption to God without physical death has already been mentioned. Chapter 7 of this book argues that verse 10 forms the basis of Rv 20.6, which is interpreted as speaking about the happiness of those whose first death and resurrection are death of the self and recovery. These will pass through their second death, which is biological death, without interruption of the rule of God or the eternal life they have been living.

However Peter may have dealt with the ending of Psalm 16, he surely connected the first five verses of the psalm with the message that Jesus had delivered at Passover fifty days before about drinking and not drinking. Perhaps Peter tried to explain, in the vocabulary of his time, how Jesus had interpreted Jewish liturgical drinking, seeing it as ordained by God to catalyze humankind's latent alcoholism and bring us to a salvific crisis. Jesus' new rite resembled the old wine rituals except for the added words of interpretation (later, Mk 14.24–25) destined to accompany all such drinking in the future. To conclude his speech Peter would have proclaimed Jesus' sobriety program as the fulfillment of Joel's recovery prophecy.

But Peter's sermon fell on deaf ears. His message made no more sense to the multitude than had the pneumatic entreaties of his fellow apostles. For Peter's proclamation occurred nineteen hundred years too soon. Humankind was fated to suffer horribly down the long and bloody centuries of the church age before it would be ready to hear the parousial message of recovery. Thus the alcoholism program that Peter and the apostles sought to inaugurate at Pentecost soon gave way to the Christian religion, which shaped its own recollection of the events of that day. As old-timer alcoholics know full well, the "street-corner evangelism" practiced by Peter and his confreres at Pentecost, while it sometimes produces religious effects, almost never sobers up drunks.

✣ 6 ✣

MARKAN SOBRIETY EMBLEMS

When you see the desolating sacrilege set up where it
ought not to be—Let the reader understand!—then let
those who are in Judea flee to the mountains.

—Mark's cryptic exhortation to the ages, Mk 13.14

This chapter, the last of the three that deal with the text of Mark specifically, examines the sobriety emblems in Mark 1–13, the narrative of Jesus' career from baptism to apocalypse, construing them as Mark's alcoholic confreres would have through their understanding of the Markan text as an encoded displacement of Jesus' sobriety story. The following items are studied: baptism, temptation, homecoming, gospel, calling followers, demons and exorcisms, the Twelve, parables and other aspects of the secrecy motif, multiplication of bread, the Passion predictions, the titles "Son of Man" and "Son of God," mental drunkenness manifest as messianism, the sermon on ego-death, Temple vessels, the vineyard allegory, rhetorical combat, apocalypse and the "desolating sacrilege," the designation "Messiah," Secret Mark, and coterie symbols including the cup, water, donkey, women, and young man in white. Also studied are the anticlerical allegories Mark has inserted into the Passion narrative, including the woman with the perfume jar, betrayal, the stricken shepherd, and denial.

In considering the elements of Mark 1–13, one should bear in mind the narrative typology governing their interpretation here, that of the drunkard who seeks help for his affliction, sobers up, undergoes a spiritual experience, attracts a following of fellow sufferers, and formulates a distinctive approach to recovery, only to see his enthusiasm give way to obsessive self-will and anger as his efforts to promote his ideas fall on increasingly deaf ears. Only when he again hits bottom, perhaps after returning to drink and acting out his anger, and then admits powerlessness a second time, surrendering not only alcohol but self, does he attain freedom from bondage. Many alcoholics recount similar stories, albeit of lesser import and unsung, of grandiose enthusiasm and subsequent humiliation en route to stage-two sobriety. Aside from chronic inebriety, the defining characteristic of the alcoholic illness, so apparent in Jesus' case, is this tendency to play God. All along Jesus knew that messiahship resided in the spiritual principles of his recovery program and not in his person as founder, yet at no time until Gethsemane was he to find relief from the addictive forces impelling him to act ever more messianically. Thus unfolded a future in which disciples who failed to remain sober, and countless others who had never known him, were to proclaim Jesus as the Messiah, thereby legitimating an ecclesiastical authoritarianism wherein humans play God in the name of religious order.

It goes without saying that the interpretations given in this chapter are not of equal certainty. Some of the symbolic equations, for example, fish to recovering persons or the man in white to the Christian deacon, are more speculative than, say, the translation of *poieō* (3.14) as "formulated" or the identity of the northern Aramaic "donkey/wine" pun (11.1–10), which rest on solid linguistic grounds. Similarly, although there can be little doubt, say, about the Markan Jesus' progression into extreme mental drunkenness, the identification of the "desolating sacrilege" (13.14) as the ritual wine cup, proposed herein, requires prior acceptance of the theory that Jesus held a particular idea about the salvific teleology of religious wine drinking. In any case, readers should gauge the validity of individual interpretations as they see fit.

Galilean Beginnings
Baptism and Temptation (1.9–13)

Following his prologue covertly signaling the "stage-twoness" of Jesus' story (explained in chap. 4), Mark presents a third-person narrative version of Jesus' account of his baptism (1.9–11) and temptation in the wilderness (1.12–13):

(1.9) In those days Jesus came from Nazareth of Galilee and was baptized by John in the Jordan. (10) And when he came up [*anabainōn*] out of [*ek*] the water, immediately he saw the heavens opened and the Spirit descending upon him like a dove; (11) and a voice came down from heaven, "Thou art my beloved Son; with thee I am well pleased." (12) The Spirit immediately drove him [*ekballei*] out into the wilderness. (13) And he was in the wilderness forty days, tempted by Satan; and he was with the wild beasts; and the angels ministered [*diēkonoun*] to him.

To religious readers the Markan scene portrays the theophanous call of a divine hero to heavenly sonship. Scholars seeking to depict the historical Jesus often speculate about the life crisis motivating his baptism. Edward Schillebeeckx, for example, calls the event "a revelatory . . . disclosure . . . [or] source experience" for Jesus, but like all commentators he concludes that the absence of data about Jesus' prior life renders it impossible to say what prompted the baptism or why the experience should have been so intense.[1] Mark's alcoholics would have known that behind this theophanic scene lay the familiar story of a wine addict banished from his home and dying of his disease, unable to drink successfully or to stop drinking.

Apart from proper names, water is the only realistic detail in Mark's description. Water is a universal countersymbol to wine figured in John's baptism ritual. Presumably, when John ministered to drunkards, he admonished them that water was not only what sealed their *metanoia* (Mk 1.4) but also the drink to which they should turn in place of wine. Alert for veiled echoes of Jesus' first-person story, Markôs readers would have interpreted verse 10a as a reference not to Jesus' immersion in water but to his having taken a drink of water. Drinking a cup of water was the entrance rite of their fellowship (see Mk 9.41). Here *anabainōn ek* can be alternatively but just as correctly translated as "rising/raising up from." Thus the Markans would have read the clause "And when he raised up from [drinking] the water, immediately he saw. . . ." This they would have recognized as a third-person version of Jesus' words recounting his conversion from wine to water. The awareness of spirit and well-being reflected here, signified by the perception of beloved sonship (1.11), is a phenomenon frequently reported by persons whose turn from drink occurred as Jesus' apparently did, suddenly and dramatically. Like alcoholics today, Jesus would have highlighted this personal memory whenever he told his story.

Moving on, the wilderness temptation recalls Elijah's symbolic forty-day journey to Mt. Horeb (1 Kgs 19.5–8) sustained only by a breadcake (word of recovery) and a jar of water (not wine). As noted, Elijah was an important sobriety exemplar to the Markans. Mark's confreres would have understood the passage as Jesus' recollection of his difficult withdrawal from his wine addiction, the first phase of sobering up. The key is seeing that the double use of *spirit* (1.10 and 12) is an implicit Latinism wherein *pneuma* refers to alcohol as well as to God. Although writing in Greek, Mark is thinking of the dual meanings of the Latin *spiritus,* which signifies both God and the intoxicating and addictive element in wine, *alcohol* in the modern lexicon.[2] He is saying that the spirit of God came to Jesus in his baptismal surrender (1.10), whereupon the spirit of wine, that is, alcoholic craving, "drove him" (*ekballō,* to cast out violently, said of demons) into the wilderness to be tempted by "Satan" (1.12), whose name means "adversary." Now "temptation" in the context of detoxification can mean only wrestling with the tendency to revert to willpower instead of continuing to rely on the grace of God in coping with residual craving for drink. Satan wins and drinkers resume drinking whenever they turn from God to self. Notice that *ekballō,* often considered an improper verb to predicate of spirit understood as God, appropriately describes the violent action of spirit understood as the effect of alcohol during withdrawal. Some drinkers suffer terribly at such times. The following colloquial remark by a former drunkard exactly catches the sense of *ekballō* intended in verse 12: "How alcohol did me when I drank was nothing to how it kicked my ass whenever I dried out."

Moreover, the details in verse 13 all point to an account of sobering up. The number forty symbolizes the duration of an oppression or curse, here the period during which Jesus suffered the wracking physical symptoms of withdrawal. Although religious readers sometimes associate the "wild beasts" with the animals of Paradise (Gn 2.19), Mark's alcoholics would have recognized that they represent the nightmare creatures of what modern medicine calls *delirium tremens.* The "angels" are not heavenly beings but human messengers of sobriety (from *angellō,* "to deliver a message"), in this case probably disciples of John the Baptist helping Jesus to stay sober during this critical period. In saying that these messengers "minister" to Jesus, Mark uses *diakoneō,* from *diakonos,* meaning "servant," a central term in Mark's theology of recovery. Shifted from a religious context to one of recovery from addiction, Mark's baptism and temptation scenes reveal themselves as paradigm descriptions of quitting drinking and drying out aided by sober alcoholics and the grace of God.

Homecoming (3.20–30)

Shortly thereafter Mark's story of the Nazareth homecoming further supports the authenticity of Jesus' reputation as an addict. Verses 20 and 21 are unique to Mark:

> (3.20) And he entered a house, and a crowd assembled so his hearers were unable to eat the bread [*artos*]. (21) Hearing [the commotion], his family came there to take charge of him, for they said, "He is *exestēmi* [bewitched, possessed, not sober]."

Depicted here is Jesus' return to his hometown and his first attempt to carry the message of recovery among people who know him as an outcast drunkard. A crowd gathers and taunts him, and Jesus and his hearers are unable to "eat the bread," that is, to share the word of recovery that *artos* in Mark always symbolizes. Hearing the commotion, his family members naturally presume that he has returned intoxicated as usual and hence set out to take charge of him. *Exestēmi*, a word with multiple meanings often translated as "beside himself" or "out of his mind," is Markan camouflage for whatever ancient Aramaic drunkenness idiom the family actually used. Examples abound in the lexicons of every age and culture. Basically what his family said was, "He's drunk again."

The story goes on to tell how some scribes from Jerusalem charge that Jesus is "possessed by Beelzebul, and by the prince of demons he casts out demons" (3.22). In Mark's secrecy scheme demon possession refers to alcohol addiction. Thus the scribes were accusing Jesus of being intoxicated. The account conceals yet another barely disguised memory of Jesus' real-life reputation as an inebriate. Jesus' reply to the scribes, "How can Satan cast out Satan?" (3.23), which he utters as a protestation of sobriety, therefore means, "How can a drunk drunk possibly cure another drunk drunk?" The parables in verses 24–30 continue the theme that exorcisms (cures of the compulsion to drink) are wrought only in cooperation with the Holy Spirit (3.29) and not by unclean spirits (3.30). This material, along with the Q saying labeling Jesus an "unbridled drunkard" (Mt 11.19/Lk 7.34; see chap. 1), comports well with the understanding of the baptism and temptation stories given here. Together they provide a basis for arguing the historicity of Jesus' alcoholism.

The Good Message (1.14–15)

After telling of the baptism and temptation, Mark recounts Jesus' return to Galilee and his initial experiences carrying the message of recovery:

> (1.14) Now after John was arrested, Jesus came into Galilee, preaching the gospel [*euangelion*, good message] of God, (15) and saying, "The time is fulfilled, and the kingdom [*basileia*] of God is at hand; repent [*metanoeite*] and believe in [*pisteuete*] the gospel."

Jesus' name for his program was the "rule/reign of God," often rendered as the "kingdom of God." This is the English version of the Greek *basileia,* which in turn translates the Aramaic *malkuta,* which lacked the spatial meaning of *basileia* and *kingdom* and conveyed only the dynamic sense of a time of reigning or ruling. Alcoholics today will equate rule of God to what they call "the program," wherein God, often designated "the higher power," is understood as the source of guidance and empowerment. *Metanoia* means an apocalyptic change of mind rather than a self-willed religious repentance. *Pisteuō* ("belief") translates the Hebrew/Aramaic *he'ᵉmin/hemin,* which means not doctrinal belief but looking for God in a crisis, trusting an other against all appearances—in this case, "grabbing hold" of the rule of God by asking for help from the depths of defeat.[3] It names the faith action of every converted person at the turning point.

Fishers of Men (1.16–20)

Behind Mark's account of the calling of the four fishermen is Jesus' story of the first drunkards he invited into recovery:

> (1.16) And passing along by the Sea of Galilee, he saw Simon and Andrew the brother of Simon casting a net in the sea; for they were fishermen. (17) And Jesus said to them, "Follow me and I will make you fishers of men." (18) And immediately they left their nets and followed him. (19) And . . . he saw James the son of Zebedee and John his brother. . . . (20) And he called them; and they left their father Zebedee in the boat . . . and followed him.

The story illustrates the truth that people normally come into recovery as a result of attraction rather than promotion. In Jesus these men beheld sobriety, something they wanted for themselves. Notice how readily and without ado they leave nets and father, thus illustrating how the desire for sobriety assumes primacy over the strongest of earthly ties, work and family. The phrase "fishers of men" looks ahead to the day when the four will begin carrying the message to other alcoholics, "catching" them from the pit of death.

Among the Markans, fish may have symbolized persons in recovery just as bread symbolized the words of recovery. This understanding would explain the presence of fish in the parables of multiplication (Mk 6.38, 8.7; Jn 6.9), just as the Markan meetings would have been characterized as "meals" of fish and bread. Scholars often remark the early Jewish-Christian tradition of Eucharists celebrated with bread and fish rather than bread and wine (Lk 24.30–31, 42–43; Jn 21.9, 12–13), but it strains credulity to imagine such meals as actual religious rites. These memories may reflect instead a primitive Markan symbolism representing the words and people of the rule of God.

The Synagogue Exorcism (1.21–28)

The theory here is that Mark has used the notions of demons (*diamōn*) and unclean spirits (*akathartos pneuma*) to personify the uncanny grip of alcohol addiction. These terms constitute the linguistic guise under which Mark reports Jesus' stories of carrying the message to drunkards seeking help. Exorcisms were widely performed by magicians in the first century, and ordinary people probably believed that conditions such as epilepsy, chorea, Tourette's syndrome, psychotic anger, and so forth resulted from demon possession. Educated people were doubtless more discriminating. Although we know little about the ancients' sense of the phenomenology of chronic drunkenness, certain reaction patterns could easily have been represented to nondrunkards as possession by a demon, for example, the contorted and frightening Jekyll-Hyde physiognomy, the incoherent rage, the striking personality change, and the withdrawal convulsion.[4] Mark may have taken his lexical cue from the mention in Isaiah's Suffering Servant poem of "a tomb among [other] demoniacs" (Is 53.9; see chap. 3). And the Prayer of Nabonidus calls the Jew who cured the possibly alcoholic king a *gzr* (see chap. 3), a word Howard Clark Kee believes should be translated as "exorcist" since it appears to derive from *g'r*, a technical term for bringing demons under control.[5] In short, demon possession provided Mark a means of describing Jesus' early ministry that was interpretable one way by his Christian readers and another by the Markôs people.

It is therefore no accident that Jesus' first work is not a healing but an exorcism performed in the synagogue:

> (1.23) And immediately there was in their synagogue a man with an unclean spirit; (24) and he cried out, "What have you to do with us, Jesus of Nazareth? Have you come to destroy us? I know who you are, the Holy One of God." (25) But Jesus rebuked him, saying, "Be silent, and come out of him!" (26) And the unclean spirit, convulsing him and crying with a loud voice, came out of him.

The demoniac's loud scream, following his alcoholic convulsion, is the gut-wrenching admission of addictive drinking the man blurts out after years of denial, an event many recovering people have experienced themselves and witnessed in others. Mark's placement of the episode in the synagogue, where the Torah is read and wine drunk, signifies that the rule of God leads to victory over a universal human illness both symbolized and realistically catalyzed by religious drink-

ing. The demon personifies this illness just as it indicates the actuality of the man's intoxication.

The Gerasene Demoniac (5.1–20)

Originally probably a parable rather than the account of an actual
event, Jesus' story of the Gerasene demoniac depicts alcoholism as a
force seeking to destroy the world, its power proportionate to the
number of victims it claims:

> (5.2) . . . there met him a man with an unclean spirit, (3) who lived
> among the tombs; and no one could bind him anymore, even with a
> chain . . . (4) no one had the strength to subdue him. (5) Night and
> day . . . he was always crying out and bruising himself with stones. (6)
> And . . . the man ran and worshipped him . . . (7) crying out "Jesus, Son
> of the Most High God." . . . (8) Jesus said, "Come out of the man, you
> unclean spirit!" (9) Then, "What is your name?" He replied, "My name
> is Legion, for we are many." [Jesus sends the legion of demons into
> the herd of swine.] (15) Then the people came to Jesus, and saw the
> demoniac sitting there, clothed and in his right mind, the man who
> had had the legion. . . . (20) And he went away and began to proclaim
> in the Decapolis how much Jesus had done for him.

Key elements in the parable are the man's outcast status, his great
strength and self-destructiveness, and the "legion" of demons inhab-
iting him. Figured here is the terrible power of collective addiction.
One alcoholic is trouble enough, but when their number becomes
legion, humankind rages uncontrollably and begins to tear itself
apart. Implicit too is the eschatological struggle between God and the
death force for possession of humans one by one and ultimately for
the race as a whole. "Tombs" again reminds us of Isaiah 53.9. The
demon's use of the title "Son of God," unrelated to the political
meaning of the term, acknowledges the sonship of powerless persons
and the superiority of divine power to that of alcohol. Jesus' casting
the demons into the herd of swine perhaps reflects teaching on his
part that the stigma of uncleanness ought no longer be attached to
inebriety. The contrast between the man's wildness and his later calm
in Jesus' presence, clothed and in his right mind, will resonate with
any recovering person who has worked with a "wet" drunk only to see
the individual later on, sober and cleaned up at a meeting. Finally,
like so many who wish to share the joy of sobriety, the man proclaims
his gratitude and his recovery wherever he goes.

Other Alcoholism Cures

The stories of the woman with the twelve-year flow of blood (5.25–34)
and the comatose twelve-year-old girl (5.22–24 and 35–42) also point

to alcoholism cures. Apparently the woman's doctors had made her what today would be called a "prescription junkie." Her symptom may have been variceal bleeding caused by high-proof alcohol primitively distilled and included in secret potions. The girl, having attained marriageable age, may have lapsed into unconsciousness after her first adult experience with wine, victim of a hypersensitivity to alcohol.[6] Both stories mention twelve, which is the number of principles in Jesus' recovery program (see "The Secret Twelve," later in this chap.), and both persons are female, the gender Mark uses at the end of his book to denote powerless persons of both sexes as distinct from the alcoholic male disciples who imagine themselves figures of power. These facts further underscore the alcoholism thematicity of the stories.

Apart from the foregoing cures, the miraculous healings Mark attributes to Jesus are either polemical (2.3–12, 3.1–5), parabolic (7.32–37, 8.22–26), or symptomatic of Jesus' messianism (9.14–29, 10.46–52). The sole exception (assuming 1.30–31 to be nonmiraculous) is the cure of leprosy in 1.40–45, notable because of variant manuscript readings of Jesus' response to the leper's petition for cleansing. Most ancient texts say that Jesus was "moved with pity," from *splanchnizomai*, to feel compassion, while some have the verb *orgizō*, to arouse to anger. Many scholars believe "anger" the original reading, seeing Jesus' ire as directed against uncharitable purity laws—an argument vitiated by the absence of witnesses to the event. From the alcoholism perspective, "anger" would echo an anecdote Jesus apparently included in his story about the emotional upset he experienced early in his career when he realized that his charisma was attracting all kinds of ill and afflicted persons besides wine addicts and that, as a result, his movement's singleness of purpose would likely be compromised and he would risk succumbing to exactly the messianism that later drove him to Jerusalem.

All things considered, the early chapters of Mark's gospel so clearly reflect Jesus' story of victory over inebriety and the beginning of his recovery program that Mark's confreres must have wondered how the truth could possibly escape detection by nonalcoholic readers.

The Secrecy Motif

One of the most widely studied elements of Mark is its secrecy motif, manifest in cryptic mentions of "the Twelve," references to mystery and to outsiders, parables, admonitions to "tell no one," drawing apart from the crowd, calling aside for special teaching, obscure Passion predictions, the disciples' strange failures to understand, the ambiguous title "Son of Man," and various clandestine symbols. Mark perhaps reckoned that his Jewish-Christian readers would regard the secrecy emblems as signs of Jesus' prepaschal reticence to divulge his identity as Messiah, whereas his alcoholic readers would understand that the real reason for this motif was Jesus' wish for anonymity, stemming from a desire to prevent his identification as the Messiah from overshadowing the principles of the rule of God, which hold the key to wellness for suffering humankind.[7]

The Secret Twelve (3.13–19 and 4.10–11)

The thesis advanced here is that the much-discussed phrase "the Twelve" actually refers not to twelve disciples Jesus appointed but to twelve sobriety principles he formulated. Although religious readers have always understood "the Twelve" to refer to the disciples named in 3.16–19, scholars have frequently noted the ambiguity surrounding Mark's use of this term. The initial mentions of twelve in 3.14 and 3.16 involve the verb *poieō*, "to make, construct, or formulate" said of things and "to appoint or ordain" said of persons, usually read "and he appointed twelve. . . ." Certain manuscripts omit this verb from 3.16, probably because it is redundant when both verses are construed as referring to the disciples. With or without *poieō*, verse 16 clearly refers to "appointing" the twelve disciples named in verses 17–19. Verses 14 and 15, on the other hand, can be understood impersonally to refer not to twelve men but to twelve principles or precepts that Jesus formulated to embody his message of victory over the alcohol demon. Like all other versions, RSV reads these verses in the personal sense of *poieō:*

> (3.14) And he appointed [*epoiēsen*] twelve, to be with him, and to be sent out to preach (15) and have authority to cast out demons.

In the absence of a stated noun as object of the verb, however, the verses can just as correctly be translated in the impersonal sense of *poieō*, with the noun *formulations* supplied as an understood cognate object of the verb *formulated:*

> (3.14) And he formulated [*poieō*] twelve formulations to have with him, and to be disseminated [*apostellō*] to announce/demonstrate [*kērussō*] (15) the authoritative [*exousia*] casting out [*ekballō*] of demons [*daimōn*].

What this retranslation indicates is that just prior to listing the names of twelve disciples for the benefit of his religious audience, Mark makes a disguised reference to the twelve recovery principles Jesus formulated. These would have been semisecret lore within the Markôs groups, imparted to newcomers on their entrance into the fellowship and constitutive of the recovery program Jesus called the rule of God.

C. S. Mann points out that the same manuscripts that omit the redundant "he appointed" from 3.16, which goes against the dual referents of "twelve" suggested here, also omit the redactional "whom he also called apostles" from verse 16, which argues *for* disciples as the sole referent of "twelve." All this suggests an uneasiness about the original text (Mann considers it "corrupted beyond our recovery") on the part of its redactors, who may have sensed the presence of a disguised intention. Mann also notes that a later mention of the Twelve in 14.17, "and when it was evening he came with the twelve," is suspect, since interpreting it as a reference to persons requires assuming that the two disciples who entered Jerusalem to make the Passover preparations (14.13) returned to Bethany to reenter the city with Jesus and the ten other disciples.[8] Verse 14.17 makes perfect sense, however, when construed to mean that Jesus arrived at this important occasion with the twelve principles of the rule of God.

Furthermore, Mark's reference in 3.15 solely to the casting out of demons, without mentioning the healing of the sick, underscores the alcoholism content of the twelve principles. It parallels his earlier altering of the stock phrase "eating and drinking" to avoid mention of drinking. Where Luke edits the Markan original to read, "your disciples eat and drink" (5.33), Mark writes, "your disciples do not fast" (2.18); where Luke writes, "why do you eat and drink" (5.30), Mark writes, "why does he eat with" (2.16). Just as Mark takes pains not to implicate Jesus in drinking in the early stage of his gospel, so here in 3.15 he is careful to point out that the Twelve pertain only to the casting out of demons, his code word for release from alcohol addiction.

Moreover, the grammatical structure of the crucial passage mentioning the Twelve in connection with the secret of the rule of God (the so-called Messianic Secret, 4.10–11) implies that the phrase refers neither to twelve disciples nor to people at all:

> (4.10) And when he was alone, those who were about him with the Twelve asked him concerning the parables. (11) And he said to them, "To you has been given the secret of the rule of God, but for those outside everything is in parables."

The passage is grammatically nuanced to distinguish three groups: the Twelve, those who were about him with the Twelve *(hoi peri auton sun tois dodēka),* and those outside *(de tois exō).* It is those about him with *(sun,* "with," understood in its possessive, not its associative, sense) the Twelve, and not the Twelve themselves, who ask the question and are the "you" of Jesus' answer. Now if "the Twelve" is taken as referring to the twelve leading disciples, the text would seem to say that Jesus meant to exclude his closest followers from the secret. Whereas the disciples' failure to understand becomes an issue later on, however, it was certainly not Jesus' original intention to keep them in the dark. All this supports a reading wherein "the Twelve" refers not to persons at all but to spiritual principles or precepts. Verse 10 may therefore be translated as follows:

> (4.10) And when he was alone, those about him who had got the Twelve asked him concerning the parables.

The sense of "had got" is that of owned knowledge or acquired understanding. "Those about him" refers to all in Jesus' recovery fellowship, including the twelve disciples named in 3.17–19, involved in following those principles or "working the Steps," as alcoholics say today. Thus what Jesus is saying in verse 11 is that the secret of the rule of God is an insider's, that is, a surrendered addict's, understanding of the twelve principles of recovery.

Arguing from another angle against the idea that "the Twelve" refers uniquely to twelve privileged disciples, Howard Clark Kee points out that Jesus repeatedly makes his special disclosures not to twelve disciples but to an inner group of three or four—at the restoration of Jairus's daughter (5.37), the Transfiguration (9.2), the apocalypse (13.3), and Gethsemane (14.33).[9] Both lines of argument indicate that there was no group of twelve individuals who alone received the secret of the rule of God. For Mark's alcoholics, once again, the "secret" *(mustērion)* of the rule of God (4.11) was that "the Twelve" referred to the twelve precepts formulated by Jesus and constitutive of their alcoholism program, whose identity and spiritual meaning were unknown or misunderstood by those outside that program.

Exactly what those principles were, and to what extent they may have prefigured the Twelve Steps of Alcoholics Anonymous, are questions lost in time, although certainly open to speculation. For example, Joachim Jeremias points out that certain manuscripts of Mark render 14.25 not in the singular but in the first-person plural, "*We* will drink no more of the fruit of the vine. . . ." Quoting Matthew Black, Jeremias says that such variants "may go back to 'extra-canonical versions' of the words of Jesus."[10] Black himself writes that "Gospel variants which may be traced to an Aramaic source are most probably survivals from the earliest period of the Gospel text."[11] Now it happens that today's Twelve Steps are also written in the first-person plural. Step one begins, "We admitted we were powerless over alcohol. . . ." If the "we" version of Mk 14.25 echoes the first precept of the Twelve, it may have begun, "We declared we would drink no more of the fruit of the vine. . . ." Similarly, Jesus' prayer in Gethsemane (14.36) may echo others of the Twelve, specifically, "Admitted that God has all power" and "Humbly asked him to remove our cup addiction."

Although the foregoing reconstructions are entirely conjectural, they are excellent candidates for consideration as numbers one, two, and three of Jesus' Twelve. What seems certain is that Jesus did formulate twelve guidelines to spiritual living within the rule of God, similar in purport if not actual content to the Twelve Steps. The mysterious Twelve would have been well known to Mark's alcoholic audience in 68 C.E. and probably had leaked out to the Christian communities as well, some of whom would have anathematized them on account of their connection to inebriety and abstinence. Presumably this gave Mark added reason to conceal all references to the Twelve beneath a veil of linguistic ambiguity. On no account should nonaddict readers be permitted to discern that his book contained the story of the writing of the Twelve.

Parables

Jesus' characteristic mode of teaching outsiders about the rule of God was by means of parables. Mark's gospel includes two types of parables, those Jesus is reported to have told as such and parabolic stories Mark's narrator tells about Jesus. Altogether the parables fall into six groups: Jesus' four parables of the rule of God, two serenity parables told by the narrator, the narrator's three stage-one/stage-two stories mentioned previously (chap. 4), the narrator's story of the Gerasene demoniac derived from an alcoholism parable told by Jesus, Jesus' two watchfulness parables in Mark 13 (discussed later in this chapter), and the narrator's three bread stories interpreted previously (chap. 2) as bread-as-word parables illustrating how the Word of God is multiplied, that is, disseminated, by the words of all recovering people rather than only by the sermons of the specially ordained.

Jesus' four parables of the rule of God are the broadcast sower (4.3–9), the lamp meant to shine (4.21–23), the seed growing in secret (4.26–29), and the small seed/large shrub (4.30–32). All four lend themselves to recovery interpretations that differ but little from their familiar meanings. The sower reflects the practice of broadcast sowing of seed. Its emphasis lies in the fact that the sower is not concerned about where the seed falls, because the ground is such that it would do him no good to try to discriminate. He is not to judge but simply to trust that the wheat that should grow will. A parable about twelfth-stepping, it means "just carry the message and leave the results to God." Jesus' explanation of the parable (4.13–20) says exactly that: some drunks are not ready to admit powerlessness and thus remain enslaved to devil alcohol. Some come to a few meetings but never really get the program and return to drink when things get rough. A third sort begins to work the program but never completes the middle steps, thus remaining a prisoner of the self and falling short of sobriety. A fourth group, however, stays with the program and achieves sobriety. These are the winners, but no one can tell at the outset who they will be, hence the maxim heard among alcoholics today: "You can only carry the message, not the alcoholic."

The parable of the lamp meant to shine suggests that the good intended for persons will show forth in due course. Things hidden will be brought out into the open. The reason we had to drink as long as we did, the reason we have certain problems, the reason things happen to us—none of this is coincidence but will be revealed as what we had to go through to attain sobriety. Much the same point is conveyed by the seed growing in secret. Many recovering people look back to an incident months or years before they quit drinking, to a chance encounter with a former addict or to hearing something about recovery, and afterward recall that occasion as "the moment the seed was planted." At the time, however, they had no understanding at all of the message growing within them. Finally, the small seed/large shrub means that the size of a movement's beginning is no indicator of its destined magnitude. Movements begun in the meeting of two persons, whether named Jesus and Simon or Bill and Bob (the names of A.A.'s cofounders), can grow into worldwide recovery programs.

Traditionally interpreted as nature miracles, the stories of the storm at sea (4.35–41) and Jesus walking on water (6.45–52) come from serenity parables illustrating a familiar recovery saying of alcoholics today, "misery is optional." Parabolically, the storm at sea and the wind against which they are rowing are in the disciples' minds. Once in recovery, which is what their boat symbolizes, the disciples ought to recognize that fears and anxieties are attitudes that they can choose to retain or to dismiss, regardless of external conditions. Persons have a choice between reacting to negative outward conditions, and thus being governed by them, or declaring their independence of such conditions. In short, serenity comes in asserting one's freedom from externals.

"Tell No One" as the Anonymity Principle

Alcoholics think of anonymity as the spiritual basis of recovery and are careful "to place principles before personalities." This is the Twelfth Tradition of Alcoholics Anonymous. The anonymity principle was important to Jesus as well. Repeatedly he tells those whom he has helped not to reveal his identity. He enjoins the leper to silence (1.44) and tells the companions of the deaf-mute not to reveal who he is (7.36). He asks the drinkers whom he brings to surrender to respect his anonymity: Galileans (1.34), Gentiles (3.12), the man from Gerasa (5.19), and the family of the comatose twelve-year-old (5.34). Scholars have interpreted these references as a Markan attempt to correct a "divine man" Christology. In stressing principles not personalities, that is exactly what the anonymity idea does. Recovery has no teachers, leaders, authorities, or specially ordained ministers. Alcoholics are looking for trouble the moment they put their faith in another alcoholic ahead of faith in the recovery program, and they have found it once they begin thinking of themselves as a guru or messiah. There are no miracle workers in recovery and no people who are cured or perfect. From an alcoholism perspective, then, it is the anonymity principle, rather than a concern for the concealment of esoteric teaching, that prompts Jesus to enjoin others to silence. In 8.30 Jesus charges his followers not to tell others he is the Messiah, the Anointed One. His point is not that they should keep his messianic status secret but rather that he is *not* King David come again, he is *not* a messianic personage. (This topic is further discussed in the sections "'Messiah' Rejected, Messianism Embraced," and "Messiah.")

"Drawing Apart" as Attending a Meeting

Mark reports that Jesus often drew apart from the crowd with his disciples, not just the twelve men named in 3.16–19, but all recovering people in his following. The purpose of this drawing apart was to hold meetings. For the Markans water symbolized recovery, and the boat their recovery program. Gathering in a boat on the water thus represents a meeting of their fellowship. When Mark's alcoholics read that Jesus and the disciples withdrew toward the lake (3.7 and 6.31–32), they understood that Jesus and his followers were going to a meeting. At the beginning of the parable discourse (4.1), Jesus' sitting in a boat and teaching the large crowd on land signifies a meeting open to everyone. The contrast between his explanation to the crowd through parables and his private teaching to his disciples

(4.33–34) is similar to the contrast in content between what alcoholics today call "open" and "closed" meetings of their fellowship.

"Calling Aside" as the Meeting Lead

Jesus repeatedly "calls aside" *(proskaleō)* his followers to impart special teaching. Christian readers sometimes interpret this teaching as privileged instructions to the prototypical clergy, whereas recovering people will see it as the "leads" (the opening remarks of the meeting leader) that Jesus gave in gatherings intended for alcoholics—"closed meetings," in today's parlance. In 3.13 he calls his followers aside to give them the twelve principles of recovery he has formulated. In 3.23 he explains the impossibility of successful twelfth-step work when drunk. In 4.10–12 he teaches that alcoholics will understand recovery in a way that outsiders cannot fathom. In 6.7 he counsels "twelfth-stepping" (carrying the message to others) in pairs, a practice followed today. In 7.14–16 he tells an open meeting that impurity results not from what one takes in through the mouth but from what comes out of it. In 8.1–3, at the beginning of the second bread parable, he informs the disciples of his wish to give the entire crowd the principles of recovery so they will not collapse when they leave him, but the disciples fail to grasp his meaning. In 8.34–9.1, at the climax of his Galilean ministry, Jesus summons both disciples and crowd for his memorable lead on ego-death, dying to self. In 10.42–45 Jesus directs the disciples away from lording it over others and toward service. In 12.43–44 he tells them a parable on the importance of being willing to let go of whatever is one's dearest worldly security. In each instance, "calling aside" indicates a meeting lead given by Jesus.

Passion Predictions

In several sayings Jesus is traditionally understood to have predicted his suffering and crucifixion (8.31, 9.12b, 9.30–31, and 10.33–34). Joachim Jeremias has form-critically identified the Aramaic kernel of one set of these predictions as "the man will be delivered up to men," and Edward Schillebeeckx identifies the second as "man must suffer much and so enter glory."[12] In working steps four through seven of their program, today's alcoholics learn that recovery requires an inventory and admission of wrongs, recognition of powerlessness over one's character defects, and prayer for their removal. The process is humiliating and painful, but it culminates in a glorious feeling of freedom. Persons experiencing this process often say, "I feel I've rejoined the human race," or, "It feels great to become a human being at last." These sayings are semantically equivalent to "the man delivered to men." Such people also say, "Pain is the touchstone of spiritual progress," "No pain, no gain," and "You gotta go through it to get out of it." These sayings equal "suffer much and so enter glory." So understood, Jesus' Passion predictions are revealed as ancient versions of modern clichés about the suffering and elation involved in spiritual growth and becoming a true human being rather than continuing to play God. Those who hold that the Passion predictions verify Jesus' putative crucifixion and resurrection must reckon with the alternative readings of those sayings brought to light here.

The Disciples' Failure to Understand

Another aspect of the secrecy motif in Mark is the disciples' failure to comprehend the significance of Jesus' teaching. Christians have conventionally explained the disciples' obtuseness by arguing, somewhat arbitrarily, that Jesus' identity needed to remain veiled until after the Resurrection. Mark's alcoholics, on the other hand, would have attributed it to the likelihood that Jesus' progressive mental drunkenness even during the Galilean phase of his career had undermined the disciples' recoveries and blurred their vision of sobriety. For Mark, however, highlighting the disciples' faulty understanding, in particular their misguided concern about hierarchical status, was an element in his critique of the clericalizing of Jewish Christianity that he believed was about to occur in his own day, which his alcoholic readers would have considered a potential threat to the clergy-free character of their recovery movement.

First of all, the disciples fail to understand that bread signifies the words of recovery spoken in meetings and that its multiplication represents comments on the presider's lead spoken by all others present (6.31–44, 6.52, 8.1–10, and 16–21). Their having only one bread loaf in their boat (8.14) signifies that the disciples grasp only one of the twelve recovery principles formulated by Jesus, which presumably dealt with carrying the message, that is, preaching. Because they lack understanding of the other eleven principles, their preaching lacks content. Hence they prepare to resort to the "yeast of the Pharisees and of Herod" (8.15), which signifies the moralistic and autocratic sermons one would expect, respectively, from puritanical Pharisees and Herodian politicos. In 8.16–21 Jesus tries to explain that the content of spiritual gatherings comes from the multiplication of bread, that is, the sharing of comments by everyone present. But the disciples do not understand.

In 9.28–29 the disciples vainly attempt twelfth-step work without prayer and wonder why they fail. In 9.32 they fail to comprehend Jesus' Passion prediction. In 7.18 they miss the point about impurity. Dominated by fear, they fail to grasp the parabolic nature of the serenity stories backgrounding 6.45–52 and 4.35–41 and hand them on as miraculous phenomena, which is how Mark depicted them for his religious readers.

In the episode that launches Jesus on his assault against the Jerusalem leaders, Peter mistakenly professes Jesus as Messiah (8.29, interpreted in the section "'Messiah' Rejected, Messianism Embraced"). Thereafter, misunderstanding Jesus' explanation that spiritual exaltation comes only after the pain of ego-death (8.31), Peter takes Jesus aside and actually tries to dissuade him from such a death, so great is his fear of self-repudiation (8.32). At this point Jesus recognizes that the disciples, as unsurrendered advocates of self-empowerment, are in fact unwitting enemies of spiritual progress:

> (8.33) But turning and seeing his disciples, he rebuked Peter, and said, "Get behind me, Satan! For you are not on the side of God, but of men."

What a look of desperate insight plays across the face of Jesus as he turns, eyes the disciples as if for the first time, and then calls Peter a "satan" (Hebrew, meaning "adversary") and orders him out of his life, saying, *hupage opisō mou*, "get thee into my past." Peter is judging not by God's standards but by those of an alcoholic man unready to admit the bankruptcy of self-sufficiency. Like so much in Mark, the skillfully rendered line is ambiguous and permits readings such as the familiar "get thee behind me" (go away for now) and the didactic "get thee into my following" (get in line with my teaching).

With this dismissal of Peter Jesus rejects his leading disciples completely, directs his memorable sermon on ego-death to the multitude instead of the disciples (8.34–9.1), and prepares for his single-handed assault on Jerusalem. The disciples figure in numerous events later in Mark, but only as foils and never again as sober recovering persons. At the Last Supper they return to drink, drunkenly sleep through Gethsemane, and run away in fear on Jesus' arrest. Although dry, spiritually awakened, and eager to carry the message of recovery fifty days later at Pentecost (see chap. 5), they ultimately deny their alcoholic origins and participate in the transformation of Jesus' recovery program into a religion.

Jesus' Titles

Yet another component of the secrecy motif is the titles assigned to Jesus. Mark uses two of these, "Son of God" and "Son of Man," to great advantage with his multiple audiences. Although "Son of God" was understood by Jews in a biblical context as a designation of corporate Israel and of the king, Mark knows that his gentile Christian audience consider it to be a mark of divinity, whereas Greco-Roman pagans will think it refers to a royal hero-ruler superior to mortal men and deserving of worshipful respect in the temporal realm. Suspicious Roman censors seeing it featured at the outset of Mark's gospel (1.1), then spoken approvingly by the Roman centurion at the end (15.39), would conclude that users of the book looked on Jesus as a figure of good Roman order. At the baptism and the Transfiguration, the voice out of heaven calling Jesus "Son" (1.11 and 9.7) is obviously meant to evoke the gentile Christology espoused by the Hellenistic churches of Mark's day that imputed to Jesus divine preexistence. In making the demons and unclean spirits recognize Jesus as "Son of God" (3.11 and 5.7), however, Mark is reminding his alcoholic readers that the authority of God comes into play most significantly in the defeat of addiction. Jesus' personal awareness of being a child of God is revealed by his Gethsemane "Abba" (14.36), a relational name antithetical in purport to the exalted meaning Christianity would later associate with "Son of God."

By contrast, "Son of Man" is the designation Jesus himself favored. Its linguistic ambiguity in Aramaic means that it can be interpreted as a self-reference by Jesus and at the same time as a general term signifying "man" or "persons."[13] From the alcoholism perspective, therefore, when Jesus speaks about the Son of Man, he is referring both to himself and to all others in recovery. This will be true of his Son-of-Man statements relativizing the law (2.10 and 2.28), pointing to the need for surrender (8.38) and for service (10.45), stressing the certainty of suffering in attaining stage two of recovery (the Passion predictions previously discussed), and describing the coming age of sobriety (8.38 and 13.26, and 14.62 as interpreted in chap. 2). In these last sayings, traditionally connected with the Parousia, or Second Coming, and assumed to refer to a messianic personage, Jesus describes recovering people as going about (*erchomai*, translated in its sense of "coming and going") in the world at the dawn of the age of recovery, empowered by God and "exalted" or "glorified" in sobriety.

The only Son-of-Man sayings that refer to Jesus alone are those concerning betrayal (14.21 and 41). Richard Longenecker's summary of scholarship on the pre-Christian use of "Son of Man" as a title, especially Dn 7.13–14, concludes that "aspects of (1) humiliation and suffering on the one hand, and (2) vindication and glory on the other, are signalled by the expression Son of Man. . . ."[14] Viewing the

Passion predictions and the eschatological/parousial sayings from the alcoholism perspective confirms Longenecker's conclusion: humiliation and suffering, then sobriety and vindication, are precisely the themes that the Markôs people would have discerned in these sayings, which they would have applied to themselves as well as to the founder of their movement, Jesus.

Clandestine Symbols and Signs

A final aspect of Mark's secrecy motif is his use of a coterie symbolism and parlance and various clandestine signs. The hypothesis here is that Mark's fellowship recognized in the following items something like the symbolic values indicated:

Markôs = general nickname of fellowship members
water = a drink opposite to wine, signifying recovery
baptism = benchmark recovery experience involving suffering
water baptism = stage one of recovery, water drinking
spirit baptism = stage two of recovery, spiritual awakening
metanoia = change from drunken thinking to sober thinking
rule of God = the recovery program
demon possession = alcohol addiction
angels = recovering persons acting as sobriety messengers
boat on water = the recovery fellowship
walking on water = serenity in recovery
bread = words of recovery spoken by meeting leaders
multiplication of bread = comments by others present
fish = persons in recovery
the Twelve = twelve precepts of recovery formulated by Jesus
drawing apart from the crowd = holding a recovery meeting
calling aside = giving the meeting lead
"tell no one" = the anonymity principle
suffering = pain of spiritual growth
Son of Man = anonymous recovering person
glory = stage-two sobriety, spiritual prosperity

From time immemorial, persons who renounce wine have identified themselves as water drinkers. In Mark water is the symbolic opposite to wine. Three occurrences of the water symbol are: (1) Jesus' water baptism, signifying release from the drink obsession and stopping drinking (1.9–11); (2) "a cup of water to drink," the entrance rite into Jesus' recovery fellowship, by Mark's time known but deprecated by Christian groups as an insult to their wine ritual and hence alluded to by Mark in the obscure and seemingly offhand manner of

9.41; and (3) the culturally anomalous "man carrying a jar of water" who shows the disciples the room for their Passover (14.13). Exegetes have always recognized the clandestine nature of the material surrounding 14.13 but have been unable to agree on its meaning. It is clearly another of Mark's "winks" to his alcoholic readers, a reminder that the Last Supper, the seder at which Jesus voiced his eschatological interpretation of Passover wine, was a meeting of their fellowship of water drinkers, albeit ironically the meeting at which the disciples cum churchmen returned to wine and so betrayed the first principle of the Twelve.

Five more secret signs important to Mark's alcoholics are: (1) the mysterious donkey of 11.2–10, interpreted later in this chapter as deriving from the northern Aramaic "donkey/wine" pun and signifying Jesus' drunkenness on the occasion of his entrance into Jerusalem; (2) the drinking vessels Jesus tries to ban from the Temple (11.16); (3) the enigmatic "desolating sacrilege" of 13.14, interpreted later in this chapter as the term Jesus uses to characterize ritual wine when recognized as emblematic of alcoholism; (4) the women at Bethany (14.3–9), at the cross (15.40–41), and at the tomb (16.1–8), who signify surrendered alcoholics of both genders; and (5) the man in the white garment, who flees naked at Jesus' arrest (14.51) and then reappears at the empty tomb (16.5–7), a self-portrait by Mark and possibly a figure of the Christian deacon, whom Mark apparently regarded as the future annunciator of the parousial recovery program he believed would appear at the Church's end time. These clandestine signs are discussed in detail further on in this chapter.

Everything considered, the secrecy motif in Mark comprises a diverse emblemology: the ambiguous Twelve, riddling parables, the anonymity mystique, symbolic in-group parlance, polyvalent titles, clandestine signs, and the theme of misunderstanding. From the perspective of alcoholism, all these point to the rule of God as a recovery program. Mark's task as writer was to allude to this secret in ways ensuring that his insider audience would not fail to recognize his book as a third-person telling of Jesus' alcoholism story while at the same time keeping his Christian readers in the dark. As a result, what the Markans saw as references to Jesus' story of his recovery and of the sobriety groups he founded, the nonalcoholic Christians saw as a hodgepodge of mysterious emblems and puzzling material lacking a single focus or explanation. Clearly, Mark knew what scripturalists and churchmen have been loath to acknowledge, that the meaning of a text does not, as the writer Joseph Conrad said, reside in a work like the kernel of a nut but is generated in the act of reading and shaped by readers' preconceptions.

Mental Drunkenness

Midway in his drunkalogue Jesus would have turned from describing his Galilean honeymoon and the founding of his sobriety fellowship to relating anecdotes about his relapse into mental drunkenness and return to drink, and ultimately his messianic assault on the Jewish leadership in Jerusalem. Lacking the third-step surrender he was to experience in Gethsemane, Jesus had begun to fail in his efforts to carry the message in his native land.

Rejection at Nazareth (6.1–6a)

The first indication of Jesus' mental drunkenness is his rejection by his townspeople during the Nazareth synagogue service. Mark places the scene at the point where Jesus presumably located it in his drunkalogue, well after his initial proclamation of the rule of God and his first return home (3.20–21), the point where his honeymoon ends and his alcoholism begins to reassert itself:

> (6.1) He went away from there and came to his own country; and his disciples followed him. (2) And on the sabbath he began to teach in the synagogue; and many who heard him were astounded, saying, "Where did this man get all this? What is the wisdom given to him? What mighty works are wrought by his hands! (3) Is not this the carpenter, the son of Mary and brother of James and Joses and Judas and Simon, and are not his sisters here with us?" And they took offense at him. (4) And Jesus said to them, "A prophet is not without honor, except in his own country, and among his own kin, and in his own house." (5) And he could do no mighty work there, except that he laid his hands upon a few sick people and healed them. (6) And he marveled because of their unbelief.

What Jesus did, according to Luke's elaborated account of the sermon (Lk 4.16–30), was in effect to proclaim himself Messiah.[15] Apparently his appearance in a sacerdotal role in his hometown, where he lacked anonymity and had earlier experienced troubles (Mk 3.20–21), triggered in Jesus an attack of fear and grandiosity. He began to press, and his preaching scandalized the people and brought healing and conversion to no one. Scholars have pointed out that the second part of verse 5, "he laid hands on a few sick people and healed them," is such an obvious redaction contrived to tone down Jesus' lack of power on this occasion that it guarantees the authenticity of the first half of the verse, "He could do no mighty work there." Verse 6 says Jesus "marveled" *(ethaumasen)* at their unbelief. In fact, this verb signifies strong emotion that will be either positive or negative depending on the context. Since Jesus' reaction here would have been alcoholic anger, the Markôs people would have read the line, "And he raged at their unbelief." Failed self-will and ensuing anger are hallmarks of mental drunkenness. Thus, beneath the disguise of ambiguity allowing Christian readers to place the blame for the Nazareth debacle on the people lies the first anecdote Jesus told describing his deteriorating sobriety and failure to carry the message, which ultimately led to his return to active alcoholism.

Sending out the Disciples (6.7–13)

Jesus responds to his rejection by sending the disciples throughout the region to proclaim the rule of God. Matthew's expanded version (10.5–23) of Mark's account of the instructions to the disciples includes Jesus' prediction that they would be persecuted but that the messianic age would dawn before their mission was finished.[16] The question here is, what is the condition of a man who sends out bearers of good news, emissaries of a program of recovery and life, but predicts their persecution and rejection? The answer is, a man wrestling with fear and resentment, acting willfully and on his own. Matthew's Jesus grandiosely predicts that God will respond to the disciples' mission with a messianic theophany of the sort predicted in Daniel (Mt 10.23), but nothing like this happens. Mark gives the disciples' return a mere mention (6.30), indicating that they had little of moment to report. Even if the healings and exorcisms referred to in 6.13 are not redactional, there was no persecution, no dawning of a messianic era. One is forced to conclude that Jesus misspoke and erred by sending out the disciples as he did. A century ago, H. J. Holtzmann and Albert Schweitzer saw this error as a crushing blow to Jesus that marked his turn to apocalyptic.[17] This episode reflects the second anecdote Jesus told about his increasing mental drunkenness.

"Messiah" Rejected, Messianism Embraced (8.27–31)

The most significant event in Jesus' progression toward relapse is his messianic decision to go to Jerusalem. His resentment at the disciples' evangelical failures unabated (Lk 10.13–15 reports that Jesus cursed the unbelieving towns),[18] his judgmentalness unchecked (7.1–23), and his anger at the disciples' myopia increasing (8.14–21 is actually a tirade), Jesus heads for the pagan territory around Caesarea Philippi. En route he discovers that the disciples are prepared to proclaim him the Messiah:

(8.27) . . . and on the way he asked his disciples, "Who do men say that I am?" (28) And they told him, "John the Baptist; and others say, Elijah; and others one of the prophets." (29) And he asked them, "But who do you say that I am?" Peter answered him, "You are the Christ [*ho christos*, Greek translation of the Hebrew *messiah*, meaning "anointed one"]." (30) And he charged them to tell no one about him/it [genitive *peri autou* means both "about him" and "about it"].

Here again, Mark faces conflicting realities. He knows that there is a radical difference between his two audiences on the Messiah question. His Christian readers hold as a central tenet of their faith that Jesus was the Messiah (see Mt 16.16–20), whereas his alcoholic confreres know that Messiah was the very *last* thing Jesus wished to be thought. For Jesus, the exalted personal status of Messiah had no place in the rule of God. As for 8.30, it is clear both from his ensuing quarrel with Peter about the kind of death he must die in Jerusalem (8.31–33) and from his upcoming sermon on ego-death (8.34–9.1) that Jesus recognizes the inappropriateness of Peter's "You are the Messiah" (8.29).

Text-grammatically, Jesus' charge "to tell no one" (8.30) may be contextualized in at least two ways. The context ordinarily assumed is, "You and I know that I am the Messiah, but for now we must keep it a secret from the people, so tell no one about me/it." By contrast, the alcoholism context is: "You may think I am the Messiah, but I consider the idea misguided, since the anonymity concept reminds us to place principles before personalities, so tell no one about me/it." Expressed colloquially, the gist of the traditional version is "keep it under your hat"; that of the recovery version, "don't spread that nonsense around." Peter's error is frequently identified as thinking in terms of a Davidic or political messiah when he ought to have realized that Jesus' messiahship was spiritual. Both concepts miss the point. The issue is principles before personalities. In the conceptuality of recovery, then as now, "Messiah" would pertain to the spiritual program Jesus announced to humankind, but not to Jesus' persona as messenger. Had Peter been thinking soberly, what he should have said, the proper answer to Jesus' question, is the following: "Who do I say you are? I say you are the same as all of us, an anonymous alcoholic with a God-given message to carry."[19]

The point is that Jesus knows perfectly well that this should have been Peter's answer. It is part and parcel of his teaching about suffering and humble service in 10.35–45. Jesus has spoken correctly in his exchange with Peter, yet the perversity of mental drunkenness is such that the sufferer can speak enlightened words but act in completely self-willed and destructive ways. Here, so distressed is Jesus at

Peter's misguided attempt to proclaim him Messiah that in a moment
of profoundly drunken thinking he rejects his closest disciples and
concludes that he alone is able to inaugurate the rule of God and that
he must do so by going to Jerusalem to convert the Jewish leaders:

> (8.31) And he began to teach them that the Son of Man must suffer
> many things, and be rejected by the elders and the chief priests and
> the scribes, and be killed, and after three days rise again.

Since it is unlikely that Jesus, even in his mentally drunken condition,
would have predicted a resurrection from physical death, the final
predicates ("be killed and rise") in this passage represent either
Mark's addition to the received story for the benefit of Christian readers who believed that Jesus' career culminated in crucifixion/resur-
rection or a redaction by the same hand that added 6.5b and 6.13.
The point in any case is that, unaware that he is victim of the paradoxical calculus of mental drunkenness, Jesus at Caesarea Philippi
ironically succumbs to fanatical messianism even as he repudiates
messiahship, absurdly announcing his intention to model self-abne-
gation by an act of colossal self-assertion.

Discourse on Ego-Death (8.34–9.1)

Jesus' drunken action, however, in no way vitiates the truth of his
subsequent teaching on the importance of ego-death. The key lines
read:

> (8.34b) If any man would come after me, let him deny himself and take
> up his cross and follow me. (35) For whoever would save his life will lose
> it; and whoever loses his life for my sake and the gospel's will save it.

Christians usually take the three imperatives in verse 34b to mean,
"Practice self-denial through willpower, bear life's pain and suffering
as Jesus bore his crucifixion, and imitate Jesus as a model of perfection." Mark's alcoholics, however, would have recognized that Jesus
intended something quite different: "Stop living by willpower (that
is, 'deny' or repudiate your self-will), cooperate with the execution
of self ('carry your cross,' in other words, voluntarily admit your powerlessness), and start working a recovery program ('follow me')."

Edward Schillebeeckx analyzes the expression "to carry one's cross"
in connection with its use in the Q community (Mt 10.38; Lk 14.27),
for whom mention of the cross was strictly metaphorical and not a
postpaschal reference to crucifixion. Schillebeeckx believes that the
idiom refers to physical death, specifically, Christian martyrdom,
whereas Burton Mack believes that it means "to bear up under con-

demnation" and "not allow the fear of being killed to affect loyalty to the movement."[20] Now when Jesus was a lad of about twelve (6 C.E.), the Romans crushed a patriot uprising in Galilee by crucifying some two thousand Jewish men. The boy Jesus must have known some of these men, must have seen their crosses, a sight no one could forget. Hence it is unlikely that he would have used "carry your cross" either in its popular sense, to refer to bearing the inevitable burdens of life, or to refer to persecution or actual crucifixion, the horrible fate from which, among other things, his sobriety program aimed to save humankind. Rather, it was self-death or ego-death to which Jesus was referring, a death that cannot occur unless one assents to and cooperates in the process, which is almost certainly what he meant by "carry your cross."

Jesus' remark about shame toward the end of his discourse has always posed a quandary to interpreters:

> (8.38) For whoever is ashamed of me and of my words in this adulterous and sinful generation, of him will the Son of Man also be ashamed, when he comes in the glory of the Father with the holy angels.

In the present context, "whoever" would refer not only to Peter and the disciples but also to anyone else ashamed to acknowledge Jesus' alcoholism ("me") or their own ("my words"), or to accept the leveling of pride and ego required in recovery. Note that the "life" in verse 35, which must be "lost" if it is to be "saved," is *psuchē*, which means "self" or "inner being" but not physical life. It is the same *psuchē* that dies in Gethsemane (14.34). Mention of "the Son of Man coming in glory" in verse 38, like those in 14.62 (see chap. 2) and 13.26 (see chap. 6), refers not to a solitary messiah personage but to people living lives exalted in sobriety, a condition that persons ashamed of admitting their powerlessness will not attain. Finally, 9.1 promises recovery to some who are present even as Jesus speaks. Overall, Jesus' discourse on ego-death, like his repudiation of the title "Messiah," represents a clear-sighted witness to the spirituality of recovery. Unfortunately he follows it by an act of utter and total messianism, going to Jerusalem. In the jargon of recovery, one would say that Jesus at this point was "talking the talk but not walking the walk."

Toward Jerusalem (9.2–10.52)

The scene of transfiguration that follows Jesus' announcement of his decision to go to Jerusalem (9.2–13) looks like a Markan invention in response to a perceived rhetorical need. In reprising the baptismal theophany in 1.10–11, which is what the Transfiguration scene does, Mark may have felt that both Christian and Roman readers needed reassurance at this point that despite Jesus' disturbing remarks about shame and loss of life (8.34–38), he really was the divine Son of God they thought him to be, who expected worship but nothing as radically humiliating as carrying crosses or dying to self.

Further on, Mk 10.35–45 conveys Jesus' discourse on the suffering entailed in stage two of recovery and on the principle that service, not hierarchical rank, is the proper end of sobriety. Otherwise, excepting only 10.35–45 and the sub rosa "cup of water" saying in 9.41, all the events between Caesarea Philippi and Jerusalem (Mark 9 and 10) reflect Jesus' increasing messianism. One notes the following: valid spiritual teaching reinforced by a questionable healing—presumably the boy in 9.14–29, whose demon appears to be epilepsy, has not gotten well but only come out of a seizure; gurulike preaching (9.33–37 and 42–50); personalist remarks on religious doctrine (10.1–31); and acceptance of the messianic designation implicit in blind Bartimaeus's salutation "Son of David" (10.46–52). Despite knowing better, Jesus succumbs completely to his alcoholic compulsion to play the part of Messiah. Afterward, in Galilee, he must have enjoyed many a laugh at his own expense in recounting these anecdotes about his unchecked self-will and messianic grandiosity en route to the Holy City.

At Jerusalem

Mark 11 begins with the following triadic sequence: Jesus' entrance into Jerusalem (11.1–11), his cursing of the fig tree (11.12–14), and his cleansing of the Temple (11.15–19). Whereas religious readers have interpreted these events as prophecy fulfillments pertaining to the Messiah (Zec 9.9 and Ps 118.26–27 in the case of the entrance, and Is 56.7 and Jer 7.11 in the Temple cleansing), Mark's insider audience would have recognized the triad as a camouflaged version of an episode in Jesus' drunkalogue, the story of how, on reaching the environs of Jerusalem, Jesus had gotten drunk on festival wine, entered the city intoxicated, and acted out his alcoholic anger. This story is one of the best-kept secrets in a gospel filled with secrecy.

First, notice how markedly the seemingly benign entrance into the city contrasts with the violent, even berserk cleansing of the Temple. Second, concerning the supposedly dishonest Temple merchants, it is known that the Roman occupiers were constantly fearful lest festival pilgrims riot and trigger rebellion. Hence the money changers and sellers of the objects of sacrifice in the Temple, who performed necessary services for the worshipers, were strictly supervised by the Temple priesthood precisely so that they would not, by crooked dealings, incite the people. They were not the "thieves" of Jer 7.11. Jesus' supposed attempt to drive these merchants from their legally occupied stalls would have been an act as ludicrous as it was rash. Third, between the entrance and the cleansing occurs the cursing of the barren fig tree, a bizarre and senseless incident that, despite Mark's interpretation contrived for the benefit of his religious readers (11.20–24), has resisted attempts by commentators to make it an allegory or to otherwise render it comprehensible. With these points in mind, we shall see how Mark has shaped the triadic event sequence in 11.1–19 to indicate Jesus' drunkenness at this juncture in his career.

Riding a Donkey (11.1–10)

The position here is that the Jerusalem entrance astride a donkey is not historical but a popular tradition that originated among nonalcoholic Christians based on their misunderstanding of what the first members of the Galilean sobriety groups had reported about Jesus. Mark's treatment of the episode implies secrecy of some sort. The mysterious directions to the disciples concerning procurement of the beast (11.2–6) have long been recognized as a signal of clandestine material whose import has remained obscure. For Mark's alcoholics the secret resided in the word *donkey* underlying verses 2, 4, 5, and 7.[21] As it happens, in the northern Aramaic dialect spoken by Jesus and the disciples, the words meaning "donkey" and "wine" were homophonic and homographic, that is, they were pronounced and written exactly the same. The two formed a paronomasia, or perfect pun, one phonemic or graphemic sequence ambiguously representing two different words. This linguistic fact, never before employed in reading Mk 11.1–10, is confirmed by the Aramaic expert George Lamsa[22] and in a Talmudic anecdote in which Jerusalem merchants ridicule a Galilean who cannot clearly pronounce what he wants to buy: "You stupid Galilean, do you want something to ride on (a donkey = *ḥamār*)? Or something to drink (wine = *ḥamar*)?"[23] Later on Mark draws attention to his knowledge of Aramaic dialect differences through his story of the serving girl's recognition of Peter's dialect in the high priest's courtyard (14.70). Mark's alcoholic readers would have understood this anecdote as both a reminder and a confirmation that Galilean Aramaic provides access to the "donkey/wine" pun, which points in turn to Jesus' drunkenness on entering Jerusalem.

The linguistic explanation of the pun is this: what speakers of other dialects and languages would regard as two different statements—in

English, "donkeyed" or "on a donkey" versus "wined" or "wine drunk"—looked and sounded the same in Jesus' Galilean Aramaic. It was, in short, ambiguous. What probably happened at the outset of the tradition is that, whereas Jesus in telling his story, and his Galilean cohort in passing it on, thought they were saying that Jesus entered the city wine drunk, their nonalcoholic compatriots, all unprepared to think of Jesus as a drunkard, understood their statement to say that Jesus entered the city on a donkey. As time passed and the Markans realized that the misunderstanding had achieved a life of its own among nonalcoholic Jesus people, they must have found the irony choice indeed. The story presumably circulated among Galilean groups, which would have recognized the paronomasia, and traveled to Judean groups, which would have needed to have its humor explained.[24] As for Mark's description of the event, since the nonalcoholic communities had long ago come to interpret "on a donkey" as a messianic prophecy fulfillment, it was only natural that the evangelist would embellish his story with trappings of the heroic legend— the unridden beast (11.2), garments and branches carpeting the hero's path (11.8), "Hosanna!" (11.9), and reference to a storied progenitor, in this case, King David (11.10).

Not only does this new understanding of the Jerusalem entry support the idea that Jesus began to drink again on reaching the Holy City at festival time and was drunk during the cursing and cleansing, it also gives parabolic significance to the entire triadic sequence mentioned above (11.1–19). First, the "donkey/wine" pun understood to mean drunkenness announces the theme of intoxication. Second, cursing the fig tree represents simple drunken behavior, the senseless blighting of a tree for barrenness in what any Palestinian native would have known was the off-season for figs. Third, cleansing the Temple depicts the danger and destructiveness that result when physical inebriation catalyzes mental drunkenness and triggers rash and violent action. Viewed as a whole, the triad acquires an integrated semiotic value: Jesus' initial deeds in Jerusalem display intoxication expressed in physical inebriation and enacted mental drunkenness. As alcoholics learn the hard way, persons who do what Jesus did, drunkenly acting out their so-called justified anger, not only wreck their serenity but also cause harm to others, fighting of all kinds, and trouble for themselves. Indeed, 11.19 reports the search by the priests and scribes for a way to destroy Jesus.

Certain collateral evidence is worth noting in support of the "donkey/wine" interpretation advanced here:

1. Justin (*First Apology*, par. 32, 262) writes that the disciples found the donkey on which Jesus rode "tied to a vine," a reference to Gn 49.11. This verse contains the rarer of two Hebrew words for ass, which, like the Aramaic example just discussed, puns with the Hebrew for wine.[25] His remark thus raises the possibility that Justin knew of a connection between Mark's donkey story and drunkenness.

2. Certain second-century anti-Christian graffiti from Rome and Carthage, discussed by Morton Smith, depict a crucified figure with the head of a donkey.[26] Smith ties these graffiti to what he believes was a pre-Christian tradition that the god of the Jews was ass-headed, but other explanations are possible. For example, wine addicts often refer to themselves as "wine heads," an epithet among drunkards perhaps as old as wine itself. The Galilean Markans, seeing that "donkey," not "wine," was the chosen understanding of the Jerusalem entrance story among their nonalcoholic compatriots, may have jokingly adopted the term "donkey heads" to refer to nonalcoholic Jesus people. By the second century this term could have spread outside Palestine as a derisive epithet used by anti-Christian pagans ignorant of its Aramaic origin and the "donkey/wine" pun.[27]

3. Origen believes that Celsus, who among his many slanders describes Jesus at the Crucifixion as "rushing with his mouth open to drink" (Origen, *Contra Celsum*, II.37, 41), was citing a familiar Greek proverb in claiming that the controversy between Jew and Christian reduced to "a fight about the shadow of an ass" (III.1, 85). Celsus may actually have been referring to the donkey story and to vague, century-old memories of disputes about Jesus' drunkenness between Jewish Markôs people (Galilean "wine heads") and gentile Christians (nonalcoholic "donkey heads").

4. Finally, a Greco-Roman slant on the donkey episode in Mark, definitely pointing to a meaning of inebriation, is the fact that the mythic Silenos, mentor of Dionysos, was depicted as riding a donkey because he was always too drunk to walk.

In any case, the "donkey/wine" pun not only indicates Jesus' intoxication at this point in his story,[28] it also explains the notoriously incomprehensible cursing of the fig tree, just as it places the Temple cleansing within a rubric of drunken anger and thereby exposes the thematic coherence of the entire entry-cursing-cleansing sequence.

Temple Vessels (11.15–16)

A close look at Mark's report of the Temple cleansing reveals the presence of yet another unrecognized ambiguity in the text, one suggesting that the Markôs community may have understood the objective of Jesus' rampage in terms entirely different from those featured in conventional translations. The RSV reads as follows:

> (11.15) . . . And he entered the Temple and began to drive out [*ekballō*] those who sold and those who bought in the Temple, and he overturned the tables of the money-changers and the seats of those who sold pigeons; (16) and he would not allow [*aphiēme*] anyone to carry [*diapherō*] anything [*skeuos*] through *[dia]* the Temple.

Interpreters have always translated *ekballein* (11.15) in its exorcism sense, "to drive out," and have concluded that Jesus' goal was to shut down all commercial activity within the Temple confines. Verse 16 is taken as an extension of this thought, with *skeuos* generically translated "thing" (RSV, NAB), "goods" (NEB, AB), and "merchandise" (NIV). *Skeuos* means "vessels," however, including specifically vessels for the storage, serving, and drinking of wine in Temple rituals. These would have ranged from the silver vessels long ago taken to Babylon and desecrated by Belshazzar (Dn 5.2), then returned to Jerusalem by Cyrus (Ezr 5.14–15), to the many vessels brought by pilgrims for drinking their private ceremonials. From the alcoholism perspective, these vessels would assume thematic centrality in the passage.

Verse 16 says that Jesus "would not allow" (*aphiēmi*, "to let, suffer, permit") the carrying of these vessels. Realistically this can only mean that he attempted to prevent it, and the clause may be so translated. "Carry" comes from *diapherō*, "to carry through," and a second *dia* follows *skeuos*. *Diapherō* can mean "carry to and fro," or "carry around," or simply "deploy," and the second *dia* can mean "for" or "with a view to." Hence the verse can be read "and he attempted to prevent anyone from carrying around [wine] vessels for Temple use." In this alternative version of verse 16, Jesus' objective in the Temple was not to suppress commercial activity but to quash religious drinking, and verse 15 merely reports the chaos he caused in violently acting out his idea. Thus *ekballein* would be translated not as "drive out" but as "knock away" or "push aside." The entire passage would read as follows:

> (11.15) . . . And he entered the Temple and began pushing aside buyers and sellers there, and overturning money-changers' tables and pigeon-sellers' seats, (16) in his attempt to prevent persons from deploying [wine] vessels for use in the Temple [rituals].

The scene is that of an intoxicated man running amok and accosting whomever he sees preparing to engage in ritual drinking, priests and people alike, drunkenly inveighing against wine and trying to snatch the cups and jugs from their very hands. Small wonder Mark reports no reaction from bystanders, who could only have looked on in amazement. One can imagine a Jewish or a Christian service today interrupted by a frenzied drunk shouting about not drinking and grabbing at kiddush cups and communion chalices. Chapter 7 discusses the possibility that Jesus' proclamation in the Temple reported in Jn 7.37, "If any one thirst, let him come to me and drink [water]," may have been a drunken tirade against wine immediately preceding this berserk attempt to seize worshipers' drinking vessels. What a stir Jesus must have caused in his rampage through the Temple, and how different his crazed action here is from his sober offer of the cup at Passover.

Warfare in the Vineyard (12.1–9)

Soon thereafter Jesus turned from lashing out physically against religious drinking to rhetorical combat on the same topic, evident in his militant recasting of the Isaian (5.1–7) allegory of the vineyard:

> (12.1) A man planted a vineyard, and set a hedge around it, and dug a pit for the wine press, and built a tower, and let it out to tenants, and went into another country. (2) When the time came, he sent a servant to the tenants, to get from them some of the fruit of the vineyard. (3) And they took him and beat him, and sent him away empty-handed . . . (5) and so with many others, some they beat and some they killed. (6) He had still one other, a beloved son; finally he sent him to them, saying, "They will respect my son." (7) But those tenants said to one another, "This is the heir; come, let us kill him, and the inheritance will be ours." (8) And they took him and killed him, and cast him out of the vineyard. (9) What will the owner of the vineyard do? He will come and destroy the tenants, and give the vineyard to others.

As conventionally interpreted, the vineyard in the allegory represents Israel, and the tenants' refusal to give the owner his harvest or obey the son represents its leaders' refusal to accept the rule of God and Jesus as Messiah.

But alcoholics who hear of a vineyard or who, like Jesus, speak about one do not imagine an idyllic picture of God's people; rather, they see the reality of viticulture and the production of an intoxicant. They see not the joys of the grape harvest but the addictive drinking that follows fermentation. The "wild grapes" of the Isaian allegory (5.2 and 4) they see as a symbol of alcoholism. The tenants in the parable refuse to yield up the owner's share because they want to

drink it all themselves. They are addicts! Prophetically the allegory
indicts not only the Jewish priests in Jesus' day, and the rising Judean
Christian clergy in Mark's time, but also an alcoholic hierarchy
throughout the church age. As in the story of the forbidden fruit of
Eden, the tenants' plan to steal the son's inheritance represents humanity's hubristic attempt to possess the secret of well-being, deludedly understood as alcohol. Alcohol, however, as an agent of God's
wrath visited on the tenants, ultimately destroys whoever seeks to
master it. So viewed, the vineyard allegory points to alcoholism from
beginning to end.

Sober, Jesus would have followed up the recast Isaian allegory by
endeavoring to carry the message of step one to the Jerusalem leaders: admission of powerlessness over alcohol and a decision to drink
no more. Drunk, he misapplied his own parable, as shown by his
subsequent efforts to convince the high priests and scribes that their
problem was the assumption of clerical rank, when in truth their first
problem was alcohol, manifest in their ritual drinking. First things
first: recovery from alcohol addiction begins with a desire to quit
drinking. This is what Jesus overlooked in his drunken anger and self-
will, apparent both in his attempts to wrest the drinking vessels from
Temple worshipers and in his bellicose midrash on Isaiah, and it
accounts for his failure to bring the Jerusalem religionists to *metanoia*.

Rhetorical Combat (11.27–12.44)

The material in 11.27–12.44 comes from Jesus' story of his rhetorical contest against the Jewish religious establishment. The reasoning
behind Jesus' position is beyond reproach. In the radical anarchism
of the rule of God, there are no clerical hierarchs interposed between
God and humankind. For Jesus as for recovering persons today, the
height of mental drunkenness is for one person in a spiritual fellowship to seek to dominate others, whether in the name of God, superior wisdom, or the common good. Yet Judea under the Romans was
in fact a theocracy. Although they were considered to be religious
figures, the leading priests, scribes, and elders of Jerusalem, who
gathered in an assembly called a sanhedrin, exercised legal authority over the people, including recommendations of excecutions, and
generally performed the functions of civil magistrates. Jesus attacks
these men not because of their venality but because, by positioning
themselves between God and persons and seeking to mediate his will
for individuals and society as a whole, they usurp the rule of God and
bring down his wrath in the enmity and warfare their domination

causes. Jesus saw this religious dominance as an important cause of humankind's troubles, and he challenged it accordingly.

Jesus' assault on the Jerusalem leaders consists of, besides the vineyard allegory, seven episodes in which, through argument and rhetoric, he seeks to confound these hierarchs and persuade them to abandon their religious offices. First, in a bold stroke Jesus unmasks the hypocrisy of the chief priests, scribes, and elders (11.27–33). By countering their question about the source of his authority with a question about John's baptisms that they are afraid to answer, Jesus exposes their supposed authority for what it is, a sham. It is a skillful rhetorical ploy, but rhetorical ploys seldom change minds.

Second, Jesus gives his "render unto Caesar and unto God" answer to the question about taxes (12.13–17). His point is that persons have only two kinds of obligations: one to the temporal order and the other to God. By omitting reference to religious authorities, Jesus means to say that if they come into the issue at all, they do so on the temporal side, however much they may seek to identify themselves with God. In other words, persons who feel themselves obligated to render to ecclesial authorities do so as if to Caesar, and what they give is Caesar's, not God's.

Third, in the dispute about marriage after death (12.18–25), Jesus explodes the idea that clergymen have knowledge about the afterlife that is unavailable to ordinary people. Then in verses 26–27 he challenges the anti-Sadducean teaching of a general end-time resurrection awaited by all the dead, substituting for it the view that what we see as biological death is in fact, for those in the rule of God, a simultaneous rising, a transition to heavenly life itself. Jesus illustrates this by citing God's words to Moses from the burning bush (Ex 3.6), which mean that since God is the God of the living and not the dead, then figures such as Abraham, Isaac, and Jacob, known to have died biologically many years before Moses' time, are alive even now and not lying dead somewhere awaiting a resurrection. To the authorities Jesus says with finality, "You are completely wrong!"

Fourth, in reaffirming the Shema and the rule of neighborly love as the epitome of God's will for humankind (12.28–34), Jesus says to the scribe who has rightly answered his question, "You are not far from the rule of God." What remains for him to do? The answer is obvious: renounce his offensive religious office. Fifth, Jesus further confirms the point by an ingenious exegesis of Ps 110.1 (12.35–37) to the effect that, because he will be not Davidic but spiritual, the Messiah will have no need of official minions.

Sixth, Jesus attacks the clergy personally, accusing them of pride, pomposity, and moral corruption (12.38–40). Seventh, as an object lesson to the disciples, he concludes his harangue with the parable of the widow's offering (12.41–44), whose point is that the way to the surrender of self is to relinquish one's dearest security. The security in question here can only be each cleric's privileged religious office. All this amounts to a titanic rhetorical assault by Jesus, brilliant but drunken, aimed at destroying the very concept of hierarchical religion.

But not one mind is changed. Once again, had Jesus been sober and "working his program," he would have remembered that alcoholics begin their journeys to recovery not by renouncing their mental drunkenness and self-will but by quitting drinking. Instead of trying to force abstinence on religious drinkers or persuade the Jerusalem leaders to abandon their clerical authority, Jesus should have concentrated on step one and witnessed to his own powerlessness over alcohol. Because he is drunk, however, both physically and mentally, Jesus takes a wrong approach, acts the part of a fanatical Galilean messiah, and only increases the resolve of the frightened Jewish hierarchs to resist him and do him harm (12.12).

Apocalypse (Mark 13)

The awful remorse experienced after a drinking bout following a period of sobriety often inspires a deeper awareness of one's illness and the vital importance of recovery. The view proposed here is that the Markan apocalypse, subject of endless speculation and dispute, originated in the revelations Jesus experienced during the hangover that concluded his Jerusalem intoxication, his last drunk before his paschal surrender. Picture Jesus on the morning after, aware of his troubles with the Jerusalem leaders but even more shaken by the realization of the gravity of his illness, saying in effect: "What have I done? I know I'm not God yet I've been suicidally playing God. I know I'm not a hero messiah, yet I've succumbed to messianism. I know the only person I can change is myself, yet I've resorted to lunatic violence and rhetorical warfare trying to reform religious drinkers and the leaders of my religion. I know that recovery can begin only with an inner desire for sobriety, yet I've ignored that truth completely in approaching my co-religionists." It is a moment of intense pain for Jesus. Here he hits bottom a second time and commences to experience the humiliation and deflation at depth that herald stage two of sobriety. Not surprisingly, it is also a time of apocalyptic insight.

As interpreted here, the Markan apocalypse revolves around the recognition of wine, specifically ritual wine, as the "desolating sacrilege" named in verse 14. This much-studied phrase, taken from Daniel 12, wherein it denotes Antiochus IV's desecration of the Temple between 167 and 164 B.C.E., is arguably the central cryptic image in Mark. The rest of the Markan apocalypse relates to the "desolating sacrilege" in various ways: hearers must endure wars and tribulations while awaiting it (13.5–13); they are admonished to "understand" when they see it (13.14b), flee to safety when the understanding comes (13.14c–20), and watch vigilantly for its arrival (13.28–37), bearing in mind that only God knows the day and hour (13.32). Owing to the siege of Jerusalem ongoing at the time of Mark's writing, the desolating sacrilege is generally assumed to refer to an imminent defilement of the Temple by Roman conquerors, yet this interpretation seems impoverished. Of all Mark's clandestine symbols, this is perhaps the most important. The culminating revelation of Jesus' career, it encodes the kernel of his message to hearers down the ages. Surely it pertains to something more important to Christian eschatology than merely another Temple desecration by invading soldiery. The following discussion explores this question and the radically different answer proposed here.

The Desolating Sacrilege as Ritual Wine (13.14)

In framing the utterance conveying Jesus' prepaschal hangover revelation and the apocalyptic admonitions Jesus subsequently included in his sobriety story (see chap. 4), Mark had to know that his exophoric reference to "the desolating sacrilege set up where it/he ought not to be" would be variously understood by the different audiences addressed in his pointed exhortation, "Let the reader understand!" (13.14). The passage reads as follows:

> (13.14) But when you see the desolating sacrilege set up where it/he ["he" agrees with the masculine participle "set up"] ought not to be— Let the reader understand!—then let those who are in Judea flee to the mountains.

Mark very likely reasoned that the Romans and the gentile Christians of his day would interpret the line as evidence of Jesus' ability to foresee the desecration of the Temple forty years before the event. To the beleaguered Judean Christians who were ostensibly his principal audience, Mark expected that the line would convey Jesus' prophetic directive to abandon Judaism and represent themselves as followers of the new religion in order to escape Roman wrath.

Mark and his alcoholics, however, would have interpreted the passage quite differently. The proposal here is that they understood

Jesus' mention of the Danielic "desolating sacrilege" as a reference to the Temple priest (or, by extension, the synagogue leader or household paterfamilias) raising the ritual wine cup. At least this is how the evangelist and his fellow Markans in 68 C.E. presumably imagined that the alcoholic hearers of Jesus' original drunkalogue had interpreted the reference. As for themselves in their own time, Mark and his cohort would have connected the passage not so much to the priests of the doomed Temple or other figures of Jewish worship as to the image of the new ritual drinker, the emergent Christian clergyman and his wine chalice. They did not think the passage an attack on ritual drinking or an attempt to curtail its practice; rather, they took it to be a reference by Jesus to the apocalyptic insight of individual persons at the moment when, touched by the grace of God, they recognize such drinking, whether Christian or Jewish, as something to forswear.

Modern interpreters agree that the line echoes Dn 12.11 and that "set up where he/it ought not to be" refers to an abomination of some kind—either a person, something connected with a person, or both—present at the Temple altar. Since seeing it should trigger precipitous flight (13.14c), "seeing" is usually taken to mean a perception that is in some way surprising and cognitively disorienting. Reasoning from the events surrounding Dn 12.11, scholars generally identify the sacrilege as referring to the standards of a conquering army erected at the Temple altar or to an "anti-Christ" figure, perhaps a statue of the Roman emperor, placed within the Temple confines.

The line can be read differently, however, to support the understanding imputed to Mark's alcoholics. Instead of indicating something usually considered an abomination (a foreign military standard, say) placed where one is shocked or surprised to see it (the Temple altar), it can indicate something in its usual place and usually considered benign (wine in the hands of the altar priest, say) newly cognized as a desecration. The beholder's cognitive reorientation would stem not from *where* a thing is newly located but from *how* it is newly perceived, not from seeing a strange or foreign object in a familiar place but from seeing a familiar object in a new and shocking light. Thus, for Mark's alcoholics to have understood Jesus as referring to ritual wine re-cognized as a sacrilege is an interpretation fully supportable from the text. The case for a surprising reading such as this, rather than the predictable understanding of military emblems based on Daniel, is strengthened by the Markan admonition, "let the reader understand." This interjection would be unnecessary and inappropriate were the familiar Danielic interpretation intended. Here the sight is ambiguous as well as surprising. Ambiguity of surprise is another of Mark's masterstrokes of secrecy.

As the central revelation of Jesus' apocalypse, recognition of the wine cup as a "desolating sacrilege" reflects the insight brought home to Jesus during his Jerusalem hangover, that the turning point of alcoholic man's recovery is seeing wine as the source of his troubles. Beholders thereupon become convinced that they must stop drinking, ritually and otherwise, and that their whole lives depend on this conviction. This apocalyptic experience triggers the drinker's admission of powerlessness over alcohol. It is the non-self-authored conceptual cataclysm awaiting all religious drinkers. As such it portends the personal revelation Jesus will soon express at the Passover supper, "This [wine] is [the cause of] my blood[shed]" (14.24a; see chap. 2). Thus the present reading harmonizes these two highly significant apocalyptic texts, 13.14ab and 14.24a, in a way no other interpretation has in the history of Markan exegesis.

In response to their alcohol apocalypse, Jesus charges his hearers to abandon the enabling structures of self-empowerment and self-management (willpower, religion, family, etc.) for the haven of surrender and recovery:

(13.14c) then let those who are in Judea flee to the mountains.

For Jesus, who is thinking here in terms of last things, the reason why wine exists at all, why it is drunk anywhere, in public houses or the streets, at festivals and celebrations, in family rituals, and particularly in religious rites, points to a single eschatology: the changing of mind and ensuing radical action entailed in the renunciation of drink. This action Jesus characterizes as "fleeing from Judea to the mountains," a phrase symbolizing the exodus from religious alcoholism to recovery. The mountain image comes from Amos, Joel, and First Isaiah, where it is connected respectively with "sweet wine" (Am 9.13; Jl 4.18) and "choice wine" (Is 25.6). Hence the image directly foreshadows Jesus' mention of "new wine" at the Last Supper (Mk 14.25), an important atonement metaphor in Mark. Thereafter, verses 15 and 16 reinforce the urgency of radical action at the apocalyptic moment, whereas verses 17 and 18 are Markan camouflage designed to keep nonalcoholic readers focused on the idea of Roman military savagery.

Further Apocalyptic Insights

Elsewhere in the apocalypse Jesus sees that recognition of the desolating sacrilege will occur in God's time, not humanity's. God alone knows the moment:

> (13.32) But of that day or that hour no one knows, not even the angels in heaven, nor the Son, but only the Father.

And in his mercy God has advanced that time so that individuals and humanity collectively will not perish from their alcoholism before their apocalypse occurs:

> (13.20) And if the Lord had not shortened the days, no human being would be saved; but for the sake of the elect, whom he chose, he shortened the days.

Paradoxically, then, the only thing persons can do to cooperate in the process is to drink, religiously and faithfully, until their turning points. This explains why Mark's Jesus at the Last Supper gives the cup to all disciples *before* he interprets the paschal drinking ritual and why liturgical drinking has always been the focal point of the Christian Eucharist.[29] Had Jesus spoken the words of interpretation and uttered his disavowal before giving the cup, many persons attempting to emulate his actions would quit drinking by self-will, thereby denying themselves the opportunity to hit bottom, admit powerlessness, and experience the gift of the rule of God and the ecstasy of new wine. This is presumably what occurred among the ascetics who overran the Markôs groups in the 60s and 70s C.E., bringing about the latter's dissolution.

Waiting for revelation will require endurance and vigilant watchfulness. Verses 7–13, 17–19, and 24–25 depict in stock apocalyptic imagery the warfare and physical cataclysm that unsurrendered humanity brings on itself, which must be suffered by those awaiting insight. Interpreted in a religious context, the verses depict a bellicose church age marked by alcoholic strife on every hand, exactly the vision elaborated in the latter part of the Book of Revelation (see chap. 7). The two watchfulness parables are the sprouting fig tree (13.28–31) and the vigilant doorkeeper (13.33–37), which indicate how persons are to keep on lookout for their apocalyptic moment. The watchfulness counseled here foreshadows Jesus' Gethsemane admonition to watch (14.34 and 38).

Early in his apocalypse Jesus warns that persons will be hated because of their association with his name:

> (13.13a) And you will be hated by all for my name's sake.

Etymologically *Jesus* means "God help!" It is a cry from the bottom, a cry of desperation acknowledging defeat by an overwhelming adversary. Ordinarily this cry is not connected with Jesus as a religious personage or icon but occurs as an unconditional call to some other, "Help me!" Not surprisingly, those who have called out "Jesus!" in this way are often feared and despised by religious drinkers and others still living by willpower and law, unknowingly awaiting their own surrender. This phenomenon would explain Jesus' remark, "hated for my name's sake."

To sum up, the key to the Markan apocalypse is Jesus' insight that the harbinger of recovery is the recognition of ritual wine, whether ministered by cultic priest, rabbi, or paterfamilias, as a "desolating sacrilege," coupled with Mark's understanding, prophetically implied in a gospel written forty years after Jesus' time, that the same recognition can occur in contexts of Christian eucharistic drinking. All else follows from this discovery. Somewhere en route from his apocalypse to the Last Supper, a sober Jesus once again humbled by alcohol drew from this insight the message he was to announce at the Passover meeting of his followers. There, after giving his drunkalogue, he would voice his recognition of alcohol as enemy, "this wine is the cause of my bloodshed," together with the Deutero-Isaian idea that it is also "covenent blood poured out for the recovery of many." In so doing, Jesus, like Isaiah, would look beyond the few who are actual addicts to the unaddicted multitudes suffering the catastrophic effects of mental drunkenness. For he had realized that the place where alcoholics unaware might ultimately discover alcohol cum self as enemy would be in a context of religious drinking. There, at the time appointed by God and on the brink of destroying themselves and their world in consequence of their unrecognized illness, ritual drinkers might experience an apocalypse illuminating their passage from religion to recovery.

Messiah

The Markan apocalypse also sheds further light on the Messiah (Christ) question. Three times, in verses 5, 6, and 22, Jesus warns against false messiahs. In verse 21 he exhorts his hearers as follows:

> (13.21) And then if any one says to you, "Look, here is the Christ!" or "Look, there he is!" do not believe it.

Like all Mark's references to the Christ/Messiah, the line is purposely ambiguous. Those who presuppose Jesus to be the Messiah will read it as an echo of 13.6, as if it said: "If anyone says to you *of anyone other than me*, 'Look, here is the Christ,' do not believe it." On the other hand, those who presuppose that Jesus neither considered himself nor wished to be considered the Messiah, and that "Messiah" does not refer to a person at all, will read the line: "If anyone says to you *of anyone at all including me*, 'Look, here is the Christ,' do not believe it." The second reading conveys Jesus' disavowal of messiahship, just as Mk 8.30 can be read as conveying Jesus' charge to the disciples not to misrepresent his identity to others by calling him Messiah. The ambiguity of 13.21 further illustrates Mark's ability to use the same words to say different—indeed, opposite—things to different audiences.

Obviously, Mark's Christian audience regarded Jesus as the Messiah, whereas his alcoholic readers believed that "Messiah" referred not to a person but to their program of spiritual principles. Presumably Mark's alcoholics in 68 C.E. would have acclaimed Jesus as founder of their movement, author of the Twelve, sacrificial way-shower, and first in sobriety. Doubtless they revered him as the archetype and epitome of recovery. Nonetheless, they would not have exalted him as a messiah or ranked him above any other member of their egalitarian fellowship, nor did they think that Jesus would have wished them to do so. As alcoholics say today, "the highest rank you get in this program is human being."

Jesus believed that the sign of God's salvation, rather than being the appearance of a solitary messiah figure, would be the sight of anonymous recovering persons going about in the world, empowered by God, glorified in sobriety, and carrying the message to other alcoholics. Thus he says:

> (13.26) And then they will see the Son of Man coming in clouds with great power and glory. (27) And then he will send out the angels [*angelous*, messengers], and gather his elect [*eklektous*, chosen ones] from the four winds, from the ends of the earth to the ends of heaven.

Verse 26 ("clouds, power, glory") anticipates the answer Jesus later gives the high priest in 14.62 ("power, clouds, heaven") and means essentially what 14.62 means, "recovering people empowered by God and coming and going with a heavenly aura" (see chap. 2). Again, the title "Son of Man" is intentionally ambiguous. To Christian readers it meant the Messiah, while to alcoholics it served as a general reference to anyone or everyone in recovery, collective witnesses to the messianic sobriety program. As is true elsewhere in Mark (see 1.13, 8.38, and 13.32), "angels" in verse 27 refers not to celestial beings but to recovering persons sent out to carry the message of sobriety and "gather in" all sufferers prepared to acknowledge their illness and ask for help.

Hence Mk 13.26–27, ordinarily considered to be a vision of the so-called Second Coming, prophesies a recovery fellowship to come not in Jesus' time or in Mark's but at some point in the indefinite future, after an interim period of tribulation within the lives of individuals and the framework of humanity's collective history. Thus the image at the beginning of the apocalypse, of the Temple buildings being thrown down and "not one stone left upon another" (13.2), although it reflects Jesus' view that his recovery movement would replace Temple Judaism, also represents Mark's prophecy of a parousial sobriety program destined to supplant the Messiah-worshiping, that is, Christian, religion emerging in Jewish Palestine even as he wrote. It is this future program and the recovering people who will enflesh it that Mark regards as Messiah and to which the vision in 13.26–27 prophetically refers. Many readers today will see the fulfillment of this prophecy in the twentieth-century fellowship known as Alcoholics Anonymous.

The Cup Image

The image of the cup in Mark appears in a constellation of significant figures. Every use is fraught with ambiguity. "Cup" can be read as a fixed expression referring to one's lot or destiny, as naming the wine chalice used in worship or the water cup of recovery, as a metonym for the wrath of God, as a synecdoche for the ocean of drink in which humanity drowns itself, and as a metaphor for salvation or for alcoholic perdition. Subject to tropological shifting and irony, the cup can be perceived one moment as a good, the next as an evil, and finally as the good beyond evil. Mark was well aware of these different valences within the discourse communities for whom he wrote.

"A Cup of Water" (9.38–41)

As stated repeatedly, "cup" appears first in the signature heading the gospel, where "Marcus" can be understood as transliterating the Hebrew *mar kôs,* "master of the cup." This phrase can signify not only a victor over alcohol but also a person designated as ritual cup minister to others, whether of wine or water. "Cup" specifically refers to the latter in a pericope of particular significance to alcoholic readers (9.38–41):

> (9.38) John said to him, "Teacher, we saw a man casting out demons in your name [Jesus], and we forbade him because he was not following us." (39) But Jesus said, "Do not forbid him. . . . (41) For truly, I say to you, whoever gives you a cup of water to drink because you bear the name of Christ, will by no means lose his reward."

Remembering that *Jesus* means "God help!," the phrase "casting out demons in your name" would signify curing inebriety by bringing drinkers to ask for help. Verse 41 identifies the action ratifying the acceptance of help, drinking water instead of wine. The clause *en onomati hoti Christou este* is translatable either as "because you are in the name of Christ," which is the traditional reading, or "that you be in the name of Christ." Now it happens that neither Hebrew nor Aramaic had a word for "meaning," and both used the expression "in the name of" to signify the meaning associated with a particular name. Hence verse 41 can be alternatively understood as follows:

> (9.41) For truly, I say to you, whoever gives you a cup of water to drink that you might know the meaning of Messiah [sobriety], will by no means lose his reward [the joy of serving as recovery messenger to other alcoholics].

Obliquely referred to here, drinking a cup of water was the entrance rite for newcomers to the Markôs fellowship, initiating them into the meaning of Messiah, their recovery program. Christians have generally interpreted this passage as merely a passing illustration of Jesus' kindness and charity. Mark's alcoholics, on the other hand, would have seen it as a bold, albeit veiled, stroke by Mark handing on the sacrament of initiation into their fellowship: exorcism of the wine demon by the giving of a cup of water, the essential first step toward wellness. Because this initiatory rite was anathematized by Christian wine drinkers (Heb 10.29 promises severe punishment for any who "deem unclean the blood of the covenant"; see chap. 4), Mark could safely refer to it only in the cryptic manner of 9.41.

The Cup of Suffering Service

Elsewhere in the gospel, the image of the cup is introduced as the wine cup (14.23), as a figure for alcoholism and the suffering associated with recovery (10.35–45 and 14.36), and as the covert referent of the main image of Jesus' apocalypse, "the desolating sacrilege set up where it ought not to be" (13.14). Mark's chief biblical source of the cup as a metaphor for alcoholism and recovery is Deutero-Isaiah, specifically the cup oracle (51.17–23), contextual with the portrait of the Suffering Servant as derelict drunkard (52.13–53.12; see chap. 3).[30]

Among the prophets who employ wine cup imagery, only Deutero-Isaiah explicitly mentions all phases of humankind's illness and recovery: the cup (a) given by God (51.17), (b) drunk by humans (51.18–20), (c) visited on nonaddicts (51.21), (d) removed by God (51.22), and (e) symbolic of the pathology of all who practice domination (51.23). These phases are discernible in Mark's three wine cup pericopes. In 10.35–45, in response to James and John's request for glorified positions at his right hand, Jesus gives his discourse on suffering service, beginning:

> (10.38) But Jesus said to them, "You do not know what you are asking. Are you able to drink the cup that I am drinking [*egō pinō*, continuous tense, in English present progressive], or to be baptized with the baptism with which I am being baptized [present tense, passive voice, signifying ongoing action]?" (39) And they said to him, "We are able." And Jesus said to them, "The cup that I am drinking you will drink; and with the baptism with which I am being baptized you will be baptized."

Here "cup" signifies alcoholic drinking and the pain it causes. Mark's use of a verb tense equivalent to the English present progressive ("I am drinking") may indicate that Jesus has already resumed drinking at this juncture en route to Jerusalem. Responding to the alcoholic thinking apparent in James and John's request for positions of authority, Jesus predicts a similar return to drink for the disciples: "The cup I am drinking you will drink." In effect he is saying what sober alcoholics often say to defiant newcomers, "You haven't drunk enough yet; alcohol hasn't fully humbled you yet." Ultimately, "baptism" refers not only to the pain of active alcoholism but also to the suffering that recovering persons undergo in repudiating the self en route to stage two of sobriety.

Jesus goes on to warn the disciples away from lording it over others and exercising clerical authority:

> (10.43) But it shall not be so among you; but whoever would be great among you must be your servant [*diakonos*, "deacon"], (44) and whoever would be first among you must be slave of all. (45) For the Son of Man also came not to be served but to serve [*diakonēsai*], and to give his life [*psuchēn*] as a ransom for many.

For Jesus, "great" and "first" pertain not to temporal or religious authority but to contented sobriety achieved through service, through carrying the message to those who still suffer. Verse 45 identifies the Son of Man as the Deutero-Isaian Suffering Servant who "gives his life" by drinking publicly for as long as he is destined to drink and then by witnessing the sacrifice of self in his recovery program. In this way the servant "ransoms" those among the many who follow his lead and admit their powerlessness over alcohol.

The much-debated *lutron* ("ransom") in verse 44 translates the Hebrew *'āšām* of Is 53.10, which refers to a substitutionary or atoning offer made to free someone or something held in bondage.[31] In the theology of recovery Jesus found in Detero-Isaiah, "ransom" refers to the advanced alcoholism the servant suffers to bring the multitude to recovery and free them from their Edenic drunkenness short of the extremes he experiences. So 10.35–45 presents three things: (1) Jesus' view of Deutero-Isaian recovery theology as regards the necessity of drinking the cup and suffering its consequences and the vicarious service of the advanced alcoholic on behalf of many; (2) Jesus' attempt to direct the disciples toward service to other sufferers; and (3) Mark's warning about the pitfalls of hierarchy, aimed at the Jewish Christians of his own day preparing to ordain clergies like the gentile churches.

Mark's second and third mentions of the cup (14.23 and 36) pertain to aspects of recovery theology missing from Isaiah's view. At the Last Supper Jesus models another kind of service implicitly associated with the Suffering Servant, ministry of the wine cup to the multitude of alcoholics unaware. Although Jesus connects his message about wine with the Suffering Servant (14.24), the idea of the servant as cup minister originates with Jesus, not Isaiah:

> (14.23) And he took a cup, and when he had given thanks he gave it to them, and they all drank from it.

Jesus' purpose in giving his followers the cup is twofold. On one hand it is, through the provision of drink, to activate real alcoholism in the many, thereby qualifying them for a recovery program to relieve their mental drunkenness without their having to experience the ruinous chemical dependence of the full-blown alcoholic. On the other hand, the cup given represents a choice offered, to drink or not to drink. It is significant that Jesus in Mark does not command the recipients to drink. Rather, he offers each person the choice. Those who choose to drink become more alcoholic, albeit unknowingly, but also come one drink nearer the time appointed for their recognition of the wine cup as the "desolating sacrilege." Those at the turning point, who see wine as the cause of their troubles, are ready to quit drinking and to choose recovery over religion. It is the latter choice that Jesus models in his eschatological words of interpretation reported in Mk 14.24–25. So the cup of 14.23 both addicts and saves. Ordinarily only its saving purpose is acknowledged. Here its addicting function is also highlighted.

Joseph's Cup (Gn 44.1–45.3)

Conceivably Jesus found in the Genesis story of Joseph's cup an archetype for this dual understanding of the cup image. In the story Joseph as Pharoah's viceroy hides his cup in Benjamin's grain sack, arrests his brothers for theft, announces that as punishment Benjamin must become his slave, and then reveals himself and welcomes his family to refuge in Egypt. The cup secreted in the grain prefigures the wine message contained in the bread-as-Word that Jesus embodies (Mk 14.22). The brothers' perception of the cup first as a cause of mortal trouble but later as a sign of Joseph's love prefigures the drinker's recognition of the wine cup first as trouble (Mk 13.14 and 14.24a) but later as a symbol of salvation (Mk 14.24b–25; Ps 116.13). When the brothers volunteer for punishment along with Benjamin, Joseph replies, "Only the man in whose hand the cup is found shall be my slave" (Gn 44.17). Jesus may have interpreted Joseph's remark as a prophecy of the Suffering Servant as a type of the few, those alcoholics destined to serve as "addiction bearers" for the many. He may also have noted the larger parallel between God's calling the Children of Israel into bondage in Egypt so that he could later free them at Passover and his calling the many into bondage to ritual wine so that later he can free them and welcome them into sobriety.

The Gethsemane Cup (14.36)

In Gethsemane Jesus models other elements of the recovery process only implied in Deutero-Isaiah: self-acceptance as a child of God, overt admission of powerlessness, request for removal of the cup, and renunciation of self-will:

> (14.36) And he said, "Abba (Father), you have all powers; remove this cup from me; yet not what I will, but what you will."

As discussed in chapter 2, the traditional paraphrase of Jesus' words takes "cup" as a locution referring to one's portion or lot: "Since you can do anything, I ask you to cancel my destined crucifixion ["this cup"], if that be your will." Alcoholics, on the other hand, will understand "cup" and the utterance as a whole thus: "Recognizing that you have all powers and admitting therefore that I have none, I ask you to remove my cup addiction ["this cup"], through your agency not mine." Etymologically, *addiction* derives from the Latin *ad*, "to," and *dicere*, "to say," meaning "assigned by decree, bound, devoted." Actually, as David Miller has pointed out, the earliest uses of the term are theological, pertaining to a relatedness to God of which addiction to alcohol or drugs is a secondary metaphor.[32] Here the Greek *parenegke to potērion touto ap emou* can be translated literally as "remove this cup which is stuck to me."[33] Hence, from the perspective of alcoholism, the translation "remove my cup addiction" seems both linguistically accurate and thematically appropriate.

Applied to Jesus, the contrast between the two paraphrases of 14.36 is that of a divine hero only seeming to be human versus an addict who has been playing God discovering that he is human indeed. The first understanding results from readers' projection of their latent alcoholism onto the text, whereas the second is available to all ritual drinkers who admit their alcohol problem and choose recovery. The plural *panta dunata soi*, "you have all powers," suggests that it is not solely powerlessness over alcohol that Jesus admits but powerlessness over the self, other people, events, and so forth. If so, Gethsemane would depict Jesus' attainment of stage two of sobriety, a possibility Mark underscores by reporting Jesus' doubling of the prayer (14.36 and 39). All things considered, the cup emerges as a polyvalent image of central importance in the Cupmaster's gospel. Ultimately, the enduring Christian fixation on the holy grail of Jesus, apparent in Scripture, history, legend, and popular devotions, reflects humankind's unquenchable desire to learn the deeper significance of the cup and the secret of its life-giving essence.

Prophetic Allegories

In addition to the scenes discussed in chapter 2 (Last Supper, Gethsemane, Crucifixion, and Empty Tomb), the Passion narrative in Mark also presents a number of prophetic allegories pertaining to the clerical religion Mark believed certain to arise in postwar Judea. Quite probably these allegories do not go back to Jesus but originated as lore within the Markan fellowship between 30 C.E. and the time of Mark's writing nearly four decades later.

The Woman with the Perfume Jar (14.3–9)

In writing of the woman disciple who anoints Jesus in 14.3–9, the feminist exegete Elisabeth Schüssler Fiorenza contrasts our lack of knowledge of the name of this disciple with our memories of the names of the men who betray and deny Jesus, Judas and Peter. Fiorenza says "the name of the faithful disciple is forgotten because she was a woman."[34] By contrast, recovery criticism sees the religiously disfranchised and male-dominated Jewish woman/women as Markan symbols of powerless alcoholics of both genders, as opposed to the Jewish-Christian men who were about to assume the same sort of clerical authority in the new religion that males were accorded in Judaism. Mark omits the woman's name not because male keepers of tradition had forgotten it but rather to evoke the theme of anonymity alongside that of powerlessness. The actions of the woman, who pours out her expensive perfume and shatters her precious alabaster jar (14.3), symbolize the sacrifice of self required for sobriety. That her act serves to anoint Jesus is Mark's way of defining Messiah ("anointed"), indicating that self-immolation is the essence of recovery and reveals messiahship wherever it is witnessed. As a prophetic prologue to the Passion story, the scene is emblematic of a Markan christology of powerlessness and anonymity.

Betrayal (14.17–20)

Mark's religious narrative identifies Judas as the disciple who betrays Jesus to the authorities (14.10–11), but his alcoholic confreres would have interpreted the betrayal differently. Notice that the betrayal story per se (14.17–20) never mentions Judas but tells of Jesus' arrival at the Last Supper with "the Twelve," which to Mark's alcoholics meant the twelve principles of recovery formulated by Jesus. Jesus says "one of you will betray me" (14.18) and then identifies "one of the Twelve" as the betrayer (14.20). So the allegorical meaning here is that *one* of the Twelve will be betrayed by *all* the disciples, which can only be the principle about drinking no more, similar to step one of today's Twelve Steps. In short, Jesus prophesies that the disciples at the Last Supper will fail to recognize wine as the desolating sacrilege and will drink the cup he gives them. This they do (14.23), betraying their recovery program and thereafter founding a religion involving liturgical drink understood via a tropology quite different from the figures in whose terms recovery criticism interprets Jesus' actions at the Supper.

The Stricken Shepherd (14.27–28)

In another prophecy Jesus quotes from Zechariah's Song of the Sword (Zec 13.7–9) and then predicts his return to Galilee:

> (14.27) And Jesus said to them, "You will all fall away; for it is written, 'I will strike the shepherd, and the sheep will be scattered.' (28) But after I am raised up, I will go before you to Galilee."

In Zechariah the stricken shepherd represents a clerical figure whose demise deprives his flock of the false security religion offers the impenitent. Two-thirds perish while one-third choose the refining fire of repentance. For Mark's religious readers, the fulfillment of this prophecy occurs following Jesus' arrest (14.43–49), in the dispersal of his followers, "and they all forsook him and fled" (14.50). From an alcoholism perspective, however, the prophecy looks into the indefinite future, to what Mark believed would be the dissolution of the Christian clergy at the end time of the Church. The references in verse 28 envision humankind's spiritual awakening ("raised up") in the new era of recovery ("Galilee") at the end of the church age (the "stricken shepherd and scattered sheep" of verse 27).

Peter's Denial (14.66–72)

Though he swore he would not (14.29–31), Peter denies Jesus ("God, help!") three times. One scarcely need mention what denial means to the alcoholic. Here Mark is prophesying that Christian clergy from Peter on will deny that their addiction to ritual wine symptomizes their alcoholism and that they need help to recover from their malady. The accusation "You also were with the Nazarene, Jesus" (14.67), spoken by the "servant girl" (*paidiskē*, 14.66), whose status as a female and a servant suggests her connection to powerlessness and recovery, actually means, "You're an alcoholic too!" But Peter denies it vehemently.

Crucifixion (15.6–39)

As already discussed, Pilate's offer of a choice of whom to crucify is an allegory of the existential decision that sooner or later confronts all people: which of our personas to submit to death, Barabbas, the self-willed and zealotic "Son of God" who inhabits every person, or Barnasha, the anonymous and sober human being ("Son of Man") awaiting discovery in us all. To satisfy the expectations of his religious readers, Mark had no choice but to portray the crucifixion of Jesus, although he took the opportunity to show Jesus twice refuse the offer of drink (15.23 and 36–37). Yet there is reason to think that Mark believed it was actually a zealotic insurrectionist and not Jesus of Nazareth who was executed (see chap. 2).

For one thing, crucifixion is not the fate of sober persons who have submitted to death of self. Nor is there any hint in Mark of crucifixion as an atoning sacrifice. Despite popular Christian belief to the contrary, crucifixion is not an Old Testament prophecy fulfillment, and scholars agree that the idea of a dying messiah is unattested in pre-Christian Judaism.[35] Crucifixion is not mentioned in the Q materials,[36] and many scholars doubt the historicity of the *privilegium paschale*, the Passover pardon for a Jewish prisoner. A crucifixion surely occurred at Passover in 30 C.E., but as to the identity of the victim, notice the confusion the appellatives would have caused. One imagines the question asked in the Jerusalem streets, perhaps by the frightened disciples themselves, "Who was crucified?" The answer "Barnasha" would have meant "some man"; the answer "Barabbas" would have indicated "a man who called himself Son of God." The referential ambiguity is obvious in either case.

From the viewpoint of recovery, the death that atones is death of self, the death Jesus died in Gethsemane, which all must die to attain sobriety/eternal life. There is no need for the crucifixion of anyone. Whereas much of the theology of crucifixion developed over two thousand years of Church history is applicable also to Gethsemane, there is an important exception: the understanding of Jesus' death as substitutionary. Recovery criticism depicts Jesus' ego-death in Gethsemane as a way-showing event illuminating the path *all* must follow, not merely symbolically but actually, en route to atonement.[37] In the end, persons bent on maintaining the traditional picture of Jesus' crucifixion must ask how much they differ from those in the Jerusalem crowd in Mark's allegory who answered Pilate by demanding death for Jesus.

From Tomb to Galilee (15.46 and 16.5–6)

Once again, the rock tomb (15.46) is a Markan allegory for the encrypting of the alcoholic Jesus within the church of Peter, whose name means "rock." The story of the empty tomb (16.5–6) represents Jesus' escape from ecclesiastical captivity and Church teachings (self-will, crucifixion, resurrection-as-resuscitation, Messiah as person, etc.) and his return to his recovery program, symbolized by Galilee. The discovery of the empty tomb by women at sunrise of the first day of the week (16.2), which was the third day of burial, can be seen as a prophecy that the story of the alcoholic Jesus would remain encrypted until the dawn of a third era or millennium, at which time it would be revealed by recovering persons.

The Young Man in White and "Secret Mark" (14.51–52 and 16.5–7)

No element of Mark has proven more resistant to interpretation than the "young man" *(neaniskos)* who escapes capture after Jesus' arrest in Gethsemane (14.51–52) and then reappears in the empty tomb (16.5–7) and announces Jesus' return to Galilee:

> (14.51) And a young man followed him, with nothing but a linen cloth [*sindōn*] about his body; and they seized him, (52) but he left the linen cloth and ran away naked. . . . (16.5) And entering the tomb, they saw a young man sitting on the right side, dressed in a white robe [*stōle*]. . . . (6) And he said to them, ". . . Jesus of Nazareth . . . is not here. (7) But go, tell his disciples and Peter that he is going before you to Galilee. . . ."

Although tradition interprets the figure in 16.5 as a heavenly being, C. S. Mann presents textual evidence that Mark intended both young men as the same person.[38] As mentioned (chap. 4, note 42), the figure in 14.51–52 is often assumed to be Mark himself. The man's conduct contrasts with that of the disciples, who flee when Jesus is arrested (14.50), whereas the man follows Jesus and escapes only when the religious authorities try to arrest him. His garment is first a linen undercloth beneath which he is naked; then, in the tomb it becomes a stole, a sign of religious office. What can be made of all this?

Relevant to this question is Morton Smith's 1958 discovery, in a Greek Orthodox monastery in Palestine, of a letter purportedly by Clement of Alexandria (ca. 150–215 C.E.) containing two brief fragments of a version of Mark that Clement calls The Secret Gospel of Mark.[39] One of these fragments, although it begins like the Lazarus story in John 11, is obviously an expanded version of Mk 14.51–52. The conclusion of this fragment reads as follows:

> And going near, Jesus rolled away the stone from the door of the tomb. And straightway, going in where the youth was, he stretched forth his hand and raised him, seizing his hand. And the youth, looking upon him, loved him and began to beseech him that he might be with him. And going out of the tomb they came into the house of the youth, for he was rich. And . . . Jesus told him what to do and in the evening the youth comes to him, wearing a linen cloth over his naked body. And he remained with him that night, for Jesus taught him the mystery of the rule of God.

Dominic Crossan cites scholarly opinion, including his own, that Mk 14.51–52 is a censored abridgment of Secret Mark prompted by a need to obviate the homoeroticism implied in the passage.[40] Acknowledging the possibility of symbolic interpretation, Crossan writes that "a story about a miraculous or physical raising from death could be used or created as a symbol for baptism or spiritual raising from death."[41] This is precisely the view here. Mark's original manuscript (Secret Mark) contained this fuller version of the evangelist's autobiographical account not of an erotic baptism but of his entrance into Jesus' recovery fellowship on the night of the Jerusalem seder.

In the passage, death symbolizes the walking death of addiction, the tomb its encrypting prison cell. The house may be the same house mentioned in Acts 12.12 as belonging to Mary, the mother of John surnamed Mark. The teaching of "the mystery of the rule of God" would have occurred in meetings of Jesus' fellowship that, like recovery meetings today, generally took place in the evening or at night, because it is then that the newly sober are most vulnerable to drink.

The linen cloth and naked body could symbolize the youth's com-
pletion of a process similar to the inventory and admission of wrongs
featured in today's recovery programs, a process involving divestiture
of all signs of wealth and station and a stripping of pride and ego as
precursor to membership in the egalitarian Markôs fellowship. The
mystery of the rule of God would have been the Twelve, the semisecret sobriety principles formulated by Jesus (Mk 3.14–15 and 4.10–
11). Finally, what some see as homoeroticism is language reflecting
the youth's desire for sobriety. Recovery operates on a principle of
"attraction, not promotion." Persons speak of wanting what the sober person has, of a desire for sobriety stronger than all other desire.
Presumably this is a timeless behavioral trait denoting onset of recovery. It is this attraction and desire that the phrases "looking upon"
and "loving" and "beseeching to be with" were intended to convey
(see chap. 7 and the discussion of Jn 1.38–39, "where are you stay-
ing?"). Mark excised them when, probably to his surprise, he found
that nonalcoholic outsiders were reading them as homoeroticism.

Mark as Deacon (16.5–7)

Whereas the young man in 14.51–52 represents Mark the initiate into
recovery (the rule of God), the figure in 16.5–7 represents Mark the
evangelist of sobriety, whose linen garment *(sindōn)* has been replaced
by a stole *(stōle)*, the sign of vocation and office. It is possible that early
in his sobriety, before the Jerusalem fellowship split along the lines
of drinker versus nondrinker, messianic versus nonmessianic, a young
Mark served as deacon in this community. Hence the figure in the
tomb may represent Mark in his role as deacon. As Christianity developed, the deacon became the sacerdotally powerless clergyman
whose title *diakonos* means "servant." The deacon is the clerical epitome of the Suffering Servant so important to Mark's theology of recovery (cf. *diakonos* in 10.43). Acts 6.1–6 is traditionally interpreted
as reporting the ordination of the first deacons in Jerusalem, and
Luke's statement that "John surnamed Mark" "deaconed" *(diakonian)*
alongside Paul and Barnabas (Acts 12.25) supports the idea that Mark
served as a deacon in the Jerusalem community. If so, the escape from
ecclesiastical capture in 14.51–52 perhaps represents Mark's renunciation of clerical office sometime before 68 C.E., presumably on account of emergent Christian teaching at odds with his experience of
the alcoholic Jesus. Assuming 16.5–7 to be an allegorical representation of the future end of the messianic (Christian) age and the freeing of the encrypted Jesus, Mark is saying that the deacon's evangelical function at that time will be to exhort recovering persons (Mark's

"women") to stop seeking the risen (sober and spiritually awakened) Jesus in the rock tomb in Jerusalem (symbolizing the Petrine church) and to look for him instead in Galilee (their recovery program).[42]

Moreover, just as Mark's allegory of the stricken shepherd predicted the dissolution of the sacrificial clergy at some future time (14.27–28), it is reasonable to assume that Mark also foresaw an early decline for the diaconate as a result of domination by higher clerical ranks. His own departure from Christian ministry, if actual, would have foreshadowed just this eventuality. The man's flight in 14.52, leaving behind a linen cloth prefiguring the stole of 16.5, thus serves as an allegorical prophecy of the demise of the diaconate as a permanent clerical order. His reappearance garbed in a clerical stole in 16.5 may be thought to prophesy the restoration of the permanent diaconate at sunrise of the third era of the Church. Historically, at least within Roman Catholicism, both scenarios have come to pass. By the sixth century the diaconate had became merely a stepping-stone to the presbyterate, but in 1964 the order was restored "as a proper and permanent rank of the hierarchy" by the Second Vatican Council, on the eve of the Church's third millennium.[43]

Although historians lack firm information about the deacon's liturgical role(s) in the earliest decades of Christianity, it is possible that already in Mark's day the deacon had begun to perform the same ministry to the cup that chapter 3 of this book ascribes to the Suffering Servant, a ministry still practiced today. In the Roman Catholic order of service, at any rate, the deacon fills the cup with wine, adds a drop of water adumbrating sobriety,[44] after the Eucharistic Prayer elevates it for all to see, and without drinking from it ministers it to the people. Each time a deacon serves the cup, he enacts the role first played by the Markan Jesus in 14.23, offering each communicant the choice either to continue drinking or, responding to the grace of God, to recognize the wine chalice as the "desolating sacrilege" of Mk 13.14a. Although Mark himself presumably had "fled Judea for the mountains" (13.14c) by the time he wrote his gospel, he may have identified the serving deacon as the *alter Christus* of Christian liturgy, the evangelist of recovery and cupmaster to the many, to whom God has entrusted the awesome ministry of the cup of drunkenness and wrath, the apocalyptic chalice of salvation. Such may be the identity of the bestoled figure in the empty tomb.

Altogether, eight prophetic allegories have been studied: woman with perfume jar, betrayal, stricken shepherd, denial, Barabbas and Barnasha, tomb and Galilee, young man in white, and Mark as deacon. What unifies these allegories is their consistent antireligion theme when read from a perspective of recovery. They look less like elements of Jesus' recovery story and more like Markan constructions conveying the evangelist's reservations about the trend toward clericalism that he saw transforming the Judean Messiah cults, and perhaps impinging on the Markôs groups, even as he wrote. The extent to which the allegories are fictions rather than versions of traditional material cannot be determined. Following the Passover and Gethsemane pericopes in Mark 14, the only material in the remainder of the gospel likely to represent historical events would be Jesus' arrest (14.43–49), the disciples' flight (14.50), the echo of Mark's entrance into Jesus' fellowship (14.51–52), Jesus' messianic profession to the high priest (14.53–62), and the references to Jesus' return to Galilee (14.28 and 16.7). Hence the allegories studied here may have been invented by Mark and readily accepted by readers hungry for descriptive detail embellishing the first real narrative of Jesus' career. On the other hand, some of this material may be traditional and may indeed have originated with Jesus in his postpaschal tellings of his story, as he reflected on such intelligence as may have come his way concerning developments in the Messiah groups and gentile Christ cults founded in his name. Barring new document finds, the various origins of these probably fictional allegories may never be identified.

Conclusion

Consistent with the theory advanced throughout this book, the interpretive basis for this chapter is that Mark 1–13 represents a veiled third-person narrative transformation of Jesus' drunkalogue: his autobiographical story of sobering up, founding an alcoholism program in Galilee, suffering fanatical mental drunkenness, succumbing again to drink, and angrily assaulting the Jerusalem religionists before getting sober for good. Jesus first gave his drunkalogue at the Last Supper, offering it as the metaphorical main meal of Passover served after the ritual bread and before the wine referred to in 14.23–25. Major crises in the story are Jesus' turn to messianism following his Galilean "honeymoon," his decision to go to Jerusalem, relapse into drinking, physical combat with Temple drinkers, rhetorical attacks on the Jewish leaders, and hangover apocalypse concerning religious wine and the crypto-alcoholism of all ritual drinkers. Prior to his rhetorical rampage in Jerusalem, Jesus' mental drunkenness is expressed more in his actions than in his sayings, many of which are constitutive of recovery. These range from his early teaching about bread, meetings, anonymity, serenity, faith-action, and the primacy of the rule of God to his formulation of the Twelve and his sermons on ego-death and service, the latter revealing the spiritual bankruptcy of ideas of messiahship and clergy based on personality and hierarchy.

In the Passion Jesus presents the cup to disciples that they might ultimately see it as the "desolating sacrilege," discloses his own recognition of wine both as "my blood" and, paradoxically, as the salvific drink of all drinkers ("covenant blood poured out for many"), and then states his intention to replace ritual wine ("fruit of the vine") by the "new wine" of recovery ("the rule of God"). In Gethsemane Jesus experiences ego-death, thus modeling for humanity step three of today's recovery program, the radical humiliation and prayer that cancel the Edenic curses and bring atonement and redemption. To the high priest who interrogates him, Jesus says that Messiah is witnessed through anonymity and exaltation in sobriety ("Son of Man . . . in the clouds of heaven"), that is, by recovering people "going about" in the world, living sober lives empowered by God.

The Crucifixion remains ambiguous in Mark's narrative, evocative of questions lacking answers. Did Mark openly reject Paul's theology of the cross? Would Mark have included the Crucifixion at all if he had not known that his Christian audience would demand it? Did he view the Crucifixion merely as the ultimate object lesson for the unsurrendered and mentally drunk? Did he regard Barabbas and Barnasha as allegorical types, as different persons, or as before-and-after personas of one individual named Jesus? Did he think of Jesus as physically killed in Jerusalem but apotheosized in the principles of his Galilean sobriety program? Or did Mark and his confreres believe (the view here) that Jesus had simply walked away from Jerusalem and returned in anonymity to his sobriety fellowship in Galilee ("flee from Judea," 13.14, and "go before you/meet with you in Galilee," 14.28 and 16.7)? However one answers these questions, recovery criticism in no way disregards or diminishes the redemptive value of Jesus' sacrificial death, but it definitely shifts its locus from Golgotha to Gethsemane, from cross to garden, from bodily death to *psuchē* death.

In addition to relating Jesus' sobriety story outwardly garbed as a messiah narrative, Mark's book also includes a number of symbols enabling recovering alcoholics to identify with the text and a series of allegories and complications depicting the alcoholism of hierarchical governance. Their themes are misunderstood spiritual dynamics, desire for domination, betrayal, denial, and the stupefying effect of mental drunkenness. Whether or not Mark feared that the recovery groups would die out in the near term, and whether or not he lived to see them overwhelmed by ascetic nondrinkers, Mark clearly believed that Jesus' sobriety movement would reappear at the end time of Christianity as God's loving response to the worsening of humankind's unrecognized alcoholism. Mark expected that the meaning of his clandestine symbols would be revealed to persons at this future time, especially the sign of the desolating sacrilege. As for religious authorities, Mark accepted their inevitability within Jewish Christianity, given the certainty of Roman victory in the ongoing war and the expected demise of regional Judaism as an agency of social order. Yet he was determined to stress the incompatibility between a clerical religion, no matter how benign its officers and rules, and the anarchical nonorganization of his recovery program, whose leaders, like those of today's Twelve-Step programs, were but trusted servants who did not govern and whose spiritual foundations, like those of Alcoholics Anonymous today, were anonymity and the placing of principles before personalities.

✤ 7 ✤

JOHANNINE WRITINGS

When the steward of the feast tasted the water, he said
to the bridegroom, "You have kept the 'choice wine'
until now."
—Unredacted excerpt from Jn 2.9–10

Happy the one who interprets this prophecy aright, and
happy those who accept its meaning, if they heed what it
says, for the crisis time is near.
—Rv 1.3

To conclude the present study of Mark, this chapter focuses the lens
of recovery criticism on the Gospel of John and the Book of Revelation. Two possibilities are suggested. The first is that the original core
of John was a collection of Markôs parables reflecting the conceptuality of recovery and going back to the sober postpaschal Jesus. The
second is that the visions in Revelation, particularly the beasts and
the seven wine bowls, are the work of an end-of-century Markan writer
who foresaw a coming church age marked by alcoholic self-will and
fighting, whose future end, the writer believed, will coincide with the
fulfillment of the prophecy in Daniel 12.5–13: the appearance of two
messengers, critical periods of 1,290 and 1,335 days, and the subsequent "cleansing of the many."

The Gospel of John
Proto-John as a Markôs Parables Collection

The Gospel of John is usually assumed to have attained final form as
late as 100 C.E. following five, six, or as many as seven decades during which its text passed through numerous stages of composition

marked by controversies among communities of differing religious casts.[1] The suggestion here is that the primitive kernel of John was actually Markan in origin, in the form of a small collection of parabolic recovery sayings for instructing the newly sober developed within the Markôs groups during the 30s C.E.. In other words, Proto-John is regarded as the work of a Markan community some thirty to forty years before Mark wrote his gospel.

These recovery parables were attributed to Jesus, and some may have been composed after his return to Galilee. The collection said nothing of Peter and the other disciples who remained in Jerusalem and, after an initial period of sobriety, became wine-drinking Messiah cultists. It lacked any mention of the Crucifixion or Resurrection, as these ideas were foreign to Markan thought. Intended for persons who had already come to a crisis and stopped drinking, the sayings contained none of the personal narrative in Jesus' drunkalogue and no material from his hangover apocalypse or from the Jerusalem Passover story. Water as a replacement for wine was a significant element in the sayings. A parable early in the collection, about a man renouncing Temple wine, echoed the memory of Jesus' encounter with Temple vessels later reported by Mark. Parables about feeding, walking on water, the desire to abide with, and raising up also made their way, later on, into Mark's gospel. Other themes in the parables were willingness to act and to change and service. Seventeen of these recovery parables, whose ghosts are discernible in the final text of John, are reconstructed here.

Formally similitudes, the parables originally would have begun with a stock phrase containing the Markans' name for their program, "the rule of God is like. . . ." Apparently the ascetic community that had gained control of the sayings collection by the 60s (see the next section) expunged the term "rule of God" owing to its connection with inebriety, with the result that the phrase occurs only once in canonical John, in the Nicodemus story (3.3 and 5). These ascetics were undoubtedly surprised, scarcely a decade later, to see nonalcoholic readers of Mark's new book, quite ignorant of the origin of "rule of God," accepting this neologism in the Jewish lexicon without raising an eyebrow. The present version of these parables uses the modern but essentially synonymous introductory phrase, "recovery is like. . . ." Each reconstructed parable is followed by a citation of the passage in John of which it was the original nucleus and a brief explanatory comment.

1. *"Recovery is like a man who desires to abide where the man of water abides"* (Jn 1.29–39). This parable indicates that recovery works

through the drunkard's attraction to the sober person. The desire to be where Jesus "abides" or "dwells" (Jn 1.38) parallels the desire of the young initiate in Secret Mark (Mk 14.51–52) who beseeches Jesus "to be with him" (see chap. 6). Both gospel sayings come from this parable, whose source may have been John Mark's initiation into the Markôs fellowship in Jerusalem in 30 C.E. The phrase "man of water" is inferred from the context of the parable as finally established in canonical John, which includes John the Baptist's oblique and non-descriptive reference to Jesus' baptism. At no time in the composition of John did its various editors introduce an explicit description of Jesus' baptism. Whether or not Jesus was actually immersed or showered in water by the Baptist, the important thing to the Markôs people was that his baptism marked the point when Jesus began to *drink* water in place of wine. This is the gist of the phrase "man of water."

2. *"Recovery is like a wedding feast where the choice wine is water"* (Jn 2.1–11). This parable anticipates the version of the Cana wedding story as it would have appeared in the early stages of John, before it became a Dionysiac wine miracle (see the discussion in the next section). It conveys exactly the meaning of that story one would expect from the Markôs fellowship. Of all the signs and mighty works ascribed to Jesus, none has captured popular imagination quite like the account of his putative changing of water to wine. Beneath its festive surface it speaks to our deepest crypto-alcoholic fantasies about controlling our own well-being. No one, on sober reflection, should be surprised to recognize the participle "made wine" as a redaction in the received version. Notice how smoothly the canonical text reads minus the inserted phrase, which is indicated by a bracketed ellipsis:

> (Jn 2.3) When the wine failed, the mother of Jesus said to him, "They have no wine." (4) And Jesus said to her, "Woman, what have you to do with me?" [literally, "what to me and to you?"] . . . (6) Now six stone jars were standing there. (7) Jesus said to the servants [literally, deacons], "Fill the jars with water." And they filled them up to the brim. (8) He said to them, "Now draw some out, and take it to the steward of the feast." So they took it. (9) When the steward of the feast tasted the water [. . .] and did not know where it came from, he called the bridegroom (10) and said to him, "Every man serves the choice wine first; and when men have drunk freely, then the poor wine; but you have kept the choice wine until now."

This unredacted version of the Cana story straightforwardly reports the replacement of wine by water, which the steward of the feast ecstatically figures as "choice wine." His parabolic phrase echoes Jesus'

Last Supper disavowal of actual wine in favor of the metaphorical "new wine of the rule of God," later recorded as Mk 14.25. As noted earlier, "choice wine" and "new wine" reflect OT wine metaphors having salvific import. Here the wedding feast symbolizes the messianic joy experienced in recovery, in turning *from* wine, not to it.

The origin of this parable may have been an actual episode in Jesus' postpaschal career. Two elements early in the canonical story are especially suggestive in this regard. The first is the term Jesus uses in addressing the unnamed person designated "the mother of Jesus," "Woman." Raymond Brown points out that the case of a son addressing his mother in this blunt manner is unattested in either Hebrew or Greek writings and concludes that there may be "symbolic import to the title, 'Woman.'"[2] The second is the odd saying, "what to me and to you?" a Semitic expression of disavowal that some readers interpret as paralleling 1 Sam 16.10, where it seems to mean "this is not our concern."[3] Now the possibility of a symbolic sense of "woman" resonates with the Markans' use of "woman/women" as a coterie term designating recovering addicts and suggests that Jesus' companion in the original episode may not have been his mother at all but a fellow exdrunkard. If so, the purport of the otherwise unexplained expression "what to me and to you?" becomes readily apparent: what indeed would a lack of wine matter to former addicts who have disavowed it for water?

Yet another enigmatic element of the Cana story is the mention of six jars in verse 6. The number six has always puzzled commentators, for in Jewish number mysticism six represents imperfection and incompleteness, whereas seven indicates wholeness and fulfillment. Why was the number of jars not seven? Where is the seventh jar? By way of prophetic answer, the seventh jar may be seen in the Christian liturgy, whose Offertory rite has always included two vessels presented to the deacon, one of wine and another of water. The wine is poured entire into the communion cup and then a few drops of the water. From the perspective of recovery, the Offertory represents an allegory of choice, not wine *and* a little water but wine *or* water, sobriety *or* further drunkenness. So viewed, the water vessel in Christian ritual reveals itself as the seventh jar of Cana water waiting to be chosen in place of wine, as a sign of the parousial fulfillment of the Eucharist. "Fill the cup with water," Jesus commands the end-time deacons, "and give it to presider of the feast."

3. *"Recovery is like a man renouncing Temple wine"* (Jn 2.13–22). Enough has been said concerning Jesus' insight that the eschatology of ritual drinking is entrance into the rule of God, recovery, mes-

sianic bliss, sobriety—whatever term one chooses. The connection of this reconstructed parable to the story of the Temple cleansing in Jn 2.13–22 is that both items derive from the memory later alluded to by Mark (11.16), that Jesus' drunken rampage in the Temple pertained to ritual drinking and specifically that it involved his attempt to wrest the drinking vessels from worshipers and forcibly stop them from drinking. Not until a generation later, in the second stage of the composition of the fourth gospel during the 50s and 60s C.E., does the story become the familiar Johannine account, which contains no mention of *skeuos*, "vessel." The original parable conveys the Markans' recollection of Jesus' own renunciation of ritual wine, his Last Supper declaration that he would drink no more of "the fruit of the vine" (later Mk 14.25). It occurs early in the parable collection because it pertains to an initiatory experience in sobriety. That early occurrence, in turn, answers a classic question about the structure of canonical John: why does the Temple cleansing come at the beginning of the gospel rather than near the end, as in the synoptics? (See the next section for further discussion.)

4. *"Recovery is like an unbeliever who comes in the night, drinks water, and is born in spirit"* (Jn 3.1–8). This parable became the Nicodemus story. It portrays the mixture of curiosity, skepticism, and desire for sobriety one sees today in persons at their first Twelve-Step meeting. The parable sought to reassure uncertain newcomers like Nicodemus that people who quit drinking ("born of water," 3.5) and come to meetings ("comes in the night," 3.2) ultimately experience their promised spiritual rebirth ("born of the spirit," 3.5).

5. *"Recovery is like a man who asks a woman at a well for water"* (Jn 4.3–42). Again, "woman" is a Markan in-group term for recovering persons, here a person who gives the newcomer water to drink. The elaborated story surrounding this woman in Jn 4.3–42 results from accretions during subsequent stages in the gospel's development. The chief term of the parable, of course, is water as opposed to wine. "Well" as a life-source symbol would have been immediately understandable. Probably the oldest material in the final story not present in the original parable is the designation of the woman as a Samaritan, which may indicate that the Markôs fellowship crossed ethnic boundaries within Palestine.

6. *"Recovery is like a sick man who wants to get well, gets up from his bed, and walks to the water"* (Jn 5.2–18). Figured in this parable is the crucial amalgam of desire for sobriety and willingness to act that is required for entry into the rule of God. Jesus' question to the man, "Do you *want* [italics added] to be healed?" highlights the importance of unreserved desire as a prerequisite to action.

7. *"Recovery is like a meal where flesh and words are shared like fish and bread"* (Jn 6.1–14). This is the parable cum allegory that becomes the feeding stories in Mark and the other synoptics, as well as in canonical John. Apparently it goes back to Jesus' prepaschal career. The meal events were fellowship meetings. "Flesh" signifies sober actions on the part of recovering persons, and "words" denotes sober thinking, respectively symbolized as fish and bread. The multiplication of fish and bread depicted in the canonical versions reflects a later insight within the Markôs groups that what today are called the "comments" on the speaker's talk by others present at the meeting represent a miraculous increase in the spiritual food distributed. In this view, the tradition of fish and bread eucharists would stem not from the Markans' liturgical practice but from metaphors in their coterie vocabulary.

8. *"Recovery is like a man eating bread of life from God"* (Jn 6.25–59). Behind the sayings in the redactionally constructed section of canonical John ultimately derived from this parable ("I am the living bread come down from heaven," etc., Jn 6.51–59; see the discussion in the next section) stands the bread metaphor so important to the Markan fellowship. The parable teaches hearers that bread represents the Word of sobriety come from God, whose "eating" (i.e., hearing, comprehending, and observing) leads to recovery and wholeness.

9. *"Recovery is like a man beset by wind and wave, who walks on the water"* (Jn 6.16–21). Also later incorporated in Mark (6.47–51) immediately following the story of feeding, as in the Johannine text, this similitude is the quintessential serenity parable. It illustrates the spiritual truism that attitude is more important than fact, that freedom from worry and fear is not contingent on external conditions. Its location after the feeding story indicates that meetings result in serenity, a fact to which today's alcoholics will readily attest.

10. *"Recovery is like a thirsty man who comes and drinks water of life"* (Jn 7.37–38). This parable uses the Jewish metaphor "living water" to contrast to wine as an expression of sobriety. Its incorporation in John 7 is the work of non-Markan writers in a later stage of the composition of the gospel, who connected it with the water ritual of the feast of Tabernacles. The passage reads as follows:

> (Jn 7.37) On the last day of the feast, the great day, Jesus stood up and proclaimed, "If any one thirst, let him come to me and drink [water].
> (38) He who believes in me, as the scripture has said, 'Out of his heart shall flow rivers of living water.'"

Although canonical John places this saying at Tabernacles, not Passover, it is possible that the parable from which it derives stems from an episode in Jesus' out-of-control Passover excursion in Jerusalem, implicit in Mark's story of the Temple cleansing, when Jesus drunkenly exhorted Temple pilgrims to abjure wine in favor of water. It may have immediately preceded his berserk attempt, covertly alluded to in Mk 11.16, to wrest the drinking vessels from the worshipers' hands, obviously an attempt to force them to stop drinking. So interpreted the parable adds yet another piece to the puzzle of what actually occurred in Jesus' fanatical assault on the Temple.

11. *"Recovery is like a blind man whose eyes are washed clear and comes to the water"* (Jn 9.1–41). Figured in this parable is the wholesale cognitive reorganization, the change of thinking, that Greek-speaking Markans called *metanoia,* here the result of renouncing wine for water. Although the concerns of Jn 9.1–41 extend far beyond the original parable, the attitude of the man born blind in the final story, unwilling to go beyond the fact of his own spiritual experience and immune to entrapment by doctrinaire religious interrogators, represents a model for the newly sober in every age.

12. *"Recovery is like a fisherman who casts on the other side and nets a great catch"* (Jn 21.1–14). This is another *metanoia* parable. "On the other side" meant such things as admitting powerlessness versus continued attempts at self-empowerment, surrender versus continued fighting, action versus continued inaction, asking for help versus continued efforts at going it alone, and so on. Church redactors in the final stage of the gospel's composition positioned this parable in chapter 21 of the canonical text, as a preamble to the so-called Easter breakfast appearance of the risen Jesus and the story of bread and 153 fish. Not surprisingly, the meaning of this enigmatic number has been pondered over the centuries. One of the observations is that 153 is the sum of all integers from one through seventeen.[4] Readers will note the coincidence that the number of sayings in the Proto-John parable collection is seventeen.

13. *"Recovery is like a man asleep in a tomb who is watered by tears and awakens"* (Jn 11.1–44). A parable for family members, this saying indicates how the love and prayer of persons in the addict's life water the soil of recovery. Notice that in the canonical version, when Jesus calls "Lazarus, come out!" (Jn 11.43), the wonder is not that a power emanates from Jesus but that Lazarus responds, he acts, he *comes out* (Jn 11.44).

14. *"Recovery is like a vine [growing out of a wine cup] whose branches are its members"* (Jn 15.1–11). This parable highlights the symbiosis between individuals in recovery and the recovery program itself. Note that the vine-and-branch metaphor excludes any possibility of hier-

archy among recovering persons. "Growing out of a wine cup" may have been part of the original saying, conveying the Markan idea that ritual drinking (the cup) leads to recovery (the vine). E. R. Goodenough points out that the first-century emblem of a vine growing out of a cup had eschatological significance, a fact heightening the plausibility of this Markan interpretation.[5]

15. *"Recovery is like a man grateful to wash another's feet"* (Jn 13.1–17). A parable about service, this saying employs the figure of the menial household slave whose job it was to wash the dust of travel from the feet of visitors. Spiritual people have always known that assuming the role of servant leads to a feeling of exaltation to which the proper response is a sense of gratitude, *eucharistia* in Greek. Recovering people look on the process as involving a kind of selfish selflessness and describe twelfth-step work, as they call service, as "keeping it by giving it away." When the abstinent ascetics who had infiltrated the Markôs groups began to transform the parable collection into a narrative, they chose this saying as the nucleus of what would later become Jn 13.1–17, the account of Jesus' actions at the Jerusalem Passover. Presumably they did so to avoid trafficking in the scandalous story of Jesus' inebriety ("this [wine] is my blood," Mk 14.24a), even though they were quite aware of the Markan memory that Jesus had not literally washed feet at the seder but rather had delivered the message about wine that later became Mk 14.22–25 (see the discussion in the next section).

16. *"Recovery is like a grain of wheat falling to the [watered] earth, dying, and bringing forth much fruit"* (Jn 12.20–26). Obviously a reference to *psuchē* death and the humiliation cum humility involved not just in recovery from addiction but in many other growth experiences as well, the parable recalls Jesus' Gethsemane experience as known to the Markans and later recounted by Mark (14.32–41). "Much fruit" points to the general benefit to humankind of each individual's conversion from self to God. "Watered" may have been included in the original parable, not from fidelity to the mechanics of germination but as a reminder to drunkards that water in place of wine is what initiates the process that leads to *psuchē* death.

17. *"Recovery is like a man lifted up [in sobriety] for all to see"* (Jn 3.13–15, 8.28, and 12.27–36). This final parable refers to the messianic sign identified by Jesus in his hangover apocalypse ("coming in clouds," Mk 13.26), cited in his reply to the high priest after his arrest ("coming with the clouds of heaven," Mk 14.62), and probably repeated whenever he told his story after his return to Galilee. It refers not solely to Jesus but to all recovering persons going about *(erchomai)*

exalted in sobriety, "raised up" for others to behold even as Deutero-Isaiah's servant was beheld by amazed onlookers (Is 52.15). Gradually, as the text of John developed, the parable was transformed into a crucifixion prediction, versions of which occur in three places in the final version of the gospel (see the discussion in the next section).

Once again, the suggestion here is that this collection of seventeen reconstructed recovery parables constitutes the elusive original kernel of the Gospel of John. These parables would have been developed during the 30s C.E. in the postpaschal Galilean Markôs fellowship for use with former wine addicts new to sobriety. Three decades later, at least five of these parables (1, 3, 7, 9, and 17) were incorporated more or less intact into Mark's gospel. Twelve of the sayings speak of water contextually understood as a drink replacing wine. All of them reflect central themes of Markan spirituality, a spirituality essentially identical to that of today's Twelve-Step programs. So viewed, the core of John turns out to be Markan in origin and connected to recovery from alcohol addiction.

Scenario of the Composition of John

Although the task of providing a detailed account of the stages comprised by the composition of John's gospel must be left to the Johannine scholar, the following scenario suggests in outline how the foregoing parable collection might have become the gospel as we know it. Apparently this slim Markan sobriety manual passed through three major recensions and a final Church redaction over a seventy-year period en route to becoming canonical John.

Events leading to the first recension began in the 50s and escalated during the 60s, as the Markôs groups were at first infiltrated and then increasingly dominated by abstinent Encratite (self-strengthened) ascetics, fellow Jews attracted by the Markans' serenity and seeking relief from anxieties attributable to the ongoing deterioration of Palestinian society—banditry, fanaticism, economic and institutional breakdown, and warfare. Originally both a real and a symbolic counter to wine, water becomes the water of purification. John the ascetic baptist becomes the Encratite hero, while the Markans continue to revere Jesus the former wine addict (see Mt 11.18–19). The term "rule of God" is downplayed owing to residual connotations of addiction. As the parable collection begins its transformation into narrative, Jesus' Temple rampage retains its position early in the text (ultimately 2.13–22) by virtue of its connection with parables 3 and 10, but putative desecration by merchants replaces ritual drinking as the target of Jesus' anger. The ascetics exclude material from Jesus' prepaschal career, as well as any reference to a Last Supper wine ritual. Into the lacuna created by the latter exclusion they introduce a narrative transformation of the foot-washing parable. There are the beginnings of a high christology aimed at counteracting Jesus' reputation as an inebriate. By 70 C.E. the Markans have ceded control of the text to the ascetics, retreated from the war-ravaged synagogues into the secrecy of home meetings, and as Mark's gospel suggests, begun to enforce powerlessness over alcohol as a qualification for membership in their fellowship. They play no further part in the development of John.

The second recension evidently grew out of postwar controversies during the 70s between the ascetics and other Jews who refused to buy into the messianic religion increasingly abroad in Jewish Palestine, including the version ostensibly advertised in the newly published Gospel of Mark, yet who were, temporarily at least, barred by Roman proscription from any public expression of their traditional Judaism. The outcome of this recension is mostly contained in 5.1–10.39 of the canonical text. Here the Jesus versus John controversy is replaced by Jesus versus Moses, which soon generalizes to Christian versus Jew. In the argument, the ascetics adopt a still-higher christology depicting Jesus as personifying a preexistent divine wisdom. The theme of replacement is imposed on the calender of Jewish feasts, Passover, Tabernacles, and finally Dedication (Hanukkah), where Jesus as Messiah replaces the altar of the now-destroyed Temple. These disputes with non-Christian Jews harden and congregational schisms occur, but the ascetics retain ownership of their text and speak of themselves as having been expelled from their own synagogues.

The third recension emerged from what appears to have been a series of trade-offs negotiated during the 80s and 90s between the ascetic Jewish Christians, increasingly branded as gnostics, and wine-drinking gentile Christians representing the emergent catholic form of the religion. The latter took their theology from Paul's letters and their narrative conception of Jesus' career from gospels such as Mark, Matthew, and Luke. At this stage a gnostic prologue is added by the ascetics (1.1–18), but so too is Passion material demanded by the catholic parties seeking to harmonize the book with the gospel stories, including conflict with authorities (11.45–47), costly ointment (12.1–8), Jerusalem entrance (12.12–19), Judas and Peter (13.21–38), arrest and trial (18.1–27), Pilate (18.28–19.16), crucifixion and burial (19.17–42), and empty tomb and appearance (20.1–18). The gnostic ascetics in turn complete their composition of the so-called

Last Discourse (14.1–17.26). Throughout they cast Jesus' speeches in poetry. Recovery parables about the woman at the well and the blind man remain, but their content is greatly expanded and they emerge as narratives depicting stages in beholders' recognition of Jesus as the Christ (4.1–42 and 9.1–41). The parables about "lifting up" also remain but take the form of crucifixion predictions (3.13–15, 8.28, and 12.27–36). The parable about fishing is inserted into a new conclusion to the book (21.1–14), which contains a justification of Petrine authority (21.15–19) conjoined with a kind of amnesty extended to the gnostic ascetics (21.20–23). Whereas the ascetics' insistence on a wine-free Last Supper leads to retention of the foot-washing parable (13.1–17), the catholic parties succeed in introducing the phrase "made wine" into the Cana wedding story (*oinon gegenēmenon*, 2.9), in one stroke converting this ancient sobriety parable into a Dionysiac wine miracle with eucharistic overtones.[6]

The end of the century saw the gospel undergo a final ecclesiastical redaction, so called, in which the ascetic Christians, by now condemned as gnostic heretics, played no part. Included is the clause "where he had made the water wine" added to the Cana reference in 4.46, evidently to counter the protests of persons still living who knew that the version of the Cana wedding story as a Dionysiac miracle ("made wine" in 2.9) was a corruption of an older parabolic text whose only mention of wine had been the metaphor "choice wine" applied to water. The Church redactors around 100 C.E., possibly aware of scandalous memories connecting the Gospel of Mark with a vanished sobriety movement, may have suspected that some readers of Mark understood the Markan Last Supper narrative as depicting the end of Jesus' drinking career. In any case, they seem to have been less concerned with ridding the Johannine text of gnostic-ascetic influence than with exploiting it to counteract material in Mark's widely circulated book. John the Baptist now gives a double witness to Jesus' divine preexistence (1.15 and 1.30, the former an obvious insertion into the prologue), thereby countering perceived Markan ambivalence on the Messiah question. The Lazarus parable is made into the story of a physical resurrection (11.38–44), and the anti-Thomasite physicalist appearance scene is introduced (20.24–29), both of which serve to countervail Mark's embarrassing silence about resurrection. Passages are brought in to correct Mark's story of Jesus' Gethsemane wavering as understood by nonalcoholics (12.27–30) and to oppose the Markan refusal of wine from the cross (19.28–30). Mark's use of "cup" as an active metaphor for addiction is countered by 18.11b, wherein "drink the cup" is not a metaphor but a fixed expression meaning lot or destiny.

Bowing to Johannine tradition, the Church redactors kept the Temple cleansing at the beginning of the gospel and stopped short of inserting a bread and wine eucharist into the Last Supper in place of the foot-washing story. They did, however, compose the passage at 6.51–59 reflecting a bread and wine communion. Here, in what is widely regarded as a constructed text,[7] Jesus is four times (6.53, 54, 55, and 56) made to utter the phrase "body and blood," a Hebrew expression that signified death. Apparently the redactors were seeking to shape a background of Christian understanding such that interpreters of Mark's account of Jesus' Last Supper discourse (Mk 14.22–25) would retroactively impose on the Markan text an implication of imminent death, presumably by crucifixion, whereas in fact Mark's phraseology does not contain the "body and blood" locution at all and (as chap. 2 of this book argues at length) need not signify physical death. The effectiveness of the redactors' strategy was confirmed for the present writer when an eminent NT scholar, on examining material from chapter 2 of this book, proclaimed its reading of Mk 14.22 and 24 "wrong because 'body and blood' means death." In the end, the Church redactors' exploitation of John to counter troubling material in Mark may have been what saved John's place in the canon later in the second century, when bishops otherwise sought to suppress it because of its gnostic content.

Overall, it is hoped that readers will consider the foregoing compositional outline, along with the parables posited as its starting point, to be important intertextual evidence bearing on the present theory of Markan audience, as well as a help in the ongoing study of Johannine composition.

The Book of Revelation

By now, readers of this book familiar with the Book of Revelation, particularly the material from chapter 10 on, should not be surprised to hear it described as a florilegium of alcohol symbols. What may prove startling is that it identifies addiction as the besetting illness of the fledgling Christian churches. The assumptions underlying these views are as follows: The writer of Revelation seems to have been an end-of-century ex-addict in a remnant Markôs group, probably some sort of elder aware of the old Markan-Christian connections. But whereas the evangelist Mark had seen the catastrophe of an alcoholic Christ cult as a future possibility likely only if postwar clergies began to operate theocratically, the writer of Revelation a quarter-century later sees this catastrophe actually occurring in the churches of his day: bishops in league with temporal authorities, advocates of dominical ecclesiastical governance addicted to ritual wine and preaching a Jesus of willpower and perfection. This he interprets as symptomizing alcoholism. But good Markan that he is, he believes that God calls no one into addiction without a plan for their subsequent recovery. This is the message he encodes in his apocalypse, the portrait of an alcoholic church and the suffering and strife it will unleash in the world, together with a promise of recovery in a rediscovered form of the Markôs fellowship. The future advent of this parousial program he sees as accompanied by apocalyptic chaos (today the term would be "paradigm shift") leading ultimately to the end of the age of the churches and the dawn of the age of sobriety. It is this discernment of illness and vision of metanoetic recovery that inform his book.

The writer calls himself "John," thereby identifying himself with John Mark and, by extension, the Galilean Markôs tradition that produced the original Johannine parables. Aware that many will interpret his message as an attack rather than a therapeutic intervention, he adopts a strategy of compositional camouflage similar to the approach successfully pursued a generation earlier by the evangelist Mark writing for an audience of Judean Christians. Whereas Mark relied mainly on linguistic ambiguities as camouflage, however, the writer of Revelation resorts to polyvalent although traditional apocalyptic symbolism and nonlinear rhetorical forms such as intercalation and interlude to ensure acceptance of his work by the Church bishops around 100 C.E.[8] Of the four main anti-Christic (anti-recovery) symbols in his apocalypse, however—dragon, beast, second beast/false prophet, and statue—all save the dragon are the writer's invention. The theory here is that these four symbols represent the pathology of the churches' alcoholism as follows: the red dragon figures wine and wine addiction per se, the beast is a personification of self-will, the second beast/false prophet is the alcoholic bishop, and the statue is a Jesus icon made to speak the bishop's image of an unsurrendered authoritarian Christ.

It is beyond the scope of this book to discuss all of Revelation, to summarize traditional interpretations, or to quote segments of the text for close reading. The approach will be simply to lay out a Markan view of key symbolism with minimum comment. In this view, the heart of the prophecy is the material from Rv 10.1–19.21. The earlier chapters will be seen as preamble-like and annunciatory, and the ending will be seen as depicting the bimillennial triumph of recovery over religion. Here, then, are the symbolic equations informing a Markôs reading of the central section of Revelation. (Text segmentation is mostly that of Elisabeth Schüssler Fiorenza.)[9]

The Writer Interprets Daniel 12 (10.1–11.13)

After presenting the seal septet prophesying an end-time unveiling of scriptural meaning (6.1–17 and 8.1) and the trumpet septet heralding a revelatory message (8.2–9.21), the writer reports a vision apprising him of "God's secret plan" (10.7) for the salvation of humanity. The plan is set forth on a "small scroll" (10.2) and voiced in "seven thunderclaps" (10.3), which the writer is instructed to keep secret and not commit to writing. His comprehension of the vision is conveyed by his "eating" the scroll (10.9). Its "sweet" taste turned "sour" (10.10) signifies the prophet's traditional ambivalence toward the message that he must announce. Next the writer is told to "measure God's sanctuary" (11.1), that is, to assess and evaluate the churches, in this case, as it turns out, in terms of alcoholism. The voice then promises to send "my two witnesses" (11.3), presumably in response to this assessment, to prophesy during three and a half years of strife.

This is where Daniel 12 comes in. The numbers here, "forty-two months" (11.2) and "one thousand two hundred and sixty days" (11.3), together with the injunction to keep the vision secret and a promise of the coming of two witnesses, link the text to Daniel 12, the mysterious addendum to Daniel that, like the material just discussed, includes a secret message, two messengers, the cleansing of many, a time period of "a year two years and a half year," and perseverance through "one thousand two hundred and ninety days" then "one thousand three hundred and thirty-five days." In effect, the Revelation writer's vision in 10.1–11.13 is his interpretation of Daniel 12. In the light of his overall apocalypse, he seems to understand the Danielic material as prophesying the still-future annunciation or founding of a spiritual movement for the good of humanity by two messengers or cofounders who must undergo a critical three-and-a-half-year period (specifically 1,290 and 1,335 days) when the survival of their movement hangs in the balance. The writer is clearly fascinated by the mysterious periods of time named in Daniel, a topic further discussed later. Again, what the writer voices here is his belief that the parousial recovery program he goes on to prophesy will, according to his interpretation of Daniel, be established by two founders and affect many people, and its survival during its first three and a half years will be touch and go.

The Seventh Trumpet (11.15–19)

With the sounding of the seventh trumpet the heralding of the apocalyptic vision is completed. It is time for the vision itself, which begins with the tableau of red dragon, woman, and child.

Red Dragon versus Woman (12.1–17)

This passage describes in mythological terms the plight of humanity caught between the mortal impulse to addiction and the heavenly call to recovery. The vision depicts a woman crowned with twelve stars confronted by a red dragon. The dragon symbolizes addiction, and the woman symbolizes recovery, the latter a Markan trademark. Their confrontal and the dragon's attempt to devour her child (12.4) represent the conflict within humanity between illness and wellness, whose object is human life itself, figured by the child. The twelve stars in the woman's crown (12.1) represent the twelve recovery principles formulated by Jesus. The dragon's red color (12.3), its warfare against the messengers of recovery (12.7–9), and its rejection of water (12.15) all point to wine addiction. Its "dragging a third of the stars from the sky" (12.4) suggests that one-third of all people somehow suffer the scourge of drink. Interestingly, researchers today estimate that one person in ten is more or less actively alcoholic, and their illness involves two others as codependents, meaning that one-third of the populace is directly affected by alcoholism, exactly the percentage suggested in Rv 12.4.

Two Beasts and a Statue (13.1–18)

Here the writer confronts the Church with a picture of its addiction. The vision shows a beast representing the churches collectively. Its seven heads represent seven communities or sees, and the coronets on its horns signify authoritarian governance (13.1). Its supposedly fatal head wound now healed (13.3) symbolizes the failure of ritual baptism, its chief sacrament, to produce the death of self (fatal head wound) required for atonement. The people's cultic prostration before the red dragon (13.4) represents the obeisance of Christian laity to the minister and his wine chalice, symbol of the latent addiction underlying clerical authority. Whereas the figures of the dragon and heavenly queen are drawn from contemporary mythology, that of the beast seems to be the writer's own creation, perhaps inspired by the sea monster Leviathan. Its meaning is psychological. The beast personifies humanity's self-will, our mortal inclination to be God for ourselves. When religion is contaminated by self-will it becomes indistinguishable from the oppressive secular institutions from which it supposedly confers spiritual freedom. So the beast's seven heads also symbolize the many manifestations of addictive self-will involved in religious governance, such as legalism, fundamentalist dogmatism, judgmentalism, perfectionism, fanatical moralism, and militancy, all of which corrupt the rule of God and undermine true spirituality.

Next a "second beast" (13.11) appears, later called "the false prophet" (16.13 and 19.20). It is a type of the Christian bishop, a magisterial autocrat in the service of the first beast (13.12), who teaches a self-empowered Jesus and claims to speak the mind of Christ. Its "two horns like a lamb" (13.11) represent the episcopal miter and a self-imputed connection with Jesus. The "noise like a dragon" (13.11) is the bishop's wine-laden exhalations proclaiming his own authority. The statue that the bishop persuades people to erect (13.14) represents a clerically fostered icon portraying a Jesus of willpower and perfection. Thus it is said to honor not God but the first beast personifying the unrepudiated self ("wounded by the sword but still lived," 13.14). The statue's ability to speak (13.15) signifies the clergy's homiletic interpretations of Jesus' sayings that make Jesus seem to proclaim a religion of self-empowerment and legalism. The number of the second beast, 666, understood as six three times, symbolizes incompleteness maximally intensified. Here the writer is not saying that churchmen are evil but only that they remain ill and untreated and their church imperfected.

An Alter-Community (14.1–5)

This vision shows a community of the redeemed, an alter-community to the churches, which can only be the Markôs fellowship parousially returned in the millennial future to which the apocalypse refers. Their number, 144,000 (14.1), represents twelve, the number of recovery principles formulated by Jesus, multiplied by itself and then millennialized. The community's avoidance of sexual defilement (14.4) symbolizes its refusal to adulterate the rule of God, its recovery program, by involvement with hierarchical religion. Its honesty and faultlessness (14.5) symbolize the continued reformation of character required in recovery. Its "new hymn" (14.3) would be devotional material of some sort unknown to Christians but heard in community gatherings. In Alcoholics Anonymous today such a new hymn is "How It Works," the opening paragraphs of chapter 5 of the book *Alcoholics Anonymous,* often read aloud at the start of meetings. "How it Works," it should be noted, concludes with the following "pertinent ideas" specifically portraying the inefficacy of self-will:

(a) That we were alcoholic and could not manage our own lives.
(b) That probably no human power could have relieved our alcoholism.
(c) That God could and would if He were sought.[10]

Judgment Announced (14.6–20)

Next the three angels in 14.6–13 announce the judgment of God on the churches. Here and in the bowl septet that follows (15.1–16.21), the dominant figure is alcohol per se—wine, the wine of God's anger, the seven wine chalices, the wine of the churches' adultery with the temporal order, the winepress, and the prostitute's drunkenness. Shifting tropes, the writer envisions a time in which wine and drunkenness will function as synecdoche, not metaphor, that is, when they will constitute not merely a figure for but also a real and considerable part of the advanced alcoholism of the Christian world, among churched and unchurched alike. In rhetorical terms, his language shifts from *poetic* imagery similar, say, to that of the Markan apocalypse (Mark 13) to *noetic* imagery denoting real-world drunkenness pervading a future church and world. The name given the Church from this point on, which to end-of-century Christian readers denoted Rome, is "Babylon, which gave the whole world the wine of God's anger to drink" (14.8).

The writer indicates that self-willed persons who try to live by auto-empowerment because they have been taught to emulate Jesus as a paragon of willpower ("worshipers of the beast and its statue," 14.9), if they continue in their present paths, are destined to become hopelessly alcoholic, "made to drink the wine of God's fury, which is ready, undiluted, in his cup of anger" (14.10). This clearly is real as well as metaphorical wine, synecdochically representing the widespread anger and death that accompany epidemic addiction. Nor is there any temporal relief from these ravages (14.11). The sole antidote is *psuchē* death: "Happy are those who die in the Lord" (14.13). And recovery *is* possible. The passage concludes by depicting dual eschatological harvests, one of grain (14.14–16) followed by another of grapes (14.17–20). Grain prefigures bread, the principal Markan symbol of the word of recovery, while grapes denote wine, symbol of God's curative wrath propelling humankind into deeper addiction as a goad to surrender. Hence the harvests represent the twin futures confronting addicts: life in recovery or further suffering in "the winepress of God's anger" (14.19). What the winepress yields is blood, enough to come "up to the horses' bridles as far away as sixteen furlongs" (14.20). This exaggerated and terrifying conceit should remove any doubt that the Markans understood Jesus' paschal words as figuratively identifying wine with human bloodshed (Mk 14.24).

The Bowl Visions (15.1–16.21)

The last of the septets in Revelation, the bowl visions open with the announcement of "the seven last plagues that will exhaust the anger of God" (15.1), followed by a reprise vision of the redeemed, whose surrenders have won them victory over the self ("fought against the beast and won") and who will be untouched by the impending cataclysm (15.2–4). Next begins the actual pouring out of the seven bowls of God's anger. The purport here is that the churches may or may not, as a result of the increase of wrath, admit their illness and come into recovery. As is true of individual drinkers, the outcome is unknown ahead of time, a fact signified by the report that persons could not enter the smoke-filled temple until the seven plagues were completed (15.8). The seventh bowl is the worst of all (16.17–21), representing either an outer global catastrophe or the wholesale inner renunciation of ego and agonism on the part of alcoholic humanity in the aggregate.

A significant element here is the interlude in 16.13–16, which shows, coming from the mouths of an alcoholic episcopate ("frog-like spirits from the jaws of the dragon, beast, and false prophet"), attempts to influence contending temporal powers ("the kings of the world"), whose results are exactly the opposite of peace. Verse 16 finds the armies of the earth arrayed at Armageddon, the mythical site of the last battle later described in 19.11–20.10. The lesson is clear: alcoholic humankind can no more achieve peace by self-will than it can quite drinking by willpower, and when authoritarian religious leaders begin to interact politically with mentally drunk temporal authorities, all hell is going to break loose. Many illustrations of this fact, past and present, might be cited. Advanced addiction in ordinary persons is bad enough, but its manifestation by organized fanatics, whether religious or secular, is terrible to behold, so clearly does it threaten all humanity.

The bowl septet suggests that the object of the wrath it depicts is the alcoholic churches—not so much the first-century communities as the increasingly diseased institution the writer sees developing in the future. In 16.4 the third bowl angel turns water, symbol of recovery, into blood by pouring wine into it, clearly a reference to the emergent Church's suppression of water-drinking communities. The "blood given them to drink" (16.6) refers not just to wine but also to the strife resulting from militant emotions catalyzed by wine. Verse 19 indicates that when its self-willed efforts to produce peace lead instead to holocaust, the Church itself, "Babylon the Great," will also be "made to drink the full winecup of God's anger."

Judgment I (17.1–18)

In the first of three judgment visions following the bowls, the Church is personified as a female figure astride the beast of the self (17.3). Her purple and scarlet vestments and gold wine cup (17.4) point to her identity, but the salient facts about the figure are her drunkenness and her adulterous relationship with temporal authority. The desire she embodies is a figure for addiction. Again, this is not metaphoric alcoholism but synecdochic—in other words, the real thing. "The wine of adultery" (17.2) and "the filth of her fornication" (17.4) refer to the adulteration of spiritual surrender with drunken self-will. This frightening figure depicts the danger of what old-timer alcoholics today call "mixing" religion and spirituality, of attempting to reconcile the irreconcilable.

The bowl angel speaks a riddle pertaining to the female and the beast (17.8), whose answer lies in the Church-sponsored view of Jesus' crucifixion and resurrection. The heart of the riddle is "beast that was, and is not, and yet is" (final predicates of verse 8). The answer to this riddle is the churches' image of a Jesus who lived, then died and was buried (placed in the "abyss" of verse 8), and then rose again. That is what "being, not being, and yet being" means. Verse 8 further states that persons who learn of this and think it miraculous will be those whose names are *not* written in the book of life. In other words, choosing to believe in Jesus' crucifixion and resurrection is a way to miss the rule of God. Yet this is precisely the belief the churches advocate, here (17.11) identified as the eighth head of the beast. It is, however, a belief that the bowl angel assures us will be destroyed (end of verse 11). So viewed, the passage represents a prophetic unmasking of a false credo Christians are admonished to cling to at all costs, a credo standing in the way of the experience of spiritual well-being.

The remainder of the first judgment vision (17.12–18) tells how the alcoholic churches will involve themselves politically in the temporal realm, seeking to maintain themselves in the world by human power, not God's. Here is the urge to self-sufficiency that fears and attacks all professions of powerlessness. This is represented by the beast and the kings making war against the Lamb (17.14). Verses 16 and 17, however, prophesy a time when temporal powers will turn against the churches in consequence of the societal chaos resulting from their attempts to play God by taking or advocating absolutist positions on causes such as social justice, objective morality, disarmament, right to life, and so on.

Judgment II (18.1–24)

The second judgment vision, again mentioning "the intoxicating wine of prostitution" (18.3), depicts the Church hitting bottom exactly as the drinking alcoholic hits bottom. Institutions do not repent, however; persons do, and one must never forget the sense in which all the events in Revelation have a possible focus entirely within the mind of the individual, whether lofty or low. The drastic action required is highlighted by a voice calling people to "come out" of the Church (18.4). This represents a call to Christians to repudiate sacramental wine, the "desolating sacrilege" of Mk 13.14, and admit their powerlessness over alcohol. Only by the actions of individual members can the Church in its illness get to recovery. Verses 9 through 23 list the fineries that the Church will lose if it abandons temporal riches in favor of spiritual. The image of the great boulder, the Church as "rock," disappearing into the sea without a ripple (18.21) shows how profound is the anonymity of true religion once shorn of visible trappings. Finally, lest anyone seriously lament the Church's loss of its worldly splendor at the hour of its repentance, verse 24 reminds one of the ills those splendors concealed, "the blood of prophets and saints, all the blood that was ever shed on earth."

Judgment III (19.1–10)

In the third judgment vision a heavenly choir praises the judgment of God in bringing the alcoholic churches to step one. The crowds in verse 6 are the Christian multitudes who have admitted powerlessness and begun working recovery programs. The wedding imagery (19.8–9) depicts the marriage of Church and Lamb. Since the Lamb symbolizes the messianic recovery program, the marriage theme indicates that the Church does in fact surrender and take step one. Although the writer of Revelation ends the bowl visions on an optimistic note, no one can predict whether the churches will in reality surrender or continue their denial and fighting. Thus one cannot tell, nor indeed did the writer know, whether the cataclysm depicted in the bowl visions represents the shattering of ego that accompanies surrender or the many kinds of outward physical destruction that finally occur if alcoholism goes untreated. In short, the alcoholic churches must choose between God's grace and ultimate wrath, and Revelation does not tell what their choices will be.

Parousia of the Messianic Recovery Program (19.11–21)

This section depicts the fulfillment of Jesus' prophecy of a future return of his recovery program, originally given in Mk 13.26–27. It shows the second coming of the Christ symbolized as a figure on a white horse at the head of a heavenly army. The image is that of a person rather than, say, the Logos, because end-of-century Christians awaiting the return of Christ-as-person would have rejected a nonpersonal image more in keeping with the "principles not personalities," focus of recovery. Here the figure is that of the anonymous Jesus, not merely Jesus of Nazareth, but the apotheosis of every anonymous alcoholic who carries the message "Yahweh saves" (the etymological "Jesus") to other sufferers. The importance of the anonymity principle is highlighted by the figure's own anonymity, "inscribed on his person was a name known to no one but himself" (19.12). The blood soaking his cloak (19.13) symbolizes not only wine and bloodshed but also the psychic carnage of ego-death. The figure is known by the name "Word of God" (19.13) because the words of the messianic recovery program come from God. The sword coming from the figure's mouth (19.15) indicates that the purpose of the Word is apocalyptic judgment, life or death. The "iron sceptre" (19.15) suggests ironlike strength, the complete reliability of the program as a way of living. His "treading out the wine of God's wrath" (19.15) represents the continuing provision of ritual wine bringing more and more people into the suffering required for recovery.

The contrasting wedding feasts, of the Lamb (19.10) and of the carrion birds (19.17–18), suggest the choice God offers between sobriety and death. Verses 19–20 depict the ultimate confrontation between the parousial Christ (the modern alcoholism program enfleshed by legions of recovering addicts) and the kings of the earth joined with the false prophet and the beast (self-will and the millions in secular and ecclesiastical institutions who embody it). But no battle ensues. Instead, the beast and false prophet are taken prisoner and thrown into the lake of burning sulfur. This signifies the victory of recovery through the surrender of the self-willed, whether in or out of religions. The only ones to receive punishment are the beast and false prophet. All others are "killed" by the sword coming from the mouth of the rider (19.21), a reference to *psuchē* death and conversion on hearing the messianic message.

Last Things

The Book of Revelation concludes with a universal final judgment (20.1–15), visionary portrayals of the New World of God (21.1–8) and the New City of God (21.9–22.9), and an appendix (22.10–21). Significantly, the vision of the City of God is revealed by one of the bowl angels (21.9). The city has no temple (21.22), a fact indicating the demise of religion. It does have twelve gates (21.12), twelve foundation stones (21.14), and twelve fruit crops from paradisiacal trees of life (22.2). Today's alcoholics will have no trouble seeing these images respectively as prefigures of the Twelve Steps, Twelve Traditions, and Twelve Promises of Alcoholics Anonymous.

The Greek text of this section, however, bears earmarks of tampering that affected the phraseology stating the time of the final judgment. The passage contains three double mentions of a thousand-year time interval (20.2–7). Each mention takes the form "a thousand years . . . until the thousand years are finished," such that the reference seems to be to a single thousand-year period mentioned twice. Yet the phrases seem oddly scattered in the passage, as if purposely disarranged. It is possible that the writer had originally juxtaposed these double mentions with the result that each pair had read, "until a thousand years . . . and another thousand years are finished," thereby denoting a two-thousand-year time period. In this case, a précis of 20.1–10 would yield the following:

> I saw an angel shackle the dragon, but only for a little time. Then he must be released until a thousand years and another thousand years are finished (20.1–3). Until this thousand years and another thousand years were finished, I saw persons who had refused to worship the beast and had died arise into new life. Happy those who so die and arise, for the second death cannot affect them (20.4–6). Until the thousand years (end of 20.6) and another thousand years are finished, the dragon will ravage the earth, but then be shackled forever (20.7–10).

If the shackling of the dragon refers to the defeat of addiction by the Markôs program, then the brief period of victory depicted in the reshaped passage ("a little time") represents the fifty or sixty years of the first-century program. The two-thousand-year rampage of the released dragon, in turn, represents unchecked alcoholism throughout the anticipated church age. The permanent reshackling of the dragon refers to the parousial return of the Markôs movement after twenty centuries and the final defeat of the illness. The writer indicates that even during the interval, persons who refuse to worship the beast will find sobriety through *psuchē* death and, echoing the psalmist's thought (Ps 16.10), that all who rise to new life after dying to the self will not be affected by "the second death," that is, physical death, but will pass directly into eternal life. As for the two-thousand-year period, the writer perhaps understood it as a millennializing of Mark's prophetic allegory of the two-day entombment of the surrendered and recovering Jesus.

Daniel 12

Once again, the theory here is that the Revelation writer understood Dn 12.5–13 as a prophecy of the bimillennial recovery movement he foresees. It would be a parousial spiritual program founded by two messengers and destined to pass through an initial period of about three and a half years when its survival would hang in the balance. As for the numbers of days given in Dn 12.11–12, 1,290 and 1,335, scholars believe them to be a gloss by an unknown redactor.[11] Ordinarily Daniel is considered a post hoc reference to the desecration of the Temple by Antiochus IV between 167 and 164 B.C.E. The facts are these: Daniel received its final redaction around 140 B.C.E., a generation after the 1,103-day Temple desecration, which lasted from 6 December 167 to 14 December 164. Now 1,103 days is a shorter time than the 1,150 days named in Dn 8.14 or the 1,260 named in 7.25, 9.27, and 12.7. These in turn are shorter than the 1,290 and 1,335 days of Dn 12.11–12. Since the latter are known to be after-the-fact redactions, they should have been, were their referent the Antiochan desecration, *reductions* of the 1,150/1,260 numbers, not increases.[12] It therefore looks as if the 1,290 and 1,335 days are indeed part of a future-oriented prophecy unrelated to the second-century Temple desecration backgrounding Daniel.

An alternative reading of Dn 12.11–12 reinforces the foregoing idea. Daniel's term for the spiritual movement he foresees is "the final phase" (12.9 and passim). Of it he knows only that it will be a time when "the multitude will be cleansed, purified, and refined" (12.10). "Multitude" looks back to Deutero-Isaiah's Suffering Servant poem and ahead to Mark's theology of service ("ransom of many," 10.45) and his idea of recovery offered to multitudes of ritual alcoholics ("[wine] poured out for [the recovery of] many," 14.24). Daniel 12.11 mentions "the abolition of the daily sacrifice," a reference to a desecration or destruction of the Temple, and "the desolating sacrilege," the same image Mark later uses in covertly referring to the emergent Christian minister and his ritual wine cup (Mk 13.14). Linguistically tortuous, the Danielic passage is ordinarily rendered as follows (syntax based on AB):

> (Dn 12.11) From the time the daily sacrifice is stopped and the desolating sacrilege holds sway there will be one thousand two hundred and ninety [1,290] days. (12) Blessed is the one who has patience and perseveres during the one thousand three hundred and thirty-five [1,335] days.

The 1,290 days, together with the 1,335 of verse 12, are invariably understood to prophesy the duration of the Temple desecration, that is, of the desolating sacrilege and the absence of the daily sacrifice construed as simultaneities. Without violating either the original Hebrew or the foregoing English version, however, verses 11–12 can be understood instead to prophesy certain numbers of days to occur not only after the point at which the daily sacrifices are stopped but also after a *subsequent* period of unstated duration following the stopping, namely, the period of the desolating sacrilege. In other words, the sense of these verses can be rendered as follows:

> (Dn 12.11–12) 1,290 and 1,335 are the days persons must have patience and persevere after the end of the period during which the desolating sacrilege will hold sway following the stopping of the daily sacrifices.

Here the 1,290 and 1,335 days refer not to the duration of the desolating sacrilege but to numbers of days to occur at the end of an interval of unspecified length following the cessation of the sacrifices. The order of events would be: (a) the cessation of the sacrifices at a point in time; (b) the period of the desolating sacrilege, understood as a sequel to the cessation and indeterminant as to duration; and (c) the 1,290 and 1,335 days as periods of precise length following the end of the desolating sacrilege. Nor would the writer of Revelation have interpreted "the stopping of daily sacrifices" to refer to the Antiochan desecration; rather, he would have taken it to mean the Romans' destruction of the Temple in 70 C.E., a generation before he wrote. Moreover, as an elder Markan he would have understood the desolating sacrilege as the Christian wine ritual. For that reason he would have fixed its duration as the two millennia he believed would pass before the return of Jesus' recovery program, Daniel's "final phase." The critical 1,290 and 1,335 days, in turn, he would have placed at the end of the two millennia. In short, the 1,290 and 1,335 days of Daniel 12 do not prophesy the length of the first-century Roman Temple desecration but rather a parlous three-and-a-half-year period at the end of a two-thousand-year church age.

Hence the question arises: assuming Alcoholics Anonymous to be the parousial Markôs program, one would expect the 1,290 and 1,335 days to appear somewhere in A.A.'s beginning history. Is there any evidence of this? It so happens that A.A. was founded by two persons on 10 June 1935. The Twelve Steps constituting the A.A. program, however, and the book *Alcoholics Anonymous* containing their exposition were not completed until December 1938 and February 1939, respectively, a little over three and a half years later. During that interval the fellowship had no name, no steps, no handbook, and members who vehemently disagreed about key aspects of their movement. Had the cofounders not "had patience and persevered" (Dn 12.12), Alcoholics Anonymous might never have been.[13] Now a first coincidence involving the Danielic numbers is that the Twelve Steps were written sometime during the two weeks before Christmas of 1938,[14] and 1,290 days from 10 June 1935 (A.A.'s founding date) was 21 December 1938. A second coincidence is that the first copies of the manuscript of *Alcoholics Anonymous* were printed in multilith and sent out over a period spanning the end of January and beginning of February 1939,[15] and 1,335 days from 10 June 1935 was 4 February 1939. Two such remarkable coincidences involving these enigmatic Danielic numbers are little short of uncanny.[16]

Overall, the foregoing discussion has portrayed the Book of Revelation as the prophetic legacy of a latter-day Markan alcoholic to the emergent Christian churches. Although OT wine-as-wrath metaphors would have been familiar to any first-century Jewish Christian, only an ex-addict could have produced the extravagant synecdoche of the bowl septet and other wine imagery of 14.6–18.24. Revelation portrays the churches' worsening alcoholism, their perversion of the Jesus message as the Markans understood it, and the troubles their unacknowledged illness would surely bring on themselves and the world. Yet the writer also foresaw a solution to their problem. He believed that Daniel had prophesied the parousial return of the largely vanished Markôs program and wellness for whoever embraces it at the hour of apocalypse. In the meantime, he felt certain that Christians reading his work would never dream of thinking that its chief figures of illness—dragon, beast, false prophet, Babylon, and prostitute—might apply to them. Moreover, the writer also seems to have believed, perhaps based on Mark's idea of a two-day entombment of Jesus, that the second coming of the Markôs program, followed by the mysterious but critical periods of 1,290 and 1,335 days, was divinely scheduled to occur two thousand years after its founding. By modern reckoning this would be the 2030s C.E. Should Alcoholics Anonymous ultimately be adjudged the parousial Markôs fellowship, its coming in the 1930s would thus have been one hundred years ahead of schedule. This eventuality, in turn, is interpretable as the fulfillment of Jesus' prophecy of a hastened parousia:

> (Mk 13.20) "And if the Lord had not shortened the days, no human being would be saved; but for the sake of the elect, those whom he chose, he shortened the days."

AFTERWORD

We must be prepared to find that the historical knowledge
of the personality and life of Jesus will not be a help,
but perhaps even an offense to religion.

—Albert Schweitzer, *The Quest of the Historical Jesus*

Operating from a reader-response stance within the perspective of recovery criticism, this book has discerned in the Markan memory of Jesus a primal scene of addiction and recovery. It has portrayed the insider audience of the Gospel of Mark as a fellowship of ex-inebriate water drinkers whose spiritual praxis resembled that of today's Twelve-Step movement. It has identified in the gospel various genre features of the former drunkard's story of illness and healing and has essayed a first-person reconstruction of Jesus' own sobriety story. In short, it has limned an entirely new image of the Markan Jesus. It has also proposed novel understandings of Mark's theology of suffering and service and of the clandestine secrecy emblems in the Markan text. In addition, it has traced a line of intertextuality linking material from Genesis, Psalms, Joel, Deutero-Isaiah, and Daniel, together with the figure of Elijah, to the core message of Mark, as well as to Proto-John and Revelation. Finally, interpreting prophecies in Daniel and Revelation, it has suggested an apocalyptic connection between the first-century Markan community and the fellowship of Alcoholics Anonymous today.

New Testament scholars will want to examine in greater depth the translational and text-linguistic ambiguities (lexis, syntax, reference, speech act, topic, figure, symbol, etc.) this book has brought to light. From a grammarian's point of view, scripturalists seem to have underestimated the problem of disambiguating the Greek text of Mark's gospel, whether that of particular manuscripts or composite versions. As demonstrated repeatedly herein, "literal translation" is often the privileging of one preconceived meaning over alternative and equally "literal" possibilities. In fact, every translation is governed by an established perspective of some sort. Such preconceptions straiten reading by blinding the translator to ambiguities in the source language and to grammatical and lexical mismatches between the source and the target languages. For example, the translation "Jesus appointed twelve [appointees]" (Mk 3.14) is neither more or less literal nor more or less correct than "Jesus formulated twelve [formulations]." The latter has simply not been seen as a possibility, except perhaps by the ancient redactors who blocked it by introducing the clause "whom he also named apostles" into certain manuscripts. Everything depends on the meaning a reader brings to the text. To be sure, individual ambiguities may be accidents unforeseen by the original writer, but when a series of ambiguities consistently reflects the same set of thematic opposites (as in Mark), one has grounds for arguing their intentionality and for positing a two-audience theory supporting the validity of alternative translations of the text. The present study has proposed two such translations, sobriety Mark and traditional Mark. Finally, the fact that received translations repeatedly favor one pole of a thematic opposition while ignoring the other is no guarantee of their correctness. Early on, for example, the Galilean Markans, hearing that outlanders were saying that Jesus had entered Jerusalem "on a donkey," whereas they knew firsthand that he had entered "wine drunk," would have thought the outsiders guilty of historicizing a ridiculous misinterpretation.

Looking back at the perennial questions about Markan rhetoric enumerated in chapter 1, readers should see that all of them are addressed, more or less comprehensively, by the interpretation advanced here. It accounts for the nicknames *Marcus* and *stump-fingered* and for Jesus' Q reputation as a drunkard. In identifying sobriety as the reward of all who recognize ritual wine as a "desolating sacrilege" and flee from hierarchical religion, it explains the peculiar form of apocalyptic present in Mark. It posits alcohol addiction as the life situation that impelled Jesus to seek help from John the Baptist. It explains the culturally anomalous phrase "this is my blood" as conveying Jesus' recognition of wine as the cause of his troubles and harmonizes that apocalyptic utterance with Jesus' prior and equally apocalyptic admonition about the desolating sacrilege. It construes the unique Markan ordering of the service of the paschal cup as signifying an offer of choice—drinking or not drinking, sobriety or further wine. It makes apparent the purport of Jesus' own renunciation of religious wine, thus sparing exegetes further embarrassing efforts to explain it as small talk or asceticism. It reveals Jesus' Gethsemane prayer as self-immolative and forever obviates the need to cast Jesus at this critical juncture in the diminished role of wavering superhero who, in the nick of time, asserts his courage and nobly carries on. And it unlocks the mystery surrounding "the Twelve" by identifying the term's possible referents not just as twelve disciples but also as twelve semisecret principles of sobriety.

As for Mark's clandestine symbols and cryptic narratives, the present interpretation points to baptismal water as a drink replacing wine, the cup of water as a Markan entrance rite, the Passover water carrier as identifying the Last Supper as a Markôs meeting, demon possession as Markan code for addiction, multiplied bread as the words of recovering people, Elijah as water drinker and sobriety exemplar, the donkey/fig tree/Temple episode as a camouflage of Jesus' wine-drunk Jerusalem rampage, wine vessels and ritual drinking as the object of his assault on the Temple, the apocalyptic discourse as a hangover revelation, the Gethsemane cup as alcoholism, the young man in white as deacon cum message bearer and cupmaster, and the cry from the cross as Jesus' emphatic refusal of the offer of wine. This interpretation also identifies pointed allegorical contrasts: female servant figures as surrendered Markôs people versus authoritarian males as unsurrendered clerical hierarchs; Barabbas as agonistic fanatic who brings violent physical death on himself versus Barnasha as anonymous recovering person who lives in peace freed from the bondage of self; Jerusalem as locus of theocracy versus Galilee as place of egalitarian sobriety; *psuchē thanatos* vs. crucifixion as the way to atonement; Messiah as a figure justifying clerical domination versus messianic witness as the service given by recovering people; the rock entombment as the encrypting of Jesus' sobriety story, and the empty tomb as a prophecy of its bimillennial manumission.

Of the other questions asked at the outset, Mark's break with Paul is explainable as a consequence of disputes over the memory of Jesus' wine addiction and of Paul's insistence on publishing theologies of messiahship, crucifixion, and substitutionary atonement contrary to Markan thinking. Familiar genre features such as triadic sequences, intercalated stage-one/stage-two progressions, unique apocalyptic, and the narrative development of Jesus' persona from euphoric to fanatic to pacific all point to Mark as a displacement of Jesus' original recovery story. The two-audience hypothesis and the profound crisis of the Roman War explain the evangelist's overarching concern for secrecy and studied ambiguity. And the disparities between Mark and the same material in the later gospels result from efforts within non-Markan communities to countervail or tone down scandalous alcoholism content in Mark. Overall, it is difficult to think of a single Markan enigma that is not solved by the interpretation presented here.

Some readers, however, may continue to wonder how the truth could have remained concealed. If Jesus was an addict, or even if only Mark and his cohorts were, would we not have known of it before? Almost certainly not. Compromised from within by ascetic abstainers, denied and censored from without by revisionist Jewish-Christian religionists, and wholly unknown to gentile Christians, the story of the Markôs fellowship and its memory of Jesus' wine addiction had no chance of survival much beyond the 70s C.E. Others will ask how people are ever to accept the idea that Jesus was alcoholic. Apparently the answer is, one grows accustomed to it, much as one grows accustomed to the idea that a spouse, parent, co-worker, friend, or minister is alcoholic. Besides, the importance of the idea as a historical datum is slight compared to its emancipatory value as an entirely new way of comprehending the witness of Jesus.

For the real "offense to religion," as Albert Schweitzer put it, is not so much the fact of Jesus' addiction as the idea of his humbled and anonymous return to Galilee. The figure of an uncrucified recovering son of man is not a likely basis for the institution of a hierarchical religion. Nor is the spirituality of this figure attractive to persons inclined toward such institutions. Our addictions to *psuchē* preservation and the morbid presumption of wellness are too powerful. Schweitzer alluded to the former in writing, "When Paul . . . did not desire to know Christ after the flesh, that was the first expression of the impulse of self-preservation by which Christianity continued to be guided for centuries."[1] And Jesus evidently had the latter in mind in his implication of illness as desideratum: "People who are well do not need a healer, but those who are ill" (Mk 2.17). Ordinarily, recognition of the need of healing is feared and resisted right up to the metanoetic moment, a fact nicely illustrated by one alcoholic's story of illness revealed: "The man said to me, 'I'm an alcoholic, I'm in Alcoholics Anonymous. Would you like to go to an A.A. meeting?' I got angry. I could have hit him. Indignation rose up in me and I mixed it with my fear and contempt and it welled up in my throat and I said . . . 'Yes.'" Such an apocalypse can ultimately lead to the same *psuchē* death and spiritual awakening Jesus experienced, yet it cannot be domesticated in religion.

What religions *can* provide, beyond the familiar comforts, is the opportunity for ritual drinking, which quickens the latent alcoholism of members and thereby hastens their recognition of illness. This is a topic likely to have proven as surprising as any in this book. In every way, Christians and Jews, even those knowledgeable about addiction, are disposed to think of religious drinking as entirely different from all other kinds of drinking, and certainly from alcoholic drinking. Just speaking of them in the same breath seems absurd and irreverent. Yet the theory here is that the genius of Jesus was to see them as one. According to Jesus' paschal insight, the ultimate purpose of ritual wine is to enable *many* persons (*huper pollōn,* Mk 14.24)—in effect, everyone—to satisfy the drinking requirement necessary for recognition of illness and entrance into the rule of God. This is a new way of construing an old idea, that of the messianic joy that religious drinking, both Jewish and Christian, is said to anticipate. Far from denigrating ritual wine, the present book completely accords with the ancient Christian belief that the most sacred and most mysterious part of the eucharistic liturgy centers on the cup of Jesus and its salvific contents.

Finally there is the question of whether the program of Alcoholics Anonymous represents the fulfillment of prophecies in Daniel, Mark, and the Book of Revelation. Simply asked, is A.A. the Messiah/Christ come again, not as a solitary personage, but as a spiritual fellowship of sober men and women detached from an addicted world and increasingly at one with God? Many commentators, while avoiding religious concepts like "Parousia" or the "Second Coming," seem to think so. Over twenty years ago, for example, the polymath Gregory Bateson argued that by virtue of discarding the first tenet of popular epistemology, the premise of a transcendent and autonomous "self," A.A. theology makes a signal contribution to the wider world in the way of conflict avoidance at every level of human interaction.[2] Similarly, the religion writer Frederick Buechner has recently said of Alcoholics Anonymous and other Twelve-Step groups, "I believe that the church has an enormous amount to learn from them. I also believe that what goes on in them is far closer to what Christ meant his church to be, and what it originally was, than much of what goes on in most churches I know."[3]

Despite the fact that A.A. is clearly the "catacombs church" of the later twentieth century, recovering alcoholics will turn a deaf ear toward proposals to extend the mission of Alcoholics Anonymous beyond its "one primary purpose—to carry its message to the alcoholic who still suffers" (A.A. Tradition Five). Hence the important issue is not history's verdict about A.A. but its judgment of the image of Jesus as an alcoholic, a sufferer who witnesses to recovery even as he ministers drink to the many. And here the crucial question is not who this image may offend but who it brings to crisis, who it convicts of powerlessness—whether drunkards, abstainers, or pious drinkers of communion or kiddush—and who it helps to live sober and joyfully in a world where multiform addiction and the violence it begets rage pandemically and where life itself grows ever more tenuous.

NOTES

Chapter 1: Interpretive Perspective

1. Howard Clark Kee, *Community of the New Age: Studies in Mark's Gospel* (Philadelphia: Westminster, 1977).

2. Vernon K. Robbins, *Jesus the Teacher: A Socio-Rhetorical Interpretation of Mark* (Philadelphia: Fortress, 1984).

3. Burton L. Mack, *A Myth of Innocence: Mark and Christian Origins* (Philadelphia: Fortress, 1988).

4. Mary Ann Tolbert, *Sowing the Gospel: Mark's World in Literary-Historical Perspective* (Minneapolis: Fortress, 1989).

5. John Bowman, *The Gospel of Mark: The New Christian Jewish Passover Haggadah* (Leiden, the Netherlands: E.J. Brill, 1965).

6. J. Duncan M. Derrett, *The Making of Mark: The Scriptural Bases of the Earliest Gospel* (Shipston-on-Stour, Britain: Drinkwater, 1985).

7. Wolfgang Roth, *Hebrew Gospel: Cracking the Code of Mark* (Oak Park, Ill.: Meyer-Stone, 1988).

8. John Dominic Crossan, *The Historical Jesus: The Life of a Mediterranean Jewish Peasant* (San Francisco: Harper, 1991).

9. John P. Meier, *A Marginal Jew: Rethinking the Historical Jesus*, vol. 1, *The Roots of the Problem and the Person* (New York: Doubleday, 1991).

10. Ronald D. Cameron, ed., *The Apochryphal Jesus and Christian Origins*, *Semeia* 49 (1990). See also E. P. Sanders, *The Historical Figure of Jesus* (New York: Penguin USA, 1994).

11. Frank Kermode, *The Genesis of Secrecy: On the Interpretation of Narrative* (Cambridge, Mass.: Harvard University Press, 1979), 138.

12. Histories of Markan interpretation (e.g., Seán P. Kealy, *Mark's Gospel: A History of Its Interpretation* [New York: Paulist, 1982]) and scholarly commentaries on Mark (e.g., C. S. Mann, *The Anchor Bible Mark* [Garden City, N.Y.: Doubleday, 1986]; W. L. Lane, *Commentary on the Gospel of Mark* [Grand Rapids, Mich.: Eerdmans, 1974]; Robert H. Gundry, *Mark: A Commentary on*

His Apology for the Cross [Grand Rapids. Mich.: Eerdmans, 1993]; and Vincent Taylor, *The Gospel according to St. Mark* [London: Macmillan, 1952]) contain nothing that would suggest the theory advanced here.

13. Historian Ernest Kurtz (*Not-God: A History of Alcoholics Anonymous* [Center City, Minn.: Hazelden Educational Services, 1979], chap. 2) describes the contributions of the Oxford Groups to the spirituality of recovery as it developed in Alcoholics Anonymous and provides bibliographical material on the Oxford Group movement.

14. Sir Edward Barry, *Observations Historical, Critical and Medical on the Wines of the Ancients, Etc.* (London: T. Cadell, 1775); Jane Harrison, *Prolegomena to the Study of Greek Religion*, 3d ed. (Cambridge: Cambridge University, 1922), chap. 8. Temperance writers regularly combed the ancients' works for alcohol references; see, for example, Daniel Dorchester, *The Liquor Problem in All Ages* (New York: Phillips and Hunt, 1887), and Richard Eddy, *Alcohol in History: An Account of Intemperance in All Ages* (New York: The National Temperance Society and Publication House, 1887).

15. R. J. Forbes, *Studies in Ancient Technology, Volume III*, 2d ed. (Leiden, the Netherlands: E.J. Brill, 1965), 80.

16. See the rabbinic material listed by Gustaf Dalman, *Jesus-Jeshua, Studies in the Gospels*, trans. Paul Levertoff (New York: Macmillan, 1929), 149–50. A popular thesis among nineteenth-century temperance advocates was that much or even most of the ancients' wine was nonalcoholic; see, for example, William Patton, *Bible Wines: On the Laws of Fermentation and Wines of the Ancients* (New York: The National Temperance Society and Publication House, 1878). Despite the methods available for preventing the fermentation of juices (Patton names filtering, boiling, subsidence, and fumigation), one assumes that the preponderance of people, then as now, preferred alcoholic to nonalcoholic wines.

17. William Richard Stegner ("The Ancient Jewish Synagogue Homily," in David E. Aune, ed., *Greco-Roman Literature and the New Testament: Selected Forms and Genres,* [Atlanta: Scholars Press, 1988], 51–61) interprets an ancient and highly entertaining homily on Noah's drunkenness and nakedness found in the Tanchuma, a collection of early sermons, as "surely . . . a warning against drunkenness" (59).

18. Eddy (*Alcohol in History,* 114) cites Tacitus, *Histories,* B, iii sect. 83.

19. Gaius Suetonius Tranquillus, *The Twelve Caesars,* trans. Robert Graves (London: Allen Lane, 1979), 264. Confirming Suetonius, Philostratus (*Philostratus and Eunapius: The Lives of the Sophists,* trans. Wilmer Cave Wright [London: William Heinemann, 1922], 85) writes that Scopelion was sent by the people of all Asia on an embassy to the emperor for the reason that "the Emperor resolved that there should be no vines in Asia, because it appeared that the people when under the influence of wine plotted revolution."

20. Erwin R. Goodenough, *Fish, Bread, and Wine,* vol. 5 of *Jewish Symbols in the Greco-Roman Period* (New York: Pantheon for the Bollinger Foundation, 1956), 102. Wine symbols on synagogue arches and door lintels, ossuaries, coins, tombs, and lamps included wine-pressing scenes, grape bunches, jars

and cups, grape leaves, and vines growing from cups, the last having eschatological significance. Among Jews, every festival, sabbath, marriage, fellowship meal, and Passover was blessed by wine. About the Jewish archeologi-
cal evidence Goodenough concludes: "One simple hypothesis, and only one,
is at hand to explain all this material, namely, that a wine-drinking ritual was
at that time [from the early Maccabees to the fall of Jerusalem in 70 C.E.] of
great importance in a mystic hope for the experience of God and for im-
mortality" (111).

21. Seán Freyne, *Galilee from Alexander the Great to Hadrian 325 B.C.E. to 135
C.E.: A Study of Second Temple Judaism* (Wilmington, Del.: Michael Glazier,
1980), 172.

22. Ruth Amiran, *Ancient Pottery of the Holy Land* (New Brunswick, N.J.:
Rutgers University Press, 1970).

23. Emil Schürer, *The History of the Jewish People in the Age of Jesus Christ (175
B.C.–A.D. 135)*, vol. 2, rev. and ed. G. Vermes, F. Miller, and M. Black (Edinburgh: T.&T. Clark, 1979), 61.

24. Freyne, *Galilee*, 171.

25. Harm Jan de Blij, *Wine: A Geographic Appreciation* (Totowa, N.J.: Row-
man & Allanheld, 1983), 44. See also D. Stanislawski, "Dionysus Westward:
Early Religions and the Economic Geography of Wine," *Geographical Review*
65 (1975): 427–44.

26. Josephus, *The Jewish War, Books I–III*, trans. H. St. J. Thackeray (London: William Heinemann, 1927), 721, 723.

27. See Richard A. Horsley with John S. Hanson, *Bandits, Prophets, and
Messiahs: Popular Movements in the Time of Jesus* (San Francisco, Harper & Row,
1985), and other related works by Horsley.

28. C. H. Dodd, *The Parables of the Kingdom* (New York: Scribner's, 1961),
97.

29. Crossan, *Historical Jesus*, 7, 10–11.

30. Ibid., 264.

31. Ibid., 334.

32. Schürer, *History of the Jewish People*, 445.

33. Josephus, *Jewish War*, III.30.

34. Bruce J. Malina, "Testing the Models: The Case of Fasting," chap. 9
of *Christian Origins and Cultural Anthropology: Practical Models for Biblical Interpretation* (Atlanta: John Knox, 1986).

35. Louise M. Rosenblatt, "Towards a Transactional Theory of Reading,"
Journal of Reading Behavior 1 (1969): 31–47; Steven Mailloux, "Learning to
Read: Interpretation and Reader-Response Criticism," *Studies in the Literary
Imagination* 12 (1979): 93–108; Susan R. Suleiman, "Introduction: Varieties
of Audience-Oriented Criticism," in Susan R. Suleiman and Inge Crosman,
eds., *The Reader in the Text: Essays on Audience and Interpetation* (Princeton, N.J.:
Princeton University Press, 1980), 3–45; and Jane P. Tompkins, "An Intro-
duction to Reader-Response Criticism," in Jane P. Tompkins, ed., *Reader-Response Criticism: From Formalism to Post-Structuralism* (Baltimore, Md.: Johns
Hopkins University Press, 1980), ix–xxvi.

36. Edgar V. McKnight, *Post-Modern Use of the Bible: The Emergence of Reader-Oriented Criticism* (Nashville: Abingdon, 1988).

37. Schuyler Brown, "Reader Response: Demythologizing the Text," *New Testament Studies* 34 (1988): 232–37. See volumes 47 and 48 of *Semeia* on reader criticism and deconstructionist work such as Stephen D. Moore's *Mark and Luke in Poststructuralist Perspective* (New Haven, Conn.: Yale University Press, 1992) and Jacques Derrida's *Glas* (Lincoln: University of Nebraska Press, 1986).

38. Stanley E. Fish, "Interpreting the Variorum," in Jane P. Tompkins, ed., *Reader-Response Criticism*, 182.

39. Kermode, *Genesis of Secrecy*, 145.

40. For example, Nan Robertson, *Getting Better: Inside Alcoholics Anonymous* (New York: William Morrow, 1988), and David R. Rudy, *Becoming Alcoholic: Alcoholics Anonymous and the Reality of Alcoholism* (Carbondale: Southern Illinois University Press, 1986). Alcoholics Anonymous and other Twelve-Step programs have been the subjects of numerous studies in medicine, addiction sciences, counseling, psychotherapy, psychology, sociology, and various other fields.

41. Author or authors unnamed, 3d ed. (New York: Alcoholics Anonymous World Services, 1976).

42. Dan O. Via, Jr., *The Ethics of Mark's Gospel—In the Middle of Time* (Philadelphia: Fortress, 1985), 212.

43. David D. Gilmore, "Anthropology of the Mediterranean Area," *Annual Review of Anthropology* 11 (1982): 175–205.

44. Seán P. Kealy (*Mark's Gospel*, 51) finds the Hebrew *mar kôs* etymology reported by the seventeenth-century exegete Cornelius à Lapide, without, of course, the interpretation proposed here.

45. Translated by Taylor, *The Gospel according to St. Mark*, 30.

46. Olaf Linton, "The Parable of the Children's Game," *New Testament Studies* 22 (1975–76): 159–79; quotation on 175.

47. Crossan, *Historical Jesus*, 262.

48. Rudolf Bultmann, *The History of the Synoptic Tradition*, 2d ed., trans. John Marsh (New York: Harper & Row, 1968), 155.

49. Norman Perrin, *Rediscovering the Teaching of Jesus* (New York: Harper & Row, 1976), 120. Perrin does not speculate about the "controversy" with which the epithet might have been associated.

50. Joachim Jeremias, *The Parables of Jesus*, 2d rev. ed., trans. S. H. Hooke (New York: Scribner's, 1972), 160. Jeremias is quoting from Dt 21.20. Since apparently he cannot bring himself to think there might have been grounds for calling Jesus a drunkard, Jeremias naturally—but not necessarily correctly—assumes that the part of Dt 21.20 applied to Jesus must have been the phrase he quotes, "refractory and rebellious."

51. Joseph A. Fitzmyer, *The Anchor Bible Gospel according to Luke I–IX*, 2d ed. (Garden City, N.Y.: Doubleday, 1983), 681.

52. Discussing the possibility for "interpretive reversals" of the original Scriptures by the Oral Torah (rabbinic commentary and interpretation),

Susan Handelman ("Jacques Derrida and the Heretic Hermeneutic," in Mark Krupnick, ed., *Displacement: Derrida and After* [Bloomington: Indiana University Press, 1983], 100–101) cites a rabbinic interpretation of Dt 21.18–21 (*Sanhedrin* 71a) so limited as to make it virtually impossible to apply the punishment of stoning. "There never has been a stubborn and rebellious son," wrote the rabbis, "and never will be." Such a view may stem from the rabbis' tacit understanding that the passage refers not to self-indulgence or disobedience per se but to the illness today's world calls alcoholism.

53. Edward Schillebeeckx, *Jesus: An Experiment in Christology,* trans. Hubert Hoskins (New York: Vintage, 1981), 102. Schillebeeckx believes that the Q materials passed from an original Aramaic phase through a Greek-speaking Jewish Christian phase, into a final editorial phase, possibly gentile Christian.

54. The framework itself presumably resulted from attempts later in Q to tone down what alcoholics would call John's "dry-drunk" fanaticism (e.g., "He shall drink no wine or beer, but even from his birth be filled with a holy spirit," Lk 1.15) and to deny Jesus' reputation as a "wet drunk" (Dt 21.20, as interpreted here) by presenting these scandalous rumors as if they indicated merely that the two men represented contrastive human types: John, the stern ascetic, and Jesus, the happy bon vivant.

55. For an illustration of the Freudian concept of "primal scene" applied to literary criticism, see Ned Lukacher, *Primal Scenes: Literature, Philosophy, Psychoanalysis* (Ithaca, N.Y.: Cornell University Press, 1986).

56. Among scholars who accept the existence of Q and the priority of Mark, B. H. Streeter (*The Four Gospels: A Study of Origins* [London: Macmillan, 1924]) was the first to conclude that Mark knew the Q materials and used some but not others. Burton L. Mack's recent conclusions about the age and widespread currency of the Sayings Gospel Q (*The Lost Gospel: The Book of Q and Christian Origins* [San Francisco: Harper, 1993]) further support the probability that Mark knew Q.

57. Gerald G. May (*Addiction and Grace* [San Francisco: Harper & Row, 1988], 11–13, 109–12) also interprets the Eden story as a source-allegory of addiction.

58. E. A. Speiser, *The Anchor Bible Genesis,* 3d ed. (Garden City, N.Y.: Doubleday, 1985), 26–27.

59. Claus Westermann, *Genesis 1–11: A Commentary,* trans. J. L. Scullion [Minneapolis: Augsburg, 1984), 241.

60. Robert P. Scharlemann ("The Being of God When God Is Not Being God: Deconstructing the History of Theism," in Thomas J. J. Altizer, et al., *Deconstruction and Theology* [New York: Crossroad, 1982], 107) describes what is intended here by the term "Living God" when he refers to "deity existing not as a transtemporal or metaphysical entity but as an actuality in life and history." Adam's statement in the Apocalypse of Adam, a Sethian gnostic document from Nag Hammadi, about the "word of knowledge of the eternal God" taught him by Eve exactly captures the alcoholic hubris of archetypal man: "for we were higher than the God who had created us and the powers with him . . ." (64.12–13, 16–18, trans. G. W. MacRae, in James M.

Robinson, general editor, *The Nag Hammadi Library* [San Francisco: Harper and Row, 1981], 257).

61. The Yahwist's original Genesis story, written early in the tenth century, is believed to have been heavily redacted during the next several hundred years. The version here ignores the familiar division of God's address in verses 15–19, first to the woman and then to the man, on grounds that it appears to be the work of sexist editors during this period.

62. Speiser, *Genesis*, 24.

63. The position here is that God's words about pain and desire were originally addressed to man and woman alike. The root for "pain" occurs twice in verse 16, both times linked with childbearing. The repetition of the pairing is a sign of tampering with the text by sexist redactors seeking to assign the verse only to woman. As to the first pair, commentators (Speiser, *Genesis*, 24, and Westermann, *Genesis 1–11*, 261) consider it an example of hendiadys (two connotative words expressing one substantive concept) meaning, "your pain resulting from childbearing." Rather than being hendiadys, however, the pairing may be a kind of simile comparing the pain under discussion to travail pain. The same may be true of the traditional gloss at the end of the verse, which compares the "desire" or "lust" mentioned there to the woman's sexual urge for her husband. The view here is that the Yahwist's original "pain" and "desire" were not of parturition and concupiscence but rather of obsessive mental drunkenness as discussed herein and common to both genders. This view comports with the conjecture by Harold Bloom (*The Book of J* [New York: Grove Weidenfeld, 1990]) that the author of the J passages was a woman, for the redactions posited here represent the sort of ploy one might expect from male editors seeking to establish male dominance within a text written by a female. It is also worth noting that Ps 16.4, which according to Mitchell Dahood (*The Anchor Bible Psalms I* [Garden City, N.Y.: Doubleday, 1965], 88) consists of the same Hebrew as Gn 3.16, refers in its context to both male and female deities, probably Baal and Astarte. This suggests that the author of this very ancient psalm, whose work likely predated the Genesis redaction, knew the traditional Eden story in a nonsexist form and so handed it on. (Chap. 5 discusses Psalm 16 at length.)

64. Gerhard von Rad, *Genesis: A Commentary*, rev. ed. (Philadelphia: Westminster, 1972), 136. Alcoholics ultimately distinguish three stages in their understanding of drink: friend, enemy, and finally and ironically, friend indeed, the agent of suffering that brought them to the joy of recovery. Thus, from an eschatological perspective, von Rad's observation is quite correct.

65. The version here ignores the much-discussed confusion of Ham and Canaan in the received text (for example, Westermann, *Genesis 1–11*, 490–91) and speaks simply of Canaan as Noah's youngest son.

66. Westermann (*Genesis 1–11*, 481–94) refers to an "outrage" on Ham/Canaan's part, which he (p. 488) identifies as the son's failure to cover the father. Others have seen Ham/Canaan's error as uncovering the father, as telling the brothers what he saw, or as an unnatural sex act he performed. All this is conjecture. Jacques Derrida ("Of an Apocalyptic Tone Recently

Adopted in Philosophy," *Semeia* 23 [1982]: 63–97) refers to the son's unveiling of the father's nakedness, despite the text's clear representation of the unveiling as Noah's own act. In any case, alcoholics will see that Noah's curse represents instead a drunkard's projective enactment of his guilt and self-contempt by angrily lashing out at those around him.

67. Elisabeth Schüssler Fiorenza, *Bread Not Stone: The Challenge of Feminist Biblical Interpretation* (Boston: Beacon, 1984), xxii.

Chapter 2: The Markan Passion

1. David L. Miller, *Christs: Meditations on Archetypal Images in Christian Theology* (New York: Seabury, 1981).

2. Joachim Jeremias, *The Eucharistic Words of Jesus*, trans. Norman Perrin (Philadelphia: Fortress, 1977).

3. Werner Kelber, ed., *The Passion in Mark: Studies on Mark 14–16* (Philadelphia: Fortress, 1976).

4. John Dominic Crossan, *The Cross That Spoke: The Origins of the Passion Narrative* (San Francisco: Harper & Row, 1988).

5. Kee, *Community*, 170.

6. Mann, *Mark*, 564–65.

7. Raymond Brown (*The Anchor Bible Gospel according to John I–XII* [Garden City, N.Y.: Doubleday, 1966], 262) cites H. L. Strack and P. Billerbeck (*Kommentar zum Neuen Testament aus Talmud und Midrasch*, 5 vols. [Munich: Beck, 1922–55], 2:483) in pointing out that "in rabbinic thought bread was a symbol of the Torah." See also Gillian Feeley-Harnik, "Food Symbolism in Judaic Tradition," chap. 4 of *The Lord's Table: Eucharist and Passover in Early Christianity* (Philadelphia: University of Pennsylvania Press, 1981). On the feeding stories as metaphor, see Jouette M. Bassler, "The Parable of the Loaves," *The Journal of Religion* 16, no. 2 (April 1986): 157–72.

8. The practice of today's Twelve-Step groups in this regard would seem to resemble that of the many second-century Christian groups ultimately anathematized under the rubric of gnosticism; see E. Pagels, "'One God, One Bishop': The Politics of Monotheism," chap. 2 of *The Gnostic Gospels* (New York: Random House, 1979), especially pp. 41–42, relating Irenaeus's account of the practices of a Valentinian group in Lyons whose leader, interestingly enough, was named Marcus.

9. Albert Schweitzer, *The Problem of the Lord's Supper*, trans. A. J. Mattill, Jr., (Macon, Ga.: Mercer University Press, 1982 [1901]).

10. Ibid., 120–21.

11. Eusebius Pamphili, *Ecclesiastical History, Books 1–5*, trans. Roy J. Deferrari (New York: Fathers of the Church, 1953), 206.

12. Susan C. Jarratt, *Rereading the Sophists: Classical Rhetoric Refigured* (Carbondale: Southern Illinois University Press, 1991).

13. Joseph Grimes, "Signals of Discourse Structure in Koine," in George MacRae, ed., *Society of Biblical Literature 1975 Seminar Papers*, vol. 1 (Missoula, Mont.: Scholars Press, 1975), 151–64.

14. František Daneš, ed., *Papers on Functional Sentence Perspective* (The Hague: Mouton, 1974).

15. See Joseph Klausner, *Jesus of Nazareth: His Life, Times, and Teaching*, trans. Herbert Danby (New York: Macmillan, 1925), 329, and C. G. Montefiore, *The Synoptic Gospels*, vol. 1, 2d ed. (New York: KTAV, 1968), 332.

16. Jeremias, *Eucharistic Words*, 209.

17. Schillebeeckx, *Jesus*, 308–9.

18. On the pros and cons of 14.25 as an avowal of abstinence, see Jeremias, *Eucharistic Words*, 207–18; J. A. Ziesler, "The Vow of Abstinence: A Note on Mark 14.25 and Parallels," *Colloquium* 5, no. 1 (1972): 12–14; D. Palmer, "Defining a Vow of Abstinence," *Colloquium* 5, no. 2 (1973): 38–41; and Joseph A. Fitzmyer, *The Anchor Bible Gospel according to Luke X–XXIV* (Garden City, N.Y.: Doubleday, 1985), 1398. In the end, regardless of the religious intentions scholars ascribe to Jesus at the Last Supper, the plain sense of his words is clear: nothing in Mk 14.24 indicates that Jesus drank from the cup, and 14.25 conveys his decision to drink wine no more.

19. Robert G. Bratcher and Eugene A. Nida, *A Translator's Handbook on the Gospel of Mark* (Leiden, the Netherlands: E.J. Brill, 1961), 441. Further translations supplying *oinos* cited by Bratcher and Nida are those of Weymouth, Goodspeed, and LaGrange.

20. See, for example, Mann, *Mark*, 569 and 580. *Anchor Bible Matthew* also reads "new wine," as does the Jerusalem Bible in both Matthew and Mark. "New" is absent from Luke, who does not recognize the metaphorical import of "new wine" (see chap. 5).

21. Jeremias, *Eucharistic Words*, 183.

22. Mitchell Dahood *(Psalms I,* 86 and 89) is the discoverer of this important but heretofore unrecognized reference to "smooth wine" in the ancient Hebrew of Psalm 16. As emended and discussed in chapter 5, Dahood's translation of Ps 16.4b–5 reads as follows:

(Ps 16.4b) I surely will not [anymore] pour libations to them [the false gods of the psalmist's Canaanite wine liturgy] from my hands, nor will I [again] raise their names to my lips [drink wine in their service].

(5) O Yahweh, you have portioned out my cup of smooth wine, you yourself have made falling low [coming to crisis, "hitting bottom"] my lot.

23. Except where emended here, the text and discussion of Psalm 116 are based on Mitchell Dahood's translation and commentary in *The Anchor Bible Psalms III* (Garden City, N.Y.: Doubleday, 1970), 144–51.

24. Discussing the root *'mn* in the sense mentioned here, Joachim Jeremias (*New Testament Theology,* trans. John Bowden [New York: Scribner's, 1971], 162) cites Ps 116.10 as an Old Testament passage that has influenced New Testament thinking.

25. C. H. Turner, "Markan Usage: Notes, Critical and Exegetical, on the Second Gospel, VIII," *Journal of Theological Studies* 28 (1926–27): 349–62.

26. H. K. Moulton, *The Analytical Greek Lexicon Revised* (Grand Rapids, Mich.: Zondervan, 1980), 308. H. G. Liddell and R. Scott (*A Greek-English Lexicon* [Oxford: Clarendon, 1925] 2:1337) give "to pass," said of time. W.

Bauer, W. F. Arndt, and F. W. Gingrich (*A Greek-English Lexicon of the New Testament*, 2d ed. [Chicago: University of Chicago Press, 1979], 625–26) give "go by, pass by," said literally of time (sense β). They also give sense γ, "to pass without touching, said of suffering or misfortune," citing Mk 14.35 and Mt 26.39 and 42. The latter is an obvious case of treating a meaning as belonging to a word in the original language solely because it has been so understood in the language of translation.

27. Gethsemane has always proved difficult to interpret. For an illustration of the scholarly wrestling it provokes, see R. S. Barbour, "Gethsemane in the Tradition of the Passion," *New Testament Studies* 16 (1969–70): 231–51. Suffice it to say that many of the questions raised by Barbour disappear in an alcoholism reading of the pericope.

28. K. G. Kuhn, "Jesus in Gethsemane," *Evangelische Theologie* 12 (1952–53): 260–85.

29. Kelber, *The Passion*, 43.

30. *Alcoholics Anonymous*, 3d ed. (New York: Alcoholics Anonymous World Services, 1976), 45.

31. Ibid., 59. Mk 9.22–24 illustrates the intimate connection between admitting powerlessness as a faith action and receipt of empowerment. The father of the epileptic boy says to Jesus, "If you can, have pity and help us." Jesus replies, "'If you can!' All power to him who believes!" Immediately the father cries out, "I believe, help my unbelief!" His admission of no faith is in reality a faith action exactly tantamount to admitting powerlessness. Also, the question arises as to whether the A.A. pioneers were at all aware of a connection between their admissions of powerlessness and Jesus' actions in Gethsemane. An anecdote in one of the original personal stories in *Alcoholics Anonymous*, "He Thought He Could Drink Like a Gentleman," suggests that at least some of them were. The writer tells of the 1938 twelfth-step visit of cofounder Bill Wilson in the writer's Cleveland home: "I did challenge Bill to tell me something about A.A. . . . . I wanted to know what this was that worked so many wonders, and hanging over the mantel was a picture of Gethsemane and Bill pointed to it and said, 'There it is,' which didn't make much sense to me" (216–17).

32. C. E. B. Cranfield, "The Cup Metaphor in Mark xiv.36 and Parallels," *The Expository Times* 59 (1947–48): 137–38.

33. Although contemporary scholarship (see Mann, *Mark*, 588, and Fitzmyer, *Luke X–XXIV*, 1436–37) interprets "Gethsemane" as a form of the Hebrew *gat-šĕmānî*, meaning "oil press," Dalman (*Jesus-Jeshua*, 29) believed the name could have signified "winepress." Dalman later suggested "press of signs," claiming to discern in the name the Greek *sēmeion*, "sign," (*Sacred Sites and Ways: Studies in the Topography of the Gospels*, trans. Paul Levertoff [London: SPCK, 1935], 340). Combining the two possibilities as "winepress of signs," or "sign of the winepress," raises the striking possibility that the name "Gethsemane," otherwise unattested, may have been coined by the Markan fellowship as an in-group reminder of the role of wine in the Passion story.

34. Chapter 4 presents the argument for locating Mark's writing within the time frame mentioned here.

35. Crossan, *The Cross That Spoke.*

36. Dahood, *Psalms III,* 114.

37. Geza Vermes, *Jesus the Jew: A Historian's Reading of the Gospels* (Philadelphia: Fortress, 1981), 160–86.

38. Matthew Black, *An Aramaic Approach to the Gospels and Acts; with an Appendix on the Son of Man, by Geza Vermes,* 3d ed. (Oxford: Clarendon, 1967), 329.

39. P. Maurice Casey, "General, Generic, and Indefinite: The Use of the Term 'Son of Man' in Aramaic Sources and in the Teachings of Jesus," *Journal for the Study of the New Testament* 29 (1987): 21–56.

40. Stevan L. Davies, "Who Is Called Bar Abbas?" *New Testament Studies* 27 (1981): 260–62.

41. Joseph Fitzmyer, *Luke X–XXIV,* 1490.

42. Crossan, *Historical Jesus,* 376.

43. The redactor of the Fourth Gospel for one; see Jn 19.30.

44. Crossan (*The Cross That Spoke,* 221–22) assumes that both "powers" in the Cross Gospel death cry (Gos. Pet. 19) are circumlocutions for "God," perhaps reflected in Mk 14.62. Nowhere does he acknowledge the possibility that the nonparallel and awkward dual vocatives in Gos. Pet. 19 may be a corruption of a text perhaps like the one suggested here, the result of a clumsy attempt to make an altogether different statement look like a rendering of Ps 22.1.

45. Crossan (*Historical Jesus,* 328–32) shows how the Secret Gospel of Mark underwent a redaction, or, as he terms it, "censorship," en route to becoming canonical Mark.

46. Jewish legend has it that Elijah will arrive for Passover riding a donkey (David Goldstein, *Jewish Legends* [New York: Peter Bedrick, 1987], 130). Chapter 6 discusses the special meaning that the locution "riding a donkey" had for Galilean Markans, in connection with the story of Jesus' entry into Jerusalem astride a donkey.

47. John Bright, *The Anchor Bible Jeremiah* (Garden City, N.Y.: Doubleday, 1965), 94.

48. Origen, *Origen Contra Celsum,* vol. 23 of Alexander Roberts and James Donaldson, eds., *Ante-Nicene Christian Library* (Edinburgh: T.&T. Clark, 1872), 2:37, 41.

49. Harry Chronis ("The Torn Veil, Cultus and Christology in Mk 15:37–39," *Journal of Biblical Literature* 101, no.1 [1982]: 97–114) discusses various explanations of the placement of the notice about the tearing of the veil.

50. Jesus' "in remembrance of her" (14.9), a reference to the symbolic recovering person depicted in the anointing, may represent a Markan counter to the Pauline eucharistic expression in 1 Cor 11.25, "in remembrance of me."

51. Josephus, *The Jewish War,* passim, tells how Vespasian, in his campaign of 67–68 C.E., annihilated whole Jewish populations from south Syria to

Judea, garrisoning the conquered towns and doubtless closing or demolishing the synagogues. The fact that postwar Judean Christianity apparently was not very successful in converting regional Jews, many of whom continued their Jewish religious practices as well as their fight against Rome, does not mean that the Messiah cult did not attempt to pursue the survival strategy hypothesized here.

52. See Mann, *Mark*, 659–72, for scholarly references on the question of Mark's ending at 16.8.

53. Thomas Sheehan, *The First Coming: How the Kingdom of God Became Christianity* (New York: Vintage Books, 1988), 170–73; emphasis in the original.

54. The various endings appended to Mark's gospel beyond 16.8 are acknowledged almost universally to be the products of hands other than Mark's. The supposedly strange "abruptness" of the ending at 16.8, which has caused many commentators to think that Mark's original ending has been lost, seems fully explained by the interpretation advanced here.

Chapter 3: Isaiah's Servant Drunkard

1. Jeremias, *New Testament Theology*, 292–94.

2. David J. A. Clines ("I, He, We, and They: A Literary Approach to Isaiah 53," *Journal for the Study of the Old Testament*, supplement series, 1 [1976]: 27–28) cites four eminent scholars who have declared themselves unconvinced that the servant actually dies: H. M. Orlinsky, G. R. Driver, R. N. Whybray, and J. A. Soggin. Clines concludes that "the references to the servant's 'death' are all ambiguous" and quotes Driver's remark, "No phrase is used which unambiguously implies his death."

3. Richard N. Longenecker (*The Christology of Early Jewish Christianity* [Grand Rapids, Mich.: Baker], 107) puts the question thus. See the later section entitled "The Scandal of Alcoholism."

4. Bernhard Duhm, *Das Buch Jesaia*, 5th ed. (Göttingen, Germany: Vandenhoeck und Ruprecht, 1968).

5. Tryggve N. D. Mettinger, *A Farewell to the Suffering Servant Songs: A Critical Examination of an Exegetical Axiom*, Publications of the Royal Society of Letters at Lund (Scripta Minora) (Lund, Sweden: CWK Gleerup, 1983).

6. John L. McKenzie, *The Anchor Bible Second Isaiah* (Garden City, N.Y.: Doubleday, 1968).

7. One of four types of parallelism in Hebrew poetry identified by C. F. Burney in *The Poetry of Our Lord* (Oxford: Clarendon, 1925). "In this form of parallelism," writes Burney, "the thought of the second line supplements and completes that of the first" (21).

8. R. N. Whybray (*New Century Bible Commentary, Isaiah 40–66* [Grand Rapids, Mich.: Wm. B. Eerdmans, 1981], 163) remarks as follows on Is 51.18: "For the image of the son who is expected to assist a drunken parent, cf. the Ugaritic *Tale of Aqhat*, where a son is promised who, among his regular duties towards his father, 'takes him by the hand when he's drunk, carries him when he's sated with wine' (*ANET*, p. 50)." (See note 14 for *ANET*.)

9. G. R. Driver ("'Another Little Drink'—Isaiah 28.1–22," in P. R. Ackroyd and B. Lindars, eds., *Words and Meanings: Essays Presented to David Winton Thomas* [Cambridge: University Press, 1968], 47–67) analyzes the drinking imagery in Isaiah 28, in which the prophet compares the Jerusalemites' drunken carousing in the face of national danger to that of the leaders of the northern kingdom before their destruction by Assyria. The drunkenness Isaiah depicts is meant to be understood as quite real. Driver lists Is 28.1–13 and 29.9–10 as instances of Isaiah's frequent use of wine imagery to "depict his defaulting fellow countrymen as drunkards" (p. 47). His analysis develops a whole lexicon of Hebrew drinking terminology. There is no indication, however, that Driver has thought of viewing this drunkenness as indicative of alcoholism, although it could hardly be otherwise.

10. Albert Champdor, *Babylon*, trans. E. Coult (New York: Putnam's, 1958), 114.

11. George A. F. Knight, *Deutero-Isaiah: A Theological Commentary on Isaiah 40–55* (New York: Abingdon, 1965), 219 n. 6. Concluding his commentary on Is 51.17–23, Knight actually refers to Israel as "an alcoholic," calling this "an amazing conception" with which Deutero-Isaiah "has now brought us face to face" (p. 221).

12. H. W. F. Saggs, *The Greatness That Was Babylon* (New York: Hawthorn, 1962), 72.

13. D. J. Wiseman, *Nebuchadrezzar and Babylon* (Oxford: Oxford University Press for the British Academy, 1985), 38.

14. J. B. Pritchard, ed., *Ancient Near Eastern Texts Relating to the Old Testament*, 2d ed. (Princeton, N.J.: Princeton University Press, 1955), 316; hereinafter abbreviated as *ANET*.

15. Wiseman, *Nebuchadrezzar and Babylon*, 91.

16. Herodotus, *The Histories*, trans. Aubrey de Sélincourt (Harmondsworth, Britain: Penguin, 1983 [1972]), I.191, 118; Xenophon, *Cyropaedia, Vol. II*, trans. Walter Miller (London: William Heinemann, 1961), 7:5, 267. Louis F. Hartman (*The Anchor Bible Book of Daniel* [Garden City, N.Y.: Doubleday, 1978], 187, 191) thinks that the "Nabonidus Chronicle" (*ANET*, 305–7) falsifies these traditional accounts, but Martin McNamara ("Nabonidus and the Book of Daniel," *The Irish Theological Quarterly* 37, no. 2 [April 1970]: 131–49) disagrees, remarking that the account in Daniel 5, and in the parallel stories in Herodotus and Xenophon, could still have "some foundation in fact" (143).

17. From the so-called "Verse Account of Nabonidus" (*ANET*, 312–15) and the so-called "Harran Inscriptions of Nabonidus," discussed by McNamara, "Nabonidus," 134–36.

18. "Verse Account," *ANET*, 312–15. McNamara ("Nabonidus," 141) examines several sources relating to Nabonidus's presumed "madness" and concludes that the king's condition was more likely an illness than mental derangement. He points out that the adjective in the sentence in "Verse Account" usually read "the king is mad" should actually be translated as "angry," "vexed," or "wroth." This comports well with the alcoholism theory.

19. Paul-Alain Beaulieu, *The Reign of Nabonidus, King of Babylon 556–539 B.C.* (New Haven, Conn.: Yale University Press, 1989).

20. McNamara ("Nabonidus," 139) quotes Nabonidus's own account from the "Harran Inscription" telling how the priests and people of Babylon "talked treason and not loyalty" in response to his rebuilding of the temple of Sin, so "I hied myself afar from my city of Babylon (on) the road to Tema."

21. Quoted in Beaulieu, *Reign of Nabonidus*, 173.

22. D. N. Freedman, "The Prayer of Nabonidus," *Bulletin of American Schools of Oriental Research* 145 (1957): 31–32. G. Vermes' translation is included in McNamara, "Nabonidus," 138, and J. T. Milik's is in Hartman, *Daniel*, 178–79. Although his affliction is generally understood as a skin disease, an ulcer or boils, the name of Nabonidus's specific malady in "The Prayer," *šᵉḥîn*, according to Hartman literally means "a burning or inflamation" (179). The king may have grown hyperallergic to wine, or the term may have been used to speak about intoxication in a figurative sense separate from its dermatological meaning.

23. McNamara, "Nabonidus," 141, and Hartman, *Daniel*, 177–80.

24. Raymond P. Dougherty (*Nabonidus and Belshazzar: A Study of the Closing Events of the Neo-Babylonian Empire* [New Haven, Conn.: Yale University Press, 1929], 105–11), who did not yet know of "The Prayer of Nabonidus," summarizes the many explanations offered for Nabonidus's odd behavior in leaving Babylon for Teima. Illness is one.

25. Gerald A. Larue, *Babylon and the Bible* (Grand Rapids, Mich.: Baker, 1969), 69.

26. This could explain the strange presence, until the time of Mohammed, of flourishing Jewish communities in the Arabian oases (five besides Teima) settled by Nabonidus (see McNamara's discussion of extrabiblical Jewish legends about Nabonidus in "Nabonidus," 141–43). It would be resonable to think that he planted them there to minister to him in his recovery, since according to "The Prayer of Nabonidus," Yahweh had become his God. Additional evidence of Nabonidus's recovery is that he finally returned to Babylon to fulfill his duties in the Marduk festival and allowed the wine to flow once more. Apparently he had learned at last, even as king, to live and let live. But by now Cyrus was rising, and Nabonidus's reign all but over.

27. Clines, "I, He, We, and They," 11–22; Mitchell Dahood, "Phoenician Elements in Isaiah 52.13–53.12," in H. Goedicke, ed., *Near Eastern Studies in Honor of William Foxwell Albright* (Baltimore, Md.: Johns Hopkins, 1971), 63–73; McKenzie, *Second Isaiah*, 129–36; David Winton Thomas, English translation of Isaiah 53, quoted in Raphael Loewe, "Prolegomenon," in S. R. Driver and A. D. Neubauer, *The Fifty-Third Chapter of Isaiah according to Jewish Interpreters* (New York: KATV, 1969), 1–38; quotation on 4–6. Also consulted: A. S. Herbert, *The Book of the Prophet Isaiah 40–66* (Cambridge: Cambridge University Press, 1975); Knight, *Deutero-Isaiah;* Christopher R. North, *The Second Isaiah: Introduction, Translation and Commentary to Chapters XL–LV* (Oxford: Clarendon, 1964); Charles Cutler Torrey, *The Second Isaiah: A New In-*

terpretation (Edinburgh: T.&T. Clark, 1928); Claus Westermann, *Isaiah 40–66: A Commentary* (Philadelphia: Westminster, 1969); Whybray, *New Century Bible Commentary*. This version is a collage of English translations taken from the foregoing sources, together with a few synonymous rephrasings of those translations explained in the notes and intended to reinforce the alcoholism interpretation explored here.

28. Jeremias, *New Testament Theology*, 292–93.

29. Mitchell Dahood (*Proverbs and Northwest Semitic Philology* [Rome: Pontifical Biblical Institute, 1963], 23) originally translated the first colon of this verse as, "With the anguish of his soul he shall be surfeited, sated," but in the version consulted here ("Phoenician Elements," 64) he emended his reading to "With the anguish of his soul he was sated, he was soaked by his sweat." In "Phoenician Elements" (72) Dahood acknowledges G. R. Driver's similar view of *yir'eh* in Driver's *In Memoriam Paul Kahle*, ed. M. Black and G. Fohrer, *Beihefte zur Zeitschrift für die alttestamentenliche Wissenschaft* 103:97

30. So Herbert, *Book of Isaiah*, 106 and 111, and Christopher R. North, *The Suffering Servant in Deutero Isaiah: An Historical and Critical Study* (Oxford: Oxford University Press, 1956), 121, 124.

31. Clines, "I, He, We, They," 37–40.

32. Morna D. Hooker, *Jesus and the Servant: The Influence of the Servant Concept of Deutero-Isaiah in the New Testament* (London: SPCK, 1959), 2–5. The scandal of alcoholism would also explain the apostle Paul's refusal to have anything to do with members of the Jerusalem church beyond brief consultations with its leaders or to make use of any biographical details of Jesus' ministry.

33. Longenecker, *Christology*, 107–8.

34. Hooker, *Jesus and the Servant*, 56.

35. Ibid., 155–58.

36. C. F. D. Moule, *The Birth of the New Testament*, 2d ed. (London: Adam & Charles Black, 1966), 81–83.

37. W. Zimmerli and J. Jeremias, *The Servant of God*, trans. H. Knight (London: SCM, 1957), 98, 104.

38. Jeremias, *New Testament Theology*, 292–93.

39. Hooker, *Jesus and the Servant*, 157–58.

40. Longenecker, *Christology*, 108–9.

Chapter 4: The Provenance, Genre, and Story of Mark

1. Howard Clark Kee, *Community*, 1.

2. Seán P. Kealy, *Mark's Gospel*.

3. Kee, *Community*, 2. For an example of the richness and complexity of the historical problems of Mark, to say nothing of literary questions, see the essay by Martin Hengel, "The Gospel of Mark: Time and Origin of Situation," in his *Studies in the Gospel of Mark*, trans. John Bowden (Philadelphia: Fortress, 1985), 1–30. See also the survey of scholarly conjectures on the date and occasion of Mark by C. S. Mann (*Mark*, 72–83).

4. Kee, *Community*, 2.

5. Dalman, *Jesus-Jeshua* and *Sacred Sites and Ways*.

6. Shailer Mathews, *The Social Teaching of Jesus: An Essay in Christian Sociology* (New York: Macmillan, 1897).

7. Shirley Jackson Case, *The Evolution of Early Christianity* (Chicago: University of Chicago Press, 1914).

8. S. G. F. Brandon, *Jesus and the Zealots* (Manchester, England: Manchester University Press, 1967).

9. Joachim Jeremias, *Jerusalem in the Time of Jesus: An Investigation into Economic and Social Conditions during the New Testament Period,* trans. F. H. and C. H. Cave (Philadelphia: Fortress, 1969).

10. E. A. Judge, *The Social Pattern of the Christian Groups in the First Century* (London: Tyndale, 1960).

11. L. E. Keck, "On the Ethos of Early Christians," *Journal of the American Academy of Religion* 42 (1974): 435–42.

12. Eduard Lohse, *The New Testament Environment,* trans. John E. Steely (Nashville: Abingdon, 1976).

13. John G. Gager, *Kingdom and Community: The Social World of Early Christianity* (Englewood Cliffs, N.J.: Prentice-Hall, 1975).

14. Abraham J. Malherbe, *Social Aspects of Early Christianity* (Philadelphia: Fortress, 1983).

15. Gerd Theissen, *Sociology of Early Palestinian Christianity,* trans. John Bowden (Philadelphia: Fortress, 1978).

16. Bruce J. Malina, *The New Testament World: Insights from Cultural Anthropology* (Atlanta: John Knox, 1981).

17. Summarized in Martin Hengel, *The 'Hellenization' of Judea in the First Century after Christ* (London: SCM, 1989).

18. A. D. Nock, *Conversion: The Old and the New in Religion from Alexander the Great to Augustine of Hippo* (London: Oxford University Press, 1933), 211.

19. Howard Clark Kee, *Christian Origins in Sociological Perspective: Methods and Resources* (Philadelphia: Westminster, 1980), 82.

20. Ibid., 84.

21. Malherbe, *Social Aspects,* and Lohse, *New Testament Environment.*

22. Gager, *Kingdom and Community,* 140.

23. Alan F. Segal, *Rebecca's Children: Judaism and Christianity in the Roman World* (Cambridge, Mass.: Harvard University Press, 1986), 103.

24. Alan F. Segal, *Paul the Convert: The Apostolate and Apostasy of Saul the Pharisee* (New Haven, Conn.: Yale University Press, 1990), 107–9.

25. Ibid., 74.

26. Rudy, *Becoming Alcoholic,* 42.

27. Mack, *Myth,* 48.

28. Ibid., 83–88.

29. Richard A. Horsley, *Sociology and the Jesus Movement* (New York: Crossroad, 1989). See also Horsley with Hanson, *Bandits, Prophets, and Messiahs.*

30. Horsley, *Sociology,* 127.

31. Mary Ann Tolbert, *Sowing the Gospel,* 73.

32. Hengel, *'Hellenization,'* 56.

33. Jacob Neusner, *Judaism in the Beginning of Christianity* (Philadelphia: Fortress, 1984), 98. Neusner cites the Babylonian Talmud, Baba Batra 60b.

34. Hengel, *'Hellenization,'* 56.

35. Vincent L. Wimbush, ed., *Ascetic Behavior in Greco-Roman Antiquity: A Sourcebook* (Minneapolis: Fortress, 1990), 4.

36. Robin Scroggs, "The Earliest Christian Communities as a Sectarian Movement," in *Christianity, Judaism, and Other Greco-Roman Cults: Studies for Morton Smith at Sixty,* part 2, *Early Christianity,* ed. Jacob Neusner (Leiden, the Netherlands: E.J. Brill, 1975), 10–11.

37. Malina, "Clean and Unclean: Understanding the Rule of Purity," chapter 6 of *Christian Origins,* 122–52.

38. Whether Mark precedes Matthew and Luke or is a post hoc abbreviation of the two is a question endlessly debated. The majority view continues to favor the primacy of Mark. Frank J. Matera (*Passion Narratives and Gospel Theologies* [New York: Paulist, 1986], 9–11) summarizes modern thinking on Mark's sources. See also John Dominic Crossan, *The Cross That Spoke;* Frank J. Matera, *What Are They Saying about Mark?* (New York: Paulist, 1987); and Joseph A. Fitzmyer, "The Priority of Mark and the 'Q' Source in Luke," in *To Advance the Gospel: New Testament Studies* (New York: Crossroad, 1981), 3–40.

39. Theissen, *Palestinian Christianity,* 117.

40. Edward S. Kilmartin ("A First Century Chalice Dispute," *Sciences Ecclésiastiques [Science et Esprit]* 12 [1960]: 403–8) discusses Jewish disputes about wine and blood drinking. Contra Crossan (*Historical Jesus,* 398–404), "bread and fish" was a Markan metaphor in Proto-John, not a eucharistic actuality.

41. Horsley with Hanson, *Bandits, Prophets, and Messiahs,* 254. As for Galilee, Burton L. Mack ("Galilee before the War," chapter 4 of *The Lost Gospel,* 51–68) highlights the cultural heterogeneity of this multiethnic region during the prewar decades.

42. T. W. Manson, *Studies in the Gospels and Epistles* (Manchester, Britain: Manchester University Press, 1962), 35. Manson points out that the anecdote is peculiar to Mark's gospel and is not likely to have come from the disciples or from Jesus.

43. At least Mark knew that Judeans could identify Galileans by their dialect, as the story of the recognition of Peter in the high priest's courtyard illustrates (Mk 14.70). See chapter 6 for the discussion of "riding a donkey" as a drinking idiom that turns on features of the northern Aramaic dialect. As for Mark's numerous Latinisms, Mann (*Mark,* 384–85) lists recent research, and Hengel (*Studies in the Gospel of Mark,* 29 and 137) cites additional studies.

44. See chapter 1, note 44.

45. See chapter 1, note 45.

46. The dispute between Paul and Mark occurred in the 40s. Paul apparently remained chary about dealing with remnants of the original brotherhood. One can imagine his chagrin, after his conversion around 32 C.E., on

first hearing that Jesus and his disciples were reputed to have been drunkards. After waiting three years to visit Jerusalem, he stayed only fifteen days and made a point of saying that he spoke with only Peter and James, brother of Jesus, but none of the other apostles (Gal 1.18–19). Günther Bornkamm (*Paul*, trans. D. M. G. Stalker [New York: Harper & Row, 1971]) repeatedly notes the oddity of Paul's refusal to hand on any biographical information about Jesus.

47. Josephus (*Jewish War*, III) describes Vespasian's campaign in such a way as to make it clear that Jewish social life in the conquered cities was traumatized and brought to a standstill.

48. The report of W. H. C. Frend (*The Rise of Christianity* [Philadelphia: Fortress, 1984]) that the Neronian persecution of 64 C.E. was not forgotten by the Roman ruling class, who thereafter associated Christianity with evil religion *(prava religio)*, might be seen as arguing against this idea. The Romans' quarrel in Galilee and Judea, however, was with insurrectionist Jews, not Christians. Hence the Jewish Christians may have believed that they stood a chance to gain Roman favor in this time of extreme peril. In the end, their real opponents turned out to be the surviving Jewish congregations. Eduard Lohse quotes the Twelfth Benediction from the end-of-century synagogue service: "Mayest thou speedily uproot the insolent government [Rome] in our days. And may the Nazarenes [Jewish Christians] and the *Minim* [Jewish heretics] die in a moment, may they be blotted out of the book of life and not be enrolled with the righteous" (*The New Testament Environment*, 163).

49. Alexandria is probably the best guess: Mark had ministered there earlier, its location would put him out of reach of the Romans waiting to resume hostilities, and it is named such by John Chrysostom against a church tradition that at the end of the century had begun to valorize what had become a somewhat suspect gospel by linking it to Peter and Rome. A copy of a letter purportedly written by Clement of Alexandria, discovered in 1958 by Morton Smith (*Clement of Alexandria and a Secret Gospel of Mark* [Cambridge, Mass.: Harvard University Press, 1973]), further supports Alexandria.

50. Dom Gregory Dix, *The Shape of the Liturgy* (New York: Seabury, 1982), 61. No sobriety program, ancient or modern, could survive a heavy influx of fanatical teetotalers seeking spiritual consolation on the cheap. As noted earlier in this chapter, the alcoholism groups may have included what are called the Thomas communities and the Ebionites mentioned by Epiphanius, both of whom followed Jesus but drank their communion in water rather than wine.

51. Horsley, *Sociology*, 106.

52. Mack, *Myth*, 71.

53. "The Gospel of Thomas (II, 2)," intro. Helmet Koester and trans. Thomas O. Lambdin, in James M. Robinson, ed., *The Nag Hammadi Library in English* (San Francisco: Harper and Row, 1981), 117–30; quotation on 121. Where the present translation has "abjure their wine," Lambdin has "shake off their wine." The versions reflect quite different perspectives on Jesus' intention.

54. Ibid., 117.

55. Kilmartin, "Chalice Dispute," 405–6.

56. Jeremias, *Eucharistic Words*, 122–25, 212.

57. Edgar Hennecke, *New Testament Apocrypha*, vol. 2, trans. R. McL. Wilson (Philadelphia: Westminster, 1965), 507.

58. Günther Bornkamm, "Introduction to 'The Acts of Thomas,'" in Hennecke, *Apocrypha*, 438.

59. Glenn Alan Koch, "A Critical Investigation of Epiphanius' Knowledge of the Ebionites: A Translation and Critical Discussion of Panarion 30" (Ph.D. diss., University of Pennsylvania, 1976), 143 n. 21.

60. Hans Lietzmann, *Mass and Lord's Supper: A Study in the History of Liturgy*, trans. Dorothea H. G. Reeve (Leiden, the Netherlands: E.J. Brill, 1979 [part 1 originally 1926]), 203.

61. Dix, *Shape of the Liturgy*, 61.

62. *Jewish War*, III, 521, Cited by Geza Vermes in *Jesus the Jew*, 48.

63. Morton Smith, *Jesus the Magician* (San Francisco: Harper & Row, 1978), 61 overleaf, 62.

64. T. Boomershine, "Mark, the Storyteller: A Rhetorical-Critical Investigation of Mark's Passion and Resurrection Narrative" (Ph.D. diss., New York: Union Theological Seminary, 1974), and Dan O. Via, Jr., *Kerygma and Comedy in the New Testament: A Structuralist Approach to Hermeneutic* (Philadelphia: Fortress, 1975).

65. Werner H. Kelber, *Mark's Story of Jesus* (Philadelphia: Fortress, 1979).

66. Frank Kermode, *Genesis of Secrecy*, 138.

67. David Rhoads and Donald Michie, *Mark as Story: An Introduction to the Narrative of a Gospel* (Philadelphia: Fortress, 1982).

68. Jack Dean Kingsbury, *The Christology of Mark's Gospel* (Philadelphia: Fortress, 1983).

69. Kee, *Community*, 17–30.

70. George A. Kennedy, *New Testament Interpretation through Rhetorical Criticism* (Chapel Hill: University of North Carolina Press, 1984). See also James Kinneavey, *Greek Rhetorical Origins of the Christian Faith: An Inquiry* (New York: Oxford University Press, 1987), and Burton L. Mack, *Rhetoric and the New Testament* (Minneapolis: Fortress, 1990).

71. Robbins, *Jesus the Teacher.*

72. Tolbert, *Sowing the Gospel*, 59.

73. Adena Rosmarin, *The Power of Genre* (Minneapolis: University of Minnesota Press, 1985), 39–40.

74. The position here is in line with the view expressed by C. Clifton Black II ("The Quest of Mark the Redactor: Why Has It Been Pursued, and What Has It Taught Us?" *Journal for the Study of the New Testament* 33 [1988]: 19–39) that redaction criticism follows from three ideas, "the Evangelist as author and theologian, his Gospel as the immediate product of his and his community's 'setting in life,' and that Gospel as a literary entity to be interpreted holistically" (22).

75. Frank Kermode, *Genesis of Secrecy*, 141. See also Robert C. Tannehill, "The Gospel of Mark as Narrative Christology," *Semeia* 16 (1979): 57–95.

76. Rhoads and Michie, *Mark as Story,* 45.

77. Hengel, *Studies in the Gospel of Mark,* 34.

78. Mann, *Mark,* 37.

79. C. H. Turner, *A New Commentary on Holy Scripture,* cited by Manson, *Studies in the Gospels,* 40–41.

80. Rhoads and Michie, *Mark as Story,* 37–38.

81. Karlyn Kohrs Campbell and Kathleen Hall Jamieson, *Form and Genre: Shaping Rhetorical Action* (Falls Church, Va.: Speech Communication Association, 1978), 19.

82. Carolyn R. Miller, "Genre as Social Action," *Quarterly Journal of Speech* 70 (1984): 151–67; quotation on 151.

83. Ibid., 158.

84. Ibid., 163.

85. "How It Works," chapter 5 of *Alcoholics Anonymous,* 3d ed., 58.

86. Rhoads and Michie, *Mark as Story,* 55.

87. Ibid., 47–49.

88. Via, *Kerygma and Comedy,* 81.

89. Ibid.

90. Jaroslav Pelikan, *Jesus through the Centuries* (New York: Harper & Row, 1985).

91. Hans Küng, *On Being a Christian,* trans. E. Quinn (New York: Doubleday, 1976), 126–44.

92. Dennis C. Duling, *Jesus Christ through History* (New York: Harcourt-Brace-Jovanovich, 1978).

93. John H. Hayes, *Son of God to Superstar: Twentieth-Century Interpretations of Jesus* (Nashville: Abingdon, 1976).

94. Patrick Allitt, "The American Christ," *American Heritage,* November 1988, 128–41.

95. Anton Wessels, *Images of Jesus* (London: SCM Press, 1990).

96. Günther Bornkamm, *Jesus of Nazareth,* trans. I. McLuskey and F. McLuskey with J. M. Robinson (New York: Harper & Row, 1960); Michael Grant, *Jesus: An Historian's Review of the Gospels* (New York: Scribner's, 1977); Paula Fredriksen, *From Jesus to Christ: The Origins of the New Testament Images of Jesus* (New Haven: Yale University Press, 1988); John Dominic Crossan, *Jesus: A Revolutionary Biography* (San Francisco: Harper, 1994); and Marcus J. Borg, *Jesus in Contemporary Scholarship* (Valley Forge, Pa.: Trinity Press International, 1994).

97. For a survey of issues in christological study see Robert Jewett, ed., *Christology and Exegesis: New Approaches, Semeia* 30 (1984). For a review of historical images, see Daniel J. Harrington, "The Jewishness of Jesus" *Bible Review* 3, no. 1 (Spring 1987): 33–41.

98. See G. Stanley Hall, *Jesus, the Christ, in the Light of Psychology,* vol. 2 (Garden City, N.Y.: Doubleday, 1917); Morton Smith, *Jesus the Magician;* Fernando Belo, *A Materialist Reading of the Gospel of Mark,* trans. M. J. O'Connell (Maryknoll, N.Y.: Orbis, 1981); Milan Machovec, *A Marxist Looks at Jesus* (Philadelphia: Fortress, 1976); John F. O'Grady, *Models of Jesus* (New York: Doubleday, 1981); William E. Phipps, *The Sexuality of Jesus: Theological*

and Literary Perspectives (New York: Harper, 1973); Edward L. Kessel, *The Androgynous Christ: A Christian Feminist View* (Portland, Oreg.: author, 1988); Arthur Drews, *The Christ Myth*, trans. C. D. Burns (Chicago: Open Court, 1911); and John Allegro, *The Sacred Mushroom and the Cross* (London: Hodder and Stoughton, 1970).

99. Robbins, *Jesus the Teacher;* Mack, *Myth;* Christopher D. Marshall, *Faith as a Theme in Mark's Narrative* (Cambridge: Cambridge University Press, 1989); Tolbert, *Sowing the Gospel;* Michael Baigent, Richard Leigh, and Henry Lincoln, *Holy Blood, Holy Grail* (New York: Dell, 1983); Barbara Thiering, *Jesus and the Riddle of the Dead Sea Scrolls: Unlocking the Secrets of His Life Story* (San Francisco: Harper, 1992); Crossan, *Historical Jesus;* Sanders, *Historical Figure of Jesus;* and N. T. Wright, *The New Testament and the People of God* (Minneapolis: Augsburg Fortress, 1992).

100. Ernest Renan, *The Life of Jesus* (New York: Modern Library, 1927 [1863]), and David Friedrich Strauss, *Das Leben Jesu* [The Life of Jesus] (Tübingen: N.p., 1835).

101. Seán P. Kealy (*Mark's Gospel,* 81–83) summarizes Holtzmann's thinking on Jesus' career.

102. Albert Schweitzer, *The Psychiatric Study of Jesus,* trans. Charles R. Joy (Gloucester, Mass.: Peter Smith, 1975 [1913]).

103. Warner Fite, *Jesus the Man: A Critical Essay* (Cambridge, Mass.: Harvard University Press, 1946).

104. Albert Schweitzer, *The Quest of the Historical Jesus: A Critical Study of Its Progress from Reimarus to Wrede,* trans. W. Montgomery (New York: Macmillan, 1961 [1906]).

105. S. G. F. Brandon, *The Trial of Jesus of Nazareth* (New York: Stein and Day, 1968). E. P. Sanders (*Jesus and Judaism* [London: SCM, 1985]) refutes the Zealot hypothesis, and Horsley (*Bandits, Prophets, and Messiahs*) has completely revised our understanding of the Zealot movement in general.

106. Adolf Holl, *Jesus in Bad Company,* trans. Simon King (London: William Collins, 1972).

107. Lee E. Snook, *The Anonymous Christ: Jesus as Savior in Modern Theology* (Minneapolis: Augsburg, 1986).

108. Edward F. Edinger, *Ego and Archetype* (New York: Penguin, 1974), chaps. 5 and 9.

109. Wolfgang Iser, "The Reading Process: A Phenomenological Approach," in Tompkins, *Reader-Response Criticism,* 50–69.

110. Jeremias (*Eucharistic Words,* 218–25) emphasizes the inadequate attention that has been paid to the omission of Jesus' Passover meditation from the eucharistic narratives.

111. Renan, *Life of Jesus;* Strauss, *Das Leben Jesu;* Albert Schweitzer, *Historical Jesus.*

112. Schweitzer, *Psychiatric Study.*

113. Brandon, *Trial of Jesus,* but also see Ernst Bammel and C. F. D. Moule, *Jesus and the Politics of His Day* (Cambridge: Cambridge University Press, 1884). The controversy over a peaceful versus a violent Jesus is longstand-

ing. Bammel discerns a sequence from peaceful to rebellious to peaceful again, which argues against zealotism and for the addiction-cum-sobriety view. And in any case, as Richard Horsley has shown (*Bandits, Prophets, and Messiahs*, 216–43), the coalition of brigands and dissidents that Josephus labels "the Zealots" was not formed until 67–68 C.E.

Chapter 5: New Wine at Pentecost

1. Works consulted include Hans Conzelmann, *Acts of the Apostles: A Commentary on the Acts of the Apostles*, trans. J. Limburg, A. T. Kraabel, and D. H. Juel (Philadelphia: Fortress, 1987); Richard J. Dillon and Joseph A. Fitzmyer, "Acts of the Apostles," in Raymond E. Brown, Joseph A. Fitzmeyer, and Roland E. Murphy, eds., *The Jerome Biblical Commentary* (Englewood Cliffs, N.J.: Prentice-Hall, 1968); Ernst Haenchen, *The Acts of the Apostles: A Commentary*, trans. B. Noble and G. Shinn (Philadelphia: Westminster, 1971); and Johannes Munck, *The Anchor Bible Acts of the Apostles* (Garden City, N.Y.: Doubleday, 1967). Conzelmann, for example, speaks of those "who think in terms of one source to which Luke has added materials, such as the miraculous gift of tongues in chapter 2" (xxxvii). All commentators acknowledge the probability of Lukan composition in Acts.

2. Mitchell Dahood, *Psalms I*, 86–91.

3. References in Dillon and Fitzmeyer, "Acts of the Apostles," 172.

4. Some commentators think that "all" in verses 1 and 4 refers to all 120 disciples mentioned in 1.15, but the position here is that "all" refers to the twelve disciples (less Judas but including Matthias) who have assumed the office that Luke refers to as "apostle." In verse 14 Peter stands "with the eleven," the "men" to whom he refers in verse 15. Justin is often quoted on the point, "For a band of twelve men went forth from Jerusalem, and they were common men, not trained in speaking" (Justin Martyr, "The First Apology of Justin, the Martyr," trans. E. R. Hardy, in Cyril C. Richardson, ed., *Early Christian Fathers* [New York: Collier, 1970], 242–89; quotation of 39.19 on 266).

5. A.A.'s step twelve reads, "Having had a spiritual awakening as the result of these steps, we tried to carry this message to alcoholics, and to practice these principles in all our affairs" (*Alcoholics Anonymous*, 60).

6. Dillon and Fitzmeyer, "Acts of the Apostles," 172.

7. C. S. Mann ("Pentecost in Acts," appendix 3 in Munck, *Acts of the Apostles*, 274–75) proposes three possible explanations of the perplexity of the crowd: (1) the apostles were actually speaking foreign languages (Mann terms this the "'minority' view" among scholars); (2) the apostles were speaking Hebrew instead of Aramaic, which surprised the Jerusalemites; (3) the apostles were speaking not new languages but different interpretations of the Pentecost Scriptures. The view here is closest to number three: that the apostles addressed individuals in the crowd in the argot of their spiritual recovery program, after which Peter's sermon presented a new interpretation of Scripture (Joel and Psalm 16) based on teachings he had from Jesus.

8. Conzelmann says, "The relationship between *pantes*, "all," and *heteroi*, "others," cannot be determined in a quantitive way. The scene is purely redactional, not historical" (*Acts of the Apostles*, 13). Not necessarily. This important referential distinction could very well have been preserved in Luke's traditional eyewitness source. Discussing the Pentecost story, G. J. Sirks ("The Cinderella of Theology: The Doctrine of the Holy Spirit," *Harvard Theological Review* 50 [1957]: 77–89) reminds us of the strong sense of contrariety conveyed in most instances by *heteroi*. Just as Sirks maintains that "'other tongues' are pericopes different from those given by tradition" (86), so is it asserted here that "others/different ones" said of the crowd refers to a subset of the multitude importantly different from the remainder.

9. Barclay M. Newman and Eugene A. Nida, *A Translator's Handbook on the Acts of the Apostles* (United Bible Societies, 1972), 41.

10. Luke presumably wrote his gospel with a copy of Mark at hand. Why he omitted what he did can never be definitively determined. In the present case, given the saying that he saw fit to include at 5.39 (see note 11), he may well have considered "new wine" to be a false note in the Markan narrative. Luke knew little of the drinking game so familiar to alcoholics. In fact, in two instances peculiar to the third gospel (12.45, which adds, "and get drunk," and 21.34, an admonition against drinking inserted into Jesus' eschatological discourse), Luke reveals his own anti-alcohol bias. He would have been appalled at an interpretation of Jesus' eucharistic words as a messianic directive to drink wine and so hit bottom as the appointed avenue to salvation.

11. A. H. Mead ("Old and New Wine: St. Luke 5.39," *The Expository Times* 20 [1989]: 234–35) wrestles with the well-known awkwardness of this saying, which in Luke immediately follows yet seemingly contradicts the Markan parable about new wine in old wineskins (Lk 5.37–8; Mk 2.22). The explanation suggested here, consistent with the alcoholism hermeneutic, is that the midcentury Hellenistic churches, completely ignorant of Jesus' identity as a drunkard, knew, yet were perplexed by, Jesus' paschal remark about drinking "new wine" (later incorporated as Mk 14.25). It's one thing, they would have said, for Jesus to tell a parable comparing the gospel to new wine (later Mk 2.22), but quite another for him to envision actually drinking new wine on the eschatological day to which they thought the disavowal saying referred, when old wine surely would be made available. It would have been an offense to the sensibilities of those who knew their wine. Hence the Hellenistic church invented a saying that became Luke 5.39 to compensate for Jesus' apparent ignorance of conventional wisdom about the relative merits of old wine versus new.

12. It is important to point out the several meanings of "new wine." It has two different literal senses. It can mean wine fully fermented but newly produced, of the current or most recent vintage, or it can mean grape juice in which the process of fermentation has only begun, sweet and still nonalcoholic, a nonintoxicant also called "sweet wine" or "must," which has to be drunk at once, before the natural grape sugar turns to alcohol. The Greek

word for the latter sense is *gleukos,* the word Luke uses in Acts 2.13, whereas *neos* modifying *oinos* ("wine") yields "new wine" in the former sense, wine of recent production. A third sense of the term results from the adjective *kainos* instead of *neos,* which means "new" in the sense of different in form, character, or quality. The "new wine" in Mk 14.25, whose metaphorical sense is discussed in chapter 2 and elsewhere, is *oinos kainos.* In the saying about not putting new wine into old wineskins (2.22), Mark uses *oinos neos.* Literally he means that fermenting grape juice will burst an old and inelastic skin, but he uses *neos* instead of *gleukos* partly as an antonym to *palaios* ("old") but mainly to reinforce the parabolic meaning that new thinking will not fit into old religious structures. *Oinos kainos* would have been inappropriate for the saying, which stresses the temporality of the new-old contrast. The saying differs completely from "new wine" as an oxymoronic metaphor for sobriety, which does require the sense "wine of a different character" as its vehicle. The latter is the sense of "new wine" *(oinos kainos)* in Mk 14.25 and also the sense that would have been understood by the "different ones" in the Pentecost crowd, Luke's use of *gleukos* to the contrary notwithstanding.

13. "Burlesque" is Conzelmann's word (*Acts of the Apostles,* 15).

14. In support of Luke's understandable misreading of his materials, commentators quote Cicero, "From the third hour there was drinking, gaming, vomiting" (Cicero, *Philippics,* trans. Walter C. A. Ker [London: William Heinemann, 1963], II.xli.104, 167). Newman and Nida point out that the Jews normally ate (and therefore drank) only after the hour of morning prayer, the third hour (*Translator's Handbook,* 41). As any alcoholic will confirm, however, if the apostles had still been actively drinking at Pentecost, they would have had no compunctions about starting before 9 A.M. Some would have been fairly sober at that hour, others would still be drunk from the night before, and others would already have begun a new day of drinking. To see the different patterns, one has only to observe skid row winos in the morning hours.

15. Carroll Stuhlmueller, "Post-Exilic Period: Spirit, Apocalyptic," in *Jerome Biblical Commentary,* 1:343. Not all apocalyptic resembles that described here. Works such as Daniel, the Enoch books, 4 Ezra, and the Testaments of the Patriarchs portray the inevitable struggle in moral terms, as a conflict between a good Israel and its evil enemies. The final victory vindicates Israel and destroys its enemies. By contrast, as Joachim Jeremias explains at length (*New Testament Theology,* 122–31), works such as Joel and the Markan apocalypse show the destruction as falling on Israel itself, in the form of a cataclysm interpretable in the alternative senses described here, either outer physical calamity or inner psychic reorientation.

16. T. W. Manson (*Studies in the Gospels,* 39–40) suggests that Mark may have visited Peter in Rome. Based on the "Papias note" in Eusebius's *Church History,* the tradition of Mark as interpreter of the elderly Peter is well established. See the detailed discussion by Martin Hengel, *Studies in the Gospel of Mark,* 47–50 and related notes.

17. J. B. Phillips's translation of Is 24.7–11 (*Four Prophets: A Translation*

into Modern English [New York: Macmillan, 1963]: 112) powerfully captures the bleakness of the alcoholic "bottom": that judgment time when wine fails as a nostrum, just before the coming of recovery and the messianic age:

(7) The wine fails, the vine is withered; the merrymakers sigh in sorrow.

(8) The joyful tambourines are silent, the shouts of the revelers have died away, and the happy notes of the harp are still.

(9) There is no more singing as they drink the wine, and strong drink is bitter to those who drink it.

(10) The city is in chaos, fallen and broken, every house is barred so that none can enter.

(11) In the streets they shout for wine. Darkness is falling on joy after joy, and laughter is banished from the earth.

No recovering person can read these lines and not recognize the prophet's firsthand familiarity with advanced alcoholism visited epidemically on his society.

18. This and all following references in this section, to Mitchell Dahood's translation and notes on Psalm 16, are from Dahood, *Psalms I,* 86–91.

19. Dahood gives Virolleaud's French translation, "Mangez ô dieux, et buvez, buvez encore." John Gray ("Canaanite Religion and Old Testament Study in the Light of New Alphabetic Texts from Ras Shamra," *Ugaritica VIII* 18 [1978]: 85) translates the same text directly into English: "Ye shall drink your fill of wine, / Even new wine till ye are drunk."

Chapter 6: Markan Sobriety Emblems

1. Schillebeeckx, *Jesus,* 137.

2. See chapter 4, note 43, on Mark's Latinisms.

3. Jeremias, *New Testament Theology,* 162. Joseph Fitzmyer says that *metanoia* "in the NT . . . is almost always used in the religious sense of a turning from sin, repentance for sin . . . a new beginning in moral conduct" (*Luke I–IX,* 237). Mark perhaps expected that his Christian audience would understand *metanoia* this way, but his insiders would have known, even as today, that it can also signify the apocalyptic reorganization of mind that occurs in sobriety.

4. Ancient healers, on the other hand, like their modern counterparts, knew perfectly well what caused inebriates' drunken contortions and that any attempt to apply their medical or magical arts in such cases was time wasted. Presumably this is why, in Morton Smith's catalogue of diseases and pathologies to which magicians and exorcists addressed themselves ("The Evidence for Magical Practices," chap. 7 of *Jesus the Magician,* 94–139), inebriety is nowhere to be found.

5. Howard Clark Kee, *Medicine, Miracle, and Magic in New Testament Times* (Cambridge: Cambridge University Press, 1986), 25.

6. An acquaintance of the writer tells of the time he and his wife returned

home one evening to find their young daughter comatose on the floor, covered with vomit and unrousable. Nothing at the scene suggested what her trouble was. A blood test at the hospital revealed an elevated blood-alcohol level. The child later admitted having experimented with the family alcohol for the first time that night.

7. Jack Dean Kingsbury evaluates research on the secrecy motif in Mark from William Wrede to the present (*Christology*, 1–45). See also Christopher Tuckett, ed., *The Messianic Secret* (Philadelphia: Fortress, 1983). The anonymity principle referred to here is set forth in A.A.'s twelfth tradition: "Anonymity is the spiritual foundation of all our traditions, ever reminding us to place principles before personalities" (*Alcoholics Anonymous*, 564).

8. Mann, *Mark*, 248 and 566.

9. Kee, *Community*, 166.

10. Jeremias, *Eucharistic Words*, 182–83.

11. Black, *An Aramaic Approach*, 279.

12. Jeremias, *New Testament Theology*, 282; Schillebeeckx, *Jesus*, 283–84.

13. See chapter 2, note 25. Barnabas Lindars's theological study (*Jesus Son of Man: A Fresh Examination of the Son of Man Sayings in the Gospels in Light of Recent Research* [London: SPCK, 1983]) essentially confirms the linguistic insights of Vermes and Black. Lindars says, "Once again, the ambiguity of this third-personal way of speaking suits Mark's purpose well" (163). Later he concludes that Jesus' uses of "Son of Man" "do not include a claim to be the Messiah" (187). See also P. Maurice Casey's "General, Generic, and Indefinite," where Casey defines the general use as occasions when a speaker wishes to say something about himself and a group of associates.

14. Longenecker, *Christology*, 88.

15. Luke makes the episode the initial proclamatory event of Messiah's career, thereby encouraging the conclusion that the rejection of Jesus was triggered by the novelty and surprise of his preaching rather than the people's perception of his deteriorating mental condition.

16. The difference between Mark's terse account of the sending out and Matthew's elaborated version, which includes the predictions of persecution and of the messianic age, need not stem from Mark's ignorance of these items of information. More likely it reflects his diffidence about whether his religious audiences would tolerate any revelation of the fear and grandiosity on Jesus' part that he knew they betokened. If Mark later on read Matthew or Luke, he learned soon enough how much alcoholic behavior persons will tolerate when they believe the perpetrator to be the Messiah.

17. Charles R. Joy, "Introduction: Schweitzer's Conception of Jesus," in Schweitzer, *Psychiatric Study*, 17–26.

18. Again, Mark presumably knew of Jesus' conduct but omitted it because he felt it too obvious an indicator of Jesus' mental drunkenness to risk highlighting. Luke has positioned the cursing of Chorazin, Bethsaida, and Capernaum (10.13–15) within the episode of the sending out of the seventy-two, but it is actually a part of Jesus' response after their return in Lk 10.17. This is shown, apart from the obvious sense of the situation, by verse

15, which quotes Is 14.13–15 and thus links the passage with Lk 10.18, which quotes Is 14.12. The point is that the towns are the ones visited by the disciples. That Jesus actually cursed them is obvious evidence of self-will run riot. Mark would have been amazed had he known that Luke would be able to recount this incident without scandalizing his audience.

19. This is the gist of Peter's phrase early in Acts (5.31) identifying Jesus as *archēgon* (founder) and *sōtēr* (savior) but not *christos* (Messiah). Logion 13 of the Gospel of Thomas, roughly parallel to Mk 8.27–30, gives Jesus' response to Thomas's use of the term *master*, couched in a bibulous terminology that also suits Peter's alcoholic craziness at this earlier juncture of his career: "I am not your master. Because you have drunk [that is, are drunkards], you have become intoxicated from the bubbling spring which I have measured out."

20. Schillebeeckx, *Jesus*, 227–28, and Mack, *Lost Gospel*, 138.

21. Strictly speaking, Mark's word is *pōlos*, meaning the colt of either an ass or a mare, but everyone from Jesus' time to the present has agreed that it was an ass's colt. Mark may have used *pōlos* in order to conform to the Zecharian phrase "a colt the foal of an ass" (9.9) and at the same time avoid *onos*, "donkey" or "ass," for fear that readers might get the Aramaic pun and become suspicious. The mysterious two-animal phrase occurring in Matthew, "the ass and the colt" (21.7), may result from a controversy over the text concerning this scandalous pun. The point in any case is that it was a donkey that nonalcoholics in Mark's audiences believed Jesus to have ridden into Jerusalem, whereas the Galilean alcoholics would have been quite aware of the "donkey/wine" pun underlying Mark's account and what it signified in Jesus' story.

22. George Lamsa, *More Light on the Gospel* (Garden City, N.Y.: Doubleday, 1968), 47–48, 74.

23. Geza Vermes (*Jesus the Jew*, 52–53) quotes this anecdote, citing the Babylonian Talmud, Erubin 53b.

24. Dialect-specific puns occur in all language communities and must be explained to outsiders. For example, midwesterners who move to Massachusetts might at first be bewildered by the schoolyard joke, "Was Lincoln tall or short?" They would later learn that eastern Massachusetts dialects do not distinguish *short* and *shot*, pronouncing both *shaht*, and thus gain a conceptual knowledge of the pun.

25. Claus Westermann, *Genesis 37–50: A Commentary*, trans. J. J. Scullion (Minneapolis: Augsburg, 1986), 219.

26. Smith, *Jesus the Magician*, 61 overleaf, 62.

27. These donkey-headed cartoons may or may not have carried associations of drunkenness. It is worth noting that Smith says of the Roman graffito that the man at the foot of the cross is looking up at the crucified figure with his hand raised in reverence, whereas closer inspection of the illustration reveals, surprisingly, the dim outlines of a wineskin in his hand, aimed at his mouth.

28. Also germane to the question of Jesus' intoxication in Jerusalem is

his remark on his arrest in Gethsemane, "Day after day I was with you in the Temple teaching, and you did not seize me" (14.49), which is odd because it seems to be a protestation of peaceableness in the aftermath of actions in the Temple that were anything but peaceful. Conceivably the statement is Mark's reminder to his alcoholic readers of a later disclosure by Jesus, otherwise unrepresented in the Markan text, that his drunken rampage occurred in a blackout of which he retained no memory.

29. Chapter 2 discusses at length the highly significant fact that Mk 14.23 presents an order of events different from that given in the other witnesses to the Last Supper. This may be the Markan "order" about which Papias says the late first-century figure John the Presbyter complained: "Mark . . . wrote down, although not in order, all that he remembered of what was either said or done by the Lord" (Eusebius, *Ecclesiastical History*, 206). As noted earlier, conflicting reports of the order of events in the Last Supper narrative would have deeply troubled an end-of-the-century elder. See Hengel, *Studies in the Gospel of Mark*, 47–50.

30. Other than Is 51.17–23, Mark doubtless identified many additional OT mentions of cups bespeaking alcoholism. Other cup references figuring alcoholic suffering are: Ps 60.5 and 75.9 (both show alcoholism as coming from God), Jer 25.15–16 (the sword metaphor implies the fighting and violence that alcoholism produces), Jer 51.7 (Babylon as a prophetic figure of authoritarian religion and the ritual drinking it promotes), and Zech 12.2 (Jerusalem as figurative cause of the strife fomented by the mental drunkenness underlying religious fanaticism). Citations of the cup as a sobriety metaphor are Ps 16.5, 23.5, and 116.13, and probably Hab 2.16.

31. Jeremias, *New Testament Theology*, 292–93.

32. D. Miller, *Christs*, 194.

33. Bratcher and Nida, *Translator's Handbook*, 448–49. The authors acknowledge this literal translation only to warn persons away from it, since they interpret "cup" in the sense of "impending affliction." Interestingly, they go on to say, "It is particularly important that in any word for 'cup' one avoid the connotations of 'cup of intoxicating liquor' (a not infrequent mistake)." This admonition, coming as it does from translators positioned at the opposite semantic pole of the ambiguity in question, seems inadvertently to confirm the legitimacy of the present reading.

34. Elisabeth Schüssler Fiorenza, *In Memory of Her: A Feminist Theological Reconstruction of Christian Origins* (New York: Crossroad, 1984), xiii.

35. Only among the monks at Qumran, as Richard Longenecker has indicated (*Christology*, 63–119), was such an idea entertained, and even there it is not fully verified.

36. Edward Schillebeeckx (*Interim Report on the Books Jesus and Christ* [New York: Crossroad, 1981], 41) writes that while the Q community had a Parousia Christology, there is no mention in Q "of a soteriology of the cross or a Christology of the resurrection."

37. On way-showing versus substitutionary atonement, see Gustaf Aulén, *Christus Victor: An Historical Study of the Three Main Types of the Idea of the Atone-*

ment, trans. A. G. Herbert (New York: Macmillan, 1969). Recovery criticism harmonizes with Aulén's third type, which he calls "the classical idea" of the atonement.

38. Mann, *Mark,* 598–601.

39. Morton Smith, *Clement of Alexandria and a Secret Gospel of Mark* (Cambridge, Mass.: Harvard University Press, 1973).

40. Crossan, *Historical Jesus,* 328–32. The excerpt from Secret Mark just quoted is taken from Crossan, 329.

41. Ibid., 330.

42. Supporting the idea of Mark as a deacon in the community, Luke implies that Mark "deaconed" *(diakonian)* with Paul and Barnabas (Acts 12.25). How long he may have continued to serve as such after his break with Paul (Acts 15.36–41) cannot be known—long enough, apparently, to interview Peter in the 50s and do missionary work in Alexandria until 63 c.e., although either of these could have been work in the service of his sobriety movement.

43. Second Vatican Council, Dogmatic Constitution *Lumen Gentium* 18: *AAS 57* (1965), 36.

44. Liturgical historians are unable to identify the source of the ancient practice, first mentioned by Justin Martyr ("First Apology," par. 67, 287), of adding a few drops of water to the eucharistic wine before its consecration, beyond attributing it to the Roman custom of cutting wine with water for table use. Juvenal and other ancient writers, after all, repeatedly admonished their readers that only alcoholics do not put water in their wine. Recovery criticism, of course, sees water as emblematic of sobriety (see the discussion of the parable of Cana water in chap. 7.)

Chapter 7: Johannine Writings

1. Since Rudolf Bultmann's landmark commentary (*The Gospel of John: A Commentary,* trans. G. R. Beasley-Murray, et al. [Philadelphia: Westminster, 1971]), a sequence-of-stages model of Johannine composition has gained favor. For example, see Raymond E. Brown, *The Community of the Beloved Disciple* (New York: Paulist, 1979); Robert Kysar, *Augsburg Commentary on the New Testament: John* (Minneapolis: Augsburg, 1986); Birger Olsson, "The History of the Johannine Movement," in Lars Hartman and Birger Olsson, eds., *Aspects on the Johannine Literature,* 1986 conference papers, *Coniectanea Biblica, New Testament Series 18* (Uppsala, Sweden: Almquist & Wiksell); and D. A. Carsons, *The Gospel according to John* (Grand Rapids, Mich.: Eerdmans, 1991).

2. Brown, *Gospel according to John I–XII,* 99.

3. Ibid.

4. For a summary of interpretations, see Raymond E. Brown, *The Anchor Bible Gospel according to John XIII–XXI* (Garden City, N.Y.: Doubleday, 1970), 1074–76.

5. See chapter 1, note 20.

6. Barnabas Lindars (*New Century Bible: The Gospel of John* [London: Oliphants, 1972], 127–28) surveys Greek and specifically Dionysiac parallels to the Cana story. See also Morton Smith, "On the Wine God in Palestine (Gen. 18, Jn 2, and Achilles Tatius)," in Saul Lieberman, ed., *Salo W. Baron Jubilee Volume, English Section, Vol. II* (Jerusalem: American Academy for Jewish Research and New York: Columbia University Press, 1974), 815–29. Quoting from Achilles Tatius's Greek romance *The Adventures of Leucippe and Clitophon*, Smith points out that Jn 2.1–11 resembles this story of Dionysus giving mortals the gift of wine at the first festival in his honor, a gift that quickens the urge to connubiality in Tatius's characters (816–17).

7. Raymond Brown (*Gospel according to John I*, 284–91) believes 6.51–58 to have been constructed of separate and originally noneucharistic Johannine sayings and cites numerous scholars of similar mind.

8. Representative research on the apocalyptic symbolism in the Book of Revelation is J. Massyngberde Ford, *The Anchor Bible Revelation* (Garden City, N.Y.: Doubleday, 1975); Adela Yarbro Collins, *Crisis and Catharsis: The Power of the Apocalypse* (Philadelphia: Westminster, 1984); Elisabeth Schüssler Fiorenza, *The Book of Revelation: Justice and Judgment* (Philadelphia: Fortress, 1985); and papers in *Interpretation* 40, no.3 (1986) and Adela Yarbro Collins, ed., *Early Christian Apocalypticism: Genre and Social Setting*, *Semeia* 36 (1986).

9. Elisabeth Schüssler Fiorenza, *Invitation to the Book of Revelation: A Commentary on the Apocalypse with Complete Text from the Jerusalem Bible* (Garden City, N.Y.: Image, 1981).

10. *Alcoholics Anonymous*, 60.

11. Alexander A. Di Lella, commentary on chapters 10–12, in *Anchor Bible Book of Daniel* (Garden City, N.Y.: Doubleday, 1978), 313–14.

12. Ibid.

13. See Kurtz, *Not-God*, chapters 2 and 3, for a description of events between the founding of A.A. and the writing of the Twelve Steps and *Alcoholics Anonymous*. See also *Alcoholics Anonymous Comes of Age: A Brief History of A.A.* (New York: Alcoholics Anonymous World Services, 1957).

14. Personal correspondence in 1982 with Nell Wing, then A.A. archivist at the General Service Office in New York City, indicates that, while the precise date of the writing of the Twelve Steps in December 1938 can never be known, various data suggest that it occurred sometime during the middle two weeks of the month.

15. Nell Wing, personal correspondence, 1982.

16. One could sift the matter even finer. Monday, 10 June 1935, A.A.'s official founding date, is said to be the day of cofounder Dr. Bob Smith's last drink. Actually Dr. Bob took his last drink in the small hours of Thursday, 6 June, four days earlier. The alcohol he consumed from then through the morning of Monday, 10 June, was administered *to* him as a detox procedure by cofounder Bill Wilson and Bob's wife, Anne Smith (*'Pass It On': The Story of Bill Wilson and How the A.A. Message Reached the World* [New York: Alcoholics Anonymous World Services, 1984], 148–49). This four-day rollback causes Daniel's 1,290 and 1,335 days to fall *precisely* at the midpoint of the two weeks

before Christmas of 1938 and *precisely* at the hinge between January and February of 1939. Coincidentally, Friday, 7 June 1935, the first day of Dr. Bob's permanent sobriety, was Pentecost Day in the Jewish calender, a reprise of Peter's sobriety proclamation on the first Christian Pentecost.

Afterword

1. Schweitzer, *Historical Jesus*, 3.
2. Gregory Bateson, "The Cybernetics of 'Self': A Theory of Alcoholism," in *Steps to the Ecology of Mind: Collected Essays in Anthropology, Psychiatry, Evolution, and Epistemology* (San Francisco: Chandler, 1972), 309–37.
3. Frederick Buechner, *Telling Secrets* (New York: HarperCollins, 1991), 93.

INDEX OF SCRIPTURES

INDEX OF NAMES

JOHN C. MELLON holds degrees from the University of Iowa and Harvard University. He is an associate professor of English at the University of Illinois at Chicago, specializing in language, literacy, and rhetoric. A longtime student of the Gospel of Mark, he is also a deacon (inactive) of the Catholic Archdiocese of Chicago and a recovering alcoholic. This is his first work of Scripture study.